The Educational Consultant

The Educational Consultant

*Helping Professionals, Parents,
and Mainstreamed Students*

Second Edition

Timothy E. Heron

Kathleen C. Harris

8700 Shoal Creek Boulevard
Austin, Texas 78758

Library of Congress Cataloging in Publication Data

Heron, Timothy E.
   The educational consultant.

   Bibliography: p.
   Includes index.
   1. Handicapped children — Education — United States.
2. Educational consultants — United States.
3. Mainstreaming in education — United States
I. Harris, Kathleen C.   II. Title.
LC 4019.H47   1987   371.9   86-30406
ISBN 0-89079-143-0

8700 Shoal Creek Boulevard
Austin, Texas 78758

10   9   8   7   6   5   4   90   91   92

TO OUR PARENTS

Raymond, Bernice, Roland, and Mary

*Who always have been and
still remain — our consultants.*

Contents

Preface

Since the enactment of Public Law 94-142, The Education of All Handicapped Children Act of 1975, an increasing number of handicapped students have been integrated into the regular classroom. The provision of appropriate education programs for handicapped students has, therefore, become the shared responsibility of regular and special educators. Planning and implementing programs for handicapped students within the mainstream school environment has presented several challenges to professionals, parents, and the students themselves.

One challenge which has surfaced has been how to help educators devise, implement, and evaluate programs that meet the unique learning needs of students. Another challenge is, of course, how to appropriately and successfully involve the parents of handicapped students in the educational process.

The second edition of *The Educational Consultant* is designed to provide educational consultants (e.g., resource teachers, coordinators, specialists, and counselors) with the information necessary to effectively consult with educators and parents regarding the design and implementation of educational programs within the least restrictive environment. The ideas, strategies, and suggestions for the second edition have come from several sources: feedback received from users of the first edition (which has been extremely helpful); our continuing experiences in consultation and clinical supervision; the research literature; practitioners; and our graduate students. We have made every attempt in the second edition to integrate these sources, because it is our belief that advances in consultation occur when individuals blend what has been empirically demonstrated as effective with their personal consulting, teaching, and parenting style.

Several new features have been added to the second edition. First, each chapter contains up-to-date references. We have added numerous references, many of which are post-1980. Second, each chapter contains a "Summary of Key Points," enumerating for the reader what we consider to be the highlights of the chapter. Third, two new chapters have been added: One chapter discusses the roles of the consultant; the other addresses consulting within a multicultural context.

The text is divided into 11 chapters. The first two chapters present information on the consultation process and the roles the consultant assumes when providing technical assistance, coordinating programs, and communicating with professionals, parents, and students. Chapters 3, 4, and 5 provide the consultant with descriptive techniques for working with teachers in mainstream settings, teachers in self-contained classrooms, and with parents. Chapters 6 and 7 discuss specific strategies for individualizing instruction at the elementary and secondary levels, respectively. In keeping with our position that career education is a life-long process, content for this area has been incorporated into the discussions presented in Chapters 6 and 7. Chapters 8 and 9 address skills the consultant needs to help teachers manage students and programs. Chapter 8 discusses various assessment strategies the consultant can use in helping teachers design, implement, and evaluate educational programs. Chapter 9 presents to the consultant strategies to select, implement, and evaluate appropriate behavior management techniques with individuals and groups. Chapter 10 addresses multicultural considerations in educational consultation, a new focus for consultants as the needs of culturally and/or linguistically different handicapped students are identified. The last chapter discusses why and how litigation and legislation affect consultation services.

The completion of this second edition could not have been accomplished without the support of our colleagues, students, friends, and families. We would like to acknowledge the assistance of our colleagues Saul Axelrod, Leonard Baca, Hanford Combs, John O. Cooper, Jill Dardig, Mary Falvey, Donald D. Hammill, William L. Heward, Richard Iano, Walter Kimball, M. Diane Klein, Steve Larsen, Belinda Lazarus, Bruce Meyer, Sister Phyllis Supancheck, Michael Skinner, Annette Tessier, and Adele Weiss for their continued support of our professional activities and for their comments on our work. We would like to express our appreciation to all of the graduate students at California State University, Los Angeles and The Ohio State University who provided us with feedback on several concepts and features of the text. In particular our special thanks go to Christina Alessi who, in addition to contributing her master's degree thesis data, typed the manuscript. Steve Mathews, Vice President of PRO-ED, and his editorial staff, especially Brenda Phillips, Marilyn Novell, and Suzanne Pustejovsky deserve our special gratitude. Their assistance with every aspect of production is appreciated.

Last, and most important, we would like to thank our parents (Raymond, Bernice, Roland, and Mary), to whom this book is dedicated; our spouses, Marge and Blaine; and Elizabeth and Edward for their continued encouragement and patience. Kathleen and Christine Heron deserve special thanks for helping their dad keep his sense of perspective during the production of this work. Without the unfailing and unwavering support of our families, the second edition of this text would not have been written.

1

The Consultation Process

Consultation involves the mutual interaction between two or more parties for the purpose of preventing or solving problems. The consultation process can be initiated by a consultant (e.g., the principal, supervisor, or resource room teacher), who might observe that a school-related problem needs attention, or by a consultee (regular class teacher, parent, or student), who might seek additional assistance with preventing or solving a problem. Regardless of whether the consultant or consultee initiates the process, it is generally accepted that both parties collaborate and share the responsibility during consultation.

The purpose of this chapter is to define consultation and the consultation process and to present several models that have been used to conceptualize and apply this process. Examples are provided to illustrate how the models have been or might be used.

OBJECTIVES

After reading this chapter, the reader should be able to:

1. define the term *consultation*.

2. define the term *developmental consultation*.

3. define the term *problem-centered consultation*.

4. distinguish between the terms *developmental consultation* and *problem-centered consultation*.

5. identify an applied example of developmental and problem-centered consultation.

6. define the consultation process and the essential components of the process.

7. list and describe a nine-step consultation process proposed by Kurpius.

1

8. identify three models for school consultation and describe the major components of each.

9. describe the relationship between the consultant and the consultee in the triadic model.

10. define the four principles of collaborative consultation implicit in the triadic model.

11. identify an applied example of the triadic model, the systems model, and the Vermont Consulting Teaching Program.

KEY TERMS

Consultation	Triadic model
Developmental consultation	Mediator
Problem-centered consultation	Target
The consultation process	Systems model
Collaborative consultation	Vermont Consulting Teacher Program
Doctrine of least restrictive alternative	Minimum rate of learning

---

DEFINITIONS OF CONSULTATION

Consultation has several definitions, varying in substance and context depending upon the target of the consultation or the intervention employed (Bergan & Tombari, 1976; Friend, 1985; Robinson, Cameron, & Raethel, 1985). According to Brown, Wyne, Blackburn, and Powell (1979), *consultation* is defined as "a process based upon an equal relationship characterized by mutual trust and open communication, joint approaches to problem identification, the pooling of personal resources to identify and select strategies that will have some probability of solving the problem that has been identified, and shared responsibility in the implementation and evaluation of the program or strategy that has been initiated" (p. 8). Idol-Maestas (1983) indicates that consultation can be considered as any support service provided to the classroom teacher for the purpose of improving academic and social behavior of all of the students. Conoley and Conoley (1982) indicate that consultation refers to a voluntary, nonsupervisory arrangement between parties to improve professional behavior. Parsons and Meyers (1984) suggest that consultation can be viewed as any professional interchange between colleagues. In their view, consultation is a collaborative interaction between two persons each of whom has expertise in a particular area. Bergan (1977), on the other hand, indicates that two forms of consultation exist — developmental consultation and problem-centered consultation. Depending on the situation, available resources, and circumstances, a consultant may need to use either or both of these approaches.

Developmental Consultation

Developmental consultation focuses on long range goals for a student. It usually involves the accomplishment of several sequenced subordinate objectives. For example, a student who has extreme social adjustment problems might be a candidate for developmental consultation. A subordinate objective might involve teaching the behavior disordered student to relax during academic work periods using systematic desensitization, a procedure whereby the student learns to work without fidgeting as other students are gradually assimilated into the classroom. Once this subordinate objective is mastered, the next objective for the student might focus on increasing appropriate verbal interactions with peers who sit close to him or her.

The consultant might collaborate with the teacher in identifying the problem, sequencing subordinate objectives, recommending intervention approaches, and evaluating the outcome. Developmental consultation, because it requires the completion of each subordinate objective to criterion, usually takes several months or longer to accomplish. Also, developmental consultation may require the collaborative efforts of other human service professionals or agents.

Problem-Centered Consultation

Problem-centered consultation is limited to solving specific and immediate problems. A learning disabled (LD) student who is aggressive or repeatedly off-task in school might be a candidate for problem-centered consultation. For example, if the LD student consistently provoked his or her classmates, immediate intervention would be required. Problem-centered consultation does not use specifically sequenced subordinate objectives; instead, the consultant and the teacher develop a mutual plan to solve an isolated problem. Long-term involvement is not anticipated with this approach.

In our view, effective consultation draws from both of the approaches described above; it is a collaborative, voluntary, mutual problem-solving process that may or may not involve the achievement of several subordinate objectives and that leads to the prevention or resolution of identified problems.

THE CONSULTATION PROCESS

The consultation process describes the relationship among the consultant, the consultee, and the client. Tharp (1975), for example, states that consultation services are provided through an intermediary — the consultee — with the expectation that behavior change will be observed in both the consultee and the client. Success with the consultation process is determined by noting improvement in both of these agents. The consultation process, however, also describes the stages these change agents encounter from the onset of consultation to its termination. At each stage in the process, a high-degree of *collaborative consultation* is essential. Unlike an "expert" model in which the consultant presumably knows something the consultee does not and the focus of the consultation is to impart that knowledge, collaborative consultation assumes that each party brings different kinds of knowledge to each stage of the process. Further, collaborative consultation implies that each party in the consultation plays an active role in the design, implementation, and evaluation of the program.

Facilitation of the Consultation Process

Collaborative consultation does not always occur spontaneously, and consultants should be prepared to handle resistance to the consultation process. Meyers (1974), for example, indicates that consultee unwillingness to work collaboratively might be overcome when consultants (a) share the responsibility for problem solving, (b) view the teacher as an expert in dealing with the student's problems, (c) de-emphasize their contribution in the consultative process, and (d) communicate to teachers that they are free to accept or reject any suggestions or recommendations made by the consultant. Nelson and Stevens (1979) state that to overcome personal as well as institutional resistance, consultants must be capable of changing a variety of behaviors and, more important, have a formal role in the school. That is, their role with respect to the rest of the school staff must be clear. Morse (1976) suggests that consultants who help teachers make their work more meaningful and productive are more likely to gain acceptance in the school and to obtain favorable changes in behavior. Idol-Maestas, Nevin, and Paolucci-Whitcomb (1984) state that resistance can be overcome when consultants treat others with respect, share information, give and receive feedback, use confrontation skills appropriately, and employ situational leadership skills effectively.

Bergan and Tombari (1976) state that the consultation process serves as a link between knowledge producers (i.e., researchers) and knowledge consumers (i.e., teachers or parents). Since teachers or parents may not have access to educationally relevant research, the consultant can help bridge the gap by informing them of new materials, methods, or technology. Teachers or parents, on the other hand, can provide specific information at each stage of the process which helps to determine the applicability of a given material, method, or technology.

A Nine-Step Procedure

Sandoval, Lambert, and Davis (1977) indicate that the consultation process is interactive. They suggest that the consultee learn to use the services of a consultant more efficiently. They feel that consultees who learn the tasks that consultants are able to perform with them and who are able to state their problems and evaluation strategies more succinctly will find the consultation process more rewarding. Kurpius (1978) outlines nine functions that define the consultation process.

Preentry. During the preentry phase, the consultant clarifies his or her own orientation toward the consultation process and various issues in the field (e.g., the relationship between the consultant and the consultee, intervention alternatives, role of related service personnel and parents in treatments, identification criteria). This self-examination forms the basis of the orientation the consultant brings to any problem-solving situation. For instance, if the consultant believes that the client should gain insight into his or her personality and that the consultant should reflect the consultee's feelings, be supportive, and improve the consultee's skill and objectivity, then a mental health orientation would be revealed. Conversely, if the consultant believes that the application of applied behavior analysis principles (e.g., reinforcement) forms the basis of consultee change, then a behavioral orientation would emerge from the self-assessment (Medway & Forman, 1980).

Entry. At the entry phase, three things happen. First, the consultant establishes rapport with the consultee, an important step if later success is to be achieved. Second, the consultant determines the conditions surrounding the problem. Finally, an agreement is reached between the consultant and the consultee on the steps for solving the problem (i.e., identifying resources, informational needs, terminal goals, and responsibility for task completion).

Gathering Information. In addition to whatever information might be available at the time consultation begins, the consultant and the consultee usually need to gather more data. The purpose of acquiring these data is to clarify the type, frequency, magnitude, or duration of the problem. Without adequate data, it is difficult to define the problem and to formulate an acceptable and effective intervention.

Defining the Problem.   Once data have been collected from a variety of sources (cf. Heron & Heward, 1982), the consultation process shifts to defining the problem in measurable terms. According to Bergan and Tombari (1976), success with problem identification invariably leads to problem resolution. Given that multiple problems might exist, it is helpful to arrange them from most to least severe. Planned interventions should be initiated for the most severe problem first.

Determining Solutions.   Several acceptable solutions might be proposed to solve any given problem. The ultimate guide in deciding which approach to use initially should be based on the *doctrine of least restrictive alternative.* Essentially, this doctrine states that the most powerful, but least intrusive, intervention should be attempted before more restrictive or time-consuming approaches are tried (Gast & Wolery, 1987; Evans & Meyer, 1985). Gaylord-Ross (1980) offers a hierarchical decision-making model for the treatment of aberrant behavior that can be applied by consultants in many field-based settings. Briefly, the model outlines a series of intervention approaches that should be used prior to initiating restrictive strategies. The Gaylord-Ross model is described in more detail in Chapter 9.

Stating Objectives.   According to Kurpius (1978), the purpose for stating objectives is to describe the conditions under which the behavior should occur, the parameters of the behavior, and the method for evaluating success.

Implementing the Plan.   Plan implementation means that the jointly agreed-upon program is placed in effect. Or, if a change is needed during implementation because the original plan was not successful, then both parties must agree to an alternative plan. The important task to accomplish at this stage is to determine that the plan is implemented as intended. No plan can be evaluated accurately if it is not carried out in the manner prescribed during the planning stage.

Evaluating the Plan.   The purpose of evaluation is to determine if a change has occurred in the desired direction. More important, the evaluation phase allows the consultant and the consultee to determine the variables that accounted for the change. A goal for every consultation project should be to determine functional or clinical significance for the intervention employed to change behavior.

Terminating Consultation.   The consultation process is terminated when both parties agree that the objective was met or that additional work is not warranted. Termination of the process should be a positive experience. Each party should recognize areas of professional growth as well as improvement in the conditions that prompted the initial consultation. Chandler (1980) found that the number of referrals for formal psychological evaluation decreased markedly after teachers had gained experience with consultation, presumably because their skill level with prevention or management had improved.

CONSULTATION MODELS

The nine-step consultation process outlined by Kurpius (1978) has been formalized and condensed into several consultation models. For instance, Gallessich (1982) refers to six broad consultation models: mental health, clinical, organizational, behavioral, program, and education and training. Babcock and Pryzwansky (1983) differentiate among collaborative, mental health, medical, and expert models. These models differ with respect to underlying assumptions, procedures, and evaluation designs. While it is beyond the scope of this chapter to discuss each of these models in depth, we take the position that a consultant's efficiency is usually increased when the appropriate model is used for the situation, because it provides the procedures within which the consultative services can be delivered.

This chapter presents three models that represent ways in which school consultation can be conceptualized: the triadic model (Tharp & Wetzel, 1969; Tharp, 1975), the systems model (Stephens, 1977) and the Vermont Consulting Teacher Program (McKenzie, 1972; Egner & Lates, 1975). These models are not intended to include all models that might be used with teachers, parents, or students. Nor are they intended to address each of the assumptions underlying the models identified by Gallessich or Babcock and Pryzwansky, although they do share many features of these models. Rather these models illustrate how consultation services can be described and evaluated with individuals, small groups, or large populations. Each of the models can be used to solve school-related problems.

Triadic Model

The *triadic model* (Figure 1.1), in its most basic form, is a linear sequence that portrays the relationships among the consultant, the mediator or consultee, and the client or target. The bracket that connects the consultant and the mediator represents the collaborative consultation process.

The triadic model describes a functional rather than an absolute sequence for consultation. That is, any professional, principal, resource room teacher, supervisor, or psychologist could serve as the consultant. The only requirement for serving as a consultant is that the individual possess the knowledge, skills, or abilities needed to work collaboratively with the mediator or the target. A regular education teacher, paraprofessional, or parent could serve

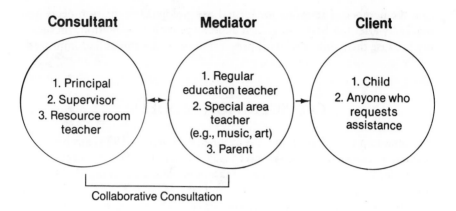

FIGURE 1.1. The triadic model of consultation showing individuals within each role. From *Behavior modification in the natural environment* (p. 47) by R. G. Tharp & R. J. Wetzel, 1969, New York: Academic Press. Adapted by permission of the publisher and authors.

as the mediator. The *mediator* has access to the target student and has some influence over him or her, while the consultant serves as a catalyst to activate the mediator. The *target* is the individual (or group) for whom the consultative service is intended, or any other person involved with the consultation (Tharp & Wetzel, 1969).

Principles of Collaborative Consultation. According to Idol-Maestas et al. (1984), four principles of collaborative consultation form the basis of the triadic model: team ownership, recognition of individual differences, application of reinforcement, and data-based evaluation.

Team ownership. The two-way arrow shown in Figure 1.1 indicates that equality and parity must exist between the consultant and the mediator for the triadic model to work effectively. According to Idol-Maestas et al. (1984), "Equality can be demonstrated by listening, respecting and learning from each other. Parity is demonstrated as the mediator's skills and knowledge are blended with the different skills and knowledge that the consultant shares" (pp. I–9).

Recognition of individual differences. This principle of collaborative consultation focuses on the effect of change on the mediator and target. That is, implicit in the implementation of the triadic model is that a change in procedure occurs. For some individuals, making a change in a routine is uncomfortable. The consultant's role in the collaboration process is to be sensitive to effects of change on the mediator and the target and to make transitions as nonthreatening as possible.

Application of reinforcement.   A distinguishing feature of collaborative consultation within the triadic model is its emphasis on the application of positive reinforcement. A basic tenet of this approach is that new behaviors are learned when their occurrence is followed by reinforcement. So, not only does the consultant use liberal amounts of reinforcement when teaching the mediator new behaviors, but also the mediator learns to use ample reinforcement with the target individual.

The emphasis on reinforcement does not mean that other behavior change principles or procedures are not used. Many educators have written extensively on how behaviors can be changed using a variety of acceleration and deceleration approaches (cf. Cooper, Heron, & Heward, 1987). The point is, positive reinforcement is a key principle in behavior development.

Data-based evaluation.   The triadic model is evaluated by determining the extent to which improved performance in the mediator and target is achieved. So, success can be analyzed using a variety of qualitative and quantitative measures (cf. Tawney & Gast, 1984; Kerr & Nelson, 1983). Specifically, the consultant has two evaluative measures to index when using the triadic model. The first measure is the extent to which the mediator acquires the knowledge or skill presented by the consultant. The second measure is whether the application of this knowledge or skill affects student performance. It is possible for gains to be obtained by the mediator when little or no improvement in student performance is realized. As Heath and Nielson (1974) indicate, the relationship between the specific performance of the teacher and the achievement of the student is uncertain. But, as Idol-Maestas et al. (1984) indicate, failure to achieve results should be interpreted as a procedural or system failure, not as a failure due to the inherent deficits of the learner.

Applied Example.   Heron and Catera (1980) conducted a study using the triadic model and incorporating the four principles of collaborative consultation described by Idol-Maestas et al. (1984). In their three-part study, the triadic model was used with three learning disabilities teachers who had expressed concern about work completion in their respective classrooms. In each classroom the consultant met with the classroom teacher to identify the problem and to outline possible solutions. During this stage, the consultant and the teacher jointly agreed that more specific information was needed. Next, after baseline data were collected by the teacher indicating that approximately 50% of the student's assigned work was completed at a criterion of 80% accuracy or higher, another meeting was held to plan an intervention. Consultation was individualized, and a different contingency was jointly agreed upon and implemented in each classroom. For instance, in classroom 1, a "punishment" contingency was used initially whereby the student stayed in for recess when he did not meet criterion (Figure 1.2 upper panel). In classroom 2, the teacher verbally praised each assignment completed to criterion and allowed the student to show his completed work to the principal at the end of the day (Figure 1.2 middle panel). In classroom 3, a "work race" was used in which a gameboard showed progress for each assignment completed to criterion (Figure 1.2 lower panel). Further, each teacher agreed to collect work samples on a daily basis which would serve as the evaluation measure.

The results across each classroom indicated that assignment completion improved over baseline levels. Of perhaps even more importance is the finding that the triadic model set the occasion for these changes to take place. In each classroom the teachers jointly developed, implemented, and evaluated the intervention. When the initial intervention did not produce the intended effect — as was the case in classroom 1 — additional collaborative consultation was necessary. It was only after the teacher and consultant reviewed the effects of the punishment intervention and discussed a reinforcement alternative that the students' performance improved. Finally, the study showed that individual differences across settings do exist, and the consultant must tailor joint interventions to accommodate these differences.

Systems Model

Stephens's (1977) describes a *systems model* for consulting with school personnel. His model is an extension of his directive teaching approach (Stephens, 1976).

Five Phases of the Systems Model.   Stephens's (1977) model involves five phases: assessment, specification of objectives, planning, implementation of treatment, and evaluation (see Figure 1.3).

Assessment.   Baseline data are collected on target behaviors — for example, the number of student talk-outs that occur during the day. Factors that may affect a planned intervention are determined, and alternative strategies are considered. Data are collected for a period of time, usually three to five days, to use as a basis for comparing treatment effects. Also, during baseline, antecedent and consequent conditions that might play a role in the planned intervention are identified. For instance, talk-outs might be related to the time of day, subject area, lack of reinforcement, or student misunderstanding of the directions.

Specification of objectives.   During this phase problem areas are specified and rank ordered from most severe to least severe. Behaviors to be modified are identified and operationally defined. An operational definition for

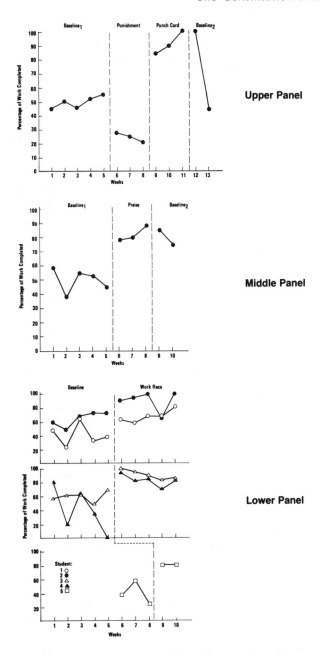

FIGURE 1.2. The percentage of work completed by seven students across three separate learning disabilities classrooms using the triadic model of consultation. From ''Teacher consultation: A functional approach'' by T. E. Heron & R. Catera, 1980, in *School Psychology Review*, 9, 283–289. Adapted by permission of the publisher and authors.

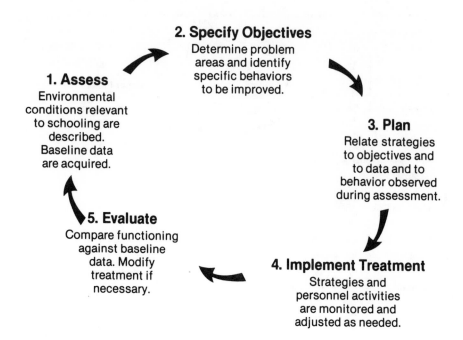

FIGURE 1.3.   A systems model of consultation. From *Teaching skills to children with learning and behavior disorders* (p. 427) by T. M. Stephens, 1977, Columbus, OH: Merrill. Reprinted by permission of the publisher.

talk-outs might be any verbalization made by the student without the teacher's permission.

Planning.   Strategies that are intended to reduce or increase the level of target behavior are outlined. Strategies are chosen so as to be consistent with the teacher's style of instruction or management yet still powerful enough to obtain the desired change in behavior.

Implementation.   The jointly agreed upon strategy is initiated, and direct and daily measurement of the target behavior is conducted. Monitoring the data on a daily basis is essential to any modifications in the treatment approach. An example of a direct and daily measure of talk-outs would be the number of inappropriate verbalizations made by the student each day. While the teacher is probably the primary person responsible for implementing a strategy in the school, both the teacher and the consultant share responsibility for monitoring day-to-day progress of the student.

Evaluation. At this stage of the consultation process, data are analyzed across baseline and treatment conditions. Again, the consultant and the teacher share responsibility for data analysis. The essential questions to be answered are: Was there a treatment effect, and was the teacher satisfied with the results of the program?

Stephens's (1977) model is an example of a systems approach, because subsequent to the evaluation stage the process loops back to Step 1 — Assessment. That is, if the planned treatment did not have the desired effect, further assessment may have to be conducted. If the plan was effective, then baseline data are collected on the next behavior targeted for change. A feature that the systems approach shares with other models of consultation is that the consultant helps the teacher devise his or her own criterion-referenced assessments or coding devices. Helping teachers rather than simply supplying an existing assessment gives them a vested interest in their projects. They feel like an integral component of the program, and they begin to acquire skills that enable them to function independently once the consultant is gone.

Applied Example. Baer and Richards (1980) conducted a study with five elementary school-aged students that illustrates the use of a systems model. In this study, the teacher was interested in increasing the students' percentage correct responses in math and English. Baseline data showed that the average percent correct for weekly assignments in math and English was 75% and 77%, respectively (Assessment). Percentage correct was defined as the number of right answers completed during daily math and English periods divided by 100 (Specify Objectives). A plan was outlined that reinforced the whole class for increased accuracy in math and English by the five students. Extra recess was awarded to the class on the basis of the five students' improved weekly scores (Plan). The contingency was placed into effect, and the percentage correct was recorded and plotted by weeks to note the trend in the data (Implement Treatment). To evaluate whether the group contingency was effective, it was terminated briefly and later reinstated (Evaluate). After the 22-week study, it was concluded that when the class reinforcer was in effect, the percentage of correct responses of the five target students increased. When the group contingency (Plan) was withdrawn, percentage correct performance in math and English decreased (Figure 1.4).

The Vermont Consulting Teacher Program

The *Vermont Consulting Teacher Program* is a collaborative effort of local school districts, the Vermont State Department of Education, and university personnel aimed at providing consultative services statewide to regular education teachers who have handicapped children in their classrooms. The program integrates the design and function components of the triadic and systems

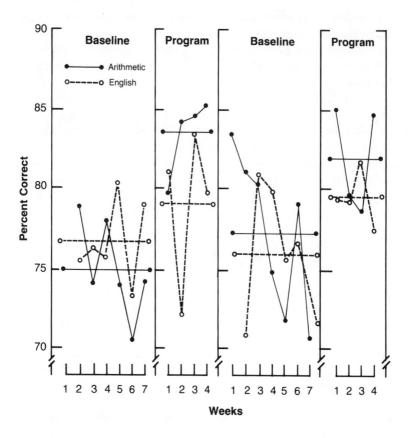

FIGURE 1.4. The percentage correct in math and English for five students using a systems model of consultation. From "An interdependent group-oriented contingency system for improving academic performance" by G. G. Baer & H. C. Richards, 1980, in *School Psychology Review, 9,* 190–193.

models and uses a behaviorally oriented approach. The underlying assumptions of the program are that all children and teachers are capable of learning skills; that teacher effectiveness can best be measured as a function of student growth; and that the systematic use of behavior analysis (procedures to determine the extent to which planned treatment affects performance) will provide the most appropriate methods of comparison (Egner & Lates, 1975).

The Vermont Consulting Teacher Program is shown in Figure 1.5. Note the similarity between the designs of the Vermont model and the systems model. Within the four-phase model is a 10-step behavioral consultation process that is implemented with the specific objective of skill acquisition by the classroom teacher (Table 1.1). The key feature of the Vermont program is that the consulting teacher must individualize the program to meet the specific needs of the regular educator.

One unique aspect of the Vermont program is the way in which evaluation of student performance is conducted. A *minimum rate of learning* is established for a given content area, specifying the number of objectives that should be mastered by a given time. For example, a school district or community might determine that a given set of hierarchically arranged instructional objectives must be mastered over the course of the year. That is, by the end of fourth grade, students must be able to complete two-step word problems, three-digit multiplication with regrouping , and long division with remainders. Students who fall below the minimum rate of learning curve not only become eligible for the supportive services of the consulting teacher, but also the minimum rate line becomes the benchmark by which future progress is determined. The trend of the student's progress compared to the rate line provides the index by which services are begun, changed, or terminated (Egner & Lates, 1975).

Advantages and Disadvantages. The Vermont program offers several advantages for consultants who work with regular education teachers. First, the program is data-based. Student performance, not categorical labels, determines eligibility for service, and entrance and existing criteria are measured

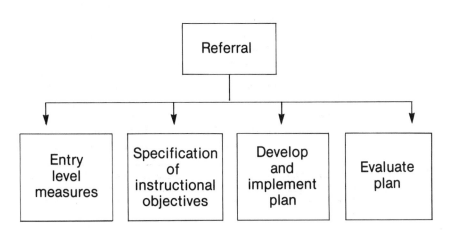

FIGURE 1.5. The Vermont Consulting Teacher Program model to provide special education in the regular classroom. From "The Vermont Consulting Teacher Program: Case presentation" by A. Egner & B. J. Lates, 1975, in C. A. Parker (Ed.), *Psychological consultation: Helping teachers meet special needs* (p. 32), Minneapolis: Leadership Training Institute in Special Education. Reprinted by permission of the publisher.

TABLE 1.1
Relation of Behavioral Model and Skills Acquired by Classroom Teacher during Consulting Steps

Behavioral Model	Consulting Steps	Skills Acquired By Teacher
Eligible learner	1. Referral procedure	
Entry level	2. Consulting teacher meetings for baseline diagnosis procedures	Defining target behaviors in measurable terms, measuring behavior reliability, collecting, recording, and graphing data daily
	3. Consulting teacher/ teacher meetings to establish eligibility	
Instructional objectives	4. Parent meeting for written permission	Involving parents in education process
	5. Consulting teacher classroom objectives	Writing individual instructional objectives
	6. Decision-making process for intervention	and procedures involving parents
Teaching/learning procedures	7. Parent information meeting for intervention procedures	Following teaching/ learning procedures precisely
	8. Implementation of intervention procedures	
Evaluation	9. Evaluation of intervention procedure	Identifying possible reinforcing consequences in the classroom
	10. Follow-through or confirmation	Responding to changes in behavior of the child

From "The Vermont Consulting Teacher Program: Case presentation" by A. Egner & B.J. Lates, 1975, in C.A. Parker (Ed.), *Psychological consultation: Helping teachers meet special needs* (p.33), Minneapolis: Leadership Training Institute/Special Education. Reprinted by permission of the publisher.

against the minimum rate line. Second, teachers and parents are active participants in the program. Recall in the consulting steps (Table 1.1) that parents provide their input to the program prior to implementation of a given plan. The Vermont program has also proven to be a cost effective approach.

Consultants are employed only for the students who need help. These services are thus allocated more efficiently.

The primary disadvantage of the program is that it requires the specification of minimum levels of achievement within certain time frames. To successfully implement the program, a task analysis of objectives must be arranged hierarchically. Also, general consensus on reasonable time frames to learn objectives must be reached by knowledgeable individuals. Given the responsibilities that regular teachers currently have, it is unlikely that many would spontaneously translate existing curriculum objectives, which are usually stated globally, into behavioral objectives. If the objectives were generated on a district-wide basis, teachers might be more willing to use the approach.

Tests of Efficacy. Knight, Meyers, Paolucci-Whitcomb, Hasazi, and Nevin (1981) conducted a four-year evaluation of the Vermont Consulting Teacher Program. Students below the 12th percentile on the Stanford Achievement Test (SAT) from six elementary schools in rural and rural-suburban Vermont served as subjects. Teachers within these schools also served as subjects. Three of the six schools, called "service schools," were randomly selected from a group of 12 schools in which the consulting teacher model had been in effect for the previous five years. The other three schools, called "nonservice" schools, did not use the consulting teacher model. Over the four-year period, teachers from the service schools participated in on-site course work, workshops, and consultations. Teachers in the nonservice schools did not.

When the data between the two schools were compared, major differences with respect to referral, assessment, curriculum, teaching, and evaluation procedures were found. That is, teachers in service schools had "institutionalized" the consulting teacher approach, meaning that collaborative decision making was evident from assessment to evaluation. In nonservice schools, the special education teacher continued to assume the primary responsibility for each area in the instructional continuum. Likewise, student data for the service schools indicated significantly greater gains in achievement, and these gains were maintained over the four-year period.

Applied Example. Figure 1.6 presents hypothetical data showing how a student's progress can be determined with the Vermont Consulting Teacher Program. Note that after the second week Sam became eligible for the consulting teacher program (see point a). The consultant, the parents, and the teacher jointly decided that intensive drill on the math facts to be learned would suffice to bring Sam's performance up to criterion. Unfortunately, this did not happen, and a second intervention — drill plus cross-age tutoring — was implemented during week six (see point b). The second intervention produced the desired result. Sam's performance reached the minimum rate line, and the special services of the consultant were no longer required. Using drill plus cross-age tutoring effectively increased Sam's rate of growth.

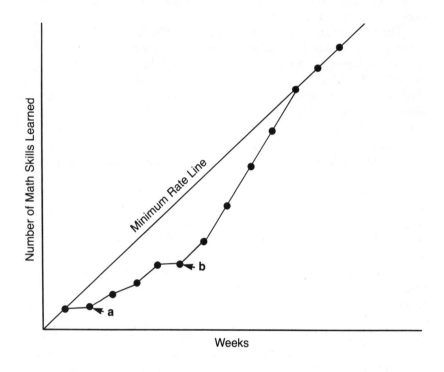

FIGURE 1.6. Hypothetical data showing Sam's rate of growth in math compared to minimum rate line using the Vermont Consulting Teacher Program.

CONCLUSION

Consultation is essentially collaborative and interactive. Each party brings to the consultation process particular expertise to solve a problem. A skilled consultant capitalizes on the knowledge and experiences of those with whom she or he works, ensuring that the intervention plan which is jointly designed has the widest possible support.

While there are a number of consultation models available for the consultant, the key steps can be crystallized into the following four components: assessment, planning, implementation, and evaluation. Using these steps, the consultant increases the probabilty of identifying the real problem and solving it.

SUMMARY OF KEY POINTS

Definitions of Consultation

1. Consultation is a collaborative, voluntary, mutual problem-solving process that may or may not involve the achievement of several subordinate objectives, and that leads to the prevention or resolution of identified problems.

2. Developmental consultation focuses on accomplishing several sequenced subordinate objectives and usually requires long-term intervention.

3. Problem-centered consultation is limited to solving specific and immediate problems.

The Consultation Process

4. The consultation process describes the relationship among the consultant, the consultee, and client and the stages these persons encounter from the onset to the termination of consultation.

5. The consultation process can be described by at least nine functions: preentry, entry, gathering information, defining the problem, identifying and selecting alternative solutions, stating objectives, implementing the plan, evaluating the plan, and terminating consultation.

6. Resistance to the consultation process may be reduced when the consultant shares the responsibility for problem solving, views the teacher as an expert, communicates that recommendations may be accepted or rejected, has a formal role in the school, and employs situational leadership skills effectively.

Consultation Models

7. The triadic model is a linear sequence that portrays the relationships among the consultant, the mediator, and the target. The relationship between the consultant and the mediator forms the basis for collaborative consultation.

8. The four principles that form the basis of the triadic model are: team ownership, recognition of individual differences, application of reinforcement, and data-based evaluation.

9. The systems model involves five phases: assessment, specification of objectives, planning, implementing treatment, and evaluation.

10. The Vermont Consulting Teacher Program is a collaborative effort among local school districts, the Vermont State Department of Education,

and University personnel. The key feature of the Vermont Consulting Teacher Program is that the consulting teacher individualizes the intervention program to meet the specific needs of the referring teacher and the student.

11. A unique feature of the Vermont Consulting Teacher Program is the minimum rate of learning line which specifies the number of objectives that should be mastered within a given time period.

QUESTIONS

1. Define the term consultation, and distinguish between two types of consultation — developmental and problem-centered.

2. How is the consulation process defined, and what are the essential ingredients that make it up?

3. After describing the three consultation models in the text, compare and contrast them with one another.

4. In what way are the four principles of collaborative consultation implicit in the triadic model applicable to other models as well?

5. Under what conditions would the triadic model, systems model, or Vermont Consulting Teacher Program be appropriate to solve a school (or home-based) problem?

DISCUSSION POINTS AND EXERCISES

1. Conduct a meeting with teachers at the elementary, junior high, and senior high levels. Determine from them their views on the consultation process. Compare their perception of the consultation process with the stages presented in this chapter.

2. Using any of the consultation models presented in the chapter, conduct a pilot study within your own district or region to determine the usefulness of the model. Evaluate your results.

3. Identify a classroom-related problem. Apply the systems model. Evaluate whether the model provides a sufficient number of components for school consultation.

2

The Consultant Role

Consultation services to students, administrators, or staff can be direct or indirect. The consultant can work individually with a student, teacher, or administrator to change their behavior, or indirectly with a mediator to change the behavior of a third party. Regardless, it is necessary for the consultant to have a clear idea of the problem to be solved, options for solving it, available resources, and evaluation techniques, prior to initiating the consultation.

The purpose of this chapter is to discuss the three overlapping roles of the consultant: providing technical assistance, coordinating programs, and communicating with professionals, parents, and students. The chapter also provides a model for communication which shows how meaning is constructed, encoded, sent, received, decoded, and comprehended. The chapter concludes with procedures to establish and maintain effective communication, including a discussion of the role and function of related-services personnel and suggestions for the consultant interested in facilitating interactions with these professionals.

OBJECTIVES

After reading this chapter, the reader should be able to:

1. describe the three overlapping roles of the consultant.

2. list and discuss how direct and indirect services can be provided to students.

3. list and discuss five direct technical services that can be provided to teachers.

4. state how direct and indirect services can be provided to administrators.

5. describe two major ways that the consultant can coordinate programs.

6. describe a model for communication that addresses all aspects of the process.

7. list four ways to establish and maintain effective communication.

KEY TERMS

Direct service	Covert modeling
Indirect service	Inservice training
Modeling	Communication

PROVIDING TECHNICAL ASSISTANCE

Consultants fulfill three overlapping roles: providing technical assistance, coordinating programs, and communicating to professionals, parents, and students (Goldstein & Sorcher, 1974) (Figure 2.1).

Technical assistance can be provided in two ways, directly and indirectly, and it can be delivered to students, teachers or parents, or administrators. Implicit in the concept of providing technical assistance is the notion that the consultant has acquired complete mastery of all areas related to the education process (i.e., assessment, planning, implementation, and evaluation) as well as being versed in other important areas (e.g., multicultural education and system analysis). The illustration shown in Figure 2.2 clarifies the distinction between direct and indirect service using the triadic model discussed in Chapter 1 as a basis.

Direct Service to Students

Direct service to students includes any task where the consultant (e.g., a school psychologist or resource room teacher) actually works with the student without a mediator. Conducting individual assessments, performing an interview, providing counseling, and, in some cases, an in-class observation are examples of direct service.

According to Bergan (1977), direct service to students is usually carried out subsequent to a referral. Additional information is required, and the consultant is called upon to obtain that information and to communicate it to those professionals (or parents) with whom the student interacts.

Let us assume that June, a learning disabled, seventh-grade student, was referred to a resource room teacher because of adjustment problems in the

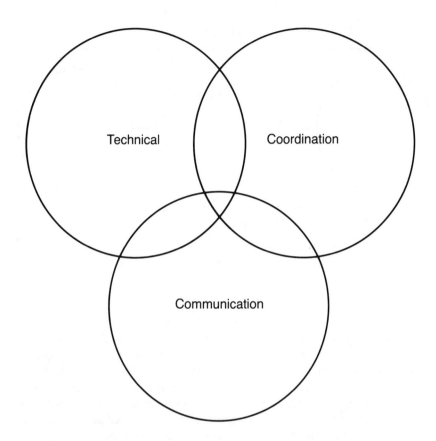

FIGURE 2.1. The three overlapping roles of a consultant: providing technical assistance, coordinating programs, and communicating to other professionals, parents, and students. From *Changing supervisor behavior* by A. Goldstein & M. Sorcher, 1974, New York, Pergamon. Adapted by permission of publisher and author.

classroom. After a discussion with the classroom teacher, the resource room teacher was able to determine that June's adjustment problems involved her interactions with other students during small group activities. She did not finish her portion of an assignment, and consequently her group was not able to complete the whole task. As a result, she was ignored by her peers.

In this example, the direct service the consultant provided was on two levels. First, she conducted an observation of the small group activity to ascertain the type of assignment June was to complete and the nature of the interactions she was having with her peers. Next, she discussed the situation with June directly. During the interview June indicated that she felt uncomfortable performing several of her tasks. She had to read, take notes, and compile

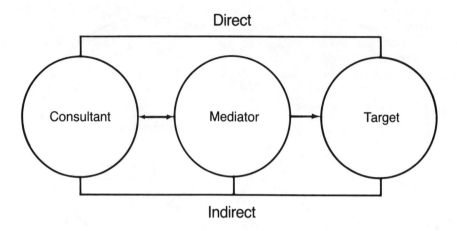

FIGURE 2.2. The triadic model showing the distinction between direct and indirect consultation.

her portion of the project for the other group members. She wanted to do her assignment but felt frustrated at being so slow. The consultant suggested that June tape-record portions of the assignment (the assignment required report writing) so that she could complete the work within the deadline. Although June still had trouble with the reading portion of the group assignment, she used a tape recorder to make notes on major points, which she later transcribed and edited for her report. Her peers reacted positively, since June's assignment was completed within the required time.

Advantages of Direct Service. Bergan (1977) indicates that direct service to students offers several advantages for the consultant. First, the consultant serves as an advocate by acting as the mediator between the student and the teacher. Hence, the student perceives the consultant as a colleague. In this sense the student becomes the consultee, and a mutual plan is decided upon in the same way it might be if the teacher were the consultee. Second, it gives the student the opportunity to engage in decision making. In June's case, she discussed the use of the tape recorder with the consultant. A final advantage is that the student gains a skill that can be applied in this situation and possibly in other situations as well.

Another example of direct service of children that may have far-reaching implications, is shown in a study conducted by Graubard, Rosenberg, and Miller (1971). In this study, students were taught techniques to gain and maintain the teacher's attention during classroom activities. Specifically, students were taught how to establish eye contact with the teacher, ask for additional assistance, nod approvingly when the teacher spoke, say "ah-hah" during a teacher explanation, and reinforce the teacher for praising them.

Teaching countercontrol techniques to the student had the effect of increasing appropriate teacher-student interaction. The obvious advantages of this technique are that students can apply these procedures in other settings, such as the home, and that it is a cost-effective way to teach students a functional coping skill.

Disadvantages of Direct Service. The main disadvantage of providing direct service to individual students is the time factor. Few consultants have the time to meet students on an individual basis.

Also, if classroom teachers receive direct service for all the student behaviors for which they may need assistance, they may never learn how to use preventative measures themselves. A teacher involved in the consultation process increases her opportunities to learn and provides the consultant with more time to work with other teachers.

Despite the cost factors involved and the potential loss of efficiency, direct service to individual students should be offered when the need arises. In cases where other professionals can be called upon to help, a referral can be made. Otherwise, the consultant might be the only person who is able to solve the student's problem.

Indirect Services to Students

Indirect service to students includes any task where the consultant works with a mediator (e.g., a teacher or parent), who in turn works to change the students' behavior. Indirect services to students are accomplished by providing direct services to teachers (or parents). Providing teachers (or parents) with recommendations or suggestions for intervention, helping to design instructional materials, or referring a teacher to another agency for additional student assistance are examples of indirect services, because the student benefits indirectly from the consultant's intervention. As mediator, the teacher (or parent) actually conducts the behavior change program.

Advantages of Indirect Service. The main advantage of providing indirect services to students is that the consultant can serve more pupils. As stated previously, time constraints and the physical limitations of travel preclude the consultant from attending personally to every student who might need assistance. With indirect service, the consultant provides technical assistance to the teacher (or parent), and they in turn provide the direct service. Second, when providing the teacher with technical assistance indirectly, the consultant sets the occasion for the teacher to use newly acquired skills in a preventative, problem-solving mode. The teacher will learn to use the skills to prevent problems rather than waiting for a problem to surface and then seeking the assistance of the consultant. Finally, indirect service sets the occasion for the teacher to generalize the skills to other students or situations in the future.

Disadvantage of Indirect Service.   The primary disadvantage of providing indirect service to students through a mediator is that it is difficult to ascertain conclusively the effects of the intervention. That is, it is difficult to determine whether improved student performance is directly related to the new instructional material or teaching procedure employed by the teacher.

Direct Service to Teachers

Direct service to teachers can be conducted with an individual teacher, small groups of teachers, or whole school staffs. The intent of direct, technical consultation could be to help a teacher prevent or solve a particular student problem, increase the teacher's level of awareness regarding curriculum issues, or conduct observations and evaluations of teacher performance. The goal of direct consultation is to improve a teacher's skill so that, in turn, she will be more proficient in dealing with student problems. Newcomer (1977) states, "The [consultant's] ultimate goal is not to remediate a particular child's learning problems, but to prevent certain problems from developing and provide the regular educator with the additional skills and competencies required to undertake remedial activities independently" (p. 161).

Direct consulting service to regular education teachers is maximally effective when the teacher wants to change his or her behavior. This perception by the regular teacher is a precondition to effective consultation. The consultee (the teacher) perceives the situation to be outside his direct control and requests assistance. In some cases, the consultee may have the skills required to do the job, but because of extraneous factors, these skills are not evident. For example, a regular educator may be able to provide individualized instruction to students if the class size is not too large. If additional students are added to the roster — especially if these students have handicaps — the teacher's ability to provide individualized instruction may decrease, and the services of a consultant must be requested to help solve the problem.

Direct and technical consulting services can be rendered in several ways: conducting observations in classrooms, modeling, providing inservice training, conducting evaluations, and providing referrals for support services within and outside the school system.

Conducting Classroom Observations.   Consultants can be of great assistance to regular educators when they conduct classroom observations for the purpose of quantifying and qualifying student and teacher behavior. A consultant can serve as another pair of eyes and ears and help a teacher determine who is receiving the teacher's attention and under what circumstances.

Skinner (1979) conducted a study that illustrates this point. A regular education teacher expressed interest in having an observer in her classroom because she was concerned about the uneven amount of attention students in her classroom were receiving. Baseline data were collected on six students in the classroom (two high achieving, two low achieving, and two learning disabled). After five sessions, the consultant met with the teacher to discuss the observational findings. The teacher felt that student 3, one of the learning disabled students, was not receiving enough teacher-initiated statements, while student 2, a nonhandicapped student, was receiving a disproportionate share of initiations. The teacher indicated that the remaining four students were receiving an appropriate number of initiations.

Beginning with week six of observation for student 3 and week eleven for student 2, the consultant met with the teacher to show her the data on her initiations. Figure 2.3 shows that the observation plus feedback phase was successful in modifying the teacher's interactions with each of the two students. The student who had received too many initiations was now receiving fewer and vice versa.

Skinner's (1979) approach to resolving this teacher's problem was successful for several reasons. First, his observational data were accurate and reliable. Second, he was able to relate to and interact with the classroom teacher. Third, he had consulting experience. As V. L. Brown (1977) stated, few professionals who express a desire to become consulting teachers have preservice training in consultation, or have the skill to provide realistic alternatives for a range of management problems. Skinner was able to combine his experiences and skill to resolve the teacher's problem.

Modeling. *Modeling*, defined as physically showing an instructional procedure to another person, is an effective procedure to use when the teacher has some prerequisite skills already in his or her repertoire, holds the model in esteem, and perceives the model as competent (Bandura, 1971; Cooper, Heron, & Heward, 1987). Modeling can be performed at any stage in the consultation process; the consultant merely instructs the teacher to imitate what he or she does. For example, a consultant could model how to dispense tokens or plan daily lessons.

Another form of modeling, referred to as surreptitious or covert modeling, also may have the potential for affecting teacher performance (Brown, Reschly, & Wasserman, 1974). During *covert modeling* the consultant performs a desired classroom behavior in the presence of the teacher but without necessarily saying, "Watch what I do, and you do the same." According to Brown et al. (1974), this procedure can be effective, even though no specific directional prompts are issued. The main advantage of surreptitious modeling

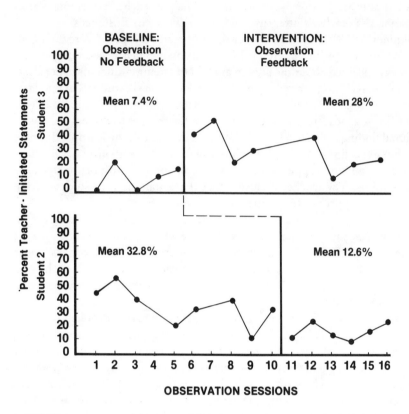

FIGURE 2.3. Percent of teacher-initiated statements to a normal and a learning-disabled student during baseline and intervention. From *Effects of an inservice program on the attitudes, knowledge, and student-teacher interaction patterns of regular classroom teachers* (p. 55) by M.E. Skinner (1979), Unpublished master's thesis, The Ohio State University, Columbus, OH: Used with permission.

is that the chances for a potentially negative "expert-subordinate" relationship between the consultant and the teacher are reduced or eliminated. Since verbal prompts are not given, the teacher does not experience the feelings of inferiority or incompetence that Oldridge (1977) indicates teachers may have during the consultation process.

Conducting Inservice Training. The need for continued teacher *inservice training*, defined as the process whereby additional skills are acquired to maintain or improve instructional effectiveness, is well recognized (Joyce & Showers, 1980; Speece & Mandell, 1980). However, few educators agree on the best method to provide this training. Shaw and Shaw (1972) state that regardless of the method for delivering inservice, the training will be effective only when the participants want to learn a new skill or method. If participants are forced to attend inservice programs in which they have no interest, it is unlikely that learning will be efficient.

On the other hand, consultants can provide teachers with inservice training by giving them reliable and credible feedback as soon after the teaching act as possible (Van Houten, 1980). Brophy and Good's (1974) research seems to indicate that an effective inservice consultation strategy is to make teachers aware of their established, but inappropriate, behavior or interaction patterns with students. Brophy and Good offer a nine-point intervention program for the consultant (see Table 2.1).

Two important functions for the consultant to consider when providing technically competent inservice training are found in points 2 and 3 in Table 2.1. Essentially, these points state that the consultant should try to focus on a few teacher behaviors at a time and find comparison groups that demonstrate good teaching technique, communicating to the teacher that he or she already has some of the skills the consultant is trying to reinforce. Teachers are more likely to have confidence in the consultant who reinforces them for the positive instructional behaviors they have instead of criticizing them for what they lack.

If positive instructional behaviors do not occur or occur only occasionally, the consultant might try to reinforce approximations of the desired behavior (e.g., "I noticed the way John smiled when you publicly praised his accomplishment in science. I bet that same strategy would work for Mario, who seems to like your attention."). The consultant is attempting to extend a demonstrated positive approach to another situation where the likelihood of success is high. The essential message the teacher gets when receiving inservice consultation using Brophy and Good's (1974) approach is that he or she has teaching competencies and skills that can be employed in other situations to prevent or solve problems. The teacher does not perceive an expert-subordinate relationship because the consultant has de-emphasized his or her role in the process (Idol, Paolucci-Whitcomb, & Nevin, 1986) and has reinforced the teacher for appropriate instructional behavior.

Conducting Evaluations. Consultants who provide technical assistance to teachers with respect to evaluation procedures perform a direct service of immeasurable importance. Not only can a functional evaluation plan determine whether a given treatment or intervention was effective in solving a current problem, but also the data collected during the course of the program might prove helpful in future situations (Alpert, 1977). For example, suppose a teacher successfully implemented a peer tutoring activity with a hearing-impaired student in the class. The knowledge gained during the tutoring session could be invaluable if the teacher decided to use a peer tutoring program with other students.

TABLE 2.1
Brophy and Good's Model for Intervention in the Classroom

1. Collect behavioral data on a representative sample of students or the entire class but maintain separate records for each individual student.

2. Identify explicit problems or possible developmental points that appear in the data.

3. If possible, find contrast groups to show good teaching behavior, making it possible to ask teachers to extend to new situations behavior that is already in their repertoire rather than to ask them to perform new behaviors.

4. Express interest in the problem, but allow teachers to give explanations before suggesting changes.

5. Pinpoint differences in teaching behavior with contrasting students and suggest change in teaching behavior with target students as a possible corrective step.

6. If the teacher is agreeable, engage in mutual problem solving until explicit treatment procedures are agreed upon.

7. Specify exactly what the teacher will do to attempt to change student behavior.

8. Arrange to get posttreatment data to evaluate success in changing teacher and student behavior and to examine the data for radiation effects.

9. Hold a debriefing session with the teacher to review the results of the study and to gain valuable clinical data from the teacher.

From *Student-Teacher Relationships: Causes and Consequences* (pp. 292–295) by Jere E. Brophy & Thomas L. Good. Copyright © 1974 by Holt, Rinehart and Winston. Reprinted by permission of Holt, Rinehart & Winston.

A key element in conducting evaluations is deciding whether the planned intervention worked. Are the students, the class, or the teacher "better" than they were prior to the intervention? How much better are they? A second key element is that evaluation helps to determine when to change a given intervention approach or when to terminate it. From an instructional standpoint, much teacher and student time would be saved if teachers had reliable timetables for knowing when to make these decisions. Cooper et al. (1987) indicate that direct and regular measures of student performance are the best indicators for deciding when to initiate, maintain, or terminate a given intervention.

By discussing the types of questions the teacher is seeking to answer, the consultant will be in a better position to recommend an evaluation plan.

Some classroom-related questions might be answered using an interview format or questionnaire. Other questions might require more systematic analysis, and several common research designs might be used (e.g., reversal, multiple baseline, pretest-posttest).

Providing Referrals. The consultant may not be able to solve many classroom-related problems, even with the assistance of a sensitive and competent teacher. Therefore, it is important for the consultant to be able to refer the teacher to other professionals who may be in a position to help. An example is the case where a student's hyperactive behavior in the room might be based on neurological or organic problems. The consultant might recommend that the student be tested for hypoglycemia, a condition that produces excessive motor behavior in some children. Also, in the case where a student's problem in school extends into the home and disrupts the family life, counseling services might be recommended. Consultants who work within specific geographical regions should be familiar with the referral resources of the community, including child protective services, mental health agencies, parent assistance programs, and counseling or clinical services.

Figure 2.4 shows an interdisciplinary team convened to review the case of a child referred to a learning disabilities clinic for suspected attention deficit disorder and hyperactivity. The members of the team — physician, psychologist, consultant, social worker, and nurse practicioner — discuss the findings from their own respective discipline and integrate these data with information received from the school or the home. The outcome of the team meeting is that a multipoint intervention program is produced which is communicated verbally and in writing to the teacher and the parent. The educational consultant assumes the responsibility for monitoring during plan implementation and conducts periodic follow-up checks to determine if the plan is working.

Indirect Service to Teachers

Indirect service to teachers occurs when the consultant provides direct service to an administrator (or other agent) who, in turn, serves the teacher. In this case the administrator would be the mediator, and the teacher would be the "target." When a consultant assists an administrator with classroom placement decisions, ecological or physical design arrangements, scheduling, or staff development, teachers receive indirect service. Indirect services to teachers share many of the advantages and disadvantages of indirect service to students. Consultants should work indirectly with teachers through an administrator but recognize the pluses and minuses of the service.

FIGURE 2.4.   An interdisciplinary team reviewing the case of a child referred to a learning disabilities clinic for suspected attention deficit disorder and hyperactivity.

Direct Service to Administrators

Administrators often seek the advice of consultants to help solve problems related to policy design, short- and long-term planning, inservice training for staff, services to handicapped and minority children, and a host of other topics. Before service can be provided, the consultant must have a clear idea of the objective the administrator has in mind. She or he must be certain that the objective is measurable and know the time frame in which the administrator wants the problem addressed. For example, the administrator might state in broad terms that she or he wants all of the teachers in the district competent in certain classroom management techniques. The following dialogue illustrates how a consultant determined the terminal objective, a procedure to measure it, and the time constraints for achieving the objective.

ANECDOTE 2.1

ADMINISTRATOR: Ruth, I asked you here today to talk over a situation I've felt many of our teachers need assistance with.

CONSULTANT: I'll be glad to help if I can.

ADMINISTRATOR: I feel we could use a refresher course on classroom management. I've noticed that several teachers at the high school were unable to handle the inappropriate behavior in their classes.

CONSULTANT *(attempting to determine the terminal objective)*: I agree that appropriate classroom management techniques are important. Which ones did you have in mind — individual or group approaches, positive or aversive techniques?

ADMINISTRATOR *(hesitantly)*: Well, all of them.

CONSULTANT *(narrowing the range)*: That's a tall order. Do you feel that we need to concentrate on group strategies to help the high school teachers with the whole class?

ADMINISTRATOR: I think that would be appropriate.

CONSULTANT: Fine. I'll work up a plan for an initial inservice program on positive group strategies for managing secondary level classrooms. *(attempting to determine time constraints)* Incidentally, what time frame did you have in mind for the teachers acquiring these competencies?

ADMINISTRATOR: I'm thinking of this program as long range. By the end of the year would be acceptable.

CONSULTANT: That's good. I'll be able to plan several mini-conferences — maybe lunch bag seminars — which will follow up on the information presented during the initial conference.

ADMINISTRATOR: Great idea.

CONSULTANT: Thank you. That leaves one more question to be resolved. What are your thoughts on evaluating the year-long inservice program?

ADMINISTRATOR: As I stated, I'd like to see better behaved students in the classes.

CONSULTANT: If students raised their hands to respond to teacher questions, waited their turn to speak, and asked permission to leave their seats, would you think their overall behavior would have improved?

ADMINISTRATOR: Without question. You cited three very troublesome matters for our teachers.

CONSULTANT: I'll plan a two-phase evaluation procedure. The first phase will assess the knowledge gained after the workshop series is over. I'll prepare a simple assessment device and interview several teachers to obtain their reactions to speakers, audiovisuals, and the rest. Next, I'd like to a schedule of short observations in each teacher's class to obtain reliability data. I'm confident the teachers can get the bulk of the data on these behaviors themselves. The real improvement you're looking for must occur in the classroom if the program is to be any success at all. My conferences with them will focus on the student's change of behavior before and after the inservice.

ADMINISTRATOR: That sounds very comprehensive.

CONSULTANT: Thank you, but there is one more thing.

ADMINISTRATOR: What's that?

CONSULTANT: I'll be meeting with the teachers collectively and individually to inform them of the purpose, scope, and expectations, and to obtain their views on the program. Also, it is important that they view this series of workshops and observations as a chance to improve and extend their management skills. They must understand my role in this process as that of a facilitator. I'll do my best to ensure that the 'evaluation' stigma which is sometimes created by these projects is avoided.

ADMINISTRATOR: I'll do everything I can to help.

CONSULTANT: I'm sure you will.

Aside from obtaining necessary information from the administrator (the terminal objective, time constraints, and evaluation procedure), the consultant shared vital information with her. She told the administrator that she viewed the teachers' reactions to the inservice plan as important. Also, she wisely established her facilitating role with the administrator and the teachers in the consultation process. As Hughes (1980) indicates, consultants must avoid alienating any organizational or philosophical factions within the school. Obtaining consensus and avoiding confrontations are important objectives for the consultant.

In our hypothetical example, the consultant indicated by her questions and responses that she was going to prepare a plan in concert with the teachers' perspectives that would help to improve the classroom management skills of the teachers. In this situation, the consultant is acting clearly in the role of a facilitator.

Consultants can perform other functions at the administration level as well. For example, they may assist with establishing and maintaining open communication between teachers and administrators. They may serve as a resource for innovative program planning, applying for and receiving grants-in-aid for experimental education research projects. They may participate in advisory meetings to design district-wide policy on a range of topics from corporal punishment in the classroom to the dress code.

Although the reasons for the interaction between the administrator and the consultant may vary, the nature of the interaction should follow a consistent path: determine the goals, identify the resources, establish the consultant role, implement the program, and evaluate the results.

Indirect Service to Administrators

When a consultant provides an indirect service to an administrator, the administrator is the target and another agent serves as the mediator. For example, an indirect service to an administrator would be provided when a consultant improved the curriculum decision making of teachers, and they in turn influenced the administrator to adopt a particular textbook series or computer-assisted instructional program.

COORDINATING PROGRAMS

Coordinating programs can be accomplished in two major ways: by facilitating the Individualized Education Program (IEP) and by managing resources.

Facilitating the IEP

Facilitating the IEP means that the consultant assumes responsibility for ensuring that all aspects of the IEP (i.e., identification through evaluation) are completed in a timely fashion and that all persons associated with completing the IEP participate fully. Turnbull, Strickland, and Brantley (1982) are emphatic that the consultant ensure full participation by all members of the IEP committee, especially the regular education teacher:

> An initial step to foster coordination is the involvement of persons responsible for implementation in the initial decision-making process of IEP development. A major consideration is to involve the teachers of the handicapped student in the development of the IEP. . . . An important system of checks and balances occurs when persons responsible for implementation participate in the planning process. (p. 231)

The IEP process is also facilitated by careful monitoring during implementation. Monitoring can occur at several levels. For instance, student progress can be monitored by determining whether the student's present level of achievement improved since the IEP was developed. Is the student able to complete tasks or assignments that he or she was unable to complete before? Likewise, how does the student perceive the implementation of the IEP? Is the student (or parent) satisfied with the rate of progress? Finally, are the methods used to reach established goals consistent with good practice? When measures are taken to determine if the goals, procedures, and outcomes of an intervention program are acceptable, the social validity of the program is being monitored.

Monitoring can also be applied to the procedural aspects of the IEP. Are students evaluated or reevaluated according to the established time lines? Are IEP meetings held annually? Are all due process measures followed? Monitoring of IEP goals, procedures, and outcomes should not be undertaken merely to identify problem areas. According to Turnbull et al. (1982), data analysis during the monitoring phase of the IEP should identify those factors of the program that work successfully. Turnbull et al. (1982) state the importance of collecting these data:

> There is a tendency to point out problems, yet rarely to highlight the successes. Educators and parents need reinforcement; they need to be recognized for a job well done. The systematic improvement of mechanics associated with the IEP process can be fostered by building on strengths and ensuring that the participants are commended for their success. (p. 240)

The IEP is facilitated also when the consultant is knowledgeable about the responsibilities of related-service personnel. By being sensitive to their roles and functions, the consultant is in a better position to know which professional might offer the maximum amount of service. Interaction with related-service personnel can be facilitated if the IEP program integrates the positive recommendations made by related-service personnel. Not all recommendations from all related-service providers need to be included in the IEP, but the major recommendations should be addressed. Another way to facilitate interactions is by planning and implementing a program that reflects a common orientation. Situations become strained when the IEP goals and short-term objectives reflect different orientations and philosophies. Strategies that are recommended by one individual might be counterproductive if they are not agreed upon by all parties; thus the program becomes fragmented.

Anecdote 2.2 indicates how an educational consultant facilitated the interaction of several related-service professionals prior to an IEP meeting. The purpose of the pre-IEP meeting was to prepare in-house recommendations so that a sample could be mailed to the guardian prior to the meeting. The student to be discussed at the conference was a behaviorally disordered adolescent who resided at a county child protective care facility.

ANECDOTE 2.2

EDUCATIONAL CONSULTANT (*chairing a pre-IEP meeting with a guidance counselor, speech clinician, school psychologist, and social worker*): Thank you for attending the meeting this afternoon. I realize that everyone's schedule is full this time of year. Let's begin with Danny O'Rourke.

SPEECH CLINICIAN (*speaking for the other participants*): Fine. Let's get started.

EDUCATIONAL CONSULTANT: As I am sure you're aware, Danny is a behaviorally disordered youth residing at the Dawn County Child Protective Services facility. He's lived there for eight months. Since the IEP conference will be the first meeting with Danny's legal guardian this year, I'd like to review last year's IEP and ask for your recommendations.

GUIDANCE COUNSELOR (*reviewing previous IEP*): Since Danny didn't arrive at our school until spring, we couldn't accomplish all the initial objectives prescribed for him. I'm in favor of addressing these objectives again this year. It is my understanding talking with his teachers that the behavioral goals mentioned on the document are still viable.

EDUCATIONAL CONSULTANT: Are there any objectives in particular which seem more important than others?

GUIDANCE COUNSELOR: Yes, I'd like Danny to be able to identify personal strengths and weaknesses so that I can begin to show him how his personality characteristics might affect his on-the-job performance after graduation. He is an adolescent. We need to focus on career expectations.

SCHOOL PSYCHOLOGIST: I agree. Danny still is all bottled up. He has difficulty communicating his feelings. I don't think he thinks of himself in very positive terms.

SPEECH CLINICIAN: You're right about his communication problem. However, I think it goes beyond any psychological disability he has. My observations indicate that he has a problem expressing his concerns and ideas. Not only does he have a slight articulation problem, but he also has difficulty sequencing his verbalizations. He jumps from thought to thought. I'd like to continue individual therapy.

EDUCATIONAL CONSULTANT: How about you, Fran? What goals do you think are appropriate for Danny?

SCHOOL PSYCHOLOGIST: I'd like to get Danny involved in group therapy as soon as possible, but it may be premature to begin in September. I'd like to see him individually to work out some of his problems.

EDUCATIONAL CONSULTANT: What is your target date for beginning group therapy?

SCHOOL PSYCHOLOGIST: January.

EDUCATIONAL CONSULTANT: Fine. Louise, you work directly with the county child care facility. What are your thoughts?

SOCIAL WORKER: I'd like to see Danny start out-patient care from a nearby mental health clinic as soon as possible. I think it will be difficult for Danny to achieve any measurable goals if only a school approach is used. Holidays and Christmas vacation come along quickly, and these breaks can stall gains. I'd like to see Danny receive services from the mental health clinic now, if he is eligible.

EDUCATIONAL CONSULTANT: OK. I'll leave it to you to check his eligibility for these services. Perhaps you could call the Director to see if Danny qualifies.

SPEECH CLINICIAN: It sounds like we are going to initiate basically the same plan for Danny this year, although some changes have been suggested.

EDUCATIONAL CONSULTANT: True. But I'd like to suggest that we consider the recommendations made by Danny's teacher at the end of last year. In her summary remarks, she indicated Danny was responding very well to a contingency contract she had negotiated. She stated that he liked the flexibility of deciding his tasks and rewards. I'd like to continue this approach. Specifically, I'd like to recommend that each of us use some form of contingency contract with Danny, at least initially, to test its effectiveness.

SPEECH CLINICIAN: That's fine with me. I can draw up a contract for Danny for several skills in therapy.

SCHOOL PSYCHOLOGIST: I can as well.

GUIDANCE COUNSELOR: I am not fond of strict contracts. I prefer a less structured program, but I'm willing to give it a try for a short time, especially if the teacher found it effective.

SOCIAL WORKER: Since I don't work directly with Danny, it's purely academic to me.

EDUCATIONAL CONSULTANT (following up on the social worker's comment): Except that if a mental health agency becomes involved, it might be important for them to consider using some form of contracting, if it eventually provided direct service.

SOCIAL WORKER: I see your point.

EDUCATIONAL CONSULTANT: In sum, we're recommending basically the same goals as last year and we'll try a contingency approach using the teacher's program as a model. Am I correct?

TEAM: Yes.

EDUCATIONAL CONSULTANT: I'll mail our sample to Danny's legal guardian so that he'll be able to review it prior to the IEP meeting. At that time we can finalize our program, and with the guardian's approval begin shortly thereafter. Thank you for your help.

This anecdote shows how a knowledgeable consultant using reliable information (the teacher's experience with contracting and the speech clinician's observations) set the stage for a consistent approach by the team. While the details of the contract were not specified, consensus was reached that this strategy should be initiated. Of course, Danny's legal guardian would have the opportunity to provide input as well, and the formal details of the IEP (long- and short-term objectives, amount of service) would have to be identified and negotiated.

The facilitating of interactions with related-services personnel is continued during the IEP implementation phases. It is important that the educational consultant monitor the progress of the student within individual disciplines and across settings. For example, if Danny were making gains in individual speech therapy sessions, were these gains evident in the classroom or at the child care facility? If gains were evidenced in therapy but not in the classroom, a revised plan might focus on generalization training.

Managing Resources

Two major resources that consultants can coordinate are personnel and information. When coordinating personnel, the consultant helps to decide who might best meet the needs of the handicapped student. "Who" in this case does not always refer to a specific person, but rather to a type of delivery system. For instance, based on the identified needs of a student, a peer tutoring program might be needed. For another student, team teaching might be the method of first choice, allowing the student to receive more individualized assistance. For a third student, a home-based education program might have to be devised so that skills learned in school can be practiced at home. The management of personnel in each of these illustrations—the students, another teacher, or the parents—is a consultant role.

Another resource that usually needs to be managed is the services of related-services personnel. Given that many special education students use the services of speech and language clinicians, counselors, adaptive physical education teachers, and so forth, the consultant's role is to orchestrate each of these separate area services so that an integrated, comprehensive program is delivered.

COMMUNICATING WITH PROFESSIONALS, PARENTS, AND STUDENTS

Of all of the consultant's responsibilities, communicating effectively with professionals, parents, and students ranks as one of the more important ones. Without effective communication, the ideas the consultant might have for changing behavior would not likely be understood, implemented as intended, or evaluated successfully. Communication is the means by which changes take place. But what is effective communication, and how is it established and maintained? The remainder of this chapter addresses these questions.

A Model of Communication

According to Parsons and Meyers (1984) *communication* is defined as a "condition in which the message perceived and responded to by the receiver corresponds to the one intended by the sender" (p. 57). Davis (1983) considers communication as the transfer of any thought, feeling, or need between people through a verbal or nonverbal channel. Figure 2.5 shows a model of communication in which meaning is conceived, encoded, and sent by the sender, and received, decoded, and comprehended by the receiver.

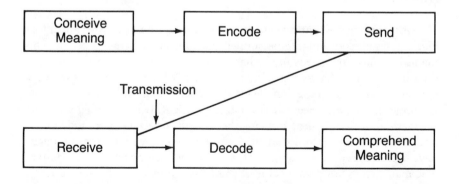

FIGURE 2.5.   A communication model illustrating the sequence by which a message is conceived, encoded, sent, received, decoded, and comprehended. From *Interpersonal communication in organizations* by O. Baskin & C. Aronoff, 1980, Santa Monica, CA: Goodyear. Adapted by permission.

According to Parsons and Meyers (1984), consultants should be aware that "miscommunication" can occur at any stage in this model because of conditions existing at the time of communication (e.g., interfering stimuli), a faulty mechanism during the communication act itself (e.g., inappropriate choice of words, gestures, or signals), or a lack of background knowledge or experience of the receiver.

> It should be apparent that the ill-chosen word, poor timing, confused mixture of verbal and nonverbal signals, and poor listening skills exhibited by the consultant . . . not only will inhibit the successful orchestration of the consultation contract at hand but will likely interfere with future referrals from that consulting source. (p. 58)

Establishing and Maintaining Effective Communication

To establish and maintain effective communication, the consultant must accomplish several interrelated objectives, including gaining acceptance, establishing credibility, providing feedback, and disseminating information (Evans, 1980; Goldstein & Sorcher, 1974; Idol et al., 1986; Speece & Mandell, 1980).

Gaining Acceptance.   Gaining acceptance and establishing rapport are important components of effective consultation (Brown et al., 1979; Idol et al., 1986). Without the acceptance of the group, even the most skilled consultant will be ineffective. Gaining acceptance and establishing rapport can be accomplished in several ways. First, Idol et al. (1986) recommend, in part, treating others with respect, shifting credit for ideas and accomplishments to others, and willingly sharing information and learning with others. Second, acceptance can be achieved when consultants participate fully in school or agency functions (e.g., serving on committees, assisting with sport or club activities). Serving in this capacity provides visibility and demonstrates to peers a commitment to the overall educational process. Finally, the consultant can gain acceptance by clearly defining, or having a superior define, the role he or she will play in the school. Letting colleagues know what the consultant can and cannot do decreases the likelihood that misconstrued expectations which could jeopardize acceptance into the social community of the school or agency will arise.

Still, the consultant should realize that gaining acceptance takes time. It is almost never achieved immediately by the newcomer. It has to be earned, and time is an important factor in this equation. As Laurie, Buchwach, Silverman, and Zigmond (1978) discovered after working with teachers in a secondary level mainstreaming program over several years:

Our experience. . . has shown us that mainstream teachers can be helped to provide more individualized educational programs for learning disabled students. . . .
But [it] took four years to accomplish, with one special educator in each high
school assigned full time to the task of working with mainstream teachers. While
these results suggested that our long-term goal of effectively mainstreaming learning disabled adolescents might be achieved, they also demonstrate that the task
we have undertaken is a formidable one. . . . To help mainstream educators
develop the attitudes, skills, and knowledge necessary to meet the challenges
of PL 94-142. . . [we] must extend our influence through direct involvement with
mainstreamed teachers. (p. 71)

Establishing Credibility.   Establishing credibility means that the consultant
is perceived as a believable person by his or her colleagues. The consultant
is thought of as a person who is knowledgeable and able to apply effective
interventions. According to Hawisher and Calhoun (1978), the consultant
must have a thorough knowledge of the dynamics of the regular classroom
in order to establish credibility:

The [consultant] skilled in teacher-to-teacher consultation has the ability to relate
to the classroom teacher in that he is able to recognize those problems of tedium,
those problems of an exceptional nature, and those problems imposed by varying
aptitudes and abilities of 30 or so active students. Without these understandings
of the classroom, the [consultant] will not be able to establish credibility and
will not be able to influence the classroom teacher to attempt new techniques
or approaches. (p. 143)

Evans' (1980) data indicate that when consulting teachers held advanced
academic degrees (i.e., master's degree or higher), they were more likely to
engage in consultation. Evans speculated that the graduate degree "might
be necessary to give resource personnel the credibility to function in the consultant role." (p. 403)

Providing Feedback.   Providing feedback to teachers or parents serves as
a mechanism to verify whether the message was received as intended. Davis
(1983) indicates that feedback can be obtained by asking the other party to
restate the communication using different words and analyzing the verbal
and nonverbal behavior of others during the communication. For example,
suppose a teacher said to a consultant, "Harry has not been behaving very
well in the classroom lately," to which the consultant replied, "If I understand what you are saying, Harry's behavior has been disruptive." The consultant's reply attempts to provide feedback to the teacher that he or she
understood the intent of the message. At this point, the teacher can either
verify that the meaning was understood ("Yes, that is what I mean") or further refine his or her original statement ("Well, it's not that he has been

disruptive, only that he is not paying attention as he used to do"). In either case, the consultant's feedback statement has served a useful purpose.

Nonverbally, the consultant must be cognizant of body position, posture, gestures, or other signals that might provide feedback that his or her intended message is not likely to be received correctly. A good example of how this happens occurs when a teacher and a consultant attempt to squeeze a mini-consultation into a cramped time frame. If the teacher is organizing papers, setting up equipment, or quickly reviewing lesson plans, it is likely that shuffling papers, poor eye contact, or physical distance will preclude the message from being received well. In this situation, the consultant is receiving nonverbal feedback that this is not the best time to try to discuss the matter.

Speece and Mandell (1980) state that teachers or parents might not have the prerequisite skills to provide effective feedback. In their view, the consultant must structure inservice programs — perhaps using role playing, videotaping, or modeling — to teach these skills. For instance, in the example above with the harried teacher and consultant, a role-playing situation might be designed whereby the consultant would say, "I recognize that this is not the best time to discuss the problem. Can I call you later today to discuss it?"

Further, Speece and Mandell (1980) believe that administrators must recognize the importance of consultant-teacher feedback exchanges and provide time during the school day for these interactions to take place. If consultant-teacher interactions occur only during crises, the full value of consultation will not be achieved.

Disseminating Information.   According to Cooper et al. (1987), "Practitioners have legal and ethical responsibilities to share data with learners, and these responsibilities extend to parents and guardians when the learners are minors and/or dependents" (p. 588). But dissemination can be defined in a broader context to include all information relative to the special education program for which the consultant is responsible. Using this broader perspective, the consultant can disseminate information in several useful ways. Informally, the consultant can talk about the program with teachers, parents, or administrators. Informal conversations that occur in the hallways, lounge areas, and parking lots of school buildings provide a valuable medium through which information flows. Formal means of communication can occur through established district-wide newsletters, school newspapers, or specially audiotaped announcements accessible through a home-school communication system (cf. Weiss et al., 1982). Likewise, a broader professional or parental audience can be reached through conferences, journal articles, or television or print media.

When providing oral or written communication to an audience, the consultant should be mindful of the audience's background knowledge, experiences, and vocabulary. The words and context of a description of a new resource room program before a school board would be stated entirely differently for teachers, parents, or the students. The context of the message would be the same, just the manner in which the content is expressed would change.

With any audience it is helpful to program for redundancy; that is, provide several ways to communicate the same message and define terms or clarify meaning with examples at every opportunity. For example, suppose that high school teachers of developmentally handicapped students wanted the consultant to advertise a new "career education" program for the students. The consultant might present the program to the school board and the Parent Teacher Association, submit an article to the school or community newspaper, and enlist faculty cooperation by presenting a slide/tape show at the teachers' meeting. For each communication medium the consultant would define the scope and sequence of the career education program and state how it would fit within the existing structure of the school and the community.

CONCLUSION

The consultant's role can be divided into three overlapping areas: providing technical assistance to teachers, parents, or administrators; coordinating the Individualized Education Program; and communicating with professionals, parents, and students. Within each of these areas, the consultant has several ways to accomplish the objective. For example, when providing technical assistance, the consultant can work directly or indirectly with others. When coordinating the IEP, the consultant can call upon teachers, parents, or students to assist with data collection, monitoring, or evaluation. When communicating to others, the consultant can use verbal and nonverbal messages, which are delivered through print, aural, or oral channels. The decision to use any of these methods or channels depends in large part on the problem the consultant is trying to solve, the resources that are available, and the time constraints that exist.

SUMMARY OF KEY POINTS

Providing Technical Assistance

1. Technical assistance can be provided in two ways — directly and indirectly — and can be delivered to student, teacher, parents, or administrators.

2. Direct service includes any task where a consultant works with another change agent without the services of a mediator. Direct service to teachers can be accomplished by conducting classroom observations, modeling,

conducting inservice training, conducting evaluations, and providing referral services.

3. Indirect service occurs when a consultant works through a mediator, who in turn tries to change the behavior of the target individual.

Coordinating Programs

4. Coordinating programs can be accomplished in two major ways: facilitating the IEP and managing resources.

5. Facilitating the IEP means that the consultant assumes responsibility for all aspects of the IEP from identification through evaluation.

6. Managing resources occurs when the consultant distributes personnel and information in a manner likely to meet the individualized needs of a handicapped student.

Communicating with Professionals, Parents, and Students

7. The term *communication* implies that a common meaning has been transmitted, received, and comprehended.

8. To establish and maintain effective communication the consultant must gain acceptance, establish credibility, provide feedback, and disseminate information.

9. Dissemination of information can occur formally or informally and take place through verbal, nonverbal, print, or tactile media.

QUESTIONS

1. Identify three ways a consultant can provide direct services to teachers. What is your reaction to these three services?

2. List and discuss the type of data a consultant must possess prior to initiating effective consultation at the administrative level.

3. What are the pros and cons of providing consultation directly to students?

4. Choose three in-school, related-service personnel. What are their potential roles in the IEP process?

5. What are the key features of Brophy and Good's (1974) intervention model?

6. Discuss how an educational consultant might enhance cooperation between diverse groups of professionals, especially as it related to IEP development.

7. Why do you think the recommendations from related-services personnel need to be integrated into a comprehensive program reflecting a specific orientation?

DISCUSSION POINTS AND EXERCISES

1. Why is it important for the consultant to establish his role in the consultation process before service is delivered?

2. Conduct a meeting with elementary and secondary level teachers to obtain their views on inservice workshops. Solicit from them alternatives to the traditional lecture format of inservice workshops.

3. Establish your own criteria for providing one-to-one consultation service to a student. Discuss these criteria with other related-service personnel.

4. Compile a list of referral agencies in your community. Conduct a meeting with key staff of these agencies to determine the type of service they provide, eligibility requirements, and free assistance they may provide.

5. During an IEP conference, collect data on the number of recommendations offered by related-services personnel. Categorize these data. Determine if the data represent a comprehensive, integrated approach to remediating the student's assessed needs.

6. Follow up the IEP conference conducted in item five above to determine the extent to which program recommendations are actually implemented. If recommendations are not followed, determine reasons for the delay or the revision.

3

Working with Teachers in the Mainstreamed Classroom

Students with handicapping conditions are being placed in regular classrooms at an increasing rate. Regular education teachers who previously believed that exceptional children and youth were the sole responsibility of special educators are now faced with the challenge of providing instruction to them. Many regular educators feel unprepared to assume the responsibility for teaching these students. Nevertheless, Public Law 94-142 clearly states that handicapped children and youth are to be educated with their nonhandicapped peers to the maximum extent possible.

Unfortunately, most regular education teachers, and many special education teachers, have only a vague understanding of the intent of the federal and state legislation. For example, many regular education teachers feel that all students who are now enrolled in self-contained classrooms will be integrated in the regular classroom. Further, many regular education teachers feel that they will be the sole person in charge of the student's education, and, consequently, they will be held accountable for the student's rate of progress — or lack of it.

This chapter begins by defining the term mainstreaming. *Concerns of teachers and parents about mainstreaming are presented. Next, the concept of the least restrictive environment is defined. Variables that affect exceptional students within a mainstreamed classroom are identified. Finally, a composite decision-making model is discussed that outlines intervention techniques a consultant can suggest to maintain mainstreamed students in the regular classroom.*

OBJECTIVES

After reading this chapter, the reader should be able to:

1. define the term *mainstreaming*.

47

2. compare concerns parents have about mainstreaming with those of teachers.

3. cite the two components of the least restrictive environment as published in the *Federal Register*.

4. identify the three aspects of Heron and Skinner's definition of the least restrictive environment.

5. cite four variables that affect exceptional students within the mainstreamed classroom.

6. describe the major component of Heron's decision-making model for maintaining mildly handicapped students in mainstreamed classrooms.

KEY TERMS

Mainstreaming	Proportional interaction
Temporal integration	Social relationships
Instructional integration	Countercontrol
Social integration	Modeling
Eligibility	Peer tutoring
Least restrictive environment	Programmed instruction
Opportunity to respond	Individualized instruction
Teacher-student interaction	Cues

MAINSTREAMING VERSUS THE LEAST RESTRICTIVE ENVIRONMENT

To discuss the concepts of mainstreaming and least restrictive environment, a definition of each must be provided, since the terms have been used interchangeably. However, there are clear differences between them.

Definition of Mainstreaming

According to Kaufman, Gottleib, Agard, and Kukic (1975), *mainstreaming* is "the temporal, instructional, and social integration of eligible exceptional children with nonhandicapped peers based on an on-going, individually determined, educational planning and programming process and requires clarification of responsibility among regular and special education administrative, instruction, and supportive personnel" (p. 4). Embedded in this definition are a number of major conditions or concepts that many professionals in special and regular education have failed to understand to the fullest. Let us examine some of the key concepts of Kaufman et al.'s (1975) definition of mainstreaming.

Temporal Integration.   *Temporal integration* is defined as the total amount of time a handicapped student spends with nonhandicapped peers expressed in "periods per day" or "academic subject areas." For example, a student might be mainstreamed for math but remain within a self-contained classroom or resource room for other academic or vocational subjects, or the student might spend a two-week trial period in a regular third grade. If at the end of the two weeks the student seems to be progressing satisfactorily, the placement is made final. Although the latter strategy has often been used, Stephens (1977) cautions against the use of trial placements for exceptional students. He feels that trial placement can be more detrimental than beneficial to students if the placement is not successful. Further, Stephens (1977) states that such placements show a lack of adequate planning on the part of a placement team. It would be better if more planning were done by the team prior to integrating the exceptional student.

It is the opinion of other researchers that temporal integration is not sufficient (Kaufman et al., 1975; Keogh & Levitt, 1976; MacMillan & Becker, 1977). In a review of research concerning the mainstreaming of mentally retarded children, Corman and Gottlieb (1978) concluded that "research on the academic achievement of integrated educable mentally retarded (EMR) pupils has yielded inconsistent results" (p. 270). Furthermore, they state that the social acceptance of retarded students by nonhandicapped peers is unrelated to the amount of time students with developmental handicaps spend in the integrated classroom.

Instructional and Social Integration.   Another key concept in the Kaufman et al. (1975) definition of mainstreaming is that of instructional and social integration. To the maximum extent possible, exceptional children should have the opportunity to benefit from academic instruction and social contact with their nonhandicapped peers.

Instructional integration is viewed by Kaufman et al. (1975) as instruction arranged so that handicapped children partake in the same educational activities as their nonhandicapped peers, but are not required to participate in areas that are too difficult for them. This may possibly be achieved by presenting information at a suitable level, through various modalities, and modifying the expected response. For example, a physically handicapped high school student may be able to successfully participate in a class science lesson if the teacher carefully structures the tasks. The physically handicapped student might have to describe the steps of an experiment and predict the outcome, while another student manipulates the apparatus and a third student takes notes on the process and writes up the results.

If a student were unable to be integrated in the nonhandicapped classroom for academic subjects because he or she lacked certain prerequisite academic skills, then an effort should be made to integrate the student in nonacademic areas, such as recess, special subjects, and physical education. Every alternative should be explored to program as much of the student's day with his or her nonhandicapped peers as possible.

Consultants are usually more successful integrating handicapped students in nonacademic subject areas when they stress the following points to the regular or special teacher. First, the handicapped student, although lacking many prerequisite academic skills, may have adequate social skills to perform satisfactorily. Second, the teacher may have successfully managed the behavior of other students (e.g., the low-achieving nonhandicapped) with traits similar to the handicapped student. Finally, a resource person is available and willing to assist if the situation warrants it.

The next concept, *social integration*, is included because it is clear that school offers more than just academic experiences. Since many mildly handicapped children have difficulty establishing and maintaining adequate social relationships with nonhandicapped peers (Bryan & Bryan, 1977; Goodman, Gottlieb, & Harrison, 1972; Gresham, 1981; Iano, Ayers, Heller, McGettigan, & Walker, 1974), one of the objectives of mainstreaming is to provide occasions where such relationships can develop. According to Gottlieb and Leyser (1981), involving students with the daily class routine increases the likelihood of their social integration with nonhandicapped peers.

The consultant can recommend a number of strategies to the regular and special classroom teacher to foster social integration, even prior to a student's placement in a regular setting. For instance, a peer group activity involving handicapped students and a regular class could be suggested. Games, athletic events, or playground activities could be arranged to maximize positive social exchanges between the two groups.

Eligibility.   The final concept of the Kaufman et al. (1975) definition of mainstreaming is *eligibility*, the criteria for placement. What does it mean to be eligible for a mainstreaming placement? Who determines eligibility?

Several authors have proposed eligibility criteria for placement (Hundert, 1982; Salend and Lutz, 1985). Overall, these criteria are based on the student's readiness to perform academic and social competencies deemed necessary for successful functioning in the regular classroom. According to Salend (1984), a competency-based approach allows a consultant to help determine who might be a successful candidate for mainstreaming and who might need additional remediation in special education programs prior to reentry.

In the final analysis, eligibility for placement of a handicapped student in a mainstreamed setting is determined by a multidisciplinary evaluation team including the student's regular teacher, the special education teacher, the school psychologist, the parents, and other persons with knowledge in the area of suspected disability (Federal Register, Vol. 42, No. 163, 121a533, August 23, 1977).

To provide effective service to eligible handicapped students, a consultant must be thoroughly knowledgeable regarding district placement criteria. Of course, since these criteria are derived from state program standards, state laws, or federal statutes, the consultant must be grounded in these areas as well.

It is interesting to note that nowhere in P. L. 94-142 or in the accompanying rules and regulations is the term *mainstreaming* used. Rather, P. L. 94-142 and the regulations speak to the issue of an educational experience within the context of the least restrictive environment (LRE). Many regular educators perceive mainstreaming to be a process whereby all exceptional children are integrated into regular classrooms. While Edwin Martin was Deputy Commissioner for the Bureau for the Education of the Handicapped in 1974, he cautioned that mainstreaming should not be a "pell-mell" process. Nevertheless, regular education teachers seem confused about the whole notion of integration. In short, regular educators are frequently less than enthusiastic about the prospects of having to teach handicapped children.

Teacher Concerns About Mainstreaming

Although reasons for the lack of enthusiasm about mainstreaming are as varied as the teachers themselves, there are some common concerns. First, many regular educators feel that they lack the specialized training needed to teach handicapped students. Second, though recommended support services can help the regular educator teach the exceptional learner, it is acknowledged that support services vary across schools and districts. Many regular educators are unfamiliar with such services or how to locate them. They are concerned that exceptional students will be simply dumped in their classrooms, and they will have to sink or swim with the added challenges. Third, the regular education teacher is concerned about accountability. Before a regular teacher accepts a child into the classroom, the teacher wants to know to what extent he or she will be held accountable if the student does not make reasonable gains.

The consultant needs to impress upon regular educators that the rules and regulations of P. L. 94-142 specify that neither the teacher nor the school district will be held accountable if a handicapped student fails to achieve the goals prescribed in his or her IEP. However, educational personnel are required to show "good faith" in their efforts to accomplish IEP goals and objectives. Despite P. L. 94-142, legal suits have been brought against schools by nonhandicapped, illiterate graduates of high schools who claim they are not educated or trained for a career. Results of such litigation may set precedents for handicapped students who, in the future, may challenge the educational process by claiming that their IEP goals were not consistently attained.

Finally, many regular education teachers feel they should share the instructional responsibility for the exceptional student with support personnel. Included in the instructional responsibilities would be planning, teaching, and evaluation. Many authors advocate shared instructional responsibility with regular educators and parents (Turnbull & Schulz, 1979; Wang & Birch, 1984).

Consultants can play an active role in the instructional process by recommending appropriate teaching strategies, materials, and evaluation techniques. At the secondary level, the offering of options for grading, credit hours, and class scheduling would be beneficial. The consultant's main task would be to act as a liaison or resource person for the regular educator.

Parent Concerns About Mainstreaming

Parents have a paradoxical view of the benefits to be gained from integration of handicapped children with nonhandicapped peers. On one hand, parents may see the integration process as a positive step. For too long they may have watched their son or daughter in a self-contained classroom be ridiculed by other students. The pain they may have felt when their child was called "dummy" or "retarded" is real. Parents may feel that an integrated program with nonhandicapped children will have a number of advantages. First, they may believe that the amount of ridicule will be reduced, since their child would be participating in a "nonhandicapped" curriculum. Second, parents may believe that the nonhandicapped students will be a good influence. They envision their child's exposure to the appropriate academic and social behavior of the nonhandicapped students as a beneficial experience. Finally, some parents may view the integration process as a valuable experience for the regular students. These parents feel the regular student will become sensitive to the individual differences of students and grow to view exceptional children as "children with a handicap" rather than "handicapped children."

Conversely, parents are often apprehensive about integration programs. They know the regular students may not accept their handicapped child. Further, they are aware that their child may precipitate problems in the regular classroom because of immaturity or lack of social skills (Bryan & Bryan, 1977; Gresham, 1982). Parents are also concerned that, given the increased ratio of students to teacher, their child may not receive the individualized assistance and special instructional programming he or she may have been receiving in the less populous self-contained classroom. Of course, closely related to the last concern is the parents' apprehension that their child may not have the same response opportunities as nonhandicapped peers in the classroom. Parents who are aware of the general nature of classroom interaction realize that the student who survives the pitfalls of education in the day-to-day world is usually the student with the fastest answer, who is passive and compliant in the room, and who reinforces the teacher (Brophy & Good, 1974). Parents of handicapped students who have characteristics different from those expected by teachers will be apprehensive about mainstreaming.

Some of the techniques and activities that consultants and supervisors could use in dealing with these common concerns are discussed further in this chapter and in greater detail later in the text.

Definition of Least Restrictive Environment

According to the final rules and regulations of P. L. 94-142 published in the *Federal Register*, the *least restrictive environment* has essentially two components. First, to the maximum extent possible the student is to be educated with his or her nonhandicapped peers; and second, the student should be removed from that setting only when the nature of his or her disability precludes an adequate educational experience even when supplementary learning aids are used (*Federal Register*, Vol. 42, No. 163, 121a550 (1), (2), August 23, 1977).

The criteria for a least restrictive environment published in the *Federal Register* can be viewed only as guidelines. They are vague and open to varying interpretations. In one sense, a general guideline permits school districts in different parts of the country to exercise a certain degree of latitude in establishing programs for exceptional students. Yet so general a guideline makes it extremely difficult for a placement team within a local education agency to determine the specific criteria for reentry and maintenance within a regular environment.

The Components of LRE. Heron and Skinner (1981) have proposed a definition of least restrictive environment that is consistent with research studies completed within the last 10 years. The use of their definition facilitates data collection on the effectiveness of the integration effort. Further, the definition proposed by Heron and Skinner (1981) is consistent with Kenowitz, Zweikel, and Edgar's (1978) concept of the least restrictive environment for severely and profoundly handicapped students. Heron and Skinner (1981) favor a movement toward programming options and social interactions with non-handicapped populations rather than thinking exclusively in terms of placement alternatives. Their definition reads:

> The least restrictive environment is defined as that educational setting that maximizes the learning-disabled student's opportunity to respond and achieve, permits

the regular education teacher to interact proportionally with all the students in the classroom, and fosters acceptable social relationships between nonhandicapped and learning-disabled students. (p. 116)

The definition has three essential components: opportunity to respond and achieve, proportional interaction between teachers and students, and acceptable social relationships between nonhandicapped and exceptional students. Each component, along with supporting documentation, is addressed in the next sections.

Opportunity to respond and achieve.   According to Greenwood, Delquadri, and Hall (1984), *opportunity to respond* is defined as "the interaction between: (a) teacher formulated instructional antecedent stimuli [the materials presented, prompts, questions asked, signals to respond, etc.] and (b) their success in establishing the academic responding desired or implied by the materials. . . . Opportunity to respond implies the use of instructional tactics that involve presenting, questioning, and correcting so that all students have, in fact, made the desired response" (pp. 64-65).

During the past 15 years educational researchers have investigated variables (such as opportunity to respond) that set the occasion for academic or social responses (Delquadri, Greenwood, & Hall, 1979; Hall, Delquadri, Greenwood, & Thurston, 1982). Despite this long-standing interest, only a handful of efforts have investigated the effects of antecedent, rather than consequent, events on academic and social performance in the classroom. For example, Massad and Edsel (1972) found in working with elementary pupils that the students' opportunity to respond to the teacher had a greater effect upon their ability to learn a language skill, such as a grapheme-phoneme relationship, than the use of positive reinforcement alone.

Similarly, Broden, Copeland, Beasley, and Hall (1977) found that inner-city high school students participated more frequently in class discussion when the teacher restated the questions to them. Further, when the time between a teacher's completion of a question and the student's response was increased from 4.5 seconds to 15 seconds, the amount of student hand-raising also increased. Both tactics are measures designed to increase student response opportunities. Again, specific reinforcement procedures were not employed; merely the opportunities for response were increased.

In an effort to determine if student opportunity to respond was equal across educational settings, Bryan, Wheeler, Felcan, and Henek (1976) compared regular and special education classrooms. It was found that response opportunities were unequal across these settings. Specifically, the learning disabled students employed in the study had more response opportunities in the special education classroom than they did in the regular classroom. Conversely, Ysseldyke, Thurlow, Mecklenburg, and Graden (1984) compared student opportunity to respond in grades 3 and 4 across special and regular education classrooms. The results of their observational study showed few differences in overall academic responding during reading. While these data should be regarded as preliminary, the potential exists in the regular education setting for a handicapped student to experience a different level of response opportunities than might be found in a more traditional special education setting.

If a consultant were assisting a placement committee with its decision, the environment in which increased opportunity to respond and achieve was greatest should be given priority. Likewise, research indicates that there is a positive correlation between achievement and self-esteem (cf. Duncan & Biddle, 1974). As students progress through the public school, it becomes important that they achieve; otherwise, they lose interest in the educational process, and their performance reflects their lack of interest.

Proportional interaction.   *Proportional interaction* means that all of the students receive the teacher's attention for appropriate behavior on a consistent enough basis to maintain performance. One way to determine how much interaction is sufficient, at least for the handicapped students, is to find out before placement in the regular classroom what the rate or percentage of teacher interactions is in the special education class. If the observations indicate that the student receives 15 direct initiations from the teacher each day in the self-contained or resource room, ideally at least 15 initiations should be provided in the regular classroom.[1] The essential contribution that this component of the definition provides is that the regular teacher is relieved of any psychological pressure to provide equal amounts of attention to all students. Rather, it provides a data-based context to determine if a student is likely to receive an appropriate amount of teacher attention. Also, it could serve to allay any fears parents might have that special education students would take the teacher's attention away from the task of educating their children.

Social relationships.   Anyone who has worked with handicapped and nonhandicapped students together realizes that the social relationships (i.e., verbal and nonverbal interactions) between these peer groups can sometimes be strained. As stated previously, several researchers (Bryan & Bryan, 1977; Gresham, 1981; Strain & Kerr, 1981) have found that handicapped students — both learning disabled and educable mentally retarded — are often rejected, ostracized, or actively ignored by their nonhandicapped peers in the regular

---

[1]Two points need to be underscored regarding the number of initiations expected from regular education teachers to mainstreamed students. First, although it is difficult to deliver 15 direct initiatives to the handicapped student in the regular classroom where 35 other students may be competing for the teacher's attention, it is not impossible. Second, the initial level of interactions would lessen as soon as the handicapped student's performance could be maintained with fewer direct contacts.

classroom. They are also less accurate perceivers of their social status within the classroom than their nonhandicapped peers (Bruininks, 1978). For example, the handicapped students often rate their social status in the classroom higher than the actual social status attributed to them by their nonhandicapped classmates. On the other hand, Kirby and Toler (1970) found that contingent upon the implementation of direct intervention approaches, the behavior of nonhandicapped peers can be changed so that a favorable attitude is held toward the exceptional student.

Of course, all interactions between nonhandicapped and exceptional students will not be positive and supportive. Such a situation does not exist in a regular classroom even if handicapped students are not integrated. The consultant should be aware of the social climate within a classroom to effectively assist the placement team with its decision. For example, it might not be desirable to place a handicapped student in a classroom if the student is actively disliked or mistreated by other students. Since peer acceptance can have a tremendous effect on academic performance and self-concept (Schmuck & Schmuck, 1975), and a positive relationship between peer status and academic achievement exists in the classroom (Lilly, 1970), the consultant must be sensitive to the social dynamics of the class.

Many consultants face situations in schools where special education students do not get along with regular students. To place a handicapped student in a regular classroom is a decision that has to be made carefully. The responsibility of being a consultant precludes the haphazard placement of students in compromising learning environments where nonhandicapped students do not accept and are not likely to work with them.

The Dimensions of Measurement of LRE.   Heron and Skinner's (1981) definition of the least restrictive environment has a number of advantages for the consultant over previous definitions. Specifically, the consultant is able to find out across three dimensions (measurable outcomes, teacher benefits, and parent benefits) whether the environment is least restrictive. Heretofore such documentation was not possible.

Measurable outcomes.   All three components of the definition (response opportunities and achievement, proportional interaction, and appropriate social exchange) are measurable. Placement team members are in a better position to determine whether a regular education setting is least restrictive if the consultant helps to provide data in these areas. The placement decision can be made on the basis of an objective analysis rather than an intuitive notion about the efficacy of a particular classroom.

Further, once integration has been completed the consultant can monitor the process more closely if measurable data are available for comparison (Cooper, Heron, & Heward, 1987). By noting differences that may arise across the three areas, the consultant is able to recommend specific interventions to the classroom teacher. For instance, suppose that prior to the integration of a handicapped student, it was found that the regular education teacher distributed her interactions equally to all students. After integration, however, she gave the handicapped student more attention than was needed to maintain performance. In this case, the consultant might recommend to the teacher that she return to the techniques she used to distribute her attention prior to placement. These might include walking around the room regularly to monitor student seatwork, using prompting strategies more effectively during class discussion, or praising all the students, not just a select few, on a regular basis.

Teacher benefits. As stated previously, the classroom teacher will not have to be under pressure to provide one-to-one instruction for the handicapped student. If proportional attention is provided in sufficient amounts to maintain the performance of students at an acceptable level, teacher anxiety should be reduced.

Also, successful integration of a handicapped student may set the occasion for the regular educator to use a wider variety of content and teaching materials as well as instructional techniques in both academic and nonacademic areas. As a result the teacher may become more sensitive to the unique learning style of the handicapped student and, with guidance from the consultant, begin to see how each student's needs can be addressed systematically.

Finally, by addressing the three areas in the definition of least restrictive environment, the consultant will be able to focus on preventive measures the regular teacher can use to reduce possible classroom management problems as well as enhance the learning atmosphere. Presently, consultants spend a disproportionate amount of time trying to help teachers solve problems that might have been prevented.

Parent benefits. Parents of handicapped students would be likely to accept Heron and Skinner's definition because of the multiple criteria used. In the past, their children have been placed in special classrooms usually on the basis of low achievement scores or poor social behavior. With the new definition the opportunity arises for children to participate in some of the regular curriculum and for the parents to monitor their child's progress. For example, during parent-teacher conferences the parents would be able to ask direct questions about the academic achievement of their child, the level of the teacher-student contacts, and social acceptance (cf. Tawney & Gast, 1984). The conference would be more structured, and the parents would be able to establish whether the goals of their child's individualized education program were being addressed.

In summary, the terms *mainstreaming* and *least restrictive environment* are not synonymous. Perhaps the best distinction between these two terms is expressed by Ysseldyke and Algozzine (1982):

Mainstreaming does not mean that all handicapped children will be retained in or returned to regular classrooms, but it does represent one aspect of the general principle of normalization, or the idea that the experiences of handicapped children should be as much like those of their nonhandicapped peers as possible. The mechanism through which proponents of mainstreaming hope to achieve normalized school experiences is the least restrictive environment (LRE.). (p. 244)

VARIABLES AFFECTING EXCEPTIONAL STUDENTS WITHIN A REGULAR CLASSROOM

Composition of the Mainstreamed Classroom

Mainstreamed classrooms are usually composed of one or more handicapped students. Seldom does the regular education teacher find more than 10% of the students in a class identified as handicapped. The high ratio of regular education students to handicapped students may be deceiving. At first glance it might appear as though only a small percentage of the class will need individualized programs or assistance. Unfortunately, the reverse is almost the case. Within any regular classroom, even without the inclusion of handicapped children, a range of abilities, skills, and interest levels exists. For example, in a given fifth-grade classroom some students will be doing sixth- or even seventh-grade work, while other students may doing third-grade work or lower. The majority of the class, however, would fall somewhere in between, as average fifth graders. So, even if handicapped children were never integrated into regular classrooms, a heterogeneous population would already exist there.

The important point here is that the inclusion of the handicapped student may not always serve to extend the heterogeneity of the class. In many cases, students are integrated for only those subject areas where they can successfully achieve. So the teacher may have an easier time instructing the handicapped student than he or she does, say, a low achiever who has been in the classroom all along. A physically handicapped student who has no loss of cognitive functioning would be able to perform the intellectual tasks, if not the motor ones, without imposing unduly on the teacher.

Another consideration may be that unidentified handicapped children are in the classroom already. Functionally, therefore, the teacher has to deal with their individual learning needs, regardless of whether they are labeled "handicapped."

Teacher Attitude

An attitude is defined as a predisposition to behave in a certain way. In the classroom, teacher attitude toward the handicapped student can greatly influence the success or failure of the mainstreaming effort. Numerous studies have been conducted that substantiate the effects of teacher attitude on main-streaming (e.g., Warger & Trippe, 1982). These studies indicate that when a handicapped student is placed in the regular classroom, a teacher may be pessimistic about the student's chance for academic or social success and may even doubt the efficacy of such an integration process. Given these factors, a climate may be established for a self-fulfilling prophecy (Jackson, 1968). That is, the handicapped student may do poorly in the regular classroom simply because the teacher acts differently toward him or her. For example, if the student had a learning disability the teacher might allow fewer learning trials, thereby precipitating lower performance.

Changing Teacher Attitudes. One of the more difficult tasks that faces a consultant is to change a teacher's attitude toward having a handicapped student in the classroom. This is a difficult task because the teacher may not have much experience with handicapped individuals. Unless there is a handicapped sibling in his family, it is unlikely that the teacher has had much day-to-day exposure to this population. Second, although many elementary and secondary teachers are required to complete courses on educating handicapped students as part of state certification, such courses may not involve direct interaction in classroom settings with these students.

The consultant has a number of options for changing the attitude of the regular educator. These include using the principal as a resource, conducting a pilot study, implementing team teaching, generating parent support, performing inservice training, and countercontrol.

Using the principal. By virtue of the principal's position as administrative and instructional leader in the school, he or she has achieved status with respect to the teachers. In most cases, principals are perceived as trustworthy individuals, and teachers are usually willing to follow their lead. A consultant can capitalize on this status by asking the principal to approach the teachers and listen to their concerns about mainstreaming handicapped students. The principal can reassure the teachers that support services and instructional materials are available to assist with the process. Further, after integration has taken place, the consultant could recommend that the principal visit the regular educator's classroom to reinforce the teaching efforts there. The visits need not be long, but they would confirm in the teacher's mind the personal commitment of the principal to see this worthwhile process implemented.

Conducting a pilot study.   Despite Stephens' (1977) caution that placements within a regular classroom should not be done on a trial basis, the consultant may choose to implement a pilot study to demonstrate that a regular educator has the instructional knowledge to successfully teach in a mainstreamed setting. For example, the consultant and regular educator might agree to conduct a study to determine if a handicapped student could function adequately within one of the classroom reading groups. If the regular educator felt that integration was not possible, the data obtained in the pilot study might persuade her or him that the handicapped student could indeed learn in the reading group. Thus, the teacher's attitude might change.

Implementing team teaching.   Team teaching is a common instructional strategy used in classrooms. It involves two or more teachers who share instructional and evaluative responsibilities for a group of students. By pairing an experienced teacher of the handicapped with a less experienced teacher, the less experienced teacher could gain the skills of the experienced teacher. The experienced teacher could model appropriate planning, instructional, and management techniques and provide the opportunity for the less experienced teacher to practice these skills in a supportive environment. After gaining confidence and experience with teaching the handicapped student, the teacher's attitude toward integration might be more favorable. Also, the teacher might be more likely to maintain a positive attitude in situations where team teaching was not used.

Generating parent support.   Many educators feel isolated from parents. They perceive the tasks the student completes in school as separate from tasks the student completes at home. By establishing lines of communication between the educator and the parent, the consultant could bridge the gap in the student's program (cf. Alessi, 1984; Weiss et al., 1982). Moreover, the teacher could perceive that the parents were concerned about their child's performance and willing to work cooperatively to help the student.

Performing inservice training.   Inservice training of teachers can have a beneficial effect on a teacher's predisposition toward the handicapped (McDaniel, 1982). When designing an inservice program, the consultant would be well advised to work closely with teachers, administrators, parents, students, and college or university faculty. Emphasis should be placed on presenting factual information, models, practice, and feedback in a systematic way (Joyce & Showers, 1980). Also, providing ample opportunity for participants to ask questions related to their own experiences and interactions with a handicapped student is helpful (Skinner, 1979).

Countercontrol.   *Countercontrol* refers to a procedure whereby students are trained to systematically employ behavioral principles to change teacher behavior (Graubard, Rosenberg, & Miller, 1971). Specifically, handicapped students might be taught ways to increase the rate of praise by a teacher or decrease the rate of criticism or warnings. In short, they would reinforce the teacher for positively attending to them. While it is acknowledged that countercontrol raises a number of ethical issues, nevertheless a consultant might want to use a modified version of it where teacher resistance has to be changed by a subtle, cost-effective, and systematic procedure.

In summary, the consultant has a variety of options at hand for changing a teacher's attitude toward the handicapped. The consultant should not hesitate to use these techniques individually or collectively.

Teacher-Student Interaction in Mainstreamed Classrooms

Data exist that quantify the type, number, and ratio of *teacher-student interactions*, defined as any verbal or nonverbal encounter, within the regular classroom (Duncan & Biddle, 1974). Unfortunately, the volume of data on teacher-student interactions in mainstreamed classrooms is only beginning to match data in regular education classrooms without handicapped children.

Several studies by Bryan and her colleagues (e.g., 1974a, 1976, 1977) represents the most consistent research effort to determine the effects of the presence of learning disabled students on teacher-student interaction in the regular classroom. Taken as a whole, her data suggest that learning disabled students receive a disproportionate amount of teacher attention. Specifically, LD students show fewer initiated statements to teachers, receive more negative comments from the teachers (warnings, criticism), and take more of the teacher's time than do nonhandicapped students. Chapman, Larsen, and Parker (1979) found similar results in a study with first-grade children. Not only did the LD students receive more teacher criticism and warnings, but they also had fewer initiations to the teachers. Likewise, Alves and Gottlieb (1986) found that handicapped students received fewer questions and received fewer feedback statements than nonhandicapped students. Alves and Gottlieb concluded from their observational study that students with mild handicaps were at a disadvantage academically, because teachers provided a less stimulating and enriching environment.

Heron and Skinner (1979), on the other hand, found that teacher-student interaction varied across regular classrooms in which LD students were integrated. One of the most important variables in determining quantity and quality of teacher-student interactions was the teacher. Thompson, Vitale, and Jewett's (1984) conclusion based on studies in two states was that no differential teacher-student interaction effects were noted between mildly handicapped and nonhandicapped students. Further, Slate and Saudargas (1986) found that teacher-student interactions were equivalent for LD and average fourth- and fifth-grade males.

The crux of the issue, however, is not whether mildly handicapped students receive more or less teacher initiations or teacher praise; it is whether each student receives enough attention to maintain and increase performance. As Brophy and Good (1974) report, two teachers might issue equal amounts of praise, yet one teacher might be distributing praise to only a small minority of students. This is not proportional interaction.

The quantity and quality of teacher-student interactions in the mainstreamed class are important variables for the consultant to consider. The consultant must be able to adequately index the level of teacher-student interaction as well as to apply the correct intervention if the level is inappropriate. A superficial view of the interaction data, based on limited observations, might give the consultant a false representation of the true interaction pattern in the classroom.

Student-Student Interaction in Mainstreamed Classrooms

Sociometric data collected in mainstreamed settings suggest that handicapped students are not readily accepted by their nonhandicapped peers. Therefore, the consultant is advised to address directly peer acceptance as part of a mainstreaming program. For example, Shotel, Iano, and McGettigan (1972) found that EMR children were frequently rejected or actively ignored by their nonhandicapped peers. They had fewer friends than nonhandicapped children, and the likelihood of their acquiring new friends in the regular classroom was slim. This finding was true for LD students as well (Gresham & Reschly, 1986; Morrison, 1981; Morrison, Forness, & MacMillan, 1983).

Bryan (1974b, 1976) conducted sociometric studies to determine if the attitudes of nonhandicapped children toward mildly handicapped children affected their acceptance. In one study, using a population of 1,200 third-, fourth-, and fifth-grade students in classrooms with at least one learning disabled student, Bryan (1974b) administered a sociometric scale designed to ascertain social acceptance and social rejection within the classroom. Social acceptance was defined by answers to the following questions: Who is your favorite friend? Who is fun to be around? Which student in the classroom does everybody like? Social rejection, on the other hand, was defined by answers to: Who is not your friend? Who is worried and scared? Which student does nobody want to have around? The results indicate first that, in general, the learning disabled student received fewer votes for social acceptance and more votes for social rejection than his or her nonhandicapped peers. Second, white LD females were the most frequently rejected population in the study. White LD boys and girls were rejected more often than black LD boys and girls.

Gresham and Reschly's (1986) data indicate that nonhandicapped peers preferred not to work with LD students on academic tasks, and they perceived the LD students as engaging in fewer positive social behaviors.

Bruininks (1978a) found that LD students, especially boys, rated themselves higher in social status in the regular classroom than nonhandicapped children of the same sex rated them. Nonhandicapped students were more accurate in estimations of their own social status in the classroom than the LD children. These findings tend to support Bryan's (1974b, 1976) research; that is, LD students are less socially acceptable than nonhandicapped students in regular classrooms.

Peterson, Dammer, and Flavell (1972) indicate that LD students may miss subtle communication cues and that poor role taking (the ability to assume the role of the other person) may account for much of the difficulty mildly handicapped children have with nonhandicapped peers. In short, mildly handicapped students may be unable to perceive the nonhandicapped student's dislike for their inappropriate behavior, and nonhandicapped students may be unable to comprehend the unique needs and problems of the mildly handicapped (Kitano, Steihl, & Cole, 1978).

Still, some studies have shown that some exceptional students can be accepted in regular class placements (Sabornie & Kauffman, 1985; Sabornie & Kauffman, 1986). In the latter study, an assessment of social acceptance was administered to 46 LD student in grades 9 through12 and a matched sample of students. The data indicated that the sociometric status of these adolescent students (LD and nonhandicapped) did not differ significantly, and that the LD students were as well known as their peers. Sabornie and Kauffman (1986) concluded:

> Our results should give educators hope that at least for some LD students the mainstream of education is socially meaningful and not rife with ostracism. . . . The picture of the LD adolescent's social skills is not as bleak as it once appeared — some exceptional students can find their appropriate social place in regular classrooms. Strategies have been devised to help mildly handicapped students become more socially adept in their relations with NH [nonhandicapped] peers. (pp. 59–60)

One strategy that the consultant might be well advised to recommend is Kitano et al's. (1978a,b) role-taking training. This training is designed to foster better social relationships between nonhandicapped and exceptional students. The role-taking training could increase taking student sensitivity toward each group's needs and feelings and add a positive dimension to mainstreaming in terms of improved self-esteem for LDs and better social relationships between LD and nonhandicapped students. Further, the consultant might be able to assist handicapped students, either directly or indirectly, to discover their social status within the classroom, develop specific behaviors that would positively affect their status, and train them to regulate their behavior.

Data obtained by Bruininks (1978b), Kitano et al. (1978), and Bryan and Bryan (1977) indicate that both the verbal and nonverbal behaviors of LD students seem to adversely affect their status and acceptability in the classroom.

Thus, the consultant and the regular education teacher need to examine the nature of the verbal and nonverbal exchanges between the handicapped and nonhandicapped students. After an analysis of the data, they could jointly plan and implement a program designed to teach each group to recognize and engage in socially acceptable and positively reinforcing verbal and nonverbal exchanges using appropriate techniques to promote social reciprocity between these groups (Strain, Odom, & McConnell, 1984). Presumably, if mildly handicapped students were taught to use verbal and nonverbal signals in a constructive fashion, their status within the classroom would be enhanced.

MAINTAINING MILDLY HANDICAPPED STUDENTS WITHIN THE REGULAR CLASSROOM

After an appropriate placement for a handicapped student has been made, what is a consultant to do if the mainstreamed child begins to present unanticipated problems in the regular classroom? The following decision-making model offers the consultant a systematic approach to solve the problem.

A Decision-Making Model

Heron (1978a) has constructed a decision-making model that supervisors, principals, consultants, or even teachers themselves can use to solve an array of problems related to integrating the handicapped (Figure 3.1).

Rationale. The strategies listed under each major target population (e.g., exceptional child, normal child, and teacher) are arranged hierarchically. The least intrusive technique is listed first, followed by more intrusive measures. More important, the strategies proposed by Heron are data based. Each has been demonstrated effective in a variety of settings, and each is relatively easy to implement, depending, of course, on the training and experience level of the teacher. Finally, the likelihood that the results will endure is enhanced with these alternatives.

Employing the Model. To use the model effectively the consultant must be able to do two things. First, he or she must be able to identify the problem. Specifically, the consultant can document the conditions under which a given behavior occurs, the variables that seem to be maintaining the behavior, and any variables that can be used to change the behavior. Of course, the latter goal speaks directly to the consultant's ability to identify reinforcers and punishers within the learning environment. Bergan and Tombari (1976) report

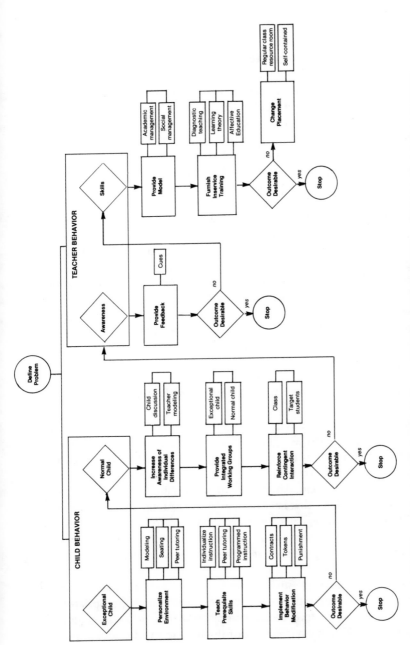

FIGURE 3.1. Process approach for maintaining mainstreamed children in regular classrooms. From ''Maintaining the mainstreamed child in the regular classroom: The decision-making process'' by T. E. Heron (1978) in *Journal of Learning Disabilities, 11*(4), 213. Reprinted by permission.

that a consultant who is able to identify the problem is more likely to come up with a solution. In their study, a consultant who could not identify the problem in concrete terms had extreme difficulty resolving it.

The second task the consultant must perform is to identify the most probable agent for change. In the regular classroom there are three change agents — the exceptional child, the nonhandicapped child, and the teacher. It is realized that classrooms are interactive environments where the rapid pace of interaction (Jackson, 1968) may make it difficult to determine who is controlling the environment. The consultant should resist applying multiple strategies simultaneously, because it would then become difficult to determine what strategy produced the effect. A sufficient number of studies have indicated that increases in the teacher's use of a specific technique produce positive, consistent, and enduring effects on student behavior.

Once the decision has been made to begin with either the exceptional child, the nonhandicapped child, or the teacher, the consultant may suggest that the teacher implement each of the alternatives listed under that population. If all of the alternatives within one category have been exhausted, the teacher would be advised to go on to the next group to resolve the problem. If, upon reaching the last alternative under a particular group (e.g., exceptional child, nonhandicapped child, or teacher), the problem continues, the teacher would be counseled to continue with another target population.

The intent of the decision-making model is to provide consultants with functional alternatives to offer regular education teachers, and preclude the premature removal of a mainstreamed student from a regular setting before a series of alternatives has been systematically attempted.

Educational Alternatives for Exceptional Students

A considerable number of mildly handicapped children and youth have been successfully integrated in the regular classroom at the elementary and secondary level. Successful entry can be attributed to such factors as the teacher's attitude and ability to provide a specific remedial approach to solve a specific academic or social problem. The following section illustrates several teacher strategies and procedures that have been used successfully. Only those instructional or behavior management strategies referred to in the model will be presented. Readers are referred to Chapter 9 for a more elaborate description of behavior management approaches.

Personalizing the Learning Environment.   Adelman (1971) indicated that a potentially effective strategy to use to reduce the level of inappropriate social behavior or increase the level of appropriate academic behavior might be to personalize the learning environment of the handicapped student. The student would be presented with tasks in a more individualized and structured fashion than before. In short, the handicapped student would perceive that he or she was receiving the teacher's personal, undivided attention. Three alternatives a consultant could recommend to a classroom teacher to personalize the environment are modeling, seating arrangement, and peer tutoring.

Modeling. One of the most effective techniques that can be used to teach new behaviors in a personalized fashion is *modeling*. Unfortunately, it is an educational strategy many teachers do not use systematically. Simply stated, when one uses a modeling approach, the target student imitates the behavior of the model.

Bandura (1969) and Cooper et al. (1987) have cited the positive, efficient, and constructive effects of modeling. In general, it has been found that modeling works best when the student is able to perform much of the required behavior. Modeling the behavior serves as a cue to perform the complete sequence efficiently. For example, Blankenship (1978) demonstrated that modeling plus feedback approach reduced the number of inversion errors made by students during subtraction computation. Essentially, what Blankenship did was write a problem, such as $37 - 9 =$ _____, and then verbalize each step of the procedure in front of the student. The student was then able to complete several examples independently.

Another interesting result was that the modeling procedure involved only an average of 35 seconds per day per child. Additionally, Blankenship (1978) noted that the skills acquired by a majority of the students during training generalized to higher order math problems and were maintained at least one month following participated intervention.

Seating. The physical size, configuration, and arrangement of seats within a classroom may be important factors in learning new behaviors. This may be especially true for low-achieving or handicapped students. Low achievers, for example, tend to improve academically as their seats are moved from the back of the room toward the front. As a rule, the closer they are to the teacher and to the stimuli to which they have to attend, the better their performance becomes.

If the teacher were interested in increasing the verbal behavior of a handicapped student during "show and tell" or classroom discussion times, the consultant might suggest that a student with high verbal ability sit across the table from a student with low verbal skills rather than beside him. Studies in group dynamics and sociometry (e.g., Steinzor, 1950) indicate that communication flows across the table rather than around it. Apparently, the low verbal student picks up gestural, facial, and verbal messages from the high verbal student, thereby increasing the likelihood of an oral response.

Peer tutoring.   For many teachers the term *peer tutoring* means one student helping another student with a given subject area or problem. The scenario in the classroom usually unfolds when the teacher says, "Sally, will you give Kristin a hand with her science project?" or "Bill, will you help Meg with her multiplication facts?"

While this type of approach may offer relief to the overworked teacher and frustrated student, the effects are only temporary, because the student will probably need help for the same problem again in the future. Further, since the teacher does not have control over the instruction, it is difficult to tell whether any substantial teaching has taken place.

Alternatively, Parson and Heward (1979), Heron, Heward, and Cooke (1980), and Heward, Heron, Ellis, and Cooke (1986) have developed and field-tested a peer-training program that consultants can teach to regular education teachers in a short time. Teachers, in turn, can instruct students in the essential components of peer tutoring — preparation, prompting, praising, testing, and plotting behaviors.

A classwide peer-tutoring program can be established after students have participated in a 30-minute orientation session and three to five 30-minute training sessions. During training, tutors learn to gather the necessary materials such as flash cards, pencils, and folders. Next, they learn to use a two-step prompting strategy that provides the student with another chance or gives the correct answer to the item the student failed to identify. Then, tutors learn to praise their student for correct responses on an intermittent basis (after every three responses) and at the end of the tutoring session (cf. Heward et al., 1986). Tutors also learn to conduct a brief test and to record the results of the test on a cumulative graph. The training can be conducted with either large or small groups using modeling, role playing, practice, and feedback. This systematic training approach can be very effective in teaching tutoring skills to children (Ellis, 1980; Heron et al., 1980; Heward et al., 1986; Parson & Heward, 1979). After training, tutors were able to perform all behaviors independently. A minimum of teacher involvement was necessary to maintain performance.

Ferrante Alexander (1986) described a classwide peer tutoring system similar to that of Heward et al. (1986) to teach math facts to sixth-, seventh-, and eighth-grade remedial students. After conducting a pretest to determine the skill level of tutor-student pairs, tutoring began. Tutor-student pairs switched roles after 5 minutes and recorded their progress and mastery of the facts. Ferrante Alexander (1986) reports that the entire peer tutoring program, including recording, can be conducted within 20 minutes and that students were eager to engage in tutoring each day.

According to Delquadri, Greenwood, Whorton, Canta, and Hall (1986), classwide peer tutoring achieves several direct instruction objectives simultaneously. First, it increases students' opportunities to respond by as much as a factor of three. Also, tutoring can be targeted to teach specific skills (e.g., textual oral reading, reading comprehension, or mathematics). Further, posting and feedback (Van Houten, 1984) are provided, enabling students to gain information on the quality of their responses. Finally, peer-mediated reinforcement for correct responses is provided, enabling a powerful reinforcer to be delivered. More information on classwide peer-tutoring approaches can be found in Chapter 6, Delquadri et al., (1986) and Scruggs and Richter (1986).

Teaching Academic Skills.   Since comprehensive data are collected during the multifactored evaluation prior to placement, it is reasonable to expect that the teacher would have an accurate indication of the student's academic strengths and weaknesses. Unfortunately, if data were derived exclusively from norm-referenced (standardized) tests, an unbalanced view of the student's performance might be obtained, because these tests usually indicate the student's frustration level. The teachers would have to translate the test findings into daily lessons.

It is possible that a student lacking specific prerequisite skills could be placed in a regular classroom. The consultant might recommend to the classroom teacher that programmed instruction, individualized instruction, and peer tutoring[2] be implemented to improve academic performance.

Programmed instruction.   *Programmed instruction* refers to the logical arrangement of material into small steps; at each step the student obtains information, responds to it, and receives feedback on his or her performance. At one time, programmed instruction was hailed as the savior of the American educational system. It seemed as though technology was finally coming to the classroom in the form of programmed readers, mathematics texts, science curricula, and a host of other computer-assisted instructional (CAI) programmed materials. For reasons that are complex and beyond the scope of this book, suffice it to say that programmed materials have remained a supplemental rather than a primary source of instruction.

Nevertheless, it should be recognized that programmed texts and CAI materials offer several advantages for the teacher and the student. First, if the programmed materials or CAI lessons are written competently, students can progress at their own pace. Within a heterogeneous class, a resource like a programmed text for teaching specific reading skills allows the teacher to give instruction to individual students without impeding the learning rate of others. Second, student frustration with difficult concepts or skills could be reduced if the frames or lessons within the program build on skills or

---

[2]The reader is referred to Heward, Heron, and Cooke (1982) for a discussion of "tutor-huddle," a key element in a classwide peer-tutoring system. Readers interested in receiving a training manual on "Classwide Peer Tutoring" should write to Timothy E. Heron at Ohio State University, Department of Human Services Education, 356 Arps Hall, 1945 N. High Street, Columbus, OH 43210.

knowledge previously learned and do not proceed too rapidly from skill to skill. Finally, programmed materials usually progress gradually, so that the correct response for an item helps the student answer the next item, or an answer key is provided for students to refer to. In either case, students are able to check their reponses.

Individualized instruction.   Ask 100 professionals what they mean by individualized instruction and you are likely to obtain 100 different responses. In this book, *individualized instruction* refers to a teacher's skill in structuring learning tasks that match student comprehension and response capabilities. For example, if a student had a short attention span and was easily distracted, the consultant might suggest that lessons be presented that are varied in format, of short duration, and limited in abstract content. The mode of presentation and the expected mode of response are integral components of individualized instruction.

Further, a teacher may require different responses from different students based on knowledge of the task and response requirements. For instance, if the teacher were having difficulty instructing a geography class at the junior high school level, the consultant might recommend that he or she require one student to supply an answer to a question, whereas another student would only have to choose among alternative answers. In the former case a recall response is required; in the latter instance a recognition is required. When individualizing instruction the teacher provides the least intrusive, yet most powerful, prompt to increase the probability that a student will respond correctly. Slavin, Madden, and Leavey (1984) sum up the contribution of individualized instruction for students reintegrated into regular programs: "In individualized instruction, mainstreamed students proceed through the same curriculum under the same guidelines as other students; they are no longer 'special'" (p. 442). The issues of individualized instruction at the elementary and secondary level are addressed more completely in Chapters 6 and 7.

Implementing Behavior Management Techniques.   The use of behavior management techniques in regular and special classrooms has increased since 1968. The use of a behavioral approach in special education settings has been shown to be consistently effective (Cooper et al., 1987). Three behavior management strategies that have been used successfully at the elementary and secondary level will be discussed below. A more thorough discussion of these and other behavior management approaches will be found in Chapter 9 and Cooper et al. (1987).

Contracts.   Contingency contracting is a term used to define a situation in which teachers (or parents) and students negotiate task and response requirements. Contracts can be either verbal or written, although most educators (e.g., Cooper et al., 1987; Dardig & Heward, 1976; Homme, Csanyi, Gonzales, & Rechs, 1969) recommend the written contract because of the documentation it provides. In essence, a contract is a "when-then" statement of agreement: "When you finish your math assignment, then you will earn 15 minutes of recess." Another term for contracting is "Grandma's Law."

Tokens.   Numerous authors have demonstrated the efficacy of token reinforcement programs in changing academic and social behavior (Cooper et al., 1987; McLaughlin, 1981). The essential feature of the token economy is that the student receives an interim reinforcer (a token, chip, or check mark), which can later be exchanged for a back-up reinforcer. For example, a behaviorally disordered student may earn three check marks for good academic behavior, which can be exchanged for three minutes of free time at the end of the period. Token programs have been successful with students who do not respond to conventional reinforcers in school, such as grades or teacher praise, and who have a long history of academic or social failure. For a review of token systems, the reader is referred to Chapter 9, Kazdin (1977), or Cooper et al. (1987).

Punishment.   The term *punishment* has a number of meanings for the educator. According to Cooper et al. (1987), if a functional definition of the term were employed at least four procedures could be considered punishing: (a) contingent application of a stimulus, (b) overcorrection, (c) contingent removal of a specific amount of reinforcement, and (d) contingent removal of the opportunity to earn reinforcement for a specific time period. If the likelihood of an inappropriate response is decreased after the application of any of these procedures, then punishment has taken place. Conversely, if one of these procedures is employed and the student's undesirable behavior continues, then punishment has not taken place, even if the procedure was used correctly. In short, punishment is defined in functional terms.

Educational Alternatives for Normal Students

One reason for the variability of behavior in the classroom is that each student enters the learning environment with different needs and expectations. Competent teachers attempt to address these needs. However, in doing so they oftentimes precipitate problems. For example, students, especially in junior and senior high school, are not always able to reconcile the teacher's differential treatment of their peers. That is, the teacher might require neater papers, faster answers, and more participation from one student and a different set of responses from others. Students often complain that the teacher is unfair, or that he or she likes one student more than another. Unfortunately, some students are unwilling to accept the teacher's actions. Hence, the sensitivity they might have to individual differences is compromised.

Increasing Awareness of Individual Difference.   Wong and Wong (1980) indicated that a prerequisite skill for developing effective interaction may be the ability to assume the role of the other person. According to Kitano et al. (1978), there is little research indicating that nonhandicapped children without training are able to comprehend the needs and feelings of handicapped children. Some strategies that have been shown to be effective in increasing student awareness of individual differences are addressed below.

Class discussion.   Class discussion can be an effective way to increase student awareness of individual differences. Using the *Peabody Language Development Kit* (PLDK), or the *Developing Understanding of Self and Others* (DUSO) kit, a consultant might recommend that the teacher structure discussions on the nature of individual differences without pointing out a particular child in the class. For instance, if the teacher were interested in having the nonhandicapped students reduce the amount of badgering they inflict on a handicapped student, he or she might present a lesson from one of the kits that portrays a handicapped student attempting to play with friends. Using a scene that shows a handicapped child being ridiculed by the other children on the block, the teacher might open the discussion by asking a question such as, "How would you feel if you were teased by your friends?"

Teacher modeling.   Modeling can be an effective procedure to use when many of the prerequisite behaviors exist in the student's repertoire. So, a consultant might suggest that the teacher model appropriate verbal and nonverbal interactions with exceptional and nonhandicapped students.

Providing Integrated Working Groups.   One way to increase the probability of mainstreaming students is to set the occasion whereby exceptional students can work on projects with nonhandicapped students. Bruininks (1978) indicates that cooperative learning in small groups fosters social integration and academic achievement. For example, the consultant might plan a newspaper project with the regular teacher where each student in the group, handicapped and nonhandicapped, is given tasks within his or her capabilities. If the exceptional student is a good artist, she might be art editor, while the nonhandicapped students might serve as proofreaders, sports editors, or circulation editors. Each group would see the other contributing a portion of work toward a common goal. Additional information about cooperative learning arrangements can be found in Chapter 6.

Exceptional child.   The benefits derived by the exceptional child while participating in a small, integrated working group are many. First, the situation provides the opportunity for exceptional students to gain public recognition from their peers for their contributions to a project. Second, it fosters the notion that school is not an environment where ridicule and rejection are constantly encountered. Third, as a member of the group, the handicapped student would not be fully responsible for the group effort. His or her successful participation in the project could be assured if the teacher structured the requirements with the exceptional child's abilities and deficits in mind.

Nonhandicapped child. In any social or academic situation where the less skilled or less talented are integrated with the more skilled or more talented, it is frequently assumed that the former group will derive all of the benefits of the interaction while the latter derive none. Unfortunately, this misconception persists despite some fairly conclusive evidence to the contrary (Greenwood, Sloan, & Baskin, 1974).

Heward, Heron, and Cooke (1982), for example, noted that academic gains were made by student tutors as well as those students who received tutoring. Also, according to Kitano et al. (1978), nonhandicapped children may need role-taking training to increase their sensitivity to the unique needs and problems of the mildly handicapped. Such training might serve to teach them about the differences that exist among people and provide them with practice in dealing with these differences on a day-to-day basis.

Reinforcing Contingent Interaction. Sometimes it is necessary for the consultant to suggest that the regular teacher structure situations so that the class as a whole or individual students earn reinforcement. Under these circumstances students would earn free time or classroom privileges or be excused from assignments (negative reinforcement) contingent upon an interaction with a mainstreamed student.

Consultants, of course, realize that the encounters between mainstreamed and nonhandicapped students may not be of long duration, perhaps just saying "hello" or asking to borrow a pencil. Therefore, the teacher needs to be aware of this behavior so that the rewards are appropriately dispensed.

Class. Having the whole class share the reinforcer earned by a student who interacted with an exceptional child is an excellent way to foster social acceptance of the mainstreamed child in the classroom. This contingency, referred to as the Hero Procedure (Kerr & Nelson, 1983), establishes that classroom reinforcers can be earned and pooled for each positive encounter with the mainstreamed student. At best, peer group pressure would be exerted to earn reinforcers for the class. At worst, the exceptional student would be tolerated rather than actively abused. If an individual within a group behaves negatively toward another person or group of persons and is subsequently reinforced for behaving positively, it is likely that the individual's attitude will become more consistent with his or her behavior (Goldstein & Sorcher, 1974).

Target students. Frequently, the successful entry of mainstreamed students is impeded by one or two nonhandicapped students who hold high status in the class and exert a great deal of influence. In this case, the consultant might recommend that the teacher consider a reinforcement approach for these individuals alone. The contingencies mentioned beforehand could be applied in much the same manner. The only difference is that the reinforcers now would be earned by individuals. (See Chapter 9 for more detail.)

Educational Alternatives for the Teacher

Thus far, we have discussed educational strategies that the consultant can recommend to the classroom teacher for consideration. If all the procedures suggested have been tried without success, the consultant's last alternative would be to provide strategies directed toward changing the behavior of the classroom teacher. While the prime targets mentioned earlier have been the students in the classroom, now the emphasis for intervention is on the regular classroom teacher.

Providing Feedback. Brophy and Good (1974) cite three reasons why the teacher's awareness of classroom interaction is frequently low: (a) the rapid pace of classroom events, (b) poor preservice training, and (c) lack of conceptual understanding by teachers of what should be going on in the classroom. Unfortunately, these three deficiencies combine in a way that promotes reactive teaching rather than proactive teaching. In reactive teaching the teacher simply responds to behavior that occurs in the classroom. In proactive teaching the teacher is constantly anticipating events and structuring tasks to maximize instruction.

Many regular education teachers are unfamiliar with the patterns of classroom interaction and consequently give more attention to some students than to others. As Brophy and Good (1974) suggest, a host of variables contribute to the disproportional interaction that occurs in the classroom. They also state that if teachers received feedback, information pertinent to improving their skills, the patterns of interaction they are displaying in the classroom would change. It is as if they were saying to themselves, "Oh, I didn't know I was doing that!" Data reported by Heron and Skinner (1979) substantiate this position. Although some techniques are more intrusive than others or require the assistance of ancillary personnel in the classroom, there are a number of ways of providing in-class feedback to teachers. All methods present cues to the teacher during rather than after the instructional period.

Cues. Educational researchers have demonstrated that providing verbal or nonverbal cues to teachers as they work can have a profound impact on the quality of instruction taking place. A cue is any prompt or instruction that sets the occasion for a behavior to occur. For example, Van Houten and Sullivan (1975) reported a procedure where, contingent upon a preestablished buzzing of the school intercom, a praise statement was issued to a target student in the class. This audio cue served as a prompt to remind the teacher to praise the target student in the class.

Other cueing strategies have used similar approaches with a similar result. Where school intercoms are unavailable or the teacher feels that the buzz would be too distracting, an alternative approach could be recommended by the consultant. Or the teacher can simply use a tape recorder with a blank tape. Every 5 minutes (or whatever other interval the teacher would prefer), he or she makes a sound on the tape. The blank tape continues, and again at the next 5-minute interval the sound is repeated. This process continues until the tape is expended. Then the teacher rewinds the tape, which has all the intervals present. When the teacher begins instruction, he or she starts the tape recorder, and the audio cues are delivered at the established intervals.

It should be realized, however, that often the regular education teacher may need to develop skills to more adequately serve the needs of the exceptional student. In no way should this statement be construed to mean that regular education teachers are unskilled. However, some teachers, although willing to accept mainstreamed students into their classrooms, lack the diagnostic and prescriptive teaching skills necessary to do a competent job. The consultant faced with this challenge has at least two alternatives. He or she can (a) provide a model for the regular classroom teacher to imitate or (b) enhance skill development in the teacher through additional inservice training.

Modeling. As stated previously, modeling can be an effective instructional strategy when the teacher already possesses many of the component behaviors. The modeling procedure involves having the consultant demonstrate the appropriate instructional behaviors for the teacher to imitate that will enhance student academic and social performance. Subsequently, the teacher receives feedback on how well the behavior was imitated.

Furnishing Inservice Training. Every school district must provide a program of continued education for its teachers. Most school districts or regions provide at least one inservice day per year where teachers attend professional meetings to enhance their teaching skills: some colleges and universities provide specific coursework for regular educators in subject areas related to exceptionality (Gallagher, 1985).

For inservice training to be optimally effective, teachers must have the opportunity to practice the skills presented, and they must receive feedback and reinforcement for their attempts and accomplishments. Wang, Vaughan, and Dytman (1985) noted the importance of inservice training with respect to the mainstreaming effort: "Research and experience have consistently suggested that staff development programs that provide ongoing training support for helping school staff to develop required implementation expertise tend to be associated with effective school improvement in general and effective mainstreaming in particular" (p. 113).

While the specific topics in any workshop should ultimately be determined collaboratively, our experience has been that workshops providing skills in diagnostic teaching, learning theory/strategies, and affective education are relevant for many teachers.

It is only after all alternatives in the model have been exhausted that a change in placement should be considered. The consultant and teacher, at this point, would attempt to determine the least restrictive environment (i.e., another setting for the student).

CONCLUSION

This chapter defined the terms *mainstreaming* and *least restrictive environment* and distinguished the differences between them. Next, the chapter addressed several factors that affect exceptional students within a regular classroom. These factors include: the composition of the mainstreamed classroom, the teacher's attitude, teacher-student interaction, and student-student interaction. Finally, the chapter presented a decision making model for a consultant to use when a student has been mainstreamed into a class but is not achieving according to expectation. The model, that divides alternatives into categories specified by the exceptional student, the nonhandicapped students, and the teacher, is a hierarchically arranged set of field-tested interventions.

SUMMARY OF KEY POINTS

Definition of Mainstreaming

1. Mainstreaming is defined as the temporal, instructional, and social integration of eligible exceptional children with nonhandicapped peers based on an ongoing, individually determined, educational planning and programming process. It requires clarification of responsibility among regular and special education administrative, instruction, and supportive personnel (Kaufman et al., 1975).

Teacher Concerns About Mainstreaming

2. Many regular education teachers feel that they do not have the specialized training necessary to teach mildly handicapped students in the regular classroom. Also, they feel that the support services will be insufficient

to meet their needs. Finally, regular education teachers believe that instructional responsibility should be shared.

Parent Concerns About Mainstreaming

3. Parents have mixed emotions about the benefits of mainstreaming. On one hand, they view the process as a way for their child to gain exposure with nonhandicapped students. On the other hand, they view the integration process as a potential source of ridicule or rejection for their child.

Definition of Least Restrictive Environment

4. According to the Federal Register (1977), the least restrictive environment is defined as the maximum amount of education with nonhandicapped peers with removal from that environment only when the nature of the disability precludes an adequate educational experience.

5. Heron and Skinner (1981) indicated that the least restrictive environment should be defined in terms of opportunity to respond and achievement, proportional interaction, and social relationships in the classroom.

Composition of Mainstreamed Classrooms

6. The composition of mainstreamed classrooms may affect the performance of exceptional students in the regular class. It is possible that the enrollment of an exceptional student in a mainstreamed class will not increase the heterogeneity of the class.

Teacher Attitude

7. A teacher's attitude is defined as a predisposition to respond in a certain way to the presence of a handicapped student in the classroom. Teacher attitudes may be changed by using the principal, implementing team teaching, generating parent support, performing inservice training, or using countercontrol.

Teacher-Student Interaction in Mainstreamed Classrooms

8. The data on the amount and quality of teacher-student interactions in mainstreamed classrooms are mixed. Some studies indicate that mildly handicapped students receive a disproportionate amount of certain kinds of interactions; other studies report no difference. The crux of the issue is whether each student receives enough attention to increase and maintain that student's performance.

Student-Student Interaction in Mainstreamed Classrooms

9. Many mildly handicapped students have difficulty with student-student interactions in mainstreamed classrooms. With proper training, mildly handicapped students can learn to improve their status within the regular classroom and be socially acceptable to peers. Likewise, with training, regular education students can learn to be more sensitive to individual difference.

A Decision-Making Model for Maintaining Mildly Handicapped Students in the Regular Classroom

10. A decision-making model was presented that outlines a series of hierarchically arranged educational and behavioral strategies for maintaining the mildly handicapped student in the regular classroom. The model uses three target audiences for intervention: the exceptional student, the nonhandicapped student, and the teacher.

QUESTIONS

1. How do Kaufman et al. (1975) define the term *mainstreaming*?

2. According to P.L. 94-142 regulations published in the *Federal Register*, the least restrictive environment is defined by two criteria. What are these criteria?

3. What are two reasons why parents might be anxious about having their son or daughter integrated in a regular classroom?

4. Differentiate between the Heron and Skinner definition of least restrictive environment and the criteria set by the *Federal Register*.

5. Give a brief synopsis of the research on teacher-student interaction in the regular classroom, especially with mildly handicapped children present.

6. What factors contribute to the social rejection of mildly handicapped students in the regular classroom?

7. Given that social interactions between mildly handicapped students and nonhandicapped students are often strained, what suggestions have been offered to improve this situation?

8. Describe Heron's model for maintaining mildly handicapped children in the regular classroom.

9. Outline several recommendations within each category of Heron's decision-making model that a consultant could offer to a regular education teacher to help manage the academic and social behavior of an exceptional student.

DISCUSSION POINTS AND EXERCISES

1. How would service delivery to mildly handicapped students be enhanced (or impeded) if Heron and Skinner's (1981) definition of the least restrictive environment were employed?

2. Inservice training for regular education teachers is essential if integration programs are going to be successful. Discuss how a consultant could determine the inservice needs for his or her teachers.

3. It is sometimes said that regular education teachers, though competent with nonhandicapped students, lack the skills to serve the mildly handicapped. What skills and attitudes are essential for a teacher if mainstreaming is to be a successful educational alternative?

4. Counter an argument offered by a regular educator who stated that the handicapped should be educated in separate facilities using specially trained teachers and unique equipment.

5. Observe in a classroom the interaction patterns existing among students. Then choose two students, one who is receiving a disproportionate amount of teacher attention and one who is not. Suggest to the regular education teacher that his or her pattern of attention be shifted to meet the assessed needs of all students.

6. Conduct a sociometric analysis of a regular classroom using a peer-nominating procedure to determine degree of social acceptance and rejection within the class. Compare these data with classroom observations. With the teacher, design an intervention to reduce or eliminate the degree of social rejection. Use modeling and integrated working groups for your intervention.

7. Collect data on teacher attitudes toward accepting handicapped children and youth in the classroom. Arrange to have the school principal visit mainstreamed classrooms regularly to reinforce teaching efforts. Reassess the teachers to note the effect of the principal's visit.

8. Present a 15-minute videotape to a group of regular educators, perhaps junior high science teachers, depicting a science class with a handicapped student. Ask the teachers to identify the positive teaching behaviors (prompts, reinforcers, etc.) that the instructor used and state how the lesson could have been presented differently. Focus the teachers' attention on specific instructional techniques that were used to enhance the lesson.

4

Working with Teachers in Self-Contained Special Education Classrooms

Despite the active efforts to mainstream handicapped students, placement within self-contained special education classrooms may sometimes be more appropriate for them. For example, a handicapped student who has chronic academic and behavior problems may be better served in a self-contained special education classroom. The student's learning potential could be seriously compromised without the special instruction offered by a teacher in a self-contained environment.

Special education classrooms have fewer students, specially trained and certified teachers, and often special equipment so that the unique learning needs of the students can be met. Programs in self-contained classrooms vary widely depending on the disabilities of the students, but one common objective is to provide intensive, diagnostic-prescriptive instruction so that students will be able to compensate for their specific disabilities. For example, a student with a visual impairment may receive mobility and orientation training so that he or she will be able to function within an academic and sighted world.

Since the ultimate goal of placing students in self-contained classrooms is to eventually move them to a less restrictive setting, a process referred to as normalization, the emphasis in this chapter is on techniques a consultant can use with special educators to develop functional Individualized Education Programs and increase generality and maintenance of skills. Ways in which a consultant can assist the special education teacher with academic and social programming are also addressed.

OBJECTIVES

After reading this chapter, the reader should be able to:

1. cite a rationale for self-contained classrooms within the service delivery hierarchy.

2. define the term *self-contained classroom* and provide two examples.

3. identify several education areas in need of assessment (e.g., academic achievement, learning style, and preferred reinforcers).

4. distinguish between an annual goal and a short-term objective.

5. provide planning and implementing suggestions for promoting generality of behavior change.

KEY TERMS

Self-contained classroom	Short-term objective
Mastery	Stimulus generality
Learning style	Response generality
Preferred reinforcer	Intermittent schedule of reinforcement
Annual goal	Maintenance

DEFINITION OF SELF-CONTAINED CLASSROOMS

According to Turnbull and Schulz (1979), *self-contained classrooms* are instructional settings that serve students who have substantial handicapping conditions and for whom placement in less restrictive settings is inappropriate. Wallace and McLoughlin (1979) state that the self-contained special education classroom is only one placement option on a continuum. Figure 4.1 shows where the self-contained special education classroom falls within the hierarchy of services for handicapped individuals. According to Wallace and McLoughlin (1979), the self-contained class offers instruction that differs in kind and intensity from other alternatives. Self-contained classrooms exist for all types of handicapping conditions (blind, learning disabled, physically impaired, etc.).

Advantages of Self-Contained Classrooms

Self-contained classrooms are usually structured to minimize distraction and increase individualized attention (Heward & Orlansky, 1984). Since the entire academic program is usually taught by one teacher, the student does not have to relate to several adults during the course of the day. For many learning

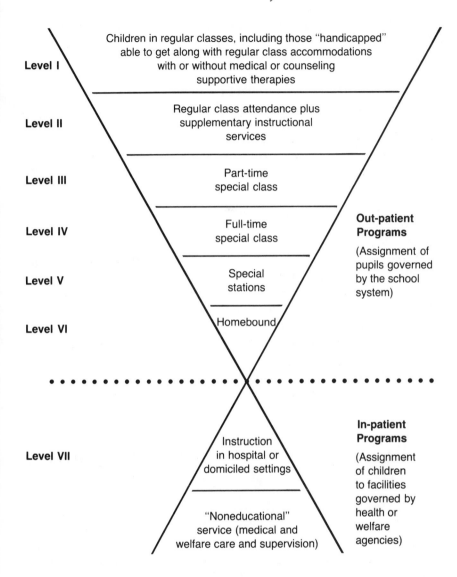

FIGURE 4.1. Cascade model of special education service. From "Special education as developmental capital" by E. Deno (1970) in *Exceptional Children, 37,* 229–237. Reprinted by permission.

and behavior disordered students who have difficulty establishing and maintaining social relationships, having one teacher can be an advantage.

In instances where special classes are formed categorically — that is, separate classes for each handicapping condition — a specific educational orientation may prevail (Stephens, 1977). A specific instructional or educational orientation, such as diagnostic-prescriptive teaching, may be of benefit to students for whom conventional approaches have failed.

Disadvantages of Self-Contained Classrooms

Several authors have indicated that one of the main disadvantages of self-contained placements for handicapped students is the likelihood that the assignment may be permanent (Heward & Orlansky, 1984; Stephens, 1977; Wallace & McLoughlin, 1979). The apprehension about permanent placement is especially critical if poor, minority group, or multiculturally diverse students are placed in this setting because of the stigma that such placements have acquired (Wiederholt, Hammill, & Brown, 1978). Generally speaking, self-contained special education teachers have fewer direct contacts with regular educators insofar as their students are concerned. Despite some inherent drawbacks with the self-contained classroom, it continues to be an option for some handicapped students. Smith and Arkans (1974) indicate that it should not be abandoned on the hierarchy of service delivery alternatives.

Assuming that a handicapped student is considered for placement within a self-contained classroom, the consultant can provide invaluable assistance to the IEP team by helping develop, implement, refine, and evaluate the student's individualized program.

HELPING TEACHERS TO DEVELOP AND EVALUATE THE INDIVIDUALIZED EDUCATION PROGRAM

Before an Individualized Education Program (IEP) can be implemented successfully, three major steps must be taken. First, initial assessment of the student's performance levels must take place. Second, assessment data must be analyzed so that annual goals and short-term objectives can be prepared and resources identified to meet these goals. Third, an IEP meeting must be planned and conducted to develop the specific program that will be aimed at remediating the student's known deficits.

Consultants can be of service to special educators in each of these areas. For example, a consultant can recommend that a draft of the IEP be mailed to the parents prior to the meeting so that they can share the teachers' view of the program. In a cover letter to parents it must be made clear that the proposed IEP is intended to set the occasion for discussion at the meeting. Affleck, Lowenbraun, and Archer (1980) make this point succinctly:

In preparing for the IEP meeting, participants should not only collect and summarize information on current functioning level, but they should also determine potential areas that might require special service programming. Written drafts of portions of the IEP, especially the long-term goals and short-term objectives, may be outlined before the meeting. While the process of participatory planning and collecting information from all parties should not be circumvented by signing of a pre-written document, we recommend prior preparation of portions of the IEP. It is important that any prepared drafts be presented only as proposals on which additional input and modifications will be accepted. (p. 27)

Figure 4.2 illustrates a working draft of this kind.

In addition, the consultant can indicate to teachers how complex, and sometimes confusing, information can be integrated so that a functional program can be developed and presented to the parents. Finally, the consultant can assist in recommending related services and provide technical assistance with developing and evaluating the IEP long- and short-term goals.

Conducting the Initial Assessment

According to Wiederholt, Hammill, and Brown (1978), assessment refers to the range of tasks a teacher performs to obtain data to enhance instruction. These tasks include administering and interpreting unbiased, nondiscriminatory norm- and criterion-referenced tests; conducting observations in the classroom; interviewing the students, the teacher, or the parents; and using analytic teaching approaches. Since each of these methods for obtaining reliable and valid assessment data has been discussed comprehensively by other authors (e.g., Cooper et al., 1987; McLoughlin & Lewis, 1987; Wallace & Larsen, 1978; Wiederholt et al., 1978), the rest of this chapter focuses on ways a consultant can assist special educators with integrating assessment data, writing goal statements, planning individual programs, monitoring and evaluating the IEP, and promoting generality and maintenance.

Integrating Assessment Data

Conducting the assessment is only half the battle; the other half is to integrate the data so that a functional program can be written. Figure 4.3 shows a summary sheet for Arlene that profiles the student's level of performance, her learning style, preferred reinforcers, objectives for instruction, materials and techniques, and evaluation measures.

Determining Strengths. An academic or social strength is the skill or cluster of skills that allows the student to perform independently. According to

INDIVIDUAL EDUCATION PROGRAM

Date ___11-25-86___

(1) Student

Name: Joe S.
School: Adams
Grade: 5
Current Placement: Regular Class/Resource Room

Date of Birth: 10-1-75   Age: 11-1

(2) Committee

Mr. Havlichek   Principal
Mrs. Snow   Regular Teacher
Mr. Bigelow   Counselor
Mr. Sheets   Resource Teacher
Mrs S.   Parent

IEP from ___12-1-86___ to ___12-1-87___   Initial

(3) Present Level of Educational Functioning	(4) Annual Goal Statements	(5) Instructional Objectives	(6) Objective Criteria and Evaluation
MATH *Strengths* 1. Can successfully compute addition and subtraction problems to two places with regrouping and zeros. 2. Knows 100 basic multiplication facts. *Weaknesses* 1. Frequently makes computational errors on problems with which he has had experience. 2. Does not complete seatwork. Key Math total score of 2.1 Grade Equivalent	Joe will apply knowledge of regrouping in addition and renaming in subtraction to four-digit numbers	1. When presented with addition problems of 3-digit numbers requiring two renamings the student will compute the answer at a rate of one problem per minute and an accuracy of 90%. 2. When presented with subtraction problems of 3-digit numbers requiring two renamings the student will compute the answer at a rate of one problem per minute with 90% accuracy. 3. When presented with addition problems of 4-digit numbers requiring three renamings the student will compute the answer at a rate of one problem per minute and an accuracy of 90%. 4. When presented with subtraction problems of 4-digit numbers requiring three renamings the student will compute the answer at a rate of one problem per minute with 90% accuracy.	Key Math (after 4 mos.) Teacher made tests (weekly) Key Math (after 4 mos.) Teacher made tests (weekly) Key Math (after 4 mos.) Teacher made tests (weekly)

FIGURE 4.2. Sample Individualized Education Program. From *Developing and implementing individualized education programs* by A. Turnbull, B. Strickland, & J. Brantley, 1982, Columbus, OH: Merrill. Used with permission.

Student's name: Arlene M.   Birthdate: 7/6/76
Date: 9/5/86   Grade level: 5th/Resource
Teacher's name: Mr. Franks   room

Reading Strengths

- Reading recog. level, 3.5
- Reading comprehension, 3.0
- Mastered all initial, medial, and final consonants and blends.
- Reads with inflection.

Reading Weaknesses

- Difficulty with inferential questions.
- Unable to apply final *e* rule
- Unable to identify word parts (syllables)
- Unable to apply plurals to *y* ending words.

Learner Style

Arlene's performance is enhanced when tasks are issued one at a time, rather than altogether. Seems to rely heavily on visual cues. Providing modes of response which allow her to write or demonstrate might be helpful.

Preferred Reinforcers

Arlene clearly enjoys free time in class. Throughout assessment she stated that playing with games (Battleship, checkers, bingo) were her favorite activities.

Annual Goals

1. By June, Arlene will be able to answer a variety of inferential questions based on her reading series.
2. By June, Arlene will gain proficiency with the application of the final *e* rule to sight vocabulary.
3. By June, Arlene will be able to identify word parts for polysyllabic words.
4. By June, Arlene will be able to use plurals correctly.

Short-Term Objectives

1. After reading a story (at least 100 words) on her independent level, Arlene will be able to answer three inferential questions with 100 percent accuracy (Target date—11/9/86).
2. Given ten words ending in final *e*, Arlene will be able to apply the final *e* rule ninety percent of the time (Target date—10/10/86).
3. Given ten compound words, presented visually, Arlene will be able to correctly syllabicate eight of them (Target date—9/21/86).
4. Given ten "y" ending words, Arlene will be able to write the correct plural form at ninety percent criterion (Target date—10/5/86).

Materials and Techniques

1. Basal reader
2. Practice worksheets
3. Use visual presentations, expect writing or demonstration responses.

Evaluation Measures

1. Tracking sheet showing date of mastery of each short-term objective.
2. Direct and daily measurement.

FIGURE 4.3. Diagnostic Summary Sheet.

Stephens (1977) a student functions independently when he or she is able to complete 90% to 95% of assigned tasks without assistance. The term *mastery* is usually reserved for completed tasks that are above 99% correct. Strengths can be delineated using a variety of formats. For example, Arlene is able to read competently at the 1.5 reading level on word recognition and comprehension. (A general rule of thumb is that the independent level is approximately two levels below the grade equivalent score on the test.) Also, she has mastered all blends and consonants in the initial, medial, and final positions (Figure 4.3).

Determining Weaknesses. Technically speaking, performance at an 80% success criterion could be considered an instructional level. This means that the student has sufficient knowledge or skill to profit from instruction. The cut-off score to determine a level is somewhat flexible and depends upon the skill to be mastered and the teacher's criterion for success. So, weaknesses are, in a practical sense, those areas or skills that may not be fully developed and that may need further remediation and instruction. In the example shown in Figure 4.3, Arlene has difficulty with words ending in final *e* and with words that change the *y* to *i* before adding *ly*. In addition, she has difficulty with inferential questions and identifying word parts.

Learning Style. According to Barbe and Swassing (1979), students have one of four basic *learning styles* — visual, auditory, kinesthetic, or mixed. While conducting assessments the teacher should note the mannerisms or behaviors the student uses to complete the task, because such information can be used in educational programming. Hawisher and Calhoun (1978) indicate that teachers need to consider the number of tasks that are assigned to students and the rate and mode with which these tasks are to be completed. Students unable to complete a task presented in one fashion might be able to do it when it is presented differently. For example, a learning disabled student may be unable to supply an answer that requires filling in the blank. However, if the student is provided with several visual alternatives, his or her performance may improve.

Other behaviors to look for might be: If a student is asked to pronounce a word, does he attempt to sound it out? Does the student seem to look at only the first part of the word and then guess at the rest? If a student consistently uses one modality (visual, auditory, or kinesthetic) to solve problems on the assessment, the teacher might infer that this sensory channel is the preferred learning modality. Instruction might be facilitated if conducted through this modality. However, the consultant must caution the teacher against wholeheartedly assuming that this is the preferred modality; rather, the teacher should be cautioned to look for a pattern of correct responses with this modality.

According to the teacher's perception, Arlene's performance is enhanced when tasks are well paced for her (Figure 4.3). Giving too many assignments at one time apparently resulted in a poorer performance. Also, providing Arlene with writing or demonstration responses seemed to increase her accuracy.

Preferred Reinforcers. *Preferred reinforcers* are consequences that students choose more frequently than other reinforcers. Teachers can determine preferred reinforcers in three ways. First the teacher can ask the students what they like. Valuable time and energy can be saved when teachers ask students what they would prefer to do contingent upon task completion. Second, the teacher can watch students to see what they like to do during free times. Third, teachers can set up a forced-choice situation (Cooper et al., 1987). For example, the teacher might say, "John, you can play a game, read a book, or help Mark with his math." If John chooses to read a book, the teacher might infer that reading was the most reinforcing activity given these options. The other two activities might also be reinforcing, but the teacher now knows which is the most powerful of the three. In our example (Figure 4.3), the teacher during the course of the assessment was able to determine that Arlene's preferred reinforcers included games and activities such as bingo, Battleship, and checkers.

Writing Goal Statements

After the assessment data have been collected and analyzed, the next step in preparing an appropriate IEP for a student is to establish goals, both long- and short-term. In addition, it is important to check periodically to ensure that these goals are being achieved.

Annual Goal. An *annual goal* is defined as a statement of the behavior the student is expected to achieve within a calendar year. It is anticipated that annual goals for each major need identified in the evaluation and placement procedures will be attained through implementation of the IEP. Turnbull, Strickland, and Hammer (1978) state the purpose of the annual goal:

> The annual goals, by necessity, must be somewhat global in nature so they can encompass the entire spectrum of short-term or intermediate objectives in a given area. They must, however, describe the educational performance to be achieved by the end of the school year. Each student must be considered individually in formulating annual goals so that realistic goals may be set and relevant teaching strategies may be determined to improve the child's functioning. (p. 22)

Given that annual goals are global in nature, the question of relative importance of one annual goal over another is raised. Consultants can assist the IEP team to develop prioritized annual goals by applying appropriate criteria. Dardig and Heward (1981) suggest a six-step process to prioritize annual goals. After introducing team members and establishing rapport (step 1), the team lists as many IEP goals as possible (step 2). Next, criteria for arranging the goals are applied (step 3). Table 4.1 shows a 9-item checklist for prioritizing the goals. These questions will provide the team with the basis for arranging goals in a hierarchical order. Steps 4 and 5 are concerned with rating the goals and synthesizing responses. The matrix shown in Figure 4.4 illustrates the outcome of this process. Finally, in step 6 a prioritized list of goals is produced. Examples of annual goals for Arlene are included on the Diagnostic Summary Sheet (Figure 4.3).

Short-Term Objectives.   Simply stated, a *short-term objective* is an intermediate step between the child's current level of performance and the annual goal. These steps are measurable and act as benchmarks for indicating progress toward the annual goal. They are less detailed than daily instructional objectives, which usually require more specific outcomes or products. The number of short-term objectives that are identified depends on several factors including the number of annual goals, the complexity of the task to be learned, and the criteria established for success. Short-term objectives are

TABLE 4.1
Criteria for Prioritizing Annual Goals

1. Will the child be able to use the skill in his/her immediate environment?

2. Is it a functional, useful skill?

3. Will the child be able to use the skill often?

4. Has the child demonstrated an interest in learning this skill?

5. Is success in teaching this skill likely?

6. Is the skill a prerequisite for learning more complex skills?

7. Will the child become more independent as a result of learning this skill?

8. Will the skill allow the child to qualify for improved or additional services, or services in a less restrictive environment?

9. Is it important to modify this behavior because it is dangerous to self or others?

From "A systematic procedure for prioritizing IEP goals" by J.C. Dardig & W.L. Heward (1981) in *The Directive Teacher*, 3(2), 6. Reprinted by permission.

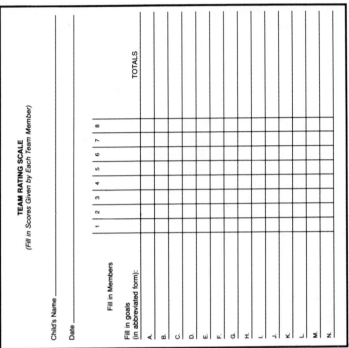

FIGURE 4.4. Individual Rating Scale. From "A systematic procedure for prioritizing IEP goals" by J. C. Dardig & W. L. Heward (1981) in *The Directive Teacher*, 3(2), 8. Reprinted by permission.

written to project student accomplishment within a specified unit of time (e.g., a report card period, quarter, or bisemester). Examples of short-term objectives for Arlene are included on the Diagnostic Summary Sheet (Figure 4.3).

Materials/Approach/Evaluation.   After conducting the assessment the teacher must make a decision about the method, duration, and location of instruction, the materials that will be used, and the process that will be used to evaluate the effectiveness of the instructional program. Since Arlene has difficulty with inferential questions, the teacher has elected to use the basal reader and individual worksheets (see Figure 4.3). Finally, the regular classroom may be selected as the site for reading instruction because of the student's ability to perform well in this setting.

Evaluation.   Evaluation of all short-term objectives should be based on measurable performance levels. Turnbull et al. (1978) recommended that continuous or direct and daily measurement be employed to increase the likelihood that short-term objectives are achieved systematically. Reviewing short-term objectives on a periodic basis, but at least on an annual basis, will help to ensure student progress. According to Sugai (1985),

> Short term objectives that have been mastered should be probed regularly and systematically to evaluate how well their achievement has been maintained and generalized. . . . The teacher should identify the conditions under which the behavior is to be demonstrated by the student and the criterion level at which the behavior is to occur. When an objective is mastered, the date of completion is noted. (p. 235)

Planning the Individualized Education Program

According to McDaniels (1980) the IEP serves six important functions. First, it is a communication vehicle for the parents and the school. Each party helps to write the IEP, and each understands the needs of the child and the goals of the program. Second, the IEP serves as the basis for resolving conflicts between the parents' desires for programs and the school's wish to serve the child. Third, resources are allocated based on the prescription in the IEP. Fourth, the IEP is a management tool for teachers; it enables them to provide appropriate education and related services. Fifth, the IEP is a compliance and monitoring document. It allows parents, schools, and government agencies to determine whether the child is receiving the appropriate service. Finally, the IEP can serve as an evaluation device to determine student progress, although teachers are not held accountable if IEP annual goals or short-term objectives are not reached by prescribed time lines.

The first three and the last functions of the IEP listed above are important for the consultant to stress to special and regular education teachers. However, the consultant must also emphasize to teachers that parents must be made to feel a part of the IEP process. Swick, Flake-Hobson, and Raymond (1980) state that the key element in the IEP conference is parent participation.

> Parents must have the opportunity to contribute their unique perspective of the child at home. To achieve a successful conference, teachers and specialists must communicate clearly and effectively with parents and make them feel that they are important members of the team. Information shared by teachers can be threatening, anxiety producing, or intimidating to parents if it is not presented in the proper atmosphere. If parents are uneasy or overwhelmed by the conference they may not be willing or able to share important information about their child. (p. 144)

Too often, parents attend an IEP meeting only to find the document has already been prepared without them. Either directly or indirectly they get the message that the educators have decided the best course of action and parental input is not needed. Anecdote 4.1 is an example of how a consultant helped a special education high school teacher plan an appropriate IEP meeting.

ANECDOTE 4.1

CONSULTANT: I understand that you'll be meeting with the Wilson family next week to discuss Fred's IEP.

TEACHER: That's correct. I was hoping that you might be able to give me some suggestions on the best way to approach the parents with the IEP goals.

CONSULTANT: I'd be glad to help. Let's start by reviewing Fred's progress.

TEACHER (*handing the Diagnostic Summary Sheet to the consultant*): I've already begun to list what I believe are appropriate long-term goals and short-term objectives, as well as the instructional approach and materials I'd like to use.

CONSULTANT: Good.

TEACHER: I don't want to complete the entire IEP document, because I'm afraid the parents might feel that I don't want their suggestions.

CONSULTANT: I couldn't agree with you more. Maybe we could outline the program, the services to be rendered, and their duration on the IEP for the parents. Put it in the mail along with a short cover letter explaining the draft so that they can review it before the meeting. Any changes that the parents recommend could be added, and if they felt strongly that any of our plans were inappropriate, we'd be able to discuss our reasoning.

TEACHER: That sounds fine.

CONSULTANT: I'd like to suggest that the annual goals and short-term objectives we list for Fred be written so that the emphasis is on application of skills and concepts in real-life situations. I think the parents would appreciate the career education emphasis and goals which will lead to better survival skills for Fred.

TEACHER: I hadn't thought of that. We have units on careers, community living, and leisure, but I've never written them directly into an IEP.

CONSULTANT: It's certainly something to consider, especially in Fred's case. He'll be graduating from high school this year, and it will be important for him to be able to apply the skills you are teaching to many situations. A career education emphasis might increase his chances of getting a job.

TEACHER: What happens if the parents refuse to sign the IEP?

CONSULTANT: You've raised a good question. The parents are not obligated to sign the IEP. Many do, of course, but there is no rule that says they must. What is required is that both parties — parents and educators — agree on the most appropriate program. Hopefully, if both parties are prepared for the meeting, we'll be able to reach consensus. We inform the parents that they'll receive a copy of the IEP for their records.

TEACHER: Thanks so much for your help.

CONSULTANT: I'll try to attend the meeting, but sometimes too many professionals at the IEP meeting inhibit communication. If you have any questions before or after the meeting, please feel free to give me a call. Remember, it's important for the parents to have the opportunity to express their views. Let them talk.

TEACHER: I'll do that. Thanks again.

In this anecdote the consultant provided three key recommendations that should greatly enhance the productivity of the conference team, and strengthen Fred's performance after the conference as well. First, the consultant suggested that a working draft be mailed to the parents so that they would be better prepared to discuss Fred's program at the conference. Several school districts currently provide this service, and according to anecdotal information, parents are responsive to this approach. Second, the consultant suggested that the annual goals and short-term objectives for Fred be written with a career education focus. Given Fred's impending graduation, it is critical that he have the opportunity to practice the survival skills he will need after leaving school. Finally, the consultant reminded the teacher to give the parents the opportunity to talk. Goldstein, Strickland, Turnbull, and Curry (1980) indicated that the two most frequent speakers at an IEP conference were the resource room teacher and the parent. However, the resource room teacher spoke twice as often as the parent. Parents must be given every opportunity to discuss their concerns, and parents whose verbal participation is low should be encouraged to express themselves.

Monitoring and Evaluating the IEP

Consultants can provide a great deal of assistance to teachers and parents by helping to monitor and evaluate the IEP. According to Turnbull, Strickland, and Brantley (1982), the monitoring process can include an evaluation of whether the goals and objectives are being met and the time table for their completion. Safer and Hobbs (1980) indicate that the majority of IEPs contain criteria for determining the accomplishment of goals and/or short-term objectives. Typically, the criteria refer to performance measures on standardized or criterion-referenced instruments.

Maher and Barbrack (1980) formalized the monitoring and evaluation process for the IEP (Table 4.2). Their system, termed A Framework for Comprehensive Evaluation of the Individualized Education Program, is designed to ensure that all aspects of the IEP are evaluated (e.g., student outcomes, consumer satisfaction, compliance with P.L. 94-142 rules). As a global source for evaluating all aspects of the IEP, the framework is helpful because it encompasses all of the critical variables required for compliance with P.L. 94-142.

At a more specific level, however, consultants can help teachers determine on a day-to-day or month-to-month basis whether IEP objectives are being met. Sugai (1985) proposed the Daily Monitoring Sheet as one method to monitor student progress on IEP objectives (see Figure 4.5). For instance, the chart shows the date on which individual objectives were addressed, a description of the teacher's activity, a statement of the expected response, the conditions under which behavior is to occur, and criteria for success. The chart also provides space for recording actual student performance and anecdotal comments.

According to Sugai (1985), "The Daily Monitoring Sheet serves as the lesson plan. When maintained on a daily basis by the resource room teacher, it functions as a dynamic record of the student's progress toward the completion of short-term objectives and as a systematic structure for sequencing instructional activities" (p. 236).

Price and Goodman (1980) suggest that another important area to consider when evaluating IEPs is the cost. According to these authors, the average

TABLE 4.2
A Framework for Comprehensive Evaluation of the Individualized Education Program (IEP)

Evaluation Aspect			
Evaluation Strategy	Area of Evaluation	Evaluation Issue	Decision Maker
Evaluability Assessment	Program Design	Program Evaluability	Planners
Process Evaluation	Program Implementation	Program Operations	Implementers
Outcome Evaluation	Pupil Progress	Goal Attainment	Planners and Implementers
Consumer Evaluation	Program Satisfaction	Program Utility	Planners

From "A framework for comprehensive evaluation of the Individualized Education Program (IEP)" by C.A. Maher & C.R. Barbrack (1980) in *Learning Disabilities Quarterly*, 3(3), 50. Reprinted by permission.

amount of time required to prepare an IEP for an exceptional student was 6.5 hours (4.5 hours at school, 2.0 hours personal time). Data such as these can be useful for the consultant, because excessive amounts of time expended to prepare the IEP may mean: (a) less direct instruction will be provided to students; (b) inservice training may be needed for staff on procedures for developing IEPs; or (c) district resources may need to be reallocated during peak IEP development times (e.g., fall and spring quarters). By gathering these data a consultant would be able to address IEP preparation needs that otherwise might go unnoticed.

GENERALITY AND MAINTENANCE OF SKILLS

Another way a consultant can help after the IEP conference is to show the teacher effective ways to promote generality and maintenance of the student's skills. This is an important task, because the student needs to use the academic or social behavior learned in the classroom in other areas or settings.

Daily Monitoring Sheet

Student Name _____ J. Caesar

Teacher Name _____ Ms. Augustus

Date	Obj. #	Plan/Schedule	Behavior	Condition	Criteria	Data	Comments
2/17	1.1	Meet with Ms. Patrick and J. to discuss J.'s progress in her classroom.	Raise hand.	When teacher asks a question.	75% 2 consecutive days 4/5 classes	80–83% 4/5 classes	*"Good* job in Ms. Patrick's class. Your objective was *met!"*
2/18	1.1	Phone J.'s parents and discuss fading of tokens and pairing more verbal praise and home activity reinforcers.	Raise hand.	When teacher asks a question.	75% 1 day 4/5 classes	85–87% 5/5 classes	"Another *great* day. Objective *met* again!"
2/19	1.1	Observe in Ms. Patrick's classroom.	Raise hand.	When teacher asks a question.	85% 4 consecutive days 5/5 classes	86–88% 4/5 classes	"Almost did it today. Try again tomorrow."
2/22	1.1	Meet with J. at 8:30 a.m. Go over progress thus far. Discuss Ms. Patrick's question-asking strategies and J.'s answering behaviors.	Raise hand.	When teacher asks a question.	85% 4 consecutive days 5/5 classes		

FIGURE 4.5. Daily Monitoring Sheet. From "Case study: Designing instruction from IEPs" by G. Sugai (1985) in *Teaching Exceptional Children, 17*(3), 237. Reprinted by permission.

Since many handicapped learners need specially designed materials and have to function in a variety of home and school settings, it is imperative that the special educator have built-in instructional strategies for promoting generality and maintenance (Baer, Wolf, and Risley, 1968). The consultant can help to increase the special educator's awareness that generality and maintenance can be part of the lesson plan.

The first step toward increasing a teacher's awareness is to let him or her know that generality can be considered in two ways: stimulus generality and response generality.

Stimulus Generality

According to Cooper et al. (1987), *stimulus generality* occurs "when a target behavior is emitted in the presence of stimulus conditions other than those in which it was directly trained. . . . The setting in which stimulus generality is desired can contain some components of the behavior change program that was implemented in the training environment, but not all of the components. If the complete program is required to produce behavior change in a different environment, then no stimulus generality can be claimed" (p. 556).

Consultants working with secondary level teachers would find the study conducted by Van Den Pol et al. (1981) a practical illustration of how stimulus generality can be assessed as part of an overall training program. In their study three adults with mental retardation and at least one other disability (deafness, epilepsy, emotional handicaps) participated in a series of class-room training activities designed to teach skill components related to restaurant behavior: locating, ordering, eating, paying, and exiting. Training consisted of role-playing a sequence of behaviors designed to simulate customer-cashier interactions. Slides were also used to show examples and of appropriate and inappropriate customer-cashier interactions. Total training time took approximately 10 hours. Generality probes, in which students were given a small amount of money and told to go to lunch, were conducted before, during, and after training. The probes were measured in McDonald's restaurant; follow-up probes were conducted at a Burger King restaurant.

Figure 4.6 shows the results of the multiple baseline analysis of stimulus generality. The data show that each adult performed approximately 40% of the correct responses during baseline. After training, the percentage of correct responses improved steadily, ending with an average of over 80% correct. Furthermore, probes taken in Burger King indicated that skills were performed correctly there as well. Finally, a maintenance check taken one year after instruction showed all adults performing over two-thirds of the behaviors.

Van Den Pol et al's (1981) study is important for consultants, because it underscores the point that simulated training, delivered by the classroom

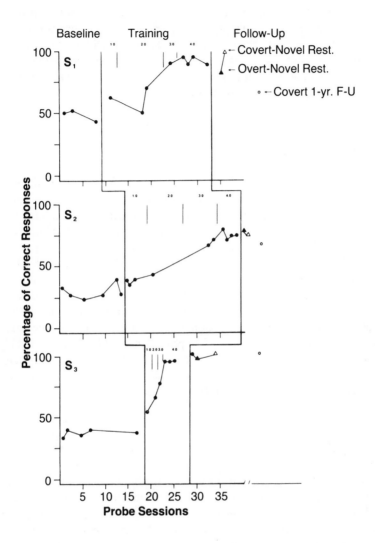

FIGURE 4.6. Percent correct responses during restaurant probes for Students 1, 2, and 3 across experimental conditions. During follow-up, closed triangles represent probes conducted at a Burger King restaurant using typical observation procedures; open triangles represent Burger King probes during which students did not know that their performance was being observed; and open circles represent covert probes conducted in a different McDonald's one year following the termination of training. From "Teaching the handicapped to eat in public places: Acquisition, generalization, and maintenance of restaurant skills" by R. A. Van Den Pol, B. A. Iwata, M. T. Ivanic, T. J. Page, N. A. Neef, & F. P. Whitley (1981) in *Journal of Applied Behavior Analysis*, 14(1), 66. Copyright 1981 by the *Society for the Experimental Analysis of Behavior, Inc.* Reprinted by permission.

teacher as part of the instructional program, may not be sufficient to produce generalized behavior. Modeling, prompting, and reinforcing correct responses in the natural setting (e.g., the restaurant) may be needed also if generalized and lasting behavior change is to take place. Consultants working with teachers and parents would be encouraged to work jointly with these agents to assess effects of training in nontrained settings.

Response Generality

Cooper et al. (1987) define *response generality* as "the extent to which the learner performs a variety of functional responses in addition to the trained response; that is, responses for which no specific contingencies have been applied are altered as a function of the contingencies applied to other responses" (p. 558). For example, suppose a teacher as part of an art project taught students how to shoot photographs with a 35mm camera at a fixed distance using fixed settings. Each clear image obtained by the students produced teacher praise (e.g., "Christine, that's a clear photo with nice sharp edges"). If Christine produced clear pictures at varying distances and settings without specific training, then response generality would have occurred. Cooper et al. (1987) summarize the key point for consultants who are helping other practitioners reinforce new forms of a behavior: "Reinforcing a few members of the response of new forms *results* in other members of the class being strengthened as well" (p. 560) [italics added].

Maintenance

Maintenance of behavior change means that the individual continues to perform the desired behavior after training has terminated. According to Koegel and Rincover (1977), for maintenance to occur it has to be programmed into the intervention by thinning the schedule of reinforcement of desirable responses and occasionally delivering noncontingent reinforcement.

PROMOTING GENERALITY OF BEHAVIOR CHANGE

Cooper et al. (1987) cite several steps and strategies that can be used to improve the likelihood of generality of behavior change. The strategies are divided into two major categories — planning and implementing — and draw on the seminal work of Stokes and Baer (1977).

Planning

As part of any behavior change program, consultants should work with teachers and parents to plan for generality of behavior change. Three questions should be asked at this phase: What are the behaviors to change? In what environments should the behaviors occur? What will be required of practitioners in those environments to support and maintain performance?

To illustrate, these questions might be addressed when planning for generality of behavior change with a learning disabled student engaged in a work study program by focusing on all behaviors (academic and social) that are likely to be required in both settings. Further, an examination of each setting should be conducted to determine if the trained behavior would have to be evident within the same setting. For instance, would the behavior need to be evident at school in the classroom, hallway, cafeteria, or gymnasium? Finally, all personnel in the school and the job site who might come into contact with the student should be aware of, and actively support, the desired behavior change. The more people that can increase opportunity to respond and deliver an appropriate consequence (e.g., feedback or reinforcement), the more likely it is that generality will occur.

Implementing

Cooper et al. (1987) list six strategies for promoting generality of behavior change. While it might be impossible for the consultant to set the occasion for all six of these strategies to be used in any given situation, the more of the strategies that can be introduced, the more likely it is that generality will occur.

Aim for the Natural Contingencies of Reinforcement. Using the natural contingencies of reinforcement means that events that might occur in any setting can be used to reinforce behavior. Events like teacher recognition, parental praise, or peer acceptance are consequences that qualify as natural contingencies of reinforcement. Teachers might have to provide extra training to students to prime these natural contingencies. For instance, a student might have to be taught to show his preoccupied father how well he did on his math paper so that his father can deliver an appropriate comment.

Teach Enough Examples. A common mistake that teachers and parents make is to teach a skill using only one or two examples, and then to expect the behavior to change over time, settings, and situations. While some authors have shown that generality of behavior change can be produced with as few as two examples (cf. Stokes, Baer, & Jackson, 1974), the more likely scenario for ensuring that generality takes place is to provide a sufficient subset of important stimuli and response examples. But how many examples are enough? Cooper et al. (1987) provide a disclaimer:

> The number of examples that must be taught before significant generality occurs varies considerably. It is a function of such variables as the target behavior(s) being taught, the instructional procedures employed, the subject's opportunities to emit the target behavior under various conditions, the existing natural contingencies of reinforcement, and the learner's history of reinforcement with regard to generality. (p. 572)

Program Common Stimuli.   There are several stimuli common across special and regular education settings. Consultants working with teachers in self-contained classrooms who anticipate mainstreaming students would be advised to focus on skill building, rules, the time and length of instruction, and the type of reinforcement.

With respect to skill building, for example, assume that a learning disabled student could perform two-digit by two-digit multiplication with regrouping, and the teacher wanted to extend the skill to three-digit by three-digit multiplication. The teacher, by focusing on the elements common to each problem (arranging the numbers according to place value and correctly multiplying and adding the columns), would be training the student for a higher order skill using a specific response generalization approach.

Likewise, if the teacher were reasonably certain that a handicapped student might be mainstreamed for specific academic periods or specific skill areas, she would be wise to consider several variables common to each setting that may affect the success of the program. For example, one of the most useful pieces of information a student needs to survive in any classroom is the classroom rules. The student needs to know what is permitted and what the consequences are for rule infraction. Often handicapped students break rules and suffer the consequences because the rules were not clearly explained or understood.

The consultant can make a teacher aware of the type and complexity of instructional materials that are used in the regular class. Again, the closer the materials in the special education class are to those in the regular class in terms of interest, readability, level of difficulty, and the skills to be learned, the greater the likelihood of generality. Wallace and Kauffman (1978) indicate that one similar instructional method or set of materials may not be enough to achieve the desired objective.

Two other factors, which can be equated across settings, are the time and length of instruction. Many handicapped youngsters have short attention spans and require their instruction in small doses over longer time periods. Also, some handicapped students perform much better in the morning than they do in the afternoon. In this case, heavy academic instruction should probably be scheduled in the morning rather than later in the day.

A final factor to promote generality is the type of reinforcement the student receives. For example, if an educable mentally retarded adolescent received points at school for appropriate behavior, a similar system could be established at home. If verbal praise is issued in the special class for appropriate behavior, then verbal praise should be included as one method of reinforcing appropriate responses in the regular classroom.

Train Loosely. To train loosely means that a wide variety of stimuli should be present at the time of training so that no one stimulus or format of instruction gains exclusive control over the behavior. The use of multiple teachers, multiple locations for lessons, types of examples, and variable noise and light levels are examples of how to train loosely.

Use Indiscriminable Contingencies. Essentially, the consultant who recommends indiscriminable contingencies would advocate the use of delayed or intermittent schedules of reinforcement. With either of these two contingencies, behaviors originally acquired under continuous reinforcement are now more likely to occur when reinforcement is no longer available for each response. Reinforcing student performance on an intermittent schedule is more advantageous to the teacher if stimulus or response generality is desired.

A consultant working with a classroom teacher should, at the least, increase the teacher's awareness of four intermittent schedules of reinforcement that can be used with relative ease in the self-contained classroom and will also benefit the student as he or she advances from one skill or one setting to another. The first two schedules (fixed interval and variable interval) are time-related. That is, reinforcement is issued for a response after a given time period has passed. The second two schedules (fixed ratio and variable ratio) are response-related. That is, the student has to perform behaviors to earn reinforcement.

Fixed interval. A fixed interval (FI) schedule of reinforcement is said to be in effect when the first response following a specific time period is reinforced (Cooper et al., 1987). For instance, a physically handicapped student who is reinforced on a fixed interval schedule of three minutes (FI 3) for appropriate object sorting would receive reinforcement for the first appropriate object-sorting behavior he or she completed following the three-minute time frame. If the behavior did not occur immediately after the three minutes, reinforcement would be withheld until it did.

While there are a few advantages the consultant could mention to the special education teacher interested in this schedule (e.g., it might be easier logistically for the teacher), there are several distinct disadvantages the consultant needs to point out. First, the schedule may become too predictable.

Students may figure out when reinforcement is likely to occur, and they may work only at that time. Second, because the schedule may be so predictable, little work may be evident soon after reinforcement has occurred. This characteristic pause tends to produce a curve, referred to as a "scallop," which shows little or no work soon after reinforcement but steady increases in performance toward the end of the interval. Finally, the student can make a great many errors during the interval for which no corrective feedback is obtained. If a behaviorally disordered student were on a fixed interval of 20 minutes (FI 20) for appropriate social behavior, not only would the teacher have to wait at least 20 minutes to deliver reinforcement, but inappropriate social behavior might go undetected during the 20-minute interval. In effect, the student might practice inappropriate behavior and receive reinforcement (perhaps from a peer in the form of attention) and completely compromise the system.

Consultants should recommend FI schedules to teachers with advice to make the intervals short. Increases in the time of the interval should only be extended as the student's behavior improves.

Variable interval.   When a variable interval (VI) schedule is used, reinforcement is delivered for the first response following the passage of a varying amount of time (Cooper et al., 1987). For example, a learning disabled student in a self-contained classroom who is on a VI 10 schedule for assignment completion would receive reinforcement for the first response that occurred following the passage of 10 minutes on the average. So, the student could be reinforced after 2 minutes, 6 minutes, 20 minutes or 12 minutes — as long as he or she performed the desired response after the passage of that time limit and the totals averaged 10 minutes.

The most striking advantage a VI schedule has over a FI schedule is that it is unpredictable. Reinforcement could occur at any time — varying around a specific average — and the behavior targeted for change is more likely to be sustained during the interval. This is in contrast to the FI schedule where the target behavior is not usually evident during the entire interval, only at the end of the interval.

Fixed ratio.   A fixed ratio (FR) schedule simply means that the student has to perform a set number of responses before reinforcement is delivered (Cooper et al., 1987). For instance, a behaviorally disordered student on a FR 14 for math would have to complete 14 math calculations before reinforcement would be delivered. Likewise, on a FR 27, the student would have to do 27 problems before earning reinforcement.

One advantage FR schedules have that the consultant can indicate to the teacher is that they are used in both special and regular classes. It is common to hear the teacher say, "When you are finished with your math worksheet, you can have free time." For the student who is likely to be mainstreamed into the regular class, the consultant might recommend that a FR schedule be introduced with low response requirements (e.g., FR 5) and later expanded to more closely match the response requirements of the classroom to which the student is going (e.g., FR 30).

Variable ratio. A variable ratio (VR) or "gambler's" schedule provides reinforcement for a varying number of responses (Cooper et al., 1987). The number of responses required to earn reinforcement varies around a specific average. For instance, a student with mental retardation in a special class who is operating under a VR 7 schedule for hand-raising would receive reinforcement following an average of seven hand-raising responses. Since the student is just as likely to earn reinforcement after 1 response as she is after 7, or 10, or 100, very high rates of responding occur.

One distinct advantage of the VR schedule is its unpredictability. Students might perform a great many behaviors anticipating that the very next response will be reinforced. Since many handicapped youngsters are integrated in the regular classrooms, the consultant would be wise to advise the special education teacher to move to a VR schedule for as many behaviors as possible. The primary reason for suggesting this strategy is that reinforcement occurs at unpredictable times in the regular classroom, and if the handicapped student is already operating under a VR schedule, it is less likely that appropriate behavior learned in the self-contained classroom will be extinguished in the regular setting. More important, generality and maintenance will be enhanced.

Teach Self-Management. By teaching self-management skills to individuals, the educator insures that the cue or prompt to occasion a behavior will reside with the person. Also, when different stimulus conditions are present, or when different responses are required, a person who has a "resident" cue to use is more likely to emit the appropriate, generalized behavior.

According to Cooper et al. (1987) self-management can be taught to students in five steps: (a) selection and definition of behaviors to change; (b) self-observation and recording of the behavior; (c) specification of the behavior change procedure; (d) implementation; and (e) evaluation. Cooper et al. (1987) provide a thorough description of how to design, implement, and evaluate self-management programs.

CONCLUSION

Consultants who work with teachers in self-contained classrooms often have to extend their services in two directions. First, they must be able to assist the self-contained teacher with tasks that are required to meet the instructional needs of students within the class. They must be able to play an active role in the IEP process, recommending assessments, providing technical assistance with administration of the tests, and interpreting the results. Also, the consultant must be familiar with the scope and sequence of the curriculum so that instructional strategies that are jointly determined by the teacher and the consultant facilitate generality and maintenance. Several key strategies are mentioned in the chapter that a consultant can use to accomplish each of these objectives.

A second task that a consultant might have to perform with the self-contained teacher would occur when a student is to be integrated in a regular classroom. The consultant can provide the needed support for the self-contained teacher in terms of preparing the student for the new environment. For example, the consultant might recommend that a different schedule of reinforcement be used, or that instructional materials be aligned more closely with the materials in the regular classroom. The important point for the consultant to remember is that he or she is serving four agents — the child, the parent, the special teacher, and the regular teacher. The strategies the consultant recommends must meet with the approval of each teacher and address the instructional needs of the student.

SUMMARY OF KEY POINTS

Definition of Self-Contained Classrooms

1. Self-contained classrooms are instructional settings that serve students who have substantial handicapping conditions and for whom placement in less restrictive settings is inappropriate.

2. Self-contained classrooms are usually structured to minimize distraction and increase individualized attention. Two disadvantages of the self-contained classroom are the likelihood that placement may be permanent and that contact with regular educators may be minimal.

Helping Teachers to Develop and Evaluate the Individualized Education Program

3. Consultants can assist special education teachers develop and evaluate the Individualized Education Program by helping with any of the following functions: the initial assessment, integrating the assessment data, writing goal statements, planning the IEP, and monitoring and evaluating the IEP process.

4. When integrating assessment data, consultants should help teachers determine each student's strengths and weaknesses, learning style, and preferred reinforcers. When writing goal statements consultants can help

in arranging annual goals, determining short-term objectives, selecting appropriate instructional materials and strategies, and designing effective evaluation procedures.

Generality and Maintenance

5. Stimulus generality occurs when a target behavior is emitted in the presence of stimulus conditions other than those in which it was directly trained.

6. Response generality is defined as the extent to which the learner performs a variety of functional responses in addition to the trained response.

7. Maintenance is defined as the performance of the target behavior after training has been terminated.

Promoting Generality of Behavior Change

8. Generality of behavior change can be promoted by focusing on planning and implementing areas prior to the initiation of treatment. When planning for generality, focus on what behavior will be changed, where the behaviors will occur, and what will be required of individuals within the environment. During implementation, focus on developing the natural contingencies of reinforcement, teaching enough examples, programming common stimuli, training loosely, using indiscriminable contingencies, and teaching self-management.

QUESTIONS

1. State two functions a consultant can perform to help self-contained teachers with the IEP process.

2. Identify and describe two types of generality.

3. Indicate procedures to follow to facilitate generality. Give a classroom-related example of each.

4. Assume that a student is to be moved from a self-contained classroom to a regular classroom. Why is it important for the two environments to be somewhat similar?

5. Define four basic schedules of reinforcement.

6. Describe a situation where instruction within a self-contained special education classroom would be appropriate for a handicapped student.

7. What factors in a student's educational program may require assessment to successfully develop and implement an Individualized Education Program?

DISCUSSION POINTS AND EXERCISES

1. Prepare a 15-minute videotape depicting a teacher who has conducted a lesson that was programmed for generality. Have participants identify key elements in the generality training. Solicit their ideas on how this approach could be used in their own classrooms.

2. Pick a child with a learning problem in your school. Identify that child's preferred reinforcers.

3. Devise a plan to maintain student academic and social gains across time.

4. The following represents an annual goal for a multiply handicapped, 6-year-old student: Sue Ellen will acquire prerequisite skills necessary for handwriting. Develop appropriate short-term objectives and indicate how these objectives might be evaluated.

5

Working with Parents of Mainstreamed Students

This chapter describes the role parents of handicapped students can assume as home-based educators, behavior managers, tutors in the classroom, and partners in the Individualized Education Program for their children. The chapter discusses ways in which consultants can access and involve parents in the education process.

A comprehensive parent program means that all parents are involved at some level of participation (Kroth, 1980). Consultants, however, should remember that not all parents will be able or willing to participate in all facets of a parenting program. As McLoughlin (1978) indicates, a parent's primary responsibility is to be a parent, not a clinician or an educator or a therapist. This chapter was written with the assumption that the consultant would consider Kroth's parent involvement model and McLoughlin's advice before embarking on any radical parent-training or intervention program.

OBJECTIVES

After reading this chapter, the reader should be able to:

1. cite the four levels of Kroth's (1980) Mirror Model of Parental Involvement from the professional and parent perspective.

2. cite three ways consultants can assist parents to become better home-based managers.

3. state several methods to initiate and maintain home-school communication programs with parents.

4. describe how a home-school communication program using a telephone answering device could be established and maintained.

5. identify key aspects in the development of parent training programs.

6. state four phases of a parent conference. Describe the function of each phase.

7. identify nine variables to consider when establishing parent training programs.

8. explain two advantages of using parents as tutors in the classroom.

KEY TERMS

Mirror Model of Parental Involvement

Home-based educator

Home-school communication

Parent conference

Parent training program

Parent tutoring program

WORKING WITH PARENTS OF MAINSTREAMED STUDENTS

Educational consultants who work with parents of mainstreamed children and youth need to understand some of the societal pressures as well as some of the individual problems such families face. As Lichto (1976) notes, feelings of social isolation or embarrassment and the potential loss of family or neighborhood assistance may place an enormous strain on parents of a handicapped child. Educational consultants need to be sensitive to these pressures so that supports can be provided for the parent and the family. Supervisors and consultants can provide special assistance in such areas as the development of an effective communication link between parent and professional, the establishment of specific behavior management approaches at home, or guidance with the IEP process.

Educational researchers and practitioners have stated consistently that parent involvement in the educational process is essential (Cooper & Edge, 1981; Heward, Dardig, & Rossett, 1979). Now, Public Law 94-142 assures the opportunity for parent involvement in the education process by mandating that identification and placement decisions be made with the consent of the parents and that safeguards be established to protect the parents' and child's right to due process.

Assuring the opportunity for parent participation and actually obtaining that participation are two different things. Participation cannot be mandated; it must be nurtured, encouraged, and reinforced. Kroth's (1980) Mirror

Model of Parental Involvement provides the consultant with an excellent perspective on the reciprocal nature of the parent-professional partnership. Also, it provides the consultant with an index to determine parent involvement and the level of that participation.

Mirror Model of Parental Involvement

Figure 5.1 shows Kroth's (1980) *Mirror Model of Parental Involvement*. Essentially, the model is divided into two major areas — professional service and parental service. Within each area there are four levels of participation designated by the terms *all, most, some,* and *few*. According to Kroth (1980), lower levels of participation need to be firmly established before higher levels of involvement can be expected. For example, all parents could probably provide information regarding the child's preschool medical and social history. Most parents could provide relevant information during the IEP process or help with an occasional field trip (e.g., prepare snacks, donate equipment, or volunteer to assist teachers). Some parents might become strong advocates for services for handicapped students. They may attend legislative hearings, initiate parent advisory groups, or volunteer as teacher's aides. Finally, only a few parents might become involved enough to form active parent groups and conduct parenting workshops themselves.

Conversely, all professionals (e.g., teachers, school psychologists) would be able to provide parents with information relative to standardized and norm-referenced tests used with their child. Most teachers are willing to call parents on the telephone to discuss pertinent happenings in school. Some teachers conduct parent education training programs to help improve the quality of service their school provides. Finally, a few teachers conduct in-depth workshops for parents and colleagues which go beyond the one-shot sessions usually offered through districts.

How is this information helpful to a consultant? First, it may dramatically change the way a consultant communicates to a teacher expectations of a successful parent-teacher partnership. Too often a consultant hears from teachers that the parents are not interested because they do not attend meetings or scheduled conferences. Teachers interpret nonattendance as disinterest and may become frustrated because they feel they are working alone to help the handicapped students. These feelings of frustration can build to feelings of resentment toward the child and the parent ("If the parents do not care how their child is doing in my class, why should I?"). If the feelings of resentment are translated into social rejection, the student's educational program may be compromised.

Parental nonattendance at scheduled meetings could be for several reasons. The time selected for the conference may have been inconvenient. Both parents may work, or each may work a different shift. Also, the parents may

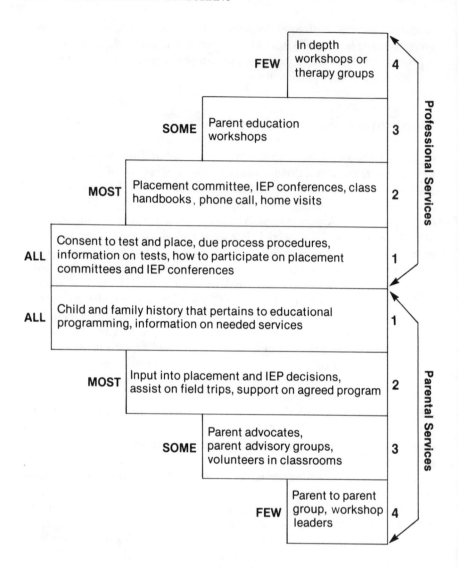

FIGURE 5.1. Mirror model of parental involvement. From "Mirror model of parental involvement" by R. L. Kroth (1980) in *The Pointer*, 25(1), 19. Reprinted by permission of Heldref Publications, 4000 Albemarle Street, NW, Washington, DC 20016.

have felt they needed to strike a balance between the help they give their handicapped child and the time they share with each other or other family members. Finally, if the distance is too great to travel or provisions cannot be made for competent babysitting, then attendance at meetings might decline.

Second, conducting a needs assessment of parent and professional concerns, strengths, and time restrictions — either directly through a telephone survey or questionnaire or indirectly by discussion with teachers or principal — will help the consultant structure a comprehensive parenting program. Resources and time can be allotted to each level to maximize parent and professional participation at that level. With parents, however, consultants should recognize that most of the organization and implementation tasks will have to be performed by them until such time as a few parents are able to carry on.

Third, when trying to determine the effectiveness of a school-, district-, or county-wide parent involvement program, single measures of evaluation (e.g., attendance at meetings or numbers of parents who volunteer as teacher aides or home-based educators) could be abandoned in favor of a more comprehensive index, the percentage of parents who participated at each level in the model. In effect, 100% of the parents could have been involved, with differing ratios of parental involvement at each level.

Anecdotes 5.1 and 5.2 describe how a consultant attempted to increase the level of participation of two parents. The first parent was at the *most* level of participation; she provided extensive input for her child's IEP. The second parent was at the *some* level; she had experience providing testimony to state legislative committees. In both cases, the consultant attempted to move the parents' involvement to the next higher level.

ANECDOTE 5.1

CONSULTANT (*a week after the IEP conference*): Mrs. Kempe, you really provided several excellent recommendations during Sal's IEP conference.

PARENT: It's important to me that Sal receive all the necessary services. He is already so far behind. I am especially eager to see him in the tutoring program.

CONSULTANT: I was quite impressed with your knowledge of school services. In fact, the reason I'm calling you is to see if you would be interested in helping Sal's teacher implement some of the objectives for Sal and for other children.

PARENT: You mean help out at school during the day?

CONSULTANT: Yes, Sal's teacher indicated he would love to have you as an assistant.

PARENT: I'm afraid that I will not be able to accept. At the time of the conference I was interviewing for a part-time job, and yesterday I was offered the position.

CONSULTANT: Congratulations! I can see where your time will be limited during the day.

PARENT: Yes, it will. Is there anything I could do for the teacher short of coming to the school?

CONSULTANT: Maybe we could set something up with you and Sal at home. I'm thinking of helping with a school-related task for only a few minutes each night.

PARENT: I already do that, but I'm open to ideas on specific things I can do. I often feel lost.

CONSULTANT: I'll set it up with the teacher. Again, good luck with your new job. I'm looking forward to working with you and the teacher on Sal's home program.

This scenario illustrates several positive consulting behaviors. First, the consultant reinforced the parent for her previous participation at the IEP conference. Second, she included the teacher in the discussion by stating that she was eager to have the parent assist in the room. Third, she reinforced the parent for getting a job offer. Instead of ignoring the parent's success, the consultant's comment expressed congratulations and empathy for the parent's position (limited time during the day). Finally, the consultant ended the conversation by reiterating that she felt her participation was still of value and that a home-based program could be explored.

ANECDOTE 5.2

CONSULTANT: Lee, I read in the newspaper last night that you provided testimony to the House Education Committee on a bill dealing with special education funding.

LEE: That's right. It is important that the bill go to the Senate with the amendments I proposed.

CONSULTANT: I realize you are busy, but I wanted to talk to you because I'd like to capitalize on your experience in an upcoming series of workshops I'm offering.

LEE: What could I do?

CONSULTANT: I'd like you to present your ideas on working with legislators to a group of parents who will be attending. I'd like them to have the total view of educating the handicapped, including the role of the legislator.

LEE: If the presentation can be scheduled at a time when I'm not required to be in session with the legislators, I'll be glad to do it.

CONSULTANT: Thank you. I appreciate your help.

In this case, the consultant achieved his objective of having Lee serve as a workshop presenter. Lee was reinforced for his expertise, and his cooperation was obtained for the presentation. Lee may have been inclined to accept the consultant's offer because the time commitment was short, or he felt a social obligation to help. Regardless of why, the consultant attained his goal.

In sum, Kroth's (1980) model can be used as a communication vehicle with regular and special education teachers and parents. Feelings of isolation and disillusionment might be prevented when teachers see that parents need not participate in all levels of the model for the total parent involvement program to be successful. Also, when Kroth's model is used with a needs assessment, the consultant is in a better position to recommend parenting resources. Existing networks of communication (e.g., school newspaper, Parent Teacher Association meetings, or regional newsletters) can be used to disseminate information about the program. Finally, once success has been achieved with a parent at a lower level of participation, increased involvement at a higher level could be planned and implemented.

Parents as Behavior Managers

All parents change child behavior. They permit some behaviors, inhibit or prevent others, and punish still more. Some parents, however, are more consistent than others about the behaviors they allow, inhibit, or punish. As a result, they become more effective behavior managers and more effective parents. Learning to become a better manager is not an impossible task for parents. O'Dell (1974) provides a review of programs in which parents have learned to use behavior management approaches in the home. Cooperatively developed plans between school-related personnel and parents have been implemented in the past (Hall, Cristler, Cranston, & Tucker, 1970; Lazarus, 1986; Weiss, 1984)

For example, Hall et al. (1970) found that when parents were given guidelines to follow with respect to executing a management program, inappropriate child behaviors were reduced or eliminated. Specifically, a parent was advised to reduce the amount of time her daughter could stay up at night contingent upon the nonoccurrence of three discrete behaviors. The parents established a rule with the child that for every minute under 30 minutes that she failed to play her clarinet, she would go to bed one minute earlier than her scheduled time.

Immediately, clarinet practice increased to the required 30-minute criterion. Subsequently, the rule was applied to two other problem behaviors with identical results. Within approximately 16 days the child was engaged in all three tasks at the required criterion level (Figure 5.2). The parent was satisfied with the results, and the child suffered no apparent side effects.

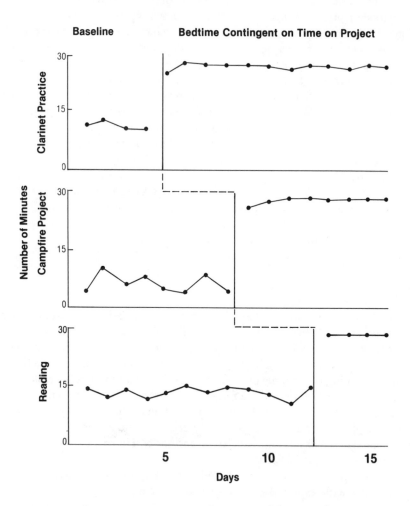

FIGURE 5.2.   Parent management of child behavior showing bedtime contingent on nonoccurrence of three behaviors. From "Teacher and parents as researchers using multiple baseline designs" by R.V. Hall, C. Christler, S. S. Cranston, & B. Tucker (1970) in *Journal of Applied Behavior Analysis, 3,* 252. Copyright by the *Society for the Experimental Analysis of Behavior, Inc.* Reprinted by permission.

Shrewsberry (1981) found that a parent could successfully reduce unpleasant, talking-back behavior by her oldest son. The mother reinforced the youth with a check mark for complying with requests without complaining. When he earned five check marks, he could exchange them for a preferred activity. On occasion when the youth did complain, the mother ignored the back talk. Figure 5.3 shows the results of the study. When the check marks plus ignoring phase were in effect, the back talk diminished. When these conditions were not in effect, it increased. In this study, the mother was the primary change agent, and the father performed reliability checks. With little guidance from a professional, the parents were able to successfully implement the change program.

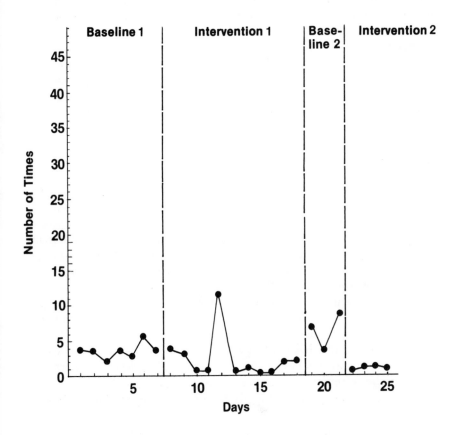

FIGURE 5.3. The number of times a 14-year-old boy talked back following a request. From *Parenting: Strategies and educational methods.* (p. 133) by J. O. Cooper & D. Edge (1981), Louisville, KY: Eston. Reprinted by permission.

Consultants can assist parents who are interested in becoming better behavior managers in a number of ways. First, specific workshop programs can be established that provide the parents with the skills they seek. The focus of the workshop might be to train parents to assess the current levels of their children's behavior, plan and execute effective interventions, and analyze the results. More important, the inservice training should provide opportunities for parents to practice the skills being taught, receive constructive feedback from a skilled supervisor or consultant, and obtain praise for improved performance.

Second, consultants can provide indirect service to parents by referring them to other sources of support or other resources. For example, many parent associations (e.g., Association for Children and Adults with Learning Disabilities) have "parent assister" programs established to help parents who have child-rearing problems or problems related to their child's performance in school. The parent assister can serve as a liaison between the parents and another agency (the school) or simply provide information or counseling to the parents.

Finally, the consultant can serve as a mediator between the school and the home. The consultant could try to initiate in the home those behavior management strategies that have been effective in school. The intent, of course, would be to provide a consistent approach at home and at school.

Parents as Home-Based Educators

Teachers and administrators frequently state that there is only so much that can be done at school to increase the academic functioning of a child. As a rule, teachers and supervisors like parents to serve as *home-based educators*, supplementing the instruction their child receives at school, but many do not know how to develop systematic methods for establishing and maintaining parental assistance. While reasons for the lack of home-school cooperation are numerous (e.g., working parents, single-parent families, multiple family commitments, and lack of parental enthusiasm), it is still possible to devise useful methods that give parents the opportunity to assist in their child's academic and social development at home.

One method that has worked well in the past has been for the teacher to model instructional strategies for the parents. Then they can incorporate the instructions from the teacher in a home-based program that may improve the child's academic performance (Kroth, 1975; Kroth, Whelan, & Stables, 1970).

It should be noted, however, that not all educators favor the use of parents as home-based educators. Barsch (1969) and Kronich (1969) suggest that parents should not attempt home-based education programs. In general, these authors feel that parents of handicapped children may be too anxious, lack the proper education skills, or simply do not have the time to do an adequate job. Further, it is felt that parents may impede the learning process by putting adverse pressure on the child or youth. In short, these authors and others (e.g., Lerner, 1976) suggest that parents remain parents and engage in family recreational or domestic activities, leaving the teaching to professionals.

We are convinced that parents can and should serve as home-based educators if guidance is provided and they feel comfortable with the task. If parents want to engage in tutoring, and many do, the consultant might conduct minitraining sessions where parents could learn tutoring techniques.

Communication Techniques with Parents

For a functional home-school relationship to develop, the opportunity to communicate must exist. *Home-school communication* is defined as a broad range of oral or written messages between parents and teachers for the purpose of exchanging information and providing training to the parents. The following section will describe a number of methods for accomplishing this objective. Documentation to support inclusion of a particular method is provided. The methods are described according to their hierarchy of intrusiveness, the least intrusive technique appearing first.

Telephone. Nearly every American family has a telephone or lives close to someone who does. Surprisingly, however, it has been only within the recent past that the telephone has come to play an important role in the home-school communication network.

A number of researchers (Alessi, 1985; Heron & Axelrod, 1976; Heron & Heward, 1982; Heward & Chapman, 1981; Lazarus, 1986; Varone, O'Brien, & Axelrod, 1972; Weiss, 1984) have used the telephone to increase parents' knowledge of school-related activities or as a method structuring home-based instruction. Heron and Axelrod (1976), for example, used a telephone to reinforce inner-city parents for assisting their children with work recognition assignments. The procedure involved calling the parents each day to tell them how well their child had done on a previous day's word recognition task and to ask them to provide the opportunity for their child to learn the next day's 10 target words.

The results of the study demonstrated that when parents were given feedback via telephone for helping with their child's work, the child's performance improved. Conversely, when the parent did not receive such feedback, word recognition performance worsened. Also, the parents reported that they like the telephone calls. In the past the only time that school personnel had called them was when a son or daughter was in trouble. This positive telephone approach was welcomed. Also, it should be noted that the parents did not receive explicit instructions on how to teach the target words to their children. Yet at least one parent stated that she told her daughter to "look for little words in the big word, write the words in the air with her eyes closed, and finally write the words in sentences." Each of these decoding strategies is a common instructional method used by classroom teachers.

Varone, O'Brien, and Axelrod (1972) conducted a similar study with children and parents of Hispanic backgrounds. Despite the fact that the parents could not read many of the English words their children brought home from school, gains in word recognition were achieved. Parents simply set the occasion for their child to study the words and to use the words in sentences. Feedback via the telephone maintained parental participation. In families where both parents work or in single-parent families, the strategy employed by Heron and Axelrod (1976) and Varone, O'Brien, and Axelrod (1972) may have to be modified, because in these studies telephone calls were made during the day while parents were home.

If the telephone system is going to be used to maximum advantage on a school- or district-wide basis, it is imperative that consultants find ways to extend this support to more parents. One way is with a telephone answering service (Alessi, 1985; Bittle, 1975; Heward & Chapman, 1981; Lazarus, 1986; Weiss et al., 1982; Weiss, 1984).

Bittle (1975), for example, demonstrated that a telephone answering service installed in the school and preprogrammed with information on school-related subjects could be used as a low-cost method to establish and maintain a parent-teacher communication network and to improve student performance in school.

As one part of the study, students were instructed to take a list of four spelling words home to their parents. The students were scheduled to be tested on the words the following day. In the next step of the study, the teacher not only sent the words home with the student but also included them on a nightly phone message to the parents. In the third phase, the word-list-only condition was reinstated for seven days. Finally, the word-list-and-telephone-message phase was repeated for six days.

Figure 5.4 shows that during the word-list-plus-telephone-message conditions, the percentage of students receiving perfect scores on the spelling test increased substantially over the word-list-alone conditions. The results indicate a functional effect between the phone message and student performance. When the spelling words were on the phone message, the level of student performance increased. When the spelling words were removed from the telephone answering service, student performance level dropped.

Heward and Chapman (1981) replicated Bittle's (1975) study. Her procedure involved taping instructions, requests, and progress notes for the parents on the school telephone answering service. The parents were free to call after school each day to obtain the data. The results of Heward and Chapman's (1981) study indicated that more telephone calls were made to the school each day when the messages were available than when they were not (Figure

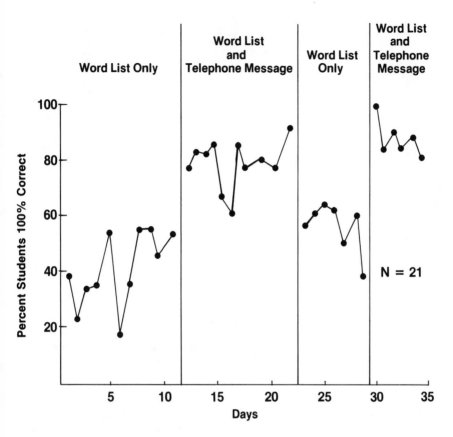

FIGURE 5.4. Daily plot of the percentage of students scoring perfectly on daily spelling tests. From "Improving parent-teacher communication through recorded telephone messages" by R. G. Bittle (1975) in *Journal of Educational Research, 69,* 91. Reprinted by permission of Heldref Publications, 4000 Albemarle Street, NW, Washington, DC 20016.

5.5). Parents reported that they liked the system, because it provided them with essential information on school events.

Hassett et al. (1984) used the home-school communication system during the summer vacation to improve the written language expression of three adolescent-aged students with learning disabilities. Essentially the procedure involved having students listen to a daily "story starter" and write for 10 minutes about the topic suggested by the story starter. Parents were instructed to count the number of words produced by their child during the 10-minute session. After collecting 12 days of baseline information on the number of words produced, parents attended a workshop where they learned how to

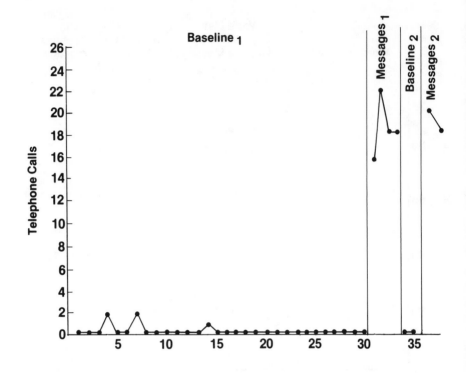

FIGURE 5.5.   Number of telephone calls made as a function of recorded messages. From "Improving parent-teacher communication through recorded telephone messages" by W. L. Heward & J. Chapman, 1981. *Journal of Special Education Technology, 4(3), 14. Reprinted by permission.*

recognize action words and adjectives and to count the total number of words written by their child. Parents also learned how to access a story starter via a teacher-produced audiotape connected to a telephone answering system, how to explain the target behavior to their child (e.g., the definition of an action word or adjective), how to record the results of their child's daily written work, and how to evaluate their child's writing. Parents also learned how to award coupons, exchangeable for free or inexpensive reinforcers, contingent upon improved production of action words, adjectives, or total words.

The results of the 9-week multiple baseline study showed that the summer writing program was successful in increasing the number of action words and adjectives used by the adolescents. Figure 5.6 shows the data for one of the students. When the home-school communication program was in effect, the number of action words and adjectives increased. When it was not in effect, the number of action words and adjectives was lower. Also, Hassett et al. (1984) indicated that the parents liked the program and that they were able to conduct it at home without problems.

Weiss (1984) conducted a study using the home-school communication program combined with home tutoring to improve the academic performance of 11 learning disabled students attending a private elementary school. During baseline, students were pretested by the teacher on their sight words, spelling words, and math facts. Prior to initiating the home-school program via the telephone, parents attended a two-hour workshop to learn how to carry out the procedures of the study (e.g., accessing words/facts via the telephone, procedures for tutoring their child, suggestions for reinforcing learning). Next, parents had access to sight words via the telephone. Each night they tutored their child on words presented by the tape and reported the results of their teaching on the "message" side of the tape. Home tutoring using the audiotape was introduced sequentially for sight words, spelling words and math facts.

The results of the study showed that phone messages produced an increase in student performance on sight words, spelling words, and math facts recognition during daily and weekly assessments (Figures 5.7 and 5.8). Further, the results showed that parents could function as home-based tutors and that parents viewed the program as successful.

Alessi (1985) conducted an interesting variation of the home-school communication program with six parents of learning disabled students. The students were enrolled in a self-contained classroom and mainstreamed in third or fourth grade for some academic skill areas. After teaching the students to correctly identify nouns, adjectives, and verbs on a story they had written in response to a story starter and setting a criterion for each variable, students learned how to make an audiotape that their parents would later hear by calling on the telephone. For instance, students made announcements like: "Hi, mom! This is [name]. I made my goal today. I wrote 8 nouns, 5 adjectives, and 6 verbs, and 43 total words today. I hope you are proud of me!" During the home-school communication phases of the program, students made audiotapes contingent upon completing their story starters at criterion with the designated number of nouns, adjectives, and verbs. Parents left a message for their child to hear the next day prior to writing that day's story (e.g., "[Name], I am proud of all the words you wrote yesterday. Keep up the good work").

Alessi's (1985) study showed that student production of nouns, adjectives, and verbs increased during home-school communication. Also, students and parents indicated on an exit interview that they enjoyed the program and found it useful, practical, and convenient. Finally, it should be mentioned that Alessi's study was conducted over a 75-day period, indicating that a home-school communication program can be carried out over extended periods of time.

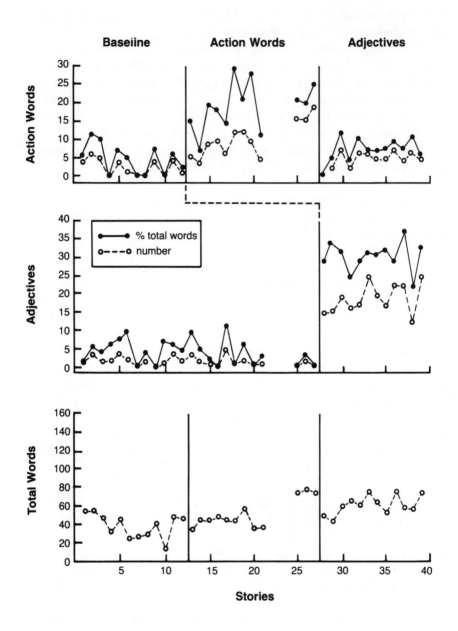

FIGURE 5.6. Action words, adjectives, and total words written by James in 10-minute stories during baseline, intervention on action words, and intervention on adjectives. From ''A telephone-managed, home-based summer writing program for LD adolescents'' by M. E. Hassett et al. (1984) in *Focus on behavior analysis in education* (p. 99), Columbus, OH: Merrill. Reprinted by permission.

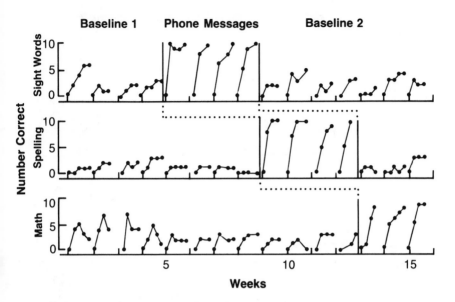

FIGURE 5.7. Number of items correctly answered on daily in-class assessments during baseline and phone messages. "The effects of a telephone-managed home-school program using parents as home-based educators on the academic achievement of learning disabled students" by A.B. Weiss (1984). Unpublished doctoral dissertation, The Ohio State University, Columbus, OH. Reprinted by permission.

Lazarus (1986) conducted a study that merged the home-school communication program with home-based education. Specifically, parents of seven children who attended a private preschool program participated in a study of their child's ability to identify word parts and sight vocabulary. During a two-hour workshop, parents learned how to access information via the telephone answering device, tutor and test their child at home, and report the results through the answering device. Nightly tutoring at home followed the same format as described by Cooke, Heron, and Heward (1983) and included six components: obtaining tutoring material, word-part and word practice, practice word testing, "bonus" word testing, recording, and reporting. After calling a designated school phone number to receive their child's word parts, practice words, and bonus words for the week, parents conducted tutoring in a three-part sequence. During "Practice: Get Ready," parents presented word parts (e.g., *ab*) and words containing those word parts (e.g., *ab*sent). The parent would say. "This says *ar* as in *car*." As the parent said this statement, she flipped the flashcard over to show the word *car*. The child imitated the parent's vocalization. During "Practice: Sequential Order," the word parts were again presented, except the parent's verbal model was

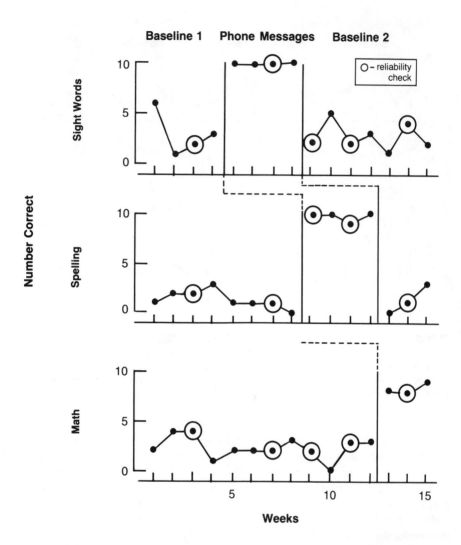

FIGURE 5.8. Number of items correctly answered on weekly in-class posttests during baseline and phone messages (open circles represent scores obtained by second observer). From "The effects of a telephone-managed home-school program using parents as home-based educators on the academic achievement of learning disabled students by A. B. Weiss (1984). Unpublished doctoral dissertation. The Ohio State University, Columbus, OH. Reprinted by permission.

omitted. If the child said the word part and corresponding word correctly, he or she was praised. If an incorrect response was made, the parent said, "Try again." This phase of tutoring lasted four minutes. During "Practice:

Random Order," the parent shuffled the cards and re-presented them to the child. Practice word testing consisted of having the parent present practice words to their child without prompts, scoring each verbal utterance as correct or incorrect by placing an X (incorrect) or an O (correct) on the back of the card. Bonus word testing was conducted in a similar fashion, only these words were not exposed to the child previously and served as a measure of response generality. Finally, the parent reported the results of the testing each night via the telephone answering device.

The results of the withdrawal design study indicated that during the parent tutoring/home-school communication phase, each of the seven students' word part and word recognition ability improved significantly. When the parent tutoring/home-school communication phase was not in effect, word part and word recognition performance dropped. The data also indicated that parents consistently reported their child's performance accurately, made use of the message side of the audiotape to leave comments to the teacher, and found the system to be a convenient and efficient means to maintain home-school communication.

Overall, the telephone system offers consultants a novel way to enlist the cooperation of parents, and it has a number of distinct advantages. First, it is flexible. Daily tapes can be generated and updated in a matter of minutes, and single-parent families or families in which both parents work can gain access to information after school without having to contact the teacher personally. Second, it is a low-cost item. The cost of the answering service, including installation, is within the budget of most school systems, and maintenance and tape costs are low. Third, it is reliable. Handwritten notes are often lost, and parents do not receive the information. Fourth, it is functional. The data indicate that parents will use the telephone to obtain important information about their child's program and may use this information in a structured home-based tutoring program. Fifth, since data on individual students are not reported on the tape, confidentiality is assured. Reporting data to parents is reserved for either a private conference or written correspondence. Finally, parents view the telephone-managed system in a positive way, perceiving that it opens another avenue for home-school communication.

Notes. Another low-cost technique that has been used repeatedly by classroom teachers over the years is to send notes home with students. The notes, unless they are of the disciplinary nature, usually are aimed at informing the parents of some accomplishment by the student in school.

Hawkins and Sluyter (1970) conducted a study that demonstrated the effectiveness of sending notes home indicating appropriate student academic performance in school. When notes were sent home, student performance improved, and when the notes were later used as tokens, exchangeable for a variety of reinforcers in the home, student performance improved even more.

Privileges (e.g., staying up later, going to a movie) or the removal of certain tasks (e.g., putting out the trash) can serve as reinforcers.

Sending notes home with students has a number of advantages. First, it is a tangible reminder from the teacher that the student's performance was acceptable. Second, the note acts as a prompt to the parents to comment on their child's performance. Finally, the note can be used as a token. A number of preprinted notes or award certificates are commercially available and can be used on all grade levels.

Parent Conferences.   A third opportunity for home-school communication is through the parent conference. According to Stephens (1977), a *parent conference* should be a goal-directed session that provides for the exchange of information between teacher and parent so that educational programming can be enhanced. The parent conference should not be considered a social visit, but rather should have specific objectives to accomplish.

Stephens (1977) indicates that parent conferences should be conducted in four phases: (a) establishing rapport; (b) obtaining information; (c) providing information; and (d) summarizing. To establish rapport it is imperative for the teacher to be able to place the parents at ease immediately. Teachers are advised to make general statements regarding neutral topics that give the parents the opportunity to speak. For example, the teacher might say, "I'm so glad we have this opportunity to meet. Were you able to find the school without much trouble?" Opening statements to avoid would include teacher questions on private family matters or controversial school or community issues. Also, to make parents more comfortable the teacher should offer them a beverage and the opportunity to smoke if they wish. The teacher must remember that parents may feel intimidated in the school, and every effort should be made to reduce their anxiety. Anecdote 5.3 illustrates how a regular education teacher established rapport with the parent of a handicapped student who attends her class.

ANECDOTE 5.3

TEACHER: Welcome to King Avenue School. It's so nice that you were able to come.

PARENT: Thank you. I have been looking forward to the meeting.

TEACHER (*offering the parent a cup of coffee*): Did you have any difficulty finding the school?

PARENT: No. The map you included in the announcement letter was perfect.

While a teacher conference usually is scheduled so that the teacher can inform the parent of the student's progress, it would be premature to begin documenting the student's performance right after establishing rapport. A better option for the teacher would be to obtain information from the parent on how the child feels about school, how the child performs at home on school-related tasks, and how he or she gets along with neighborhood children. It is imperative for the teacher to have these data if successful programming is to be accomplished. Of course, the teacher need not continue to ask leading questions of parents to obtain every bit of information possible. Rather, the teacher should wait until there is a natural break in the conversation to provide school-related information to the parents. Anecdote 5.4 describes a scenario where such a break occurs.

ANECODTE 5.4

TEACHER: How does Sally handle money while she is shopping alone? (*teacher obtaining information.*)

PARENT: Not too well. She often does not count her change, and I'm afraid to trust her with large bills.

TEACHER: Yes, I've observed a similar pattern in the classroom while we were working on paper money, coins, and giving change. Hopefully, we'll begin to see a change in this area, because I've introduced a store in the classroom. Students can buy things from the store — like pencils, chalk, and erasers — with play money. To keep whatever they buy, they have to be able to count the change correctly, name the coins they get as change, and give an equivalent value for the coins. (*teacher providing information.*)

PARENT: That sounds like the kind of practice she needs.

The dialogue continues with teacher and parent exchanging information until all the teacher's objectives (outlined prior to the conference) are met. Parents should be given every opportunity to ask questions, provide alternatives, and challenge the type of programming their child receives. Teachers need not feel defensive about the educational experiences they are providing, rather they should state as clearly and as straightforwardly as possible the rationale for their approach. If parents object, the teacher should pursue a line of questioning that will elicit from the parents their specific objections. Anecdote 5.5 provides such an example.

ANECDOTE 5.5

TEACHER: Are there other questions you have regarding Girard's progress?

PARENT: Yes, I don't feel that the math instruction he is receiving is doing him any good. He seems to be going nowhere.

TEACHER (*reflecting the parent's statement*): You feel that your son has not made adequate progress in math?

PARENT: That's right. He continues to have trouble telling time, measuring distances, and dealing with money.

TEACHER: Let's just explore one of these areas. When Girard arrived in the class in September, he could not tell time to the hour, half hour, or quarter hour. Presently, he is able to tell time to the hour and half hour. Have you noticed this at home?

PARENT: Well, yes, but he still cannot tell time.

TEACHER: If I understand you correctly, you mean Girard cannot tell time to the quarter hour and the minutes. Is that correct?

PARENT: Yes.

TEACHER: I wish we had been able to make faster progress, Mrs. Carn, but, as I think you see, Girard has made some progress, although not as fast as we would like.

PARENT: Yes, that's right.

TEACHER: Since I've had some success with Girard teaching him time to the hour and half hour, I think I'll continue a similar technique with the quarter hour and minutes. Maybe we can work out a program for Girard at home.

The final phase in the parent conference is the summary. It is important that the parents hear a review of the major points discussed in the conference prior to their departure. The summary provides an opportunity to bring closure to the meeting by restating all the important items of discussion.

More important, perhaps, than simply recounting the major discussion points of the conference, the summary sets the occasion for the teacher to perform two additional tasks. The first is to provide some degree of training for the parents so that they will be better able to carry on the school program at home. For example, the teacher may show the parents a simple way to teach their child to tell time or give correct change, or the teacher may show the parent how to make interesting word or sound games. Further, the teacher may demonstrate how to set up a contingency contract with a child so more productivity is achieved in the home (see Chapter 9 for more details on contingency contracting).

The second task is for the teacher to set a firm plan for follow-up consultation. The follow-up plan need not be elaborate, rather the teacher should mention to the parents when they can expect it. In those instances where the teacher has demonstrated a new strategy to the parent, or where a different course of action is being engineered, it is critical that the follow-up occur soon after the conference. It might be as early as the next day. Of course, if the problems are not pressing, the follow-up could be postponed until a later time. Anecdote 5.6 shows how the last two items of the parent conference — training and follow-up — can be incorporated in the summary of the conference.

ANECDOTE 5.6

TEACHER: Unfortunately, we are running short of time, but before you go let me take a minute to summarize what we have discussed so far.

PARENT: Fine.

TEACHER: One of the points of concern for both of us is Harry's need to learn more sight vocabulary words. While he has made progress this term, his reading recognition and comprehension might be increased if he had more knowledge of basic sight vocabulary.

PARENT: That's right. He seems to miss many words that I feel he should know by the beginning of the third grade.

TEACHER (*about to provide a minitraining session*): Agreed. One of the activities I've found successful with Harry is a word game. He seems to like to play this type of game. Let me take time to share with you some of the games you can play at home that will complement what I'm doing here at school. (*Teacher shows the parents how they can play word bingo, concentration, and lotto games. Then goes on to share another observation.*) Another item that we discussed was Harry's unwillingness at times to follow instructions. While I don't consider this a chronic problem, it seems to be occurring with sufficient frequency to call attention to itself.

PARENT: That's true. We've noticed similar behavior at home. We figured that he was imitating his friends in the neighborhood, because in the past he would usually follow instructions without too much fuss.

TEACHER: Well, why don't we just wait awhile to see what happens. If possible, let's say that we arrange a follow-up contact in two weeks. If Harry's performance with following directions has not improved we might be able to plan a joint strategy to resolve the problem. In the meantime, would you be able to count the number of times per day Harry is given an instruction and the number of times he fails to carry it out in a reasonable amount of time? I'll do the same with him in school. In two weeks I'll call you and we can compare notes to see if the trend is increasing, decreasing, or staying the same.

PARENT: Fine, that sounds like an excellent idea. We'll do our best.

TEACHER: Very good. Do you have any additional questions you'd like to bring up at this time?

PARENT: That just about covers it.

TEACHER: O.K. If you have any questions or if you would like any additional suggestions on sight vocabulary games, please feel free to call me. If not, you can expect a telephone call from me two weeks from today. Would 7:30 p.m. be a good time to call?

PARENT: That would be fine.

TEACHER: Again, I appreciate your willingness to come in for the conference. I learned a great deal. I hope you have a nice day.

PARENT: Thank you. I learned quite a bit as well. We'll hear from you in two weeks. Goodbye.

This conference was closed in a nonthreatening manner for the parents. The teacher did not tell the parents what to do, rather she suggested alternatives for the parents to consider (word bingo, lotto games, etc.). Finally, the teacher made it clear to the parents that follow-up contact would be made in two weeks.

The parents' perception of this meeting more than likely was positive. One could speculate that the parents perceived the teacher as very interested in the development of their child, knowledgeable about instructional activities, and willing to assist them to ensure that progress was made. With the positive feelings that have been generated, it is likely that, if two weeks hence a behavior management program is implemented for Harry's problem, a joint strategy can be achieved without too much difficulty.

Parent Training. Numerous publications, workshops, and commercial materials are available to teach parents how to rear their children from birth to adulthood. Some references (e.g., Spock, 1976) provide not only medical information, but also information about developmental milestones and behavior to be expected at each stage of maturation. More recently, a number of authors with a behavioral orientation (e.g., Cooper & Edge, 1981; Dardig & Heward, 1981a; Heward, Dardig, & Rossett, 1979) have outlined specific strategies for parents to employ to solve a number of common problems that arise in the home.

Dardig and Heward (1981a), for example, offer parents and children the opportunity to learn contracting strategies. The major theme of the book is that many home-based problems can be precluded or overcome if parents and children establish and implement effective contingency contracts.

Cooper and Edge (1981) offer specific suggestions to the parents for problems such as toileting, not eating food at mealtime, discipline, and a host of others. In their text is a discussion of the principles of learning as well as case studies in which these principles were applied.

Establishing Parent Training Programs

To establish an effective *parent training program*, Stephens (1977) offers the following guidelines: (a) use a consistent theoretical model, (b) determine parental skills to be mastered in advance, (c) allow for varying rates of learning by parents, (d) employ a systematic and functional approach, and (e) provide follow-up.

By using Stephens' (1977) guidelines a consultant can provide and individualized parent training program. The program will be based on the assessed needs of each parent and will be tailored to their individual learning styles and rates. Providing follow-up training or a refresher course is essential if the skills acquired during the initial training are to be maintained. While Stephens's suggestions are consistent with a behavioral orientation, the success or failure of parent training programs rests to a large extent on the variables listed below.

Time of Meeting. Meeting times should be scheduled so that the maximum number of parents can attend consistently. Meeting times set on different days from week to week often lead to poor attendance and a lack of continuity in program. If possible, parents should have a choice of times to accommodate their particular needs. Consideration should also be given to scheduling meetings during the day so that parents who work nights or single-parent families can attend.

Length of Sessions. Each instructional session should range from one to two hours. The length of individual meetings should be based on the number of parents there and how far they have to travel to attend. If parents have to travel a considerable distance, it would be better to schedule longer meetings. Obviously, these parents would think twice about attending if the meetings were too brief to appear worthwhile.

Number of Sessions.   Patterson's (1975) training program is accomplished within a 5- to 15-week period. The total number of sessions to schedule may be determined by a needs assessment, a procedure to decide the number of skills to be mastered by parents. Keeping in mind Stephens's (1977) advice that parents will learn the skills at different rates, the consultant can establish a flexible schedule with respect to the number of sessions required. To do this the consultant can give the parents a pretest on the course syllabus at the first session. Based on the data obtained in the test, the consultant can then calculate the number of sessions he or she feels will be required to achieve competency. For a general guide on the number of sessions to use, the content to cover in each session, and the instructional and evaluation materials to employ, the reader is referred to Cooper and Edge (1981).

Location of Sessions.   To the maximum extent possible, the location of the training sessions should be central and easily accessible to the participants. School buildings, churches, or community auditoriums provide the consultant with the optimum amount of flexibility. For example, if the meetings are held in a school or community facility, there is usually access to audiovisual equipment, chalkboards, and ample space. Although the informal atmosphere in someone's home may initially be more conducive to discussion, it is generally not a good idea to use homes because of the potential distractions and the logistical problems of transporting equipment and materials.

Grouping.   Although there are no clear rules on the optimum number of people in a parent training group, experience seems to indicate that small groups, ranging from 8 to 12 people, are best. Small groups offer more opportunity for each parent to participate. Further, if role playing and behavior rehearsal are part of the training, and they should be, small groups facilitate these exercises. Frequently, individuals who are meeting to discuss problems become inhibited if the group is too large. Also, larger meetings can be dominated by a few outspoken parents, and less verbal members do not participate as much.

Finally, groups should remain intact for the length of the training program. The rationale, of course, is that personal relationships develop among the parents and they become more willing to confide in each other.

Cost.   There a number of ways to reduce or eliminate the cost of parent training programs to the school. First, one can obtain the training through a university or college. Frequently, colleges offer course work or practicum experiences that require graduate students to actively engage in parent programming. Under the supervision of faculty members, parent training is offered at minimal cost or no cost at all. Second, apply for grant money. Many national, state, and local sources offer grant money to organizations involved in parent training. A reference list of sources can be obtained at a public library. Third, seek funds through corporations or private individuals. Many national and local corporations have funds budgeted for community projects. Guidelines are often available to help organizations apply for these sources of money, and private individuals have been known to donate funds for parent training programs. Fourth, secure volunteer assistance. Teachers or administrators interested in establishing parent training programs can often be enlisted to run the groups without charge.

Structure of Sessions. While the topics from session to session will vary, it is important that the structure of the session remain consistent. During each session the parents should receive information that will help them at home, have the opportunity to ask questions and discuss issues related to it as well as the chance to practice skills taught in the session, and receive feedback and reinforcement on their performance. It is one thing for the parents to gain the cognitive knowledge associated with the curriculum; it is quite another for them to gain the practical skill needed to execute the curriculum at home. Training sessions that emphasize the former at the expense of the latter provide the parents with only half of the skills they need.

The initial session should be devoted to having the parents get to know one another. Effective consultants have a battery of "icebreakers" they employ to encourage parents to meet one another.

The Final Session. The final session should be reserved for distributing certificates of achievement (Figure 5.9) and answering any questions that parents may have. Plans for follow-up can be discussed, and individual parent concerns can be addressed.

The Team Leader. To a large extent the success or failure of a parent-training program can be traced to the effectiveness of the team leader. Just as teachers are willing to accept the suggestions of supervisors they perceive as competent, so, too, will parents accept the recommendations and suggestions of a parent trainer they feel is trustworthy and expert. Parents must feel that the trainer cares about their problems and is a person in whom they can confide. Also, the parents must feel that the trainer has had experience with the types of problems they are encountering. If parents do not have confidence in the trainer's ability to help them, little progress is likely to be made.

THE OHIO STATE UNIVERSITY

COLLEGE OF EDUCATION

Department of Human Services Education

Hereby acknowledges that

KATHLEEN CHRISTINE LEE

Has successfully demonstrated the competencies of the

Parenting Skills Workshop

— PARENTING SKILLS ACQUIRED —

* PINPOINTING SPECIFIC CHILD
  BEHAVIORS

* OBSERVING & RECORDING CHILD
  BEHAVIOR

* GRAPHING BEHAVIORAL
  INFORMATION

* SELECTING & USING STRATEGIES
  FOR ACCELERATING APPROPRIATE
  & DECELERATING INAPPROPRIATE
  BEHAVIORS

* CONTINGENCY CONTRACTING

* EVALUATING THE EFFECTS OF
  BEHAVIORAL STRATEGIES

Awarded On: 1/5/87
DATE

THOMAS H. STEPHANS, CHAIRMAN
DEPARTMENT OF HUMAN SERVICES EDUCATION

WORKSHOP LEADER

WILLIAM L. HEWARD
PARENT TRAINING CO-ORDINATOR

FIGURE 5.9. A sample certificate of achievement to be presented to the parent at the completion of a parent training program.

Parents in the Classroom

Until recently the classroom was thought to be the exclusive domain of the classroom teacher. The teacher was responsible for planning and teaching lessons and evaluating performance of each student. Clearly, there are teacher responsibilities, but just as clearly some duties can be accomplished by parents who volunteer in the classroom.

Parent volunteers, though they require instruction and supervision by the teacher, can perform essential jobs for the teacher. For example, parent volunteers could write or explain directions to students, correct papers and provide reinforcement, or give one-to-one remedial instruction. However, without a well thought-out plan for working with parents as paraprofessionals, many of the possible benefits would be lost.

Fortunately, a number of educators have recognized the need to provide training for parents who assume the duties of a paraprofessional. Strenechy, McLoughlin, and Edge (1979), for example, identified guidelines for a *parent tutoring program*. In general, these authors feel that potential parent tutors should receive an in-service orientation, support from the school administration, and supervision from the teacher or consultant. Further, they recommend that parents not tutor their own children.

Many parents would be unable to participate in such a program because of family or work responsibilities, but even if a few parents were able to volunteer, the teachers, pupils, and parents would gain the following advantages: (a) Given a reduced teacher-student ratio, the teacher would be free to provide more direct remedial assistance to the students most in need; (b) parents would become better acquainted with the problems of the mildly handicapped and more knowledgeable about methods for remediating or coping with these problems; (c) parent input in the Individualized Education Program (IEP) process would be enhanced; and (d) if the program incorporates "foster grandparents," capable senior citizens would have the opportunity to contribute their time and talents in a worthwhile project. For them, an increased feeling of self-worth could be a valuable spin-off advantage.

CONCLUSION

This chapter suggested a number of ways in which consultants can work with parents of handicapped children. A model was presented that describes the types of services professionals and parents can perform and the levels of that service. Techniques for increasing parent involvement as behavior managers and home-based educators were presented. A telephone answering service was suggested as a means by which consultants can help to increase home-school communication and student academic performance. Procedures for conducting effective parent conferences were described and several recommendations were proposed for establishing and implementing functional parent training programs. Finally, the use of parents as in-school tutors was discussed.

SUMMARY OF KEY POINTS

Mirror Model of Parental Involvement

1. The Mirror Model of Parental Involvement is divided into two reciprocal areas: professional services and parent services. Within each area are four levels defined by the terms *all, most, some,* and *few.*

2. The Mirror Model of Parental Involvement is helpful to the consultant because it changes the way the consultant communicates to a teacher expectations of a successful parent training partnership. Also, it shifts the emphasis of evaluation from single measures to multiple measures.

3. The Mirror Model of Parental Involvement can serve as a communication vehicle for teachers and parents.

Parents as Behavior Managers

4. Consultants can assist parents to become better behavior managers in three ways. First, workshop programs can be offered that provide parents with skills. Second, consultants can refer parents to support groups (e.g., ACLD). Third, consultants can serve as mediators between the home and the school.

Parents as Home-Based Educators

5. Parents serve as home-based educators when they supplement the instruction their child receives during the day at home.

6. Parents can serve as appropriate home-based educators if guidance and/or minitraining sessions are provided to them.

Communication Techniques with Parents

7. Home-school communication techniques with parents can be faciliated using the telephone, notes, parent conferences, and parent training. Each of these techniques has advantages, and the techniques can be combined.

8. Home-school communication programs managed by a telephone answering device offer consultants several advantages not available through conventional avenues.

Establishing Parent Training Programs

9. To establish an effective parent-training program, use a consistent theoretical model, determine parental skills to master, allow for varying rates of learning, employ a systematic approach, and provide for follow up.

10. Effective parent-training programs must also consider variables such as the time of the meeting; the length, number, location, and structure of sessions; grouping; cost; and qualifications of the team leader.

Parents in the Classroom

11. Parents can be effective assistants in the classroom by helping with one-to-one instruction, giving feedback to students orally and in writing, and preparing materials.

12. Parents in the classroom have the advantages of reducing teacher-student ratios, acquainting parents with remedial strategies for mildly handicapped students, potentially improving the IEP process, and setting the occasion for senior citizens to engage in a meaningful activity.

QUESTIONS

1. Identify the four levels of parent involvement in Kroth's (1980) Mirror Model of Parental Involvement. What types of activities could professionals and parents do at each level?

2. Provide two examples that show how parents used behavior management techniques to change inappropriate child behavior.

3. List three advantages of using the telephone to enhance student academic achievement. Cite variations of how a home-school communication program could be used with a telephone answering device.

4. According to Stephens (1977) what are the key phases or components of an effective parent conference?

5. What guidelines does Stephens offer for establishing an effective parent-training program?

6. Name two ways to help reduce the cost of parent training programs.

7. What advantages can be obtained from having parents participate as in-class tutors?

DISCUSSION POINTS AND EXERCISES

1. Argue for or against the use of parents as in-school tutors. State your reasons and provide documentation for your positions.

2. Conduct an in-service training program based on the recommendations of Cooper and Edge (1981); Heward, Dardig, and Rossett (1979); or Stephens (1977). Note the effects. Rewrite inservice training components based on your experience.

3. Conduct an informal meeting with teachers, parents, and administrators. The topic of the meeting is "Managing Students' Behavior at School and at Home." Record comments from each participant. Obtain consensus on a course of action with a current problem.

4. Discuss the special problems handicapped students have inside and outside the regular classroom environment. Identify at least three recommendations you could offer to teachers and other support personnel for dealing more effectively with these students.

5. Present a videotape of a parent conference. Have teachers identify the four phases outlined by Stephens (rapport building, obtaining information, providing information, and summarizing). Follow up the videotape training by observing teachers during a conference. Provide appropriate praise and feedback.

6

Modifying Curriculum and Instructional Strategies at the Elementary School Level

One objective of the consultant at the elementary school level is to help the teacher individualize a curriculum that integrates academic skills, social development, and career education. The purpose of this chapter is to describe ways in which a consultant can assist elementary teachers with that process. After discussing the concepts of effective instruction and procedures to facilitate mainstreaming, the chapter focuses on ways to enhance the academic, social, and career education skills of elementary students. Next, specific methods to individualize instruction will be presented. Several strategies related to grouping techniques, curriculum adaptations, and technology will be addressed.

OBJECTIVES

After reading this chapter, the reader should be able to:

1. define the activities of consultation at the elementary level.

2. discuss ways in which an elementary teacher can incorporate social development and career education within an academic curriculum.

3. identify and discuss at least three grouping techniques that elementary teachers can use to individualize instruction.

4. provide two suggestions for curriculum adaptations at the elementary school level to meet the individualized needs of handicapped learners.

5. list and describe two sources of technical equipment that an elementary teacher could use to supplement basic instruction.

141

KEY TERMS

Effective instruction	Small group instruction
Affective education	Peer tutoring
Social skills training	Cross-age tutoring
Career education	Cooperative learning
Individualized instruction	Jigsaw method
Remedial teaching model	Curriculum adaptations
Large group instruction	Technology

EDUCATIONAL CONSULTATION AT THE ELEMENTARY LEVEL

Over the past few years research has indicated that if regular educators receive appropriate training, they can successfully meet a wide variety of student needs in the regular education classroom (Stainback, Stainback, Courtnage, & Jaben, 1985). The consultant can help the regular educator receive appropriate training. Educational consultants are often called upon to conduct inservice activities to provide information regarding appropriate instructional techniques for teachers. However, consultants also have available to them a more frequent, informal, and effective opportunity to assist regular educators. Consultants at the elementary level are encouraged to work collaboratively with elementary teachers to develop programs that will meet the individual needs of students. To achieve this objective, consultants should consider at least two aspects: effective instruction and procedures to facilitate mainstreaming.

Effective Instruction

The recent research on teacher effectiveness and the effective schools movement (e.g., Englert, 1984; Goodman, 1985) provide the basis for making suggestions to improve teacher behavior. The major findings of teacher effectiveness research suggest that *effective instruction* occurs when teachers (a) maximize the amount of time students are actively involved in academic tasks; (b) provide direct instruction; (c) maintain a brisk lesson pace; (d) help students obtain a high accuracy in their responses to teacher questions and provide prompts to help students determine correct responses; and (e) monitor the performance of each student carefully. This chapter considers instructional techniques to assist the teacher in meeting these objectives.

Procedures to Facilitate Mainstreaming

In addition to helping the teacher provide effective instruction, consultants must also be aware of procedures to facilitate the successful mainstreaming of mildly handicapped students into the regular education environment. It is important to note that teacher objectives for effective instruction in regular education are consistent with teacher objectives for special education. That is, both require direct instruction, successive approximations to skill mastery, and monitoring of student performance. However, to facilitate mainstreaming, the consultant should consider other activities as well. In addition to helping the elementary teacher provide effective instruction for students, the consultant should (a) collaborate with the elementary teacher to assess and define problems; (b) prepare the handicapped student for mainstreaming; (c) prepare the nonhandicapped students for a mainstreamed student; and (d) collaborate with the elementary teacher to evaluate the success of the mainstreaming effort (Ottman, 1981; Salend, 1984).

In facilitating the mainstreaming of a handicapped student, it is important for the consultant to determine collaboratively with the elementary teacher those student behaviors considered most important. In general, teachers consider the following student behaviors important for successful mainstreaming: interacting positively with other students, following class rules, displaying proper work habits, and coping (Walker et al., 1983). The educational consultant can work with the special education teacher so that the handicapped student exhibits these appropriate student behaviors. In addition, the educational consultant can work with the regular elementary teacher in constructing classroom situations that will facilitate the ability of the mainstreamed handicapped student to work successfully in individual and small and large group situations. The consultant should realize that to effect successful mainstreaming, he or she will need to consider all the relevant people in the student's environment (e.g., the handicapped student, the special education teacher, the administrator, the parents) in addition to the regular educator and nonhandicapped students.

CURRICULUM

Effective instruction at the elementary level incorporates academic skills, social development, and career education. The academic curriculum involves the mastery of reading, writing, spelling, and arithmetic as well as the development of concepts in other content areas such as social studies and science. School districts usually follow a curriculum guide so that teachers can follow a scope and sequence for teaching. To assist the student's social development, a number of curriculum guides are also available (cf. Stephens, 1981; Walker et al., 1983). Finally, the elementary teacher can set the occasion for the development of career education skills by referring to competency lists (Brolin & Kokaska, 1979), developing appropriate work attitudes and habits (Kolstoe, 1976), and engaging in career exploration and awareness activities (Brolin & Kokaska, 1979).

Since other authors have addressed the topic of the academic curriculum (e.g., Lowenbraun & Affleck, 1976; Morsink, 1984; Turnbull & Schulz, 1979), the next section focuses on ways in which the consultant can help the elementary teacher address social development and career education. These two areas are especially important for the mainstreamed handicapped student's success.

Social Development

There is ample literature to document that learning disabled students experience social problems. They seem to have difficulty understanding nonverbal communication (Bryan, 1977) as well as using verbal communication (Bryan & Bryan, 1978). They are, generally, unpopular with their peers (Bruininks, 1978a, b; Bryan, 1974a, b; Bryan, 1976; & Siperstein, Bopp, & Bak, 1978), and they are at risk for social neglect or rejection (Bryan, 1982). It is therefore imperative that elementary teachers attend to the social development of learning disabled students who may be mainstreamed into their classrooms. Given that the elementary classroom is the least restrictive alternative for the mildly handicapped student, it is an appropriate setting to foster the development of social skills.

Programs for Social Development. A variety of programs are available to help the elementary teacher facilitate the social development of students (cf. Walker et al., 1983). According to Wood (1982), there are two major types of programs: (a) those that focus on *affective education* and stress the development of thoughts, feelings, and interpersonal relationships and (b) those that focus on *social skills training*, the achievement of established goals related to socially acceptable behavior. Whether the consultant and the teacher decide to implement one type of program or another is not as important as recognizing that social development is an important aspect of the elementary curriculum and that, especially for the mainstreamed handicapped student, direct instruction is essential for social development (Gresham, 1984). Ultimately, the teacher must decide which social development goals are most important and how these goals can best be achieved.

Procedures to Develop Social Skills. According to Strain, Odom, and McConnell (1984), there are three basic procedural variations to teach social skills to students. First, the students can be taught using the so-called "pull-out" program, whereby the student leaves the classroom for a period of time and receives instruction in another location. Second, social skills can be taught in the regular classroom by the teacher, but only those students needing instruction (e.g., the mildly handicapped students) would be engaged. Finally, instruction can be delivered in the regular classroom to all students, the implication being that social skills are learned and maintained in a specific context, so all students should participate in the training. Strain et al. (1984) report that the last variation is programmatically superior to the other two, because it sets the occasion for the generalization of skills and places the mildly handicapped students in direct contact with the natural community of reinforcers, their classmates.

Strain and Odom (1986) worked with nonhandicapped children to develop communication skills with handicapped children. The nonhandicapped children were taught and encouraged to initiate social overtures to handicapped students. After training, positive social behavior change was noted, and there were no negative side effects for the nonhandicapped students. Further, it was found that the handicapped students increased their social responding, social initiations, and the length of time they interacted with their nonhandicapped peers.

The consultant and teacher may also find it useful to use naturally occurring situations in the classroom as opportunities to develop the social and communication skills of students. Cavallaro (1983) suggests that teachers combine the prompting of appropriate language with reinforcement. She suggests that teachers become aware of those naturally occurring situations in which children are expected to communicate their needs (e.g., instruction situations) as well as engage in conversation (e.g., during snacks and meals). She then suggests that teachers, when interacting with students in these naturally occurring situations, apply the following general rules: obtain the student's attention at the beginning of the interaction, perhaps by looking at the child and remaining silent for a few seconds until the child responds; systematically prompt the child to respond correctly; use concise language; keep interactions brief and pleasant; and, most important, wait for the child to respond.

In summary, the educational consultant is encouraged to work with students, teachers, and parents in helping elementary students to develop socially. He or she can develop programs for nonhandicapped students to initiate and maintain social interactions with their handicapped peers and vice versa. The consultant can also work with the elementary teacher to develop goals for social development, taking advantage of naturally occurring classroom situations.

Career Education

The recent interest in career education as a curriculum approach and instructional orientation was initiated at the national level in 1971 by former U.S. Commissioner of Education, Sidney Marland (Brolin & D'Alonzo, 1979). To date several professionals at federal, state, and local levels have endorsed career education and have worked to include the concept in school programs.

According to Gillet (1980, 1983), *career education* at the elementary level consists of the following: developing social skills, understanding oneself, developing communication and computation skills, learning about the world of work, and exploring a variety of career opportunities. Gillet (1980) suggests that elementary teachers establish goals for career education that will help the student to understand that work is a part of one's daily activities and that learning about communities and their resources can be useful for enjoyable leisure activities.

Consultants are encouraged to help teachers to incorporate career education goals into the regular elementary curriculum. For example, elementary teachers can take advantage of field trips that provide opportunities to discuss jobs available in the community (Gillet, 1983) and the leisure activities afforded by parks and community centers. In addition, the consultant can help the elementary teacher make job charts that show the relationship between school tasks and future jobs. For example, pouring juice during snack is similar to being a cafeteria helper, a bus boy, or a waiter (Gillet, 1980).

In summary, career education at the elementary level focuses upon developing the students' awareness of careers and community opportunities. Consultants are encouraged to assist elementary teachers in developing career education goals that are consistent with student needs and, like social development, can be incorporated into the regular elementary curriculum.

INSTRUCTION

To provide effective instruction in basic skills, social development, and career education, the consultant must help the elementary teacher attend to the individual needs of all students in the classroom. Individualized instruction has several meanings for educators. For some teachers it means that each student has his or her own work folder containing assignments designed to meet his or her personal needs. Other teachers consider individualized instruction in the context of a teaching method. Modes of presenting instructional tasks and expected modes of response are programmed so that the student has the maximum opportunity for success.

Like most educational concepts, individualized instruction can be conceptualized in a number of ways, and the consultant must be able to relate to the way a regular educator applies the term to the actual learning needs of the student. For example, if a regular educator's perception of individualized instruction is that each student has his or her own folder, yet each folder contains the same work for all students, the consultant may have to explore with the teacher other ways to meet the assessed needs of the student.

Several definitions of individualized instruction will be provided in this section along with a model for remedial instruction that can be used to meet the individualized learning needs of all students.

A Definition of Individualized Instruction

The definition of *individualized instruction* has evolved over several years. According to Good, Biddle, and Brophy (1975), individualization became a popular educational approach when school districts started to abandon their strict adherence to an age-graded curriculum. Teachers began to concentrate on teaching skills, regardless of the grade level children were assigned. For example, children in the second, third, or fourth grade who may have lacked a specific academic skill may have been grouped together in a nongraded classroom or taught by a team of two teachers.

Since the mid1960s, an era marked by significant legislative and litigative milestones for the handicapped, individualized instruction has come to mean that each student will progress through a specifically designed curriculum to meet goals identified for that student. Generally agreed upon educational goals for all students have been replaced by prescribed objectives to meet individually assessed needs.

To cite an example, a handicapped student in the 1950s might have been taught the same social studies curriculum in the same way as the other students. In the 1960s that curriculum still might have been taught to the student, except a battery of technological hardware (tape recorders, computers, etc.) would have been used to help the student learn the material. Today, the handicapped student might receive instruction in social studies only if it matched the goals and objectives specified by his or her Individualized Education Program (IEP).

Some authors (notably Minskoff, 1975) define individualized instruction as the teaching act that occurs between one teacher and one student for 100% of the time. According to Turnbull and Schulz (1979), when individual differences among students are considered along with their interest level, age, learning styles, and abilities, individualized instruction takes place. These authors contend that individualized programs can be used successfully in classrooms with large numbers of students, but teachers will need the assistance of consultants to redesign the instructional strategies.

A Model for Individualizing Instruction

Regardless of the definition one uses for individualized instruction, a *remedial teaching model* developed by Wallace and Kauffman (1978) can be employed. The model is based on a series of instructional decisions that enable a teacher to meet long-range goals (Figure 6.1).

The model begins when the teacher collects Type I data — information from test results, observations, and records — to formulate the instructional plan. Type II data, not illustrated on the graph, are obtained as soon as the student enters the system and begins to make responses based on the presentation of instructional tasks. Type II data refers to the information a teacher uses to correct a previous teaching approach or strategy. It serves a feedback function in the system.

After long-range and immediate goals are selected, the first instructional task is presented. If the student accomplishes this task, the next task in the sequence is presented. This process continues, assuming the student meets the criteria, until all of the instructional tasks and immediate goals have been achieved. At this point, the first long-term goal should have been accomplished. Another long-term goal is then selected, and the process is repeated.

If the student makes an error after the initial instructional task has been presented, the teacher's first responsibility is to analyze his or her own behavior. The teacher must determine whether the presentation was appropriate, whether the student had sufficient feedback, or whether the classroom arrangement needs changing. For example, if a teacher called on a learning disabled student to answer a question during a discussion period and the student was attending to events going on elsewhere in the room, the teacher might elect to move the student's seat closer to the teacher so that the student would not be so distracted. If the student's future responses were appropriate, the teacher could be reasonably confident that the change made was effective. If student errors persisted, regardless of seat arrangement, the teacher should look closer at the student's response to see if the task was appropriate. For instance, if the student was still unable to supply the correct answer during the discussion, the teacher might give the student clues. The clues might serve to help the student recognize the correct response, thereby increasing the likelihood of success.

The teacher decides, based on an analysis of teaching behavior and the student's responses, whether to modify the present task, present the next task in the sequence, or, if the long-range goal is unrealistic, to write a new long-range goal. We take the position that consultants should be aware of the steps that are available in this remedial model, because it serves as an excellent starting point for individualizing instruction.

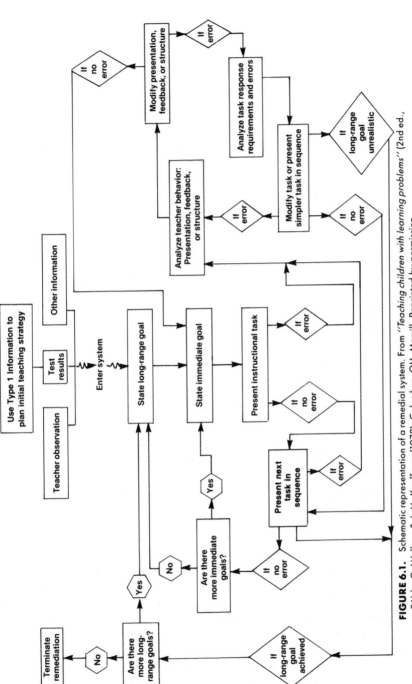

FIGURE 6.1. Schematic representation of a remedial system. From *"Teaching children with learning problems"* (2nd ed., p. 96) by G. Wallace & J. M. Kauffman (1978), Columbus, OH: Merrill. Reprinted by permission.

Using Individualized Procedures in the Regular Classroom

One reason a regular education teacher may be reluctant to accept a handicapped child into the elementary classroom is that the teacher might feel unable to meet the student's learning needs. The teacher might feel that the time required to teach 30 or more students would preclude the individualizing of instruction.

A teacher who expresses negative feelings about "having to go it alone" can be helped. The consultant can increase the teacher's awareness of effective teaching strategies, curriculum adaptations, and technological hardware. The consultant's ultimate objective would be to help the teacher develop the necessary knowledge and confidence to direct a program so well organized that it appears to run itself (Turnbull & Schulz, 1979).

There are a number of strategies teachers can use to increase the level of individualized instruction in the regular classroom. The strategies mentioned in this section have been used successfully in regular education classrooms or have been validated by experimental research. In either case, their potential for increasing individualized instruction at the elementary level has been demonstrated.

Grouping

The general characteristics of effective instruction include individualization, teacher direction, and grouping (Stevens & Rosenshine, 1981). Polloway, Cronin, and Patton (1986) discuss the positive benefits of grouping for instruction. Grouping generally promotes better use of teacher time and more efficient management of students, increases instructional time and peer interaction, and facilitates overlearning and generalization. However, providing individualized instruction in group arrangements requires the effective application of various types of grouping techniques. In this chapter we discuss large group instruction, small group instruction, peer and cross-age tutoring, and cooperative learning, because these grouping arrangements are frequently found in elementary classrooms.

Large Group Instruction.   Many regular educators may feel that it is impossible to individualize using *large group instruction,* where one teacher is directing a lesson with 30 or more students. Individualized instruction, however, can be provided if the modes of presentation and expected student response modes are matched. For instance, suppose that a teacher in an elementary school class were introducing a geography unit on the Nile Valley. Some students in the class might be required to give oral responses to the teacher's question. Other students (e.g., a cerebral-palsied student with articulation problems) might be required to demonstrate or point. Anecdote 6.1 illustrates how this geography lesson might take place.

ANECDOTE 6.1

TEACHER (*calling on April*): April, tell the class why the Nile River is so important to the economy and well-being of Egypt.

APRIL: The river is important because it serves as a source of water for irrigation and transportation for people up and down the valley.

TEACHER: Very good. Since much of Egypt is arid, the Nile provides the necessary water to raise crops and livestock.

TEACHER (*calling on Richard, the cerebral-palsied student*): Richard, please turn on the overhead projector. You'll notice that an outline map of Egypt and a grease pencil are on the stage. I'd like you to do the following: first, draw the location of the Nile; second, shade the area around the Nile that was once known as the flood plain; and last, locate the series of dams that have been constructed along the river to prevent flooding and provide hydroelectric power.

RICHARD (*takes the grease pencil in his hand and performs the tasks*)

TEACHER: Excellent! Class, notice that Richard has shaded a large area of the river valley. Prior to dam construction projects, this shaded area represented the land that was flooded annually by the Nile. (*Teacher continues with the rest of the lesson*).

The teacher in this anecdote provided individualized instruction to a handicapped student in a large group setting. She knew the content she wanted to teach and the expected student responses. April had to supply an answer orally, while Richards's participation in the same activity was tailored so that he could be successful. He did not say a word, yet he performed exactly what was required. The teacher's verbal praise not only reinforced Richard's performance, but also publicly announced his success to the class. Especially for handicapped students, public recognition for acceptable performance can be a definite boost to confidence.

Small Group Instruction. In graded classrooms it is not surprising to find a wide range of student abilities, interests, and rates of learning. When faced with such heterogeneity, teachers usually divide the students for *small group instruction*. While the teacher is working with one group, the other students may be assigned seat work, board work, or independent activities. To provide individualized instruction to all students, including the handicapped, the teacher must be able to manage each group simultaneously. As Mercer (1979) states, "small group instruction is essential in mainstreamed classrooms" (p. 320). Anecdote 6.2 describes a conversation between a consultant and a teacher who was having difficulty with her classrooom, which contained two developmentally handicapped students.

ANECDOTE 6.2

TEACHER (*talking to consultant*): Mr. Krebs, I'm having trouble with my reading groups, and I'm really lost for ideas on what to do with Dale and Joe while I'm with a reading group. They seem to demand so much attention.

CONSULTANT: Tell me about it.

TEACHER: Right after morning exercises and announcements I explain all the board work to the class, and I try to take extra time with Dale and Joe. I go over each assignment and ask if there are any questions.

CONSULTANT: Do many students ask questions?

TEACHER: A few do, but most wait until I take my first reading group. Then they'll raise their hand or come back to my desk to ask for help with a problem I just explained.

CONSULTANT: I know what you mean. I used to have the same problem, and it wasn't just the handicapped students who would interrupt.

TEACHER: What did you do?

CONSULTANT: Well, I started the morning the same way you do. But I told the students that I wasn't to be interrupted while I was with a reading group. If they had questions they were to put their names on the board, and continue with the work they could do. I made quick trips to a student who needed help when I thought it was necessary.

TEACHER: How do you do that without interrupting the flow of instruction?

CONSULTANT: Suppose the first group you had was reading a story. One thing you could do is have the students read the next paragraph of the story to themselves. Tell them to read to find out why something happened or read to find what the paragraph was about. While they are reading silently, slip off to the student whose name appears first on the board to provide individual help. While you are at the student's desk, praise the student for his or her work. The system should reduce the number of interruptions you have, and the students' on-task behavior should improve because you will be praising their effort and achievement.

TEACHER: That sounds like a great idea. I think I'll try it.

CONSULTANT: It worked for me when I taught. I'm sure it will work for you. You may have to make extra trips to Dale's and Joe's desks to help them, but as you gain experience you'll find ways to cut down the number of times you have to visit their desks during the reading period.

In this case the consultant provided a functional suggestion on how individualized instruction could be handled in a classroom where students were having difficulty with their daily assignments. Further, the consultant indicated that Dale and Joe may need more assistance initially, but that later this direct help with seat work assignments could probably be reduced.

Peer Tutoring.　An often forgotten resource for providing individualized instruction is the students themselves. Research on *peer tutoring*, defined as same-age students teaching one another, has demonstrated that it is an effective strategy for increasing academic skills of both students (Allen & Boraks, 1978; Conlon, Hall, & Hanley, 1972; Harris, Sherman, Henderson, & Harris, 1972;) and tutors (Davis, 1972; Dinnen, Clark, & Risley, 1977; Parson & Heward, 1979). According to Lovitt (1977) tutors learn because they have additional practice with the skill and may have to look up answers for questions or defend their reasoning if challenged by a student.

Clearly, peer tutoring has several distinct advantages over other techniques. First, tutors are available. Teachers do not have to rely on volunteers, parent-aides, or paraprofessionals. Second, when tutors and students switch roles both benefit. Custer and Osguthorpe (1983) reported an interesting project in which mildly mentally retarded fifth- and sixth-grade students trained their nonhandicapped peers to use sign language. After tutoring, it was found that the nonhandicapped students did learn how to use sign language. In addition, during recess, the social interaction time between the two groups increased, and the nonhandicapped peers reported that they felt much more friendly toward the handicapped students. It seems that peer tutoring can be used to enhance academic skill mastery as well as the social development of elementary students.

Although peer tutoring is used in regular education classrooms, it is usually done on a limited and impromptu basis. Typically, the teacher assigns a proficient pupil to tutor a student who has yet to master a skill or concept, and the tutor-student pair work together without direct teacher supervision (Deterline, 1970).

To use peer tutoring on a classwide basis, a procedure needs to be employed that will enable the tutor to learn the new skill and simultaneously to teach it to his student. To achieve this objective, Heward, Heron, and Cooke (1982) devised a procedure known as *tutor huddle*.[1]

To form a tutor huddle, a class is divided into tutor-student pairs. The division can be based on achievement scores or compatibility. A handicapped student may serve as either tutor or student depending upon the goals of the tutoring program. Once the tutor-student pairs are formed, they are combined in groups of three to five pairs. For example, if there were 32 students in the class, 16 tutor-student pairs might be arranged in four tutor huddles.

At the beginning of each tutoring session, the tutors from each huddle meet for five minutes to review the material they are to present to their respective students. As Figure 6.2 illustrates, the tutors are presenting sight-word vocabulary to one another — the same sight words that they will present to their students during the 5-minute practice session that follows.

---

[1]A complete description of the classwide peer tutoring training package can be obtained by writing Timothy E. Heron, Department of Human Services Education, The Ohio State University, 1945 N. High St., Columbus, OH 43210.

FIGURE 6.2. Four first-grade children participating in a tutor huddle.

During tutor huddle, the tutors confirm each other's responses to the sight vocabulary words by saying "yes." If a tutor makes a mistake, the other tutors provide corrective feedback. If none of the tutors is able to provide the word, a tutor raises his or her hand to obtain teacher assistance. While the tutors are reviewing in the huddle, their students are engaged in seat work at their desks.

At the teacher's signal, a five-minute practice session begins. Each tutor is joined by his or her student for flash card drill (Figure 6.3). The tutor presents the cards to the student as quickly as possible. If a student is not able to identify a word or says a word incorrectly, the tutor uses a two-step prompting procedure to help. At the end of the five-minute practice session, the student is tested by the tutor, and the result is graphed. During practice and testing, the student receives verbal reinforcement from the teacher for looking at the flash cards and following the tutor's directions.

In a tutor-huddle procedure, "a tutoring system within a tutoring system" is arranged (Heward et al., 1982, p. 9). Tutors learn from one another, and the consequence of having to teach their students the assignment within a matter of minutes may add an extra incentive to learn.

FIGURE 6.3. A first-grade tutor presenting sight-word vocabulary to her student.

Heward, Heron, Ellis, and Cooke (1986) demonstrated that a classwide peer tutoring program can be enhanced further by training tutors to praise their partners on an intermittent schedule of reinforcement. Essentially, the procedure involved training 26 first-grade students to say "Good," "Great," "Super" when their partner emitted a correct response. Training was conducted within the context of the existing classwide system and proceeded from one tutor huddle to the next in a stepwise fashion. After reviewing all previously trained tutor behaviors, the tutors (a) viewed a model, the teacher, praising a student after every third trial (FR 3); (b) practiced with the teacher; and then (c) practiced with one another.

Figure 6.4 shows the percentage of student responses praised by each of the four observed tutors. During baseline, none of the tutors praised their partners. After training, all tutors improved their praise levels and approached an FR 3 schedule (i.e., praise delivered after every third trial). In short, a functional relationship between tutor praise training and student correct responses praised was evident. According to Heward et al. (1986), "The results show clearly that a peer tutor training package of modeling, role playing, and practicing with feedback . . . can also be used to teach peer tutors to provide verbal praise on a simple intermittent schedule" (pp. 11–12).

Cross-Age Tutoring.   Some regular education teachers, especially those at earlier grade levels, may feel that the students within their classroom are not ready to teach one another, yet they still want a tutoring program to individualize instruction. *Cross-age tutoring* (older students helping younger ones) can effectively solve the teacher's problem if some logistical hurdles can be overcome. For example, if a sixth grader were to tutor a second grader in math on Monday from 9:00 a.m. to 9:30 a.m., the teacher would have to resolve any scheduling conflicts for the sixth grader. According to Dineen et al. (1977), special arrangements may have to be made for missed class time. Also, it is highly unlikely that more than several older students could be used at once. So, the chances of having a classwide program using cross-age tutors are slim. However, if the teacher is interested in cross-age tutoring a few students, the technique can be effective (Cloward, 1967; Frager & Stern, 1970; Johnson & Bailey, 1974).

Some teachers may feel that peer or cross-age tutoring would be a beneficial experience but hesitate to do it because of the time it takes to prepare tutoring materials. Because this concern is clearly legitimate, the consultant must help the elementary teacher identify those situations in which it would be appropriate for the students to prepare their own materials. Pierce and Van Houten (1984), for example, describe several situations in which it would be appropriate for students to prepare tutoring materials. For instance, students could construct their own flash cards. The teacher could make one sample set of cards and place each card at a separate work station. Students could move from station to station copying each card. Consultants are urged

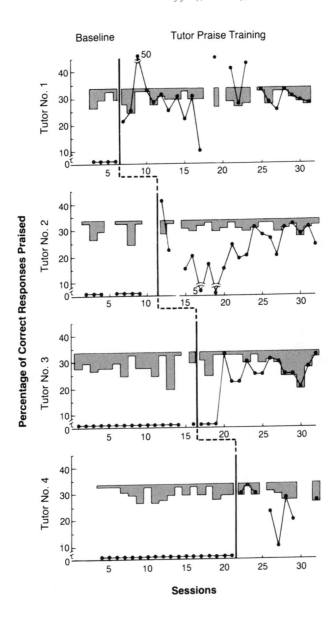

FIGURE 6.4. Percentage of correct student responses verbally praised by tutors during baseline and after training. The bottom edge of the shaded portion of each tutor's graph represents the percentage of student responses the tutor needed to praise each session in order to deliver praise at an equivalent FR3 schedule. Gaps in the data represent absences. From "Teaching first grade tutors to use verbal praise on an intermittent schedule" by W.L. Heward, T.E. Heron, D.E. Ellis, & N.L. Cooke (1986) in *Education and Treatment of Children*, 9(1), 5–15. Reprinted by permission.

to help elementary teachers establish criteria for successful task completion (e.g., neat flash cards, correct information recorded) and monitor students' activities while performing the task.

Cooperative Learning.   Kagan (1986) defines *cooperative learning* as "the structuring of classrooms so that the students work together in small cooperative teams" (p. 231). There are a number of cooperative learning methods, including those developed by Johnson and Johnson at the Cooperative Learning Center at the University of Minnesota (Johnson & Johnson, 1975). Johnson and Johnson incorporate the development of social and communication skills as part of the goals for cooperative learning. In contrast, the development of social and communication skills is not inherent in the cooperative learning methods developed at the Center for Social Organization of Schools at Johns Hopkins University (Kagan, 1986). Whether social and communication skills are incorporated into the cooperative learning goals, the one feature that distinguishes cooperative learning methods from large or small group instruction is that the class is divided into small teams whose participants are dependent upon one another (Kagan, 1986). The goals for students are common and individual students achieve these goals only if all members of the team achieve the goals (Knight, Peterson, & McGuire, 1982).

Using Kagan's (1986) definition of cooperative learning, peer tutoring arrangements can represent a cooperative learning situation if the students are dependent upon one another to master common goals. In cooperative projects, students work together to produce a common product such as a written paper. Another cooperative learning method is the *jigsaw method.* Students are required to operate as a team in that each member is responsible for teaching other members of the team some unique skill that only that team member knows, thereby encouraging a positive interdependence among the group. An example of the use of a jigsaw method may be having each team of students assigned the common goal of learning the location of a state, the size of the state, the principle product produced by the state, and the state capital. Each team would be composed of five students. Each of the five students would be assigned a group of states (e.g., northeast, southeast, central, northwest, and southwest) and become an expert in the assigned states. The first activity for students would be to regroup by assigned states. For example, all students who were assigned the northeast states would group together. In each of these new groups, students would help each other become experts about their assigned states. Once students achieved that goal, they would then return to their original team and assume responsibility for teaching the other team members the knowledge they obtained in their expert group. In this way, each team member possesses a unique bit of information unknown by the other team members. Team members become interdependent to learn what each other knows to achieve the goals of the lesson.

According to Knight, Peterson, and McGuire (1982), the teacher's role in cooperative learning includes specifying goals and objectives, selecting the size of each team, arranging the classroom and obtaining materials, observing the student-student interaction, helping student teams to work cooperatively, and evaluating the group product.

Consultants can set the occasion for elementary teachers to use cooperative learning methods. First, they can help elementary teachers to determine how to group students so that each group can have common goals while attending to the needs of each individual student, an especially important consideration when mainstreamed handicapped students are involved. Several studies indicate that students with handicaps are more successfully mainstreamed into regular classrooms when cooperative learning methods are used (e.g., Bryan, Cosden, & Pearl, 1982; Cooper, Johnson, Johnson, & Wilderson, 1980; Johnson, Johnson, DeWeerdt, Lyons, & Zaidman, 1983; Rynders, Johnson, Johnson, & Schmidt, 1980). Research indicates that achievement, as well as interpersonal relations among students, can be enhanced through the use of cooperative learning methods.

Second, the consultant can work with the teacher in identifying appropriate methods to observe student-student interaction and evaluate the success of each group. The discussion of assessment techniques presented in Chapter 8 should prove helpful to the consultant in this regard.

Third, the consultant can help the elementary teacher to teach students appropriate communication skills so that the students will be able to work together as a group. As indicated by Johnson and Johnson (1975), cooperation is essential. Cooperative skills include communication skills and skills in building and maintaining trust. The consultant uses these skills when engaging in collaborative consultation activities. Therefore, the consultant should be an excellent resource to the elementary teacher.

Johnson and Johnson (1975) suggest that teachers use the following procedures to assist students to develop cooperative skills: (a) ask students to identify the skills they think they will need to cooperate with each other; (b) help the students to define the skills; (c) set up situations for the students to practice the skills; (d) provide each student with feedback regarding use of the skills; (e) encourage continued use of the skills; (f) orchestrate situations where each student will be able to successfully use the skills and therefore be reinforced for using the skills; (g) require that the skills be used frequently so that they become part of each student's behavioral repertoire; and (h) establish use of the skills as an expectation in the class.

Finally, the consultant can assist the elementary teacher in obtaining materials that will help the teacher to learn more about cooperative learning methods. As indicated by Kagan (1986), many resources are available to teachers to help them incorporate cooperative learning in their classrooms. Some of the resources provided by Kagan (1986) are listed in Table 6.1.

TABLE 6.1
Cooperative Learning Resources

Aronson, E., Blaney, N., Stephan, C., Sikes, J., & Snapp, M. (1978). *The jigsaw classroom*. Beverly Hills, CA: Sage.

Dishon, D., & O'Leary, P. W. (1985). *A guidebook for cooperative learning: A technique for creating more effective schools*. Holmes Beach, FL: Learning Publications.

Johnson, D. W., & Johnson, R. T. (1975). *Learning together and alone: Cooperation, competition, and individualization*. Englewood Cliffs, NJ: Prentice-Hall.

Johnson, R. T., & Johnson, D. W. (Eds.). (1984). *Structuring cooperative learning: Lesson plans for teachers*. Minneapolis: Interaction.

Michaelis, B., & Michaelis, D. (1977). *Learning through noncompetitive activities and play*. Palo Alto, CA: Learning Handbooks, Pitman Learning.

Moorman, C., & Dishon, D. (1983). *Our classroom: We can learn together*. Englewood Cliffs, NJ: Prentice-Hall.

Orlick, T. (1977). *Winning through cooperation: Competitive insanity: Cooperative alternatives*. Washington, DC: Hawkins.

Orlick, T. (1982). *The second cooperative sports and games book*. New York: Pantheon.

Schmuck, R. A., & Schmuck, P. A. (1983). *Group processes in the classroom*. Dubuque, IA: William C. Brown.

Sharan, S., Hare, P., Webb, C. D., & Hertz-Lazarowitz, R. (Eds.). (1980). *Cooperation in education*. Provo, UT: Brigham Young University Press.

Slavin, R., Sharan, S., Kagan, S., Hertz-Lazarowitz, R., Webb, C., & Schmuck, R. (Eds.). (1985). *Learning to cooperate, cooperating to learn*. New York: Plenum.

Curriculum Adaptations

While the school curriculum may be outlined by the district, the choice of instructional materials and methods is usually left to the teacher (Turnbull & Schulz, 1979). The teacher selects materials based on several criteria, including the publisher's guidelines, previous experience teaching the skill, availability, and the student's individual needs. *Curriculum adaptations* refer to changes in instructional methodology or materials to meet the unique learning needs of students.

Unfortunately, the match between the first three variables and student need is often imprecise (Lovitt, 1977), or there are units of instruction for which materials do not currently exist. Sometimes the teacher must make the materials or forego teaching the unit. For a teacher to adapt existing curriculum materials that meet the predetermined needs of handicapped students, it is essential that the teacher have a clear idea of the content to be taught and the best method for teaching it to an individual student. In adapting curricula, the consultant should help the teacher identify those aspects of the task that are problematic for the student. With a minimum of changes in the teacher's behavior, the consultant helps the teacher develop ways for the student to cope with identified problems. There are several strategies a teacher can use to do this.

Reducing Distractions.   A number of special educators have indicated that some handicapped children (e.g., the learning disabled, behaviorally disordered) are distracted by stimulation in their environment (Stephens, 1977; Wallace & McLoughlin, 1979). By adapting the method by which the handicapped student is required to complete an assignment, the teacher might reduce or eliminate the distractibility. Lambie and Hutchens (1986), for example, discuss ways in which an elementary school teacher can adapt mathematics materials to minimize distractions and help students complete assignments. For instance, with paper and pencil tasks, the teacher can fold the page like an accordion and ask the student to complete one column at a time, or the teacher can draw different colored boxes around groups of problems and ask the student to complete one color at a time. Both of these techniques can help the student minimize distractibility by limiting or changing the amount of stimuli on a page.

Another way to reduce distractions is to have the student complete assignments in a study carrel. As Haubrich and Shores (1976) found, LD students who worked in enclosed carrels had higher attention spans, though not necessarily higher achievement scores, than when they worked at conventional desks. The carrels effectively screen distracting visual stimuli.

Pacing Lessons.   Another way that the existing curriculum can be modified for the handicapped student is to pace the activities or tasks the students are required to complete. Instead of issuing one major assignment (e.g., completing five pages of math), the teacher might assign three shorter tasks involving the same skill, but not requiring the same sustained concentration. Further, the teacher might modify an assignment so that the student is not penalized for his or her disability. For example, suppose that a cerebral-palsied student, integrated in the regular classroom for math, had to complete 25 math problems that were written on the board. While the other students in the class might be required to copy the problems and solve them without a manipulative device or a calculator, the cerebral-palsied child could work directly from the board, using a calculator or an abacus. In this way, he is not penalized for his inability to copy the problems. To the contrary, he would be demonstrating to the teacher that he had mastered the mathematical operation required.

Promoting Overlearning. Generally, skill instruction in the regular classroom proceeds in a vertical fashion. That is, once a student has mastered a lower-order skill, instruction begins on the next higher-order skill. With many handicapped students, however, it is necessary to overlearn a skill, so that proficiency and long-term retention is enhanced. The teacher can adapt the existing scope and sequence of a curriculum and promote overlearning by giving handicapped students additional practice and review with previously learned skills.

Modifying Delivery of Content. Unquestionably, most of the goals established by a teacher for students are achieved through some type of verbal behavior (Popham & Baker, 1970). While lecturing to students can be an effective technique for presenting new ideas, it does not usually provide the students with the opportunity to practice the skills the teacher is attempting to teach. Further, if the teacher gives a lecture to the class and fails to ask the students pertinent questions after the talk, it is unlikely that they will remember much of what was said.

On the other hand, a class discussion can be a valuable learning experience for the handicapped student as well as the rest of the class. If the students have sufficient background on the topic and the teacher has the ability to lead the group, a discussion can lead to affective changes in learners (Popham & Baker, 1970). For example, suppose that a teacher were leading a discussion on the effects of poverty on individuals. During the discussion the teacher could raise additional questions about how the lack of resources — monetary, physical, or social — reduces a person's ability to participate in the mainstream of the society. If the teacher is skillful, students might begin to gain an understanding of how the handicapped, for example, must make use of all the resources at their disposal to succeed. Nonhandicapped students might come to sense that the problems that face sensorially, physically, and emotionally handicapped individuals are not so different from those affecting the poverty-stricken. Both groups suffer social alienation and rejection.

Finally, according to Popham and Baker (1970), lectures and discussions need to be supplemented with demonstrations that show students the tasks that the teacher wants them to learn. Consultants need to remind teachers that to use demonstration as an instructional method they must (a) make sure they can perform the demonstration; (b) have all necessary apparatus available; (c) schedule practice sessions after the demonstration so that students can imitate the behavior, and (d) provide feedback to the students on their ability to imitate the demonstrated tasks.

For further discussion regarding effective group instruction to meet the needs of all students, the reader is referred to Chapter 7.

Technology

Each year computers and related hardware are produced that are smaller, more efficient, and less expensive; and educational publishers are using highly sophisticated computer systems to program educational lessons on a wide range of topics. Still, microcomputers represent only one aspect of technology that can be used to improve instruction. In this chapter, *technology* refers to the full range of educational media, materials, hardware, and software that can be used to affect academic, social, or career education gains.

Tape Recorders. The cassette tape recorder is an excellent device for individualizing instruction in any classroom. It has several uses. For example, the teacher can record review lessons, stories, tests, and directions for completing assignments. Students who have difficulty comprehending oral instructions are able to use the tape recorder effectively, because they can replay the instruction several times. Further, the teacher can pace an exercise with the recorder so that students with lower rates of learning can be challenged while faster students can be moved ahead. Sample teacher directions to a handicapped student are found in Anecdote 6.3.

ANECDOTE 6.3

(Student turns tape recorder on.)

TEACHER: Good morning. Today we are going to take our practice spelling exam. I'll say one word at a time, use the word in a sentence, and then say the word again. After I have pronounced each word the second time, turn off the recorder and write the correct spelling. When you are finished, turn the recorder back on and I'll spell the word. You can correct your own paper. The first word is *typhoon*. A typhoon is a fierce storm. *Typhoon. (Student turns off tape recorder and writes the response; then turns on the tape recorder to hear the teacher spell the word.)*

TEACHER: Typhoon, t-y-p-h-o-o-n.

In this anecdote the teacher programmed a written response for the student. Perhaps for another student she may have programmed an oral response, and the student would have spelled the word directly onto the tape.

The tape recorder, when used in combination with other materials such as the microcomputer or paper and pencil exercises, can be the cornerstone of a self-instructional package. These packages, that contain the student's assignment, mode of response, and self-checking component, can be of great value in helping the handicapped student remain within the mainstream (deGrandpré & Messier, 1979).

One potential disadvantage of the tape recorder is that it takes time to produce the tapes. The teacher may be able to ask students, assistants, paraprofessionals, or volunteers to help make the tapes. For suggestions on development of instructional tapes, the reader is referred to the discussion of compensatory techniques in Chapter 7.

Overhead Projector. Next to the tape recorder the piece of instructional hardware most common to individual instruction is the overhead projector. It can be used in a group lesson as we noted in Anecdote 6.1. Also, the overhead can be used to introduce new lessons, review key points prior to an exam, or as a way to observe an individual student's response.

One advantage of the overhead is its low cost. By using write-on transparencies and washable pens, teachers can reuse transparencies almost indefinitely. Like audiotapes, transparencies can be catalogued and filed according to the skill or content they are designed to teach.

Filmstrips and Recorders. For students who have poor reading skills, filmstrip-tape packages offer the opportunity to participate in an individualized program. Students listen to a tape of a story or lesson while simultaneously viewing the filmstrip. Students enjoy using the filmstrip projector with the tape recorder. The teacher can use this approach to review lessons or as an independent seat-work assignment. If deaf or hard-of-hearing students are integrated in the regular classroom, the consultant might recommend that captioned films or filmstrips be used so that these students will be able to participate as well.

Computers. Currently, computer technology is present in almost all aspects of society. As indicated by Wiegner (1982), the decision of the educational community is not whether or not to use computer technology but rather how to use computer technology to the best possible educational advantage. Research indicates the following: (a) microcomputers can assist learners in reaching instructional objectives; (b) students who receive computer-assisted instruction (CAI) are are able to retain information after the CAI ends; (c) CAI can improve the speed at which students learn a given amount of material; and (d) students react positively to well designed CAI programs and tend to reject poorly designed CAI programs (Edwards, Norton, Taylor, Weiss, & Van Dusseldorp, 1975; Gleason, 1981; Kulik, Bangert, & Williams, 1983). Since the achievement of many handicapped students is linked to educational objectives, improving retention, overlearning, and motivation via the computer can further refine the individual program for the handicapped student (Hannaford, 1983).

These findings provide challenges to teachers, especially teachers who wish to incorporate exceptional students into the elementary classroom, and suggest that the computer is a viable instructional tool in mainstreamed settings. For the consultant to best help the elementary teacher use the computer as an instructional tool with mainstreamed students, the consultant should be able to answer several questions. What can a computer do? How much adaptation to the hardware or software will be necessary to use the system in the classroom? How can the computer be used to compensate for the problems mainstreamed handicapped students experience in the classroom?

The microcomputer can be used to teach, to drill, to simulate, and to communicate. There are microcomputer programs developed to teach new concepts and review previously taught ones. In addition, there are microcomputer programs designed to provide the necessary drill and practice for students to overlearn and master concepts. Given the expanding array of software programs available, consultants can assist regular education teachers by suggesting that a data-based evaluation guide be used to assess the potential programs. Test (1985) outlined a multistep procedure to evaluate programs.

Step 1. Read the documentation that accompanies the program carefully, paying attention to objectives, field-test data, and instructional claims.

Step 2. Use an evaluation form to document the assessment.

Step 3. Run the program and test how it responds to correct and incorrect responses.

Step 4. Observe a student as he or she completes the program to determine those features of the program that seem to set the occasion for, and maintain, responding.

Microcomputers can also be used as a motivator to students. Most students find using the computer reinforcing. Therefore, it is possible for the teacher to also use the microcomputer as a reinforcement for task completion. Students may be permitted to use the microcomputer contingent upon completing another classroom task. Microcomputers can also be used to compensate for a skill deficit. For example, the microcomputer can be used as a word processor. Students who have difficulty writing, because of either poor motor coordination or poor organizational skills, can use the computer to complete written assignments. Students who experience disabling conditions, such as orthopedic, visual or auditory impairments, can use the computer to help compensate for their disability. For example, an orthopedically handicapped student who does not have adequate fine motor control or speech can, with a pointer applied to the computer keyboard, use the computer to receive instruction as well as to communicate with the teacher and other students in the class.

For the consultant, the key point is to help the teacher integrate microcomputer technology with existing strategies — that is, helping the elementary teacher recognize that a new strategy can be incorporated into his or her existing repertoire. The teacher does not have to abandon everything he has done to date to effectively use a new instructional strategy. For instance, the consultant could help the teacher apply the skills used to evaluate paper and pencil instructional materials to the evaluation of computer programs. First, the consultant should identify how the teacher currently evaluates materials. Once this information is known, the consultant can help the teacher refine his or her criteria with microcomputer materials. Consultants are urged to help teachers answer two questions about microcomputer instructional uses: Does the computer program do what you want it to do well; and is the computer the best medium for the job?

When computer programs are used to provide instruction for students, there are several considerations to address. First, identify what the program is intended to do. For example, if the program is designed to provide drill and practice for mastery of multiplication facts, then evaluate it according to how well it helps the student master multiplication facts. Second, decide whether this lesson can be taught more effectively with another method. That is, in light of instructional objectives and individual students' learning styles, should textbooks, worksheets, manipulative materials, filmstrips, tape recorders, or some combination be used instead? Finally, as consultants, you can help elementary teachers develop and apply criteria that will effectively evaluate whether the computer program is designed well. Some of the things to consider in making this decision follow:

1. Is the software program user-friendly? For example, are prompts provided to students to tell them what to do to work the program? Is there a minimum number of key strokes needed to execute the program? How much time is taken in starting the program and moving to each of its parts? Is the student able to operate the program independently or will it require teacher intervention?

2. Does the computer provide the student with sufficient opportunities to respond (OTR)? For example, does the computer give the student more than one choice to respond to a given command? What is the computer's response when a student does not answer correctly? Does the computer provide hints? Does the computer model the correct response? Depending

on the purpose of the lesson and the needs of the student, the teacher may want the instructional program to provide different types of responses/commands/questions to the student's response. Another question may then be asked about the program: Is the program modifiable? Would it be possible for the teacher to override commands to the computer program to change the list of words that are practiced or to change parameters of the situation being simulated? These modifications may be necessary to effectively use the program with some of the students in the class.

3. Does the computer program use graphics or sound? Is the reinforcement appropriate with respect to frequency and duration? Is it age-appropriate? Is the reinforcement related to the skills to be learned in using the program or is it external to the program's purpose? For example, some programs provide reinforcement in the way of a game. When students complete a lesson, they have some time away from the lesson and are provided with the opportunity to play a game. Other programs provide immediate reinforcement when a student correctly responds (e.g., a display of color graphics or sounds). The teacher needs to evaluate what type of reinforcement is appropriate for a given situation and if the computer delivers that reinforcement satisfactorily.

In summary, there are many considerations in deciding how best to use technology with students. The teacher must make the decision, based on the availability of the technology, just what its use will be. Once that purpose is determined for each situation, the teacher must decide whether or not the technological device meets that purpose well. It is important for teachers to make judgments based upon their knowledge of effective instructional strategies, their knowledge of individual students' strengths and weaknesses, and their knowledge of the capability of technology. Consultants should try to help teachers increase their knowledge in each of these areas as well as evaluate the effectiveness of the technology used.

Consultants interested in referring teachers to sources of information on the use of microcomputers with exceptional individuals could suggest Bowe (1984), Budoff, Thormann, & Gras (1984), Hagen (1984), Taber (1983), and Torgesen (1986). Also, Becker (1984) indicated that there are at least six national periodicals written for school teachers and administrators interested in the educational uses of computers. In addition, there are newsletters, books, organizations, computer networks, and projects designed to address computer use with exceptional populations (Bailey & Raimondi, 1984).

CONCLUSION

A regular education teacher with a handicapped student enrolled in the classroom must be able to provide individualized instruction so that the assessed needs of the student can be met. The success of the child's program will be determined in large part by the ability of the teacher to use grouping techniques, adapt the existing curriculum and instructional methods, and use technology. Consultants should be ready to work jointly with regular class teachers to devise individualized programs using each of these alternatives.

SUMMARY OF KEY POINTS

Educational Consultation at the Elementary Level

1. Consultation at the elementary level requires the consultant to help the teacher provide an individualized program for elementary students that integrates the mastery of academic skills with social development and career education.

2. Research regarding effective instruction suggests that teachers should maximize the amount of time students are actively involved in academic tasks, provide direct instruction, maintain a brisk lesson pace, help students respond accurately to teacher questions, provide prompts to help students respond correctly, and monitor each student's performance.

3. To facilitate mainstreaming of handicapped students, consultants should collaborate with elementary teachers in defining and assessing any possible problems the mainstreamed student may present, work with the handicapped student to prepare for mainstreaming, work with nonhandicapped students to prepare them to receive a handicapped student, and collaborate with the elementary teacher in evaluating the success of the mainstreaming effort.

Curriculum

4. Curriculum at the elementary level includes basic skills mastery, social development, and career education.

5. The social development of elementary students can be enhanced by affective education or social skills training.

6. Consultants are encouraged to help teachers decide the most appropriate goals for social development, how those goals can be interfaced with instructional goals, and what intervention strategy will best help students to accomplish those goals.

7. The social development of mainstreamed students includes the development of communication skills.

8. Teachers are encouraged to provide direct instruction to meet the goals of social development.

9. Career education at the elementary level includes the development of social skills, self-concept, communication skills, computation skills, and learning about the world of work and career opportunities.

10. Consultants are encouraged to help elementary teachers incorporate career education goals into the regular elementary curriculum.

Instruction

11. When individualizing instruction, elementary teachers attend to the needs of individual students in the class.

12. Individualized instruction can be accomplished in a variety of ways, including grouping techniques, curriculum adaptations, and technology.

13. Individualization can occur in large group instruction when the teacher matches modes of presentation with expected student response modes.

14. Small group instruction can facilitate individualization, because it allows students to work on different activities at the same time.

15. Peer tutoring requires students to teach one another. It facilitates individualization, because it allow pairs of students to work on different activities at the same time.

16. Cooperative learning methods structure the classroom so that students work together in small cooperative teams. It facilitates individualization, because it allows groups of students to work on common goals while attending to the individual needs of students within the group.

17. The consultant can help the elementary teacher group students by helping the teacher determine how to structure groups to meet the individual needs of students; by helping the teacher identify and use appropriate methods to observe student-student interaction and evaluate the success of the grouping; and by helping the teacher teach the students appropriate communication skills so that the students will work well as a group.

18. Curriculum adaptations refer to changes in instructional methodology or materials to meet the unique learning needs of students.

19. Curriculum adaptations to reduce distractions include limiting the amount of material to be completed at a given time and using a study carrel.

20. Other curriculum adaptations include pacing lessons, promoting overlearning, and changing the ways in which content is delivered.

21. Technology can facilitate the individualization of instruction by providing materials that will help students to compensate for skill deficits and/or provide instructional experiences designed for the needs of specific students.

22. Teachers can use tape recorders for a variety of purposes, including reviewing lessons, individualizing tests, and/or recording directions for assignments.

23. Overhead projectors can help the teacher individualize instruction by providing a modified presentation of content in a group lesson or by operating as the response tool for a student.

24. Filmstrips and recorders can assist the teacher in individualizing instruction by providing a modified presentation of content and additional opportunity for the student to overlearn the content.

25. Computers can assist teachers in individualizing instruction by providing drill and practice opportunities for students, teaching content not taught to the entire class, providing the teacher with a reinforcer for students, and providing students with another response mode.

26. Consultants should help elementary teachers to decide how to make the best use of technology for the individualization of instruction by providing the elementary teacher with information regarding individual student needs, technological materials and their educational uses, and classroom arrangements that will facilitate the appropriate use of technology.

QUESTIONS

1. What activities does a consultant perform at the elementary level?

2. Discuss at least two ways in which an elementary teacher could incorporate social development into a basic skills curriculum.

3. Discuss at least two ways in which an elementary teacher could incorporate career education into a basic skills curriculum.

4. Define individualized instruction and discuss at least three techniques for individualizing instruction at the elementary level.

5. Define and discuss three types of instructional grouping techniques.

6. List two ways a regular education teacher could adapt an existing curriculum.

7. State how the following pieces of equipment could be used to individualize instruction for handicapped students: tape recorder, overhead projector, computer, filmstrips.

DISCUSSION POINTS AND EXERCISES

1. Conduct a meeting with the special and regular education teachers to determine how existing curriculum materials in both classrooms could be adapted to meet the needs of a specific handicapped student.

2. Conduct a pilot study with a group of elementary education teachers to determine the efficacy of various pieces of instructional hardware (e.g., tape recorder, microcomputer). Include in the study a complete evaluation of how individualization was enhanced.

3. Show a videotape of a teacher instructing the class in social studies, science, or math. Obtain the views of the audience of regular and special teachers on how the lesson could have been better individualized.

7

Modifying Curriculum and Instructional Strategies at the Junior and Senior High School Level

To provide appropriate instruction for secondary-level handicapped students can be a challenging task for regular education teachers. Unlike their elementary colleagues who are responsible for 30 students per day, teachers at the secondary level are usually responsible for up to 180 students per day. To assist them with effective teaching programs for handicapped students, the consultant needs a thorough understanding of the secondary-level classroom and how it works.

The purpose of this chapter is to examine ways that a consultant can assist the secondary educator in the provision of appropriate and effective instruction for students who have problems learning. The chapter provides a framework for educational consultation at the secondary level; discusses curriculum modifications, academic as well as nonacademic; and explores instructional strategies designed to meet the needs of handicapped youth. Examples of the use of curriculum modifications and instructional strategies are provided throughout. The emphasis of the discussion is to suggest ways that the educational consultant can help the secondary educator, despite the problems of large enrollment and the heavy emphasis on content acquisition.

OBJECTIVES

After reading this chapter, the reader should be able to:

1. discuss a framework for providing educational consultation at the secondary level.

1. identify academic and nonacademic curriculum modifications for secondary students.

2. compare and contrast the advantages and disadvantages of curriculum modifications.

3. identify three types of instructional strategies for secondary students.

4. discuss applications of curriculum modifications and instructional strategies for handicapped youth.

KEY TERMS

Remedial curriculum

Tutorial curriculum

Locational study skills

Organizational study skills

Career education

Career awareness

Career exploration

Career preparation

Functional curriculum

Communication skills

Social skills

Learning strategies

Compensatory techniques

EDUCATIONAL CONSULTATION AT THE SECONDARY LEVEL

Consultation at the secondary level involves the facilitation of an individualized program that integrates school and home/community resources. The same process occurs at the elementary level; however, at the secondary level the social system has changed into a complex interaction of people and programs. The consultant is no longer involved with primarily one regular or one special education teacher trying to implement a basic curriculum. Now the consultant faces several different content-oriented teachers, curriculum changes that include academic and nonacademic modification, varied levels of family/community involvement, and handicapped adolescents. The adolescent with a handicap not only has problems learning but also experiences the turmoil of adolescence. In short, the consultant faces the problem of helping to implement a program for the handicapped adolescent that considers the learning problems of the student, attends to the professional concerns of secondary educators, meets the expectations of the family, and provides a realistic curriculum with respect to post-secondary outcomes.

People in the Adolescent's Community

Table 7.1 shows the people in the adolescent's community. These individuals include the adolescent, the secondary educators, and the youth's parents and community members. A consultant working at the secondary level must be knowledgeable about each of these individuals to deliver effective service.

Adolescent.   Mercer (1979) stated that the handicapped youth is an adolescent first and an exceptional individual second. Therefore, the handicapped adolescent is expected to accomplish the tasks of adolescence—that is, forging new and mature relationships with peers, developing emotional independence from adults, and accepting one's sexuality (Havighurst, 1952). However, a handicapping condition may make the accomplishment of these developmental tasks difficult. For instance, the handicapped secondary student usually fails academically (Carlson & Alley, 1981). Academic failure often results in frustration, which can lower self-confidence and can result in less willingness to accept and perform any task.

Table 7.2 provides a comparison of expected and exhibited school behavior of adolescents. Handicapped adolescents tend to be low achievers (Deshler, Schumaker, Alley, Warner, & Clark, 1982); inactive learners (Hallahan & Reeve, 1980); and they are poorly motivated (Adelman, 1978). Yet they are expected to be good listeners, readers, and writers (Matthews, Whang, & Fawcett, 1980; Moran, 1980; Schumaker, Sheldon-Wildgen, & Sherman, 1980); active learners (Schumaker, Deshler, Alley, & Warner, 1983); and self-motivated students (Nesselroade & Reese, 1973).

TABLE 7.1
People in the Adolescent's Community

Adolescent	Educators	Parents/ Community Members
Physical Changes growth sex	Content specialists Lecturers	Approach—Avoid protection negative perception pessimistic involvement
Cognitive Changes other-centered abstract thought	Monitors—Independent work	
Social-Emotional parental independence peer dependence		Mores community work systems

TABLE 7.2
Comparison of Expected and Exhibited
School Behavior of Handicapped Adolescents

	Expected Adolescent Behavior	Exhibited Adolescent Behavior

School	good listeners
	good readers
	good writers
	self-controlled
	independent
	initiators
	organized
	accumulators of
	   academic credits
	test takers
		low achievers
		few basic skills
		   5th grade—reading, writing
		   6th grade—math
		inactive learners
		low motivation
		low self-esteem
		high off-task behaviors
		increased behavior problems
		poor test takers

Work	good listeners good readers good writers self-controlled independent initiators good speakers	occupationally immature immature social perceptions problems—interpersonal relationships poor social skills

Secondary Educator. At the secondary level knowledge accumulation is assumed by more than one teacher, and there is a shift in teacher expectations, both from the student's perspective and the teacher's perspective. The teacher no longer guides the student through a variety of learning experiences. Rather, the secondary teacher is a specialist in a given content area, and the student obtains knowledge from a variety of specialists. Moran (1980) indicated that secondary educators deliver that body of knowledge through lecturing and monitoring of independent student work.

Parents/Community Members. Parents of handicapped adolescents are generally pessimistic about the future of their handicapped children (Smith, Robinson, & Voress, 1982). Parents often perceive their handicapped offspring negatively (i.e., they question their abilities and doubt that the youth will succeed in life). Parents face a difficult situation in that they want to foster independence for a child who they doubt will function independently.

In addition to parental concerns, the environment of the handicapped adolescent includes members of the community, employers, and social service staff. These individuals reflect the mores of the environment that may or may not accommodate the behavior of a handicapped youth easily.

Program

Two general social systems exist within which the student functions: the school and the home/community. If the consultant is to provide effective services within these settings, three areas generally need to be considered: (a) the content of the setting, (b) the activities of the setting, and (c) the evaluation of the success in that setting. Figure 7.1 presents a graphic representation of the environments to consider when implementing a program for a handicapped youth. Characteristics of high school programs and home/commuity programs as reflected in Figure 7.1 follow. The characteristics of an individualized program, combining elements of the high school and the home/community are also presented.

High School Program. Boyer (1983), in his extensive study of American high schools, acknowledges that each secondary school is unique in that it is designed to serve a specific population in a given geographic area. However, most secondary schools share many features. The content of most American high schools is that of a comprehensive curriculum (i.e., academic

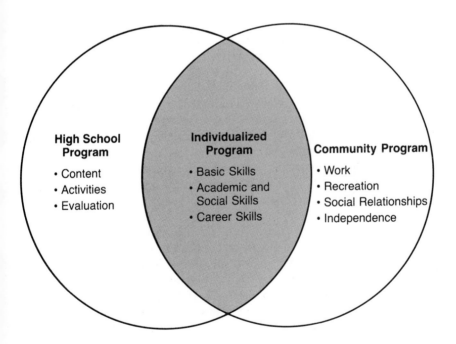

FIGURE 7.1. Environments of handicapped adolescents.

programs for the college-bound student, vocational education programs for those students seeking employment immediately after high school, and general studies programs for those students who have not made a post-secondary plan). Students usually have access to traditional academic courses (English, mathematics, science, and social studies); vocational courses (e.g., agriculture, distribution and marketing, health, business and office occupations, industrial arts, trades and industry, and consumer and homemaking); and general courses often described as "personal service and social development" (Boyer, 1983, p. 73). General courses sometimes include music performance and training for marriage/adulthood. Courses are generally offered in secondary institutions servicing more than 600 students with approximately 50 teachers. Usually, instructional services are provided in 50-minute periods with six to seven periods a day.

The traditional instructional activities used to present this content are lecture and laboratory experiences, evaluated through standardized competency tests. The indicator of success for the high school student is graduation.

Home and Community Program. The content of the community program usually includes work, acceptance by the peer group, and possibly learning experiences provided by agencies such as social service and juvenile justice. The activities related to this content are job-related activities as well as recreation activities such as dance and sports. The community evaluates the attainment of skills by noting sustained social relationships, independent functioning, and the acquisition of financial resources.

Individualized Program. The individualized program should incorporate content, activities, and evaluation procedures of both the school and the community. Why? Because if the handicapped student is to succeed to any degree in a regular education setting, then direct, individualized instruction in all relevant areas must be provided. One cannot assume that skills learned in one situation will automatically generalize to another situation (Cooper, Heron, & Heward, 1987). So, the individualized program must incorporate the academic content of the high school with the content of work and leisure activity. It is generally agreed that basic academic skills and nonacademic social and interpersonal skills, as well as career education and specific vocational skill development, should all be provided in an integrated program leading to successful employment after graduation from high school (Brolin & Kokaska, 1979; Committee on Youth Development of the President's Committee on Employment of the Handicapped, 1984; Epstein, 1982). Mastery of basic academic skills is important for all students. Brown and Yuh-Sheng Chang (1982) suggest that secondary graduates who do not adequately master basic skills, such as reading, may experience reduced employment opportunities. Social and interpersonal skill development relate directly to a handicapped individual's success on the job and in life adjustment (Greenspan

& Shoultz, 1981; Zetlin & Turner, 1983). Specific vocational training is essential for handicapped individuals, as unemployment is a common outcome for many of these persons (Bowe, 1980; Levitan & Taggart, 1976). Consequently, adequately preparing handicapped youth for future employment is a priority in special education (Will, 1984).

Content in an individualized program is provided via activities that use direct instruction techniques (i.e., through individual and small group situations, using multimodality presentations and compensatory techniques). However, it is also clearly recognized, especially at the secondary level, that if the student is to be integrated into mainstream society, it will be necessary to teach the adolescent how to successfully engage in the activities of the high school program and the community program. This requires the consultant to work with regular educators, special educators, and community members to help the student generalize skills across high school programs, community programs, and individualized programs.

To accomplish the goal of the secondary consultant (i.e., the successful implementation of an individualized program at the secondary level), the consultant must be able to function in two modes: as problem solver and as problem preventer. The educational consultant at the secondary level must be skilled in problem resolution. However, even more so, the consultant at the secondary level must understand the secondary environment and be able to orchestrate situations that will prevent problems. Educational consultants at the secondary level might apply Adamson's (1983) advice: The secondary educational consultant must be "willing to step into the world of the regular teacher both as an advocate (for handicapped adolescents) and as a colleague" (p. 71).

The curriculum for secondary handicapped students should be individualized to meet each student's needs. There are several different types of curricula educators can consider when designing a program for a secondary student. In this chapter, only academic and nonacademic curriculum options are discussed, because these options represent commonly used approaches available to consultants. The purpose of this discussion is not to exhaust all possible alternatives but to provide the secondary consultant with ideas that may be helpful in designing appropriate educational programs for secondary youth.

ACADEMIC CURRICULUM

The remedial and tutorial curriculum options for secondary handicapped students are discussed in this section. The remedial approach represents a curriculum consistent with the recent "back to basics" movement (Sewall, 1982). The back to basics movement in education reflects a national concern that many high school graduates do not have the reading, writing, or mathematics skills necessary for success in occupational settings.

The tutorial approach is implemented at the secondary level for a number of different reasons (Deshler, Schumaker, Lenz, & Ellis, 1984). The increased emphasis on competency testing has resulted in an increased interest by teachers in attending to the skills students will need to pass those competency tests. In addition, there is an increased emphasis on completion of a "core curriculum" (Boyer, 1983; Gardner, 1983; Shelby & Coleman, 1983). Teachers are often requested to tutor students to meet the demands of the core curriculum. Another reason for developing tutoring programs is the high dropout rate of learning disabled adolescents (Schumaker, Warner, Deshler, & Alley, 1980). It is felt that if learning disabled adolescents are tutored, they will be more successful in school and retention will be improved. Finally, it has been reported that secondary teachers use a limited number of instructional techniques when teaching content area subjects (Goodlad, 1983). As a consequence, it may be very difficult for secondary mainstreamed students to learn when a limited number of instructional strategies are used. Therefore, tutoring these students could facilitate their ability to learn secondary content.

Remedial Curriculum

In a *remedial curriculum*, educators provide remedial instruction for basic academic skill deficits (Deshler et al., 1984; Marsh & Price, 1980). The basic skills of reading, writing, and mathematics are usually taught at a level commensurate with the achievement level of the student. For example, if a junior in high school read on a fifth-grade level, a remedial reading program would be designed to improve reading skills on a fifth-grade level. The reading ability of the student would be systematically developed according to a scope and sequence plan for each grade level.

Educators who advocate using a remedial model at the secondary level make several assumptions. First, they assume that the skills that the student lacks can be identified through assessment. Second, they assume that the student will benefit from instruction despite a past history of poor performance. Third, they agree that the missing skills are necessary for success in secondary school and later in life (Alley & Deshler, 1979).

Alley and Deshler (1979) provide a thorough treatment of basic skills remediation at the secondary level. The types of skills that should be remediated as well as instructional strategies for the remediation of these skills are discussed. Regardless of the remedial curriculum developed, the following suggestions are offered consultants who wish to implement a remedial curriculum at the secondary level. First, use direct instructional procedures that emphasize mastery of basic skills to a prespecified level (Engelmann &

Carnine, 1982; Goodman & Mann, 1976). Second, strive to provide an intensive remedial experience to maximize mastery of the basic skill (Meyen & Lehr, 1980). Third, consider the use of strategies that will serve to motivate the student to engage in the remedial tasks (Cox, 1980). Learning disabled students, in particular, are noted for poor motivation in performing tasks that they have attempted and failed in the past.

Teaching Strategies for the Special Educator.   The consultant working with a special educator at the secondary level who uses the remedial model is faced with two important considerations. As stated previously, many handicapped students at the junior and senior high level have gaps in their academic and social repertoires. The difference between what they might be expected to perform and what they actually perform is large, and the gap grows larger with each passing year. The question that the consultant and the special educator need to answer is, "Where should instruction begin?" The second concern deals with the most appropriate teaching strategies to use. Positive reinforcement, modeling, and contingency contracting are examples of the techniques that could be used to help close the gap. The strategy that the consultant and special educator elect depends on several variables, including the degree of handicap exhibited by the student, the amount of time the teacher has available for instruction, and the resources the consultant and teacher can muster to provide supportive services for other environments, such as the regular classroom or the home.

Jerry, an LD adolescent mainstreamed in a secondary-level English class, illustrates a case that consultants and remedial-model teachers frequently encounter. Jerry's listening comprehension is adequate. His verbal skills are above average, but his written expression is poor. He has difficulty writing essays, themes, book reports, and narratives. He has trouble organizing his thoughts on paper, and he has little knowledge of punctuation and grammar. Consequently, he is at a severe disadvantage compared to other students in the class. He does, however, maintain a C or better average in other assignments, such as oral reports and group projects.

To assist Jerry, the consultant and special education teacher worked out a program where he wrote several essays and stories each week similar to the ones required of him in the English class. The stories were assigned to assess the magnitude of Jerry's problem. The data confirmed not only that Jerry's writing ability was poor but also that Jerry's attitude toward writing was extremely negative — a factor that Irmscher (1972) indicates must be addressed before formal instruction can begin on the writing skills themselves.

Given Jerry's poor attitude toward writing assignments, the teacher began a four-step plan, recommended by Alley and Deshler (1979), to improve his attitude.

1. In step one, daily writing assignments were issued with the instructions to write as quickly as possible about any ideas on the topic at hand. Jerry was told not to worry about punctuation, grammar, and spelling. He was reinforced (praised) for generating ideas and expressing his ideas as well as he could.

2. In step two, the teacher planned a five-minute, small group meeting with two other students to assist Jerry with generating ideas. The purpose was to talk about ideas. The ideas could be related to family, sports, work, future goals, and so on. Once the students had the opportunity to discuss their ideas, they were directed to write them on paper. Step two provided the pool of ideas on which the writing assignment could be based.

3. In step three, the teacher gave Jerry a tape recorder. He was told to express his ideas on tape and later to transcribe these ideas on paper. Initially, step three required only that Jerry copy his thoughts onto the paper from the tape. Later, he would be asked to generate an outline of his ideas from the tape and edit his outline to improve its organization.

4. In step four, Jerry kept a journal. The journal contained a brief synopsis of his daily activities. Elbow (cited in Alley & Deshler, 1979) states that daily writing activity in a journal can be an important aspect of a writing program, because it provides another opportunity for self-expression.

The special education teacher and the consultant also worked on two other deficiencies in Jerry's writing. These were his inability to organize sentences and paragraphs and his poor skills in grammar, punctuation, and spelling. Of course, intensive work on these skills did not begin until Jerry had experienced success with the four-step program just mentioned.

One strategy that the teacher and the consultant found most useful was a prompting plus differential reinforcement procedure. Jerry received points for those sentences (or paragraphs) that logically followed one another and expanded upon the topic sentence. If consecutive sentences were not related, Jerry received no points. When teaching grammar and punctuation, the teacher would initially indicate the number of punctuation marks or capitals required in the sentence. For example, in the sentence, "the boy said i am hungry (6)," the number six in parentheses served as a cue to Jerry that there were six punctuation marks or capitals to be identified. As Jerry's skill improved, the numerical cue was eliminated.

The consultant and teacher agreed that the instructional sequence should begin with an improvement in Jerry's attitude toward writing, hence the four-step program. Both realized that there was little hope of improving Jerry's writing ability as long as he was so negative. They felt that a plan was needed that progressively reinforced Jerry for writing anything — even sketchy ideas —

if, over time, those ideas could be structured and used as a way to teach organizational and mechanical skills. In behavioral terms, the plan called for the reinforcement of successive approximations to a terminal goal, a process referred to as shaping.

Teaching Strategies for the Regular Educator.   Because of the nature of a handicapped student's problem, the consultant must be prepared to use the remedial model with regular education teachers. To do so, the first objective the consultant might set would be to inform the regular education teacher of the scope and sequence of the handicapped student's program in the special education classroom. After doing so, the consultant could discuss with the teacher how the problem might be addressed within the regular class. Anecdote 7.1 continues our example with Jerry and illustrates what might be said.

ANECDOTE 7.1

CONSULTANT (*just finishing a description of Jerry's program in the special education classroom*): Mr. Holbrook, do you have any questions about the program the resource room teacher and I established?

MR. HOLBROOK: No. It seems like a good idea. I just hope there's enough time left in the school year to see an improvement.

CONSULTANT: I do, too. The year is going very fast, which brings up my reason to meet with you. As Jerry's English teacher, you can play an important part in the program.

MR. HOLBROOK: Me! I'm responsible for teaching junior English to 180 students. I don't have the time to teach Jerry the proper use of commas and periods. Besides, he can hardly write anyway.

CONSULTANT (*resolutely*): I am well aware of the limitations on your time, Mr. Holbrook. You have a difficult job, and I don't mean to imply that you should take primary responsibility for Jerry's instruction.

MR. HOLBROOK (*straightforwardly*): Then what are you asking?

CONSULTANT: I'd like to discuss some ways that you might individualize Jerry's instruction and at the same time reinforce the program we've established in the special education class.

MR. HOLBROOK: Sounds like I am going to have to do more work.

CONSULTANT: Maybe. But try to think in terms of helping Jerry.

MR. HOLBROOK: I'm listening.

CONSULTANT: I understand that Jerry, along with other students in the class, has written and oral assignments to complete each marking period

MR. HOLBROOK: That's right.

CONSULTANT: One way to individualize Jerry's program would be to issue all, or most, of his writing assignments at one time. He could work on them in the resource room. Not only would he be able to schedule his work over the marking period, but also the smaller group in the resource room would serve as a source of ideas for writing. The resource teacher could use your assignments as a base for offering remedial help.

MR. HOLBROOK: That doesn't sound too difficult. Anything else?

CONSULTANT (*feeling more confident*): Yes. I understand students in your class earn extra points for additional work.

MR. HOLBROOK: That's right. I frequently give bonus points for extra assignments.

CONSULTANT: Good. I'd like you to think about doing that in Jerry's case so that he could earn extra points when consecutive writing assignments show improvement.

MR. HOLBROOK: You mean he wouldn't have to do extra work, just show improvement from assignment to assignment?

CONSULTANT: That's right.

MR. HOLBROOK (*hesitating*): Well, that's a bit different than my normal procedure, but I guess I could work it out.

CONSULTANT: The last two items refer to testing and evaluation. Until Jerry's writing begins to show improvement, I'd like to reduce the number of written tests he has to take. I realize it's not possible to eliminate all of them. But I think Jerry's attitude toward writing, evidenced by his procrastination, doodling, and poor performance, suggests that we should ease off on the number of writing tasks he has to complete — at least right now.

MR. HOLBROOK: Maybe the resource teacher can help with some of the tasks.

CONSULTANT: That's a good idea. I'll ask Mrs. Graham. I'm sure she'd be willing. Finally, is there any way that Jerry could be assigned to a discussion group for his writing tasks the same way he is in the special education room?

MR. HOLBROOK: I haven't used discussion groups lately. But come to think of it, it might be a good idea for all the students. The group might help to clarify the topics.

CONSULTANT: Precisely.

MR. HOLBROOK: I'll do what I can with the suggestions you've made.

CONSULTANT: I couldn't ask more. I'll stop around next week to see how it's going. In the meantime, maybe you can meet informally with Mrs. Graham so that you get a better idea of Jerry's whole program.

MR. HOLBROOK: I'll try to meet her this week.

CONSULTANT: Thank you. Good luck.

To begin to individualize Jerry's instruction in the regular classroom, the consultant met with the English teacher to explain the program in the resource room. He wanted the English teacher to know that a plan was already in effect to improve Jerry's writing skills. The consultant knew if Jerry's program was to succeed he needed the English teacher's help. The tasks he asked the teacher to assign were designed not only to individualize the English class but also to reinforce Jerry's program in the resource room. To accomplish one of his objectives (having Jerry earn bonus points), the consultant suggested an extension of the teacher's plan to give bonus points for extra work. Because the consultant was aware of this plan, he was able to secure the teacher's cooperation. As Heron and Catera (1980) indicate, consultants who are able to match proposed interventions with class strategies already in effect are more likely to be successful. Finally, the consultant was able to convince the English teacher that testing and evaluation procedures needed to be adjusted if individualization was going to work in this case.

The four parties to Jerry's program — the consultant, the special educator, the English teacher, and Jerry himself — recognize that there is a long way to go before the goals for writing skills are met. The consultant may even realize that they may never all be fully met. In a remedial model, teaching follows assessment, and a systematic program is designed to increase the probability of skill acquisition.

Advantages and Disadvantages. Despite the inherent strengths in the remedial approach (i.e., providing increased competence in skills that may, in turn, increase the student's ability to learn content-related material), there are several shortcomings. First, the curriculum materials developed for use with this approach are generally materials that were developed for elementary students. Even though some materials, usually termed "high interest, low level" materials, are designed to remediate basic skills, there is little data available to indicate which of these materials are best able to produce quick gains for the secondary student with learning problems (Deshler et al., 1984). Second, limited instructional time at the secondary level precludes closing the gap to any significant extent between the present levels of student performance and the hoped-for grade level placement (Deshler, Alley, & Carlson, 1980). Third, with characteristically low motivation for academic tasks, learning disabled students may become bored with the rehashing of the same old skills, even with the high-interest, low-level materials. Fourth, since lower-order basic skills have yet to be mastered, little time is spent on the more advanced skills that the student's peers are acquiring. The student, who will probably be in school a few more years at best, is restricted from exposure to the content and general information his or her peers are acquiring. Finally, since a remedial curriculum is usually provided in a pull-out instructional situation (i.e., the student is removed from the regular classroom to receive remedial instruction), it is difficult for educators to demonstrate to the student how to incorporate the skills learned through the remedial model in the regular classroom or in real-life experiences (Alley & Deshler, 1979). If a handicapped student is not provided with direct instruction in the generalization of skills across situations, it is unlikely that the student will indeed be able to transfer skills learned in one situation to another situation.

Deshler et al. (1984) indicate there are little data available related to the efficacy of a basic skills remediation approach. However, about 51% of secondary learning disabled programs emphasize this approach (Deshler, Lowrey, & Alley, 1979). Research reporting the basic skill gains of secondary learning disabled students indicate that students reach a plateau, in junior high school, at about the fifth-grade level in the achievement of the basic skills of reading, math, and writing (Warner, Schumaker, Alley, & Deshler, 1980). If most of the secondary instruction is remedial in nature and students do not achieve above about a fifth-grade level in those skill areas that are being remediated, there is a serious need to consider the effectiveness of a remedial curriculum as it is currently being implemented in pull-out resource programs and self-contained special education classes.

Tutorial Curriculum

In the *tutorial curriculum* the emphasis of instruction shifts from teaching basic skills, such as decoding words, to teaching content, such as identifying the factors that led to the Civil War. Specifically, the students are taught academic content by a special education teacher or tutor. The goal of this approach is to help the mildly handicapped student receive a passing grade in the regular classroom (Deshler et al., 1979). There are no special curriculum materials used in this approach. The tutor generally uses the regular education materials with an appropriate variety of instructional methods.

If it is decided that tutoring would be beneficial for a handicapped adolescent, it is recommended that several teaching strategies be considered when using a tutorial approach.

Content Determination. It is suggested that the consultant work jointly with the special educator or tutor to determine the scope and sequence of the content that the regular classroom teacher uses. Once the content is identified, it is possible to make decisions regarding the teaching of the content within the tutorial sessions. For example, if a handicapped student integrated in a junior high school geography class was required to learn map reading, the tutor might concentrate instruction on the key skills of reading a legend, orientation, and direction and distance. After basic map-reading was acquired, more complex skills could be introduced. Consultants can also help the tutor guide the student's program in the area of testing. The tutor should know how the handicapped student is going to be tested in class before direct instruction begins. Will the student have to supply answers to questions in writing or orally? Will the student have to recognize the correct answers from among alternatives? Is the exam a true/false test? Answers to these questions are important, because they help the tutor determine how to prepare the student.

Study Skills. It is suggested that the tutor consider teaching and demonstrating the use of study skills when using a tutorial approach with a handicapped adolescent. To master academic content areas, students have to apply study skills. If the tutor teaches the handicapped adolescent how to use study skills with the content being tutored, it may facilitate the student's ability to use study skills with other content areas that are not being tutored (Stokes & Baer, 1977).

Alley and Deshler (1979) discuss the ability of study skills to help students acquire, organize and retrieve information. There are generally two types of study skills — locational skills and organizational skills.

Locational study skills can be defined as those skills that help the student find and understand material that can assist the student's comprehension of the content to be mastered. For example, if a student is studying biology, the tutor may want to help the student use the biology textbook to determine where the different topics can be found by teaching the student to use the table of contents or the index of the textbook. Or the tutor may want to help the student locate definitions of words with which the student is unfamiliar by showing the student how to use the textbook glossary or a dictionary. In addition, it is often helpful to teach students how to locate, read, and understand graphic aids such as tables, figures, and diagrams. These graphic aids can be very helpful to the handicapped student, because they can summarize a lot of information and show relationships between concepts in a compressed fashion.

Organizational study skills that can be addressed in a tutorial approach include survey skills and note-taking skills. Survey skills are used to give the student a preview of the content material. It is suggested that students be taught to survey material based on their own individual strengths and weaknesses. Any or all of the following techniques for surveying material may be used by the student, depending upon individual learning styles and needs (Graham, cited in Alley & Deshler, 1979):

1. skim the section
2. read the heading sections
3. read summary sentences
4. read topic sentences
5. interpret graphs and aids
6. read the picture captions (p. 9)

Kline (1986) compared a lecture–take notes format (baseline) with guided notes on high school students' performance on American History daily and unit quizzes. In the lecture-take notes condition, students initially read assigned pages with the teacher. Then the teacher presented an overhead transparency of important information from the reading and provided the students with the opportunity to take notes from the overhead. At the end of each session, a 10-point quiz was issued over the material covered that day. During guided notes, students followed the same procedure, except now students had a copy of the information from the transparency on their desks and they filled in the key material as the teacher spoke.

The results indicate that student performance was higher on daily and unit tests under the guided notes condition than under the lecture–take notes condition (Figure 7.2). The data also indicate that the students preferred the guided notes conditions, saying that it helped them to remain interested in the material.

Saski, Swicegood, and Carter (1983) report that notetaking skills are useful to recall information, and the use of some note-taking strategy is better than using no note-taking strategy (Devine, 1981). Saski et al. (1983) suggest the use of a note-taking format that can serve as a guide to organize and classify information. They suggest that effective note-taking formats are those that help the student to incorporate print cues from the text with verbal cues obtained in class. They further suggest that any note-taking format consider the following: space, subordination, division, question, and connections. tions, and connections.

If the note-taking format is spatially organized, it will facilitate efficient note-taking and content will be placed in a way that will be comprehensible at a later date. Subordination and division will help to make clear the concepts and their relationships to each other. Questions are useful, because they help students check on understanding of content as well as identify those areas for which the student requires additional information. Questions can also be a useful tool for test preparation. Connections help the student relate current information to previously learned concepts. Figure 7.3 provides an example of a lesson plan for a tutorial session. An example of note-taking is included within the lesson plan.

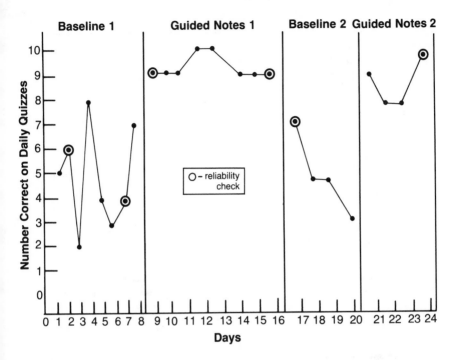

FIGURE 7.2. Number correct for student on daily quizzes. Open circles represent scores obtained by second observer. From "Effects of guided notes on academic achievement of learning disabled high school students" by C. Kline (1986). Unpublished master's thesis. The Ohio State University, Columbus, OH. Reprinted by permission.

Advantages and Disadvantages. The tutorial approach has two advantages. First, it addresses the student's immediate needs (i.e., helping the student to obtain a passing grade in class). Second, it allows the student to remain in the regular classroom with age-appropriate peers. For handicapped adolescents, the opportunity to interact with peers can enhance feelings of self-esteem.

However, the consultant should realize that there are disadvantages to this approach as well. Several authors have noted that it is a short-term solution at best (Alley & Deshler, 1979; Laurie, Buchwach, Silverman, & Zigmond, 1978). The student's skill deficit is not addressed. Rather, the student receives instruction in the courses in which he or she is enrolled. If enough credits are generated, the student is promoted and eventually graduates from high school. Although the student may have graduated, he or she may still lack important skills.

Second, the tutorial model may inadvertently reinforce the regular education teacher's failure to provide an individualized approach for the student.

Subject: Political Systems

Content Determination: The student will be able to:

1. identify the presidency as the most important and powerful office in the political system of the United States.
2. define and discuss at least one role of the presidency.

Tutoring Session Activities:

1. Identify and discuss key vocabulary words, such as:

president	chief executive	veto
presidency	executive	role
office	laws	

2. Read the section from the text chapter, "The Presidency," which discusses the roles of the presidency.
3. Outline one role of the presidency.

Outline

Purpose: define and discuss one role of the Presidency

Old Information	New Information
1. Congress consists of Senators and Representatives.	1. The President is the chief executive.
2. Congressmen make the laws.	2. The current President is Ronald Reagan.
3. The people are represented by Congress.	3. The President executes the laws of Congress.
	4. The President has the power to veto proposed laws before they are passed.

Questions/Answers

1. What is the role of the Presidency?
   (The President executes the laws of Congress.)
2. What is meant by the sentence: "The President executes the laws of Congress?"
   (The President is responsible for making sure laws are enforced.)
3. Why is the President more powerful than Congress?
   (The President has the power to veto a proposed law before the law gets passed.)

FIGURE 7.3. Example of a lesson plan for a tutorial session. From "Notetaking formats for learning disabled students" by J. Saski, P. Swicegood, & J. Carter (1983) in *Learning Disability Quarterly*, 6(3), 269. Reprinted by permission.

The regular teacher may feel that the tutor will review the requisite material with the students, and therefore the regular education teacher may feel that it is not necessary to provide any individualized assistance for the student.

Third, the major responsibility for delivering content is shifted from the regular teacher, who is the content expert, to a tutor, who is more than likely not a content expert, as it is almost impossible for any one tutor or special educator to be a content expert in all fields of study at the secondary level. Therefore, a situation could arise where the regular educator, who is able to teach content, does not do so, and the tutor, who is skilled at individualizing instruction, lacks the background in certain areas to put his or her skill to work. Under these circumstances the student loses, twice.

NONACADEMIC CURRICULUM

This section addresses the following nonacademic curriculum areas: career education, functional curriculum, and social/communication skill development. For some students, an academic curriculum at the secondary level is no longer sufficient, since an academic curriculum may not adequately prepare them for a successful transition to a post-secondary environment. In such cases, a career education or functional curriculum may be a viable alternative. This section will also consider another curriculum area, which is not academic in nature but that may be incorporated into existing curricula (i.e., social/communication skill development).

Career Education

Career education programs have been developed for many reasons. For instance, high schools were graduating students deficient in basic skills; schools were failing to keep pace with industrial and technological changes; minority, disadvantaged, and students with special needs were being neglected; and high school graduates were entering adult society without saleable vocational skills, career decision-making skills, or appropriate habits, attitudes, and values for making the transition (Mori, 1982). Since the 1970s, school-based career education models (e.g., Clayton, 1983; Mori, 1980), experience-based career education models (e.g., Bucknam & Brand, 1984), and competency-based career education models (e.g., Brolin & Carver, 1982; Brolin & Kokaska, 1974) have been developed.

Mesa Public Schools developed a school-based career education program for secondary students that included the following components: career and vocational development; career guidance and placement; community resource service for observations, speakers and interviews; staff development; and program evaluation (D'Alonzo, Marino, & Kauss, 1984). A program that combined the community and school resources was Project CAST (1981) which was developed in Maryland. This program was divided into four phases, one for each year of high school. In the first phase, students concentrated on developing their career awareness by learning about various types of occupations and by visiting job sites. In phase two, students explored specific careers, depending upon their own interests and abilities, and observed employees who worked in careers that students identified as interesting. In the third phase, students were provided with job experiences and developed their abilities to seek and maintain jobs. During the last phase of this program, students received on-the-job training/work study. The objectives of this last phase were to obtain employment in a self-selected occupation, to become trained in a self-selected occupation, to continue adjustment to the working world, and to further growth of independent living skills.

Most *career education* programs combine career awareness, career exploration, and career preparation. *Career awareness* activities provide students with information for specific job clusters as well as help students understand their own skills and interests as they are related to different adult roles (Kolstoe, 1976). Through *career exploration* activities, students are directed to examine more closely the alternatives that they may eventually select within occupational, recreational, or familiar areas related to career development. Students are encouraged to refine their skills, abilities, and interests through hands-on activities. For example, practical experiences may be provided so that students learn specific strategies for managing personal finances. These activities may include generating a personal budget, beginning and managing a checking account, and using newspaper want ads to compare prices of necessary items. It is at this level that students begin to identify, learn, and master a variety of living skills.

In the *career preparation* stage, students learn specific occupational and living skills through work experiences, vocational courses, or academic coursework. See Project CAST (1981) for specific objectives for career preparation.

Career preparation is the final level of career education in the public schools. Cegelka (1979) pointed out, however, that the tasks encompassed by these career education levels do not end for the individual upon leaving high school. The process of becoming aware of, exploring, and preparing for the multitude of tasks associated with living in society never ends.

Teaching Strategies.   Current law requires the participation of special educators, parents, and other education professionals in the identification, programming, and placement of handicapped students. The requirement for generating an Individualized Educational Program (IEP) for each handicapped student, together with the required provision of vocational guidance and education services, suggests that the inclusion of career education concepts and competencies in education for the handicapped might logically begin with the IEP development process. Some ways in which consultants can participate in the assessment, program writing, and program placement are discussed.

Assessment.   Special education professionals can contribute to the assessment process in two important ways. First, as potential IEP team members they can be advocates for assessments in the daily living, personal-social, and occupational preparation and guidance areas. For example, a special education teacher serving on an IEP team that is reviewing the referral of a 13-year-old with a tested IQ of 65 may request assessment information in the areas of manual dexterity and ability to work with others. Information on levels of performance in these areas would assist the team in developing a program to prepare the student for entrance into a vocational program.

The second contribution special educators can make in the area of assessment is to provide the IEP team with evaluative data on performance levels of handicapped students in career education areas. For example, suppose a special education teacher for the partially sighted is planning a unit on buying and preparing food at an awareness level of instruction. The teacher might collect data that indicate that a 15-year-old student in the class is ready to proceed to the orientation level of instruction. The teacher might consider changing the IEP program to reflect the new instructional need and recommend placement in a regular education homemaking class. With the assessment data from the teacher in hand, the placement team can make program placement decisions relative to the handicapped student's career needs.

Program writing. Consultants, as members of the IEP team, could help to formulate long-term goals and short-term objectives related to career education. They could also suggest the time required to meet the short-term objectives, given the current performance levels of the individual and the scope and sequence of instruction. Table 7.3 presents an example of the specification of long-term goals and short-term objectives using the Brolin and Kokaska (1979) curriculum.

Program placement. Placement of handicapped students depends on the program specified for them in the IEP process. It is not the availability of placement that dictates the nature of the program. Rather, placements

TABLE 7.3
Example of Long-Term Goals, Short-Term Objectives, and Time Estimates (expressed in months) in an IEP

Curriculum Areas Requiring Special Education and Related Services	Annual Goals	Short-term Objectives	Time Required
Daily Living	Buying and preparing food	1. Demonstrate appropriate eating skill	9-15 to 10-31
		2. Plan balanced meals	11-3 to 12-15
		3. Purchase food	
Occupational	Selecting and planning occupational choices	1. Identify major occupational interests	9-15 to 10-15
		2. Identify occupational aptitudes	10-16 to 12-1

must be determined and then designed to meet the needs of individual handicapped students. The consultant, with knowledge of the learning, skill, and interest characteristics of the handicapped student, can be a valuable resource for the IEP team in making a placement decision. The sharing of the characteristics with educators from regular academic and vocational classes will help the team determine whether a regular class would meet the program needs of a handicapped student. The following anecdote provides an example of the participation of the consultant in IEP placement decisions for a 14-year-old physically handicapped student.

ANECDOTE 7.2

TEAM CHAIRPERSON: We have considered Allen's current performance levels and have written annual goals and short-term objectives related to family finances. What placement alternatives can we recommend to meet these goals and objectives?

CONSULTANT: The assessment data indicate that Allen is capable of performing the math skills necessary to calculate taxes and manage a bank account. In addition, his social skill levels are appropriate for regular class placement.

BUSINESS TEACHER: I teach units in those areas in our ninth-grade business math sections. I think that Allen could do the math. However, I wonder about his ability to take notes in class and complete homework assignments given his physical limitations. The assessment report indicates difficulty in writing. Since my course requires homework and note taking, he may not be able to do all the assignments.

CONSULTANT: I've noted that Allen has had great success when he either uses a tape recorder for note taking and homework assignments or when a nonhandicapped peer assists him with note taking. Would either of these arrangements be acceptable to you?

BUSINESS TEACHER: Certainly.

PARENT: I'm in favor of Allen receiving instruction in banking and tax computation. I can take him to the bank to open an account and provide the tape recorder he'll need for class.

TEAM CHAIRPERSON: We are in agreement then that Allen could be placed in the ninth-grade business math class for instruction related to calculating taxes and managing a bank account. He may use a tape recorder or peer to assist in note taking and homework assignments.

In this anecdote the consultant suggested a placement alternative (a regular class in business math) based on the assessment data, knowledge of class curriculum, and the compensatory strategies known to be successful with Allen. The business teacher was concerned about the student's physical abilities but found the compensatory measures acceptable. The parent agreed to provide the needed recording equipment and a practical experience related to banking. This example points out another function the consultant can serve in IEP team meetings: The consultant can suggest ways in which regular educators can modify existing classes or assignments to accommodate a handicapped student.

Advantages and Disadvantages. A career education curriculum has the distinct advantage of preparing students for transition into the world of work. An experience-based career preparation program also has the advantage of providing students with the opportunity to obtain on-the-job experience while they are still under the sponsorship of the educational system. The curriculum is geared toward increasing skills that are likely to be needed in the students' working careers. Also, it provides the opportunity for the handicapped students to earn money at a time when their nonhandicapped peers are probably doing the same. It is difficult to assess the impact that earning money has on handicapped adolescents, but presumably it benefits their social position with their nonhandicapped, secondary-level peers.

The obvious disadvantages to an experience-based career preparation program relate to the type of jobs that are available to handicapped students. According to Alley and Deshler (1979), handicapped students are typically hired for menial jobs in the food and restaurant industry. They are, therefore, exposed to a limited repertoire of job possibilities, and the likelihood of promotion is also limited. The chance for students to find positions with better career potential is usually related to the personal initiative and community contacts of the work-study coordinator.

Functional Curriculum

According to Alley and Deshler (1979), the *functional curriculum* is designed to help students acquire independent-living skills. The functional curriculum assumes that the scope and sequence of the regular curriculum is inappropriate. A new curriculum is generated that attempts to provide students with the skills necessary to obtain a job, find a place to live, and function independently.

Bender and Valletutti (1982) present a functional curriculum guide for adolescents and young adults. The curriculum guide is designed from the perspective of the functional roles that an individual assumes when involved in any one or more of the following situations: (a) as a resident of a home,

(b) as a student in school, (c) as a member of a community, (d) as a consumer of goods and services, (e) as an employee, and (f) as a participant in leisure activities.

In designing a functional curriculum for an adolescent with learning problems, Bender and Valletutti (1982) recommend assuming a sociological perspective and first determining the environmental contexts within which the adolescent will function. Once the environmental contexts have been decided, one should determine the skills needed to function effectively in each of these environments, determine the skill deficits of the adolescent for each specific environment, and then develop an instructional plan that will remediate these skills deficits.

Teaching Strategies.   Consultants working with special educators using the functional curriculum model need a thorough understanding of skills the teachers are trying to develop. Consultants are encouraged to help teachers to use the strategies for functional curriculum development suggested by Bender and Valletutti (1982).

Ernie is a 16-year-old retarded student enrolled in a suburban high school. His academic skills have developed slowly but steadily throughout his elementary and junior high years, but his achievement has reached a plateau. Socially, Ernie is very immature. He has difficulty making and keeping friends, and his interactions with peers are tentative and awkward. His special education teacher used a functional curriculum model to try to teach essential vocabulary words (e.g., danger, poison, flammable), the bases of banking (using a checkbook and savings account), and how to complete necessary forms and applications (e.g., job and driver applications, apartment leases, and credit applications). The teacher requested help from the district's consultant because Ernie was having trouble learning these skills. Anecdote 7.3 describes a conversation the special education teacher had with the consultant about Ernie. tant about Ernie.

ANECDOTE 7.3

TEACHER *(expressing frustration):* I'm not making much headway with Ernie on his survival skills.

CONSULTANT: What skills do you consider survival skills?

TEACHER: Basically four skills — essential sight vocabulary, banking and finance, completing forms, and consumerism.

CONSULTANT: That's an ambitious plan. But since Ernie will be graduating soon, I can understand your reasoning. Tell me how you've been teaching finance and banking. Maybe we can start with these skills.

TEACHER: Well, I got sample checkbooks from the local bank. I use the checkbooks in class to teach the unit. Ernie has learned the location of his account number and how to write a check. Also, I taught him how to make deposits and withdrawals and how to balance his checkbook.

CONSULTANT: Is Ernie able to use calculators to do the math that's required?

TEACHER: No. Since his skills are so poor in basic addition and subtraction, I try to give him as much practice as I can. I have him check the balance using paper and pencil.

CONSULTANT (*recognizing that the teacher mixed the remedial model — teaching basic skills — with the functional model*): Does it take a long time for Ernie to balance his book using paper and pencil?

TEACHER: It sure does.

CONSULTANT: Maybe letting him use a small calculator would reduce the time it takes to do the addition and subtraction.

TEACHER: Maybe so. But how's he to learn the basic skills if he doesn't practice them?

CONSULTANT: Chances are if he hasn't mastered them by now it's unlikely that he's going to. Besides, calculators are so small these days he could carry one with him to use whenever he needed it.

TEACHER: I see your point.

CONSULTANT: Also, you might plan a field trip to the bank. Students, including Ernie, could set up an account and make an actual deposit. Before the field trip they could role play the behaviors that would be required in the bank.

TEACHER: Sounds like a good idea.

CONSULTANT: Also, if you can get the form the bank used to open an account, you could build a lesson around completing the form.

TEACHER: That's a great idea.

CONSULTANT: You might let the bank know before the visit that several of your students are planning to open accounts. With advance notice, they might be able to offer help when you arrive.

TEACHER: Sounds ideal. What's the first step?

(*The consultant spends the rest of the time explaining how to set up the lesson on completing the bank forms. Also, the consultant carefully describes how a role-playing-behavioral rehearsal situation could be structured so that each student, including Ernie, has the opportunity to practice and receive feedback on his or her performance.*)

The consultant has helped the teacher focus on developing skills needed for one environmental context and has made two notable suggestions to the teacher. First, the consultant recommended the hand-held calculator, because its use is consistent with the functional skills curriculum. At this point in Ernie's life, it is probably more practical for him to learn to use a calculator effectively than it is for him to struggle with math calculations.

Second, the consultant recommended role playing to give students the opportunity to practice the skills required in a new setting. Students can learn what to expect from the tellers prior to interacting with them. Finally, asking the students to complete the same forms in class and at the bank promotes generalization of skills (Cooper et al., 1987).

Advantages and Disadvantages.   One obvious advantage of the functional curriculum is that it facilitates the secondary handicapped student's transition into a post-secondary environment. The functional curriculum can directly address the development of skills necessary for successful functioning in environments the student will probably experience after high school. The belief that all handicapped individuals, regardless of the nature or degree of their disability, have the capacity to work and function as independently as possible in society underlies much of the current activity in secondary special education (Wehman, Kregel, & Barcus, 1985; Will, 1984).

According to Alley and Deshler (1979), there are two potential disadvantages to the functional curriculum. The survival skills, that allegedly should sustain the students for life, may fall victim to technological advances. What is thought essential today may be considered irrelevant tomorrow. Also, since the functional curriculum is taught almost exclusively in self-contained classrooms, there is little potential for interaction with regular education students.

Communication and Social Skills Development

There are many reasons for addressing *communication* and *social skills* development for adolescents, including the low social status of handicapped students and the relationship between social and communication skills. As indicated by Donahue and Bryan (1984), the relationship between communication skills and peer group membership is very strong during adolescence. The one activity essential to adolescent friendship is shared talk, yet a characteristic of unpopular students is talkativeness and difficulty understanding conversational rules. Low social status is frequently attributed to learning disabled adolescents (Schumaker, Hazel, Sherman, & Sheldon, 1982; Smith et al., 1982). Because of this low status, and because one cannot assume that learning disabled adolescents will inferentially learn appropriate social skills, there is a need to directly address social skill development. To ensure that social skills are mastered, teach these skills directly. Further, after careful examination of the nature of social skills, it is apparent that adequate communication, including listening and speaking, are essential components of appropriate social skills.

There are curricula designed to develop the social skills (e.g., Goldstein, Sprafkin, Gershaw, & Klein, 1980) as well as the communication skills (e.g., Wiig, 1982) of adolescents. It is suggested that the secondary consultant be familiar with these curricula when working with regular and special educators in developing the social and communication skills of adolescents. However, since it is often difficult for secondary educators to address all the components of an existing curriculum, they may be reluctant to adopt yet another content area to teach. Therefore, it is recommended that the secondary consultant attempt to help educators develop social and communication skills within the curriculum being implemented for each secondary student.

Teaching Strategies. The secondary consultant can help the secondary educator develop the social and communication skills of students when students are interacting with their peers. Or the consultant can help the secondary educator facilitate appropriate social behavior and communication skills when the adolescent is assuming the role of student in an instructional situation. In a study of teacher-student interaction in a junior high school special education classroom, Klein and Harris (1986) found that students who were considered of low ability by the teacher seemed to demonstrate little ability to use language as a tool, to initiate a topic, or to obtain information through questioning. This study suggests that the teacher's judgment of a student's ability may be influenced by the student's ability to use language to control the environment.

Tables 7.4 and 7.5 provide two excerpts from tape transcriptions. They demonstrate the difference in verbal interaction between a lower-ability black student and a higher-ability black student in the same classroom participating in the same language arts activity.

In the excerpt in Table 7.4, the class is reading about movies. The teacher is specifically addressing the low-ability student, and she is trying to help the student decode a sentence. The teacher asks the student several questions at one time. The student's response is a guess (i.e., "Children"?). The student does not articulate her confusion or formulate a specific question for the teacher that will address her needs. Though this is only an excerpt, it is representative of this student's lack of ability to use language to help her function successfully in the classroom.

By contrast, the excerpt found in Table 7.5 demonstrates the greater verbal repertoire of the high-ability handicapped black student in the same class. The class is still reading about movies. The target student (i.e., the high-ability student) uses several different types of verbal behavior in her effort to communicate with the teacher. She is able to initiate topics (e.g., "It say

TABLE 7.4
Language of Low Ability Student and the Teacher

Context: Reading About Movies

TEACHER: OK, L--, what does this say? We saw it right up here. What is it?

STUDENT: *Junior.*

TEACHER: Junior. Where do you see the word *junior*? That's not junior. What does that say?

STUDENT: *Children?*

TEACHER: Children. Children under blank may go free. What age must you be to go free?

STUDENT: *Five.*

TEACHER: Under five. Would you write that on the line?

TABLE 7.5
Language of High Ability Student and the Teacher

Context: Reading About Movies

TEACHER: Do you think you would like to see a picture of Jungle Cowboy?

OTHER STUDENT: No.

TEACHER: Huh? OK.

TARGET STUDENT: *It say producer.*

TEACHER: Awright, where's producer? Where's the word producer? Where's producer? That say producer there.

OTHER STUDENT: Directed

TEACHER: Directed OK. Awright, so they told us who's starring in the movie. Here they tell us who directed the movie. What do they mean by directed?

TARGET STUDENT: *Like.*

OTHER STUDENT: Telling what to do.

TARGET STUDENT: *Standing up.*

TEACHER: Huh?

TARGET STUDENT: *Standing up?*

TABLE 7.5   continued

TEACHER: OK and what, D———?

OTHER STUDENT: Telling what to do.

TEACHER: Awright, the people who tell them how to act and give them instruction. Huh?

TARGET STUDENT: *What's a producer?*

TEACHER: What does the word produce mean?

TARGET STUDENT: *Like you.*

TEACHER: When you pruh.

TARGET STUDENT: *Like you be saying something.*

TEACHER: When you produce something what did you do?

TARGET STUDENT: *Present it?*

OTHER STUDENT: *Get it down.*

TEACHER: No.

OTHER STUDENT: *Like you give them orders.*

TEACHER: No. If you were made. If you were, uh creating a product and they said this produced by S———A———, what did you do?

TARGET STUDENT: *I made it.*

TEACHER: Awright. You were the one that was in charge of the making of it, the production. OK?

---

producer") as well as use appropriate forms for questions ("What's a producer?"). Though this student is not representative of a highly verbal junior high school student, she was one of the more verbal students in the self-contained special education class and illustrates how a student can use language functionally. Anecdotally, it was also apparent from this study that when students used language appropriately, the teacher judged them to be of high ability. Thus, the teacher's perception may influence how he or she interacts with the student to produce a more productive communicative environment in the classroom.

Spekman and Roth (1982) indicate that students can be taught to speak more informatively, listen more carefully, and follow social norms such as turn-taking and maintaining conversational flow within classroom situations. In the example presented here, the teacher could attempt to understand the communicative intentions of the lower-ability student and model, for the student, an appropriate way to communicate his or her intentions. In addition, the teacher could attempt to pick up on nonverbal (i.e., gestural) cues from the student that suggest confusion and model for the student how to ask for assistance.

An example of another situation where the teacher attempted to increase the social skills of adolescents in an instructional setting is provided by a special education teacher who worked with mildly handicapped students in a special education class on a junior high school campus. In this example, academic and social skills objectives are combined. The social and academic goals for these students can be found in Table 7.6.

The teacher implemented a remedial curricula and wished to have two students work together on a common academic area. Dale was strong in addition and subtraction skills but rushed through assignments and often made careless mistakes. Dale tended to complain and give up when frustrated. However, Dale was friendly with the other special education students. Charles had strong addition skills but was just learning to regroup in subtraction. Charles was friendly with the teacher. He was not a complainer but would give up and sit quietly when the work was difficult. Charles did not play with the other students during break, preferring to spend time with the teacher. However, Charles was observed talking with Dale on occasion.

The teacher incorporated principles from the social skills curriculum of Goldstein et al. (1980). That is, first she worked with both students, modeling appropriate behavior for giving instructions, asking for help, following instructions, and so on. She also reinforced students for engaging in these behaviors with her and then with each other. Then the teacher withdrew from the group, and the two students worked together. The common project for both students was subtraction crossword puzzles. Both students received points on a daily behavior management system for being on-task (i.e., talking about math problems or writing down math work) and completing the

TABLE 7.6
Social and Academic Goals

Dale
Academic goal: to work regrouping subtraction with 80% accuracy
Social goals: to give instructions, to concentrate on a task, to help another student complete a task

Charles
Academic goal: to regroup subtraction problems, 3-digit by 3-digit; to pass a quiz on regrouping with 80% accuracy
Social goals: to concentrate on a task, to ask for help, to follow instructions, to work with another student

---

work with 80% accuracy. The teacher found this program to be effective in developing the social and communication skills of these two adolescents as well as fostering a friendship between the two boys.

Advantages and Disadvantages. The advantages for developing social and communication skills are obvious. Since consultants are encouraged to help teachers develop these skills within the implementation of the existing curriculum, there is no need to sacrifice development of any other skill to develop social and communication skills. The consultant is cautioned, however, to help teachers receive the necessary support and knowledge to implement these techniques in an effective fashion. For example, a teacher who is learning how to develop appropriate communication skills within a small group instructional situation may require any one or more of the following: assistance in teaching the rest of the class, feedback on the nature of the teacher-student interaction, coaching regarding use of communication techniques, and so on (Spekman & Roth, 1982.)

GENERIC INSTRUCTIONAL STRATEGIES

In this section, instructional strategies that can be used with individual students and groups of students are discussed. These strategies can be used by regular educators or special educators and are suitable for use with any content material.

Learning Strategies

The *learning strategies* approach is an intervention model for learning disabled adolescents developed by the University of Kansas Institute for Research in Learning Disabilities (KU-IRLD) (Schumaker et al., 1983). The approach was designed to address the following characteristics of adolescents who have learning problems: limited basic skills, deficiencies in study skills and strategies, and social skills deficits.

The learning strategies approach is designed to teach students how to learn and how to use these learning skills to perform academic tasks (Deshler et al., 1984). The model basically assumes that (a) knowledge is transitory; (b) current educational practice fails to teach students how to relate what they know to real-life problems; (c) learning strategies can be taught directly; and (d) these skills can be demonstrated in the regular classroom.

Four major components of the learning strategies approach are the curriculum component, the instructional methodology, the motivation system, and the evaluation system (Schumaker et al., 1983). Specific instructional procedures and materials have been developed. In an effort to standardize the approach and collect data regarding its effectiveness, it is suggested that teachers who wish to use a learning strategies approach receive training in its use. What follows is an example of the logic that drives the approach. For an in-depth understanding of the learning strategies procedure, the reader is referred to the work of Schumaker et al. (1983).

Learning Strategies Procedure.   The strategies in the model proceed through five steps: (a) pointing out to the student the ineffective strategy that is currently in use; (b) demonstrating the new strategy; (c) applying the strategy in controlled settings or situations; (d) tranferring the new strategy to the regular classroom; and (e) grouping for practice and reinforcement.

Pointing out the ineffective strategy.   Suppose, for example, that a college-bound, learning disabled student in the special education class was asked to identify three articles in popular magazines that were related to the topic of ecology and to write a brief synopsis of them. To start his assignment, the student began to thumb through magazines in the library. The special educator might intervene and point out that this method was time-consuming, laborious, and potentially ineffective. He or she could tell the student that only by chance would he find the articles he needed using this approach.

Demonstrating the new strategy.   The special education teacher could then show the LD student where to find the cumulative index for the magazine or journal and explain that the index lists all of the articles by subject and author for a given year. Next, the teacher might obtain an index, open it to the subject section, and check for the term ecology. The teacher would point out that ecology is a broad term that describes the relationship among many environmental factors. The student could be taught to use a thesaurus to find synonyms for the main term. Next, the student would be shown how to locate the articles he or she identified through the index. Once the student found the periodicals in the library, he or she could learn how to use a table of contents to locate the pages needed. Of course, if the school library had a computerized system, the student would be shown how to use the terminal.

Applying the strategy in controlled settings.   The special teacher, assisted by the consultant, should plan to have students practice their newly acquired skills in a controlled way. This means that the student should be given additional assignments, within a restricted range, so that the likelihood of success is increased. Returning to our previous example, the LD student could research articles but now the topic would be more specfic—say, air pollution—and he or she would be told to use only the 1987 index to *Time* magazine. Thus, potentially confusing variables (e.g., multiple indexes and years) are eliminated. The student has the opportunity for intensive practice on his or her own within a well-structured area.

Transferring the new strategy to the regular classroom. Students need to demonstrate skills learned in the special classroom in the regular setting. If LD students have received sufficient practice and reinforcement within the special class, they should now be ready to apply their knowledge to curriculum-related tasks in the regular class. Again, it is important for students to practice in the regular class because potentially more topics and more research will be expected of them with less time to complete the assignments. If the special and regular education teachers worked together on the way in which the tasks were presented, the student should be able to respond to the new tasks without much difficulty.

Grouping for practice and reinforcement. The regular teacher would be advised to establish groups for the purpose of practicing and reinforcing the newly acquired skill. Students could learn from one another how to expand their skills.

Advantages and Disadvantages. The main advantage of the learning strategies approach is that students are taught how to access and process information in ways they may use later in life. In addition, this approach can be used with any academic content and could help the student to learn mainstream coursework. However, there are potential disadvantages. Effective use of this intervention requires reading skills at a fourth-grade level. Further, to use the intervention as designed, the special educator or tutor must instruct the student in the use of the technique, and this instruction takes time.

Compensatory Techniques

Compensatory techniques are those strategies that help a person overcome or circumvent the lack of a specific skill. For example, to compensate for a poor sense of direction, one might do the following: (a) develop map reading skills; (b) always outline the route after referring to a map; (c) follow the outlined route; and (d) carry a map just in case one encounters a detour and needs to develop a new route.

Unlike the learning strategies approach, use of compensatory techniques as an instructional tool does not require extensive training. It does, however, require thoughtful planning, because often it is necessary to develop or modify materials.

Why would a teacher consider using compensatory techniques with handicapped adolescents? Well, in addition to poor reading and writing skills, handicapped adolescents often experience poor memory and poor organizational skills. Compensatory techniques can help the secondary student compensate for these deficits.

Basic Skills Techniques. To compensate for poor basic math skills, the student may be taught to use a hand-held calculator. Russell (1982) discusses how mildly mentally handicapped students can be taught to effectively use a calculator with a minimum amount of time, certainly less time than it would take to develop mastery of basic number facts with this group of students. By the time a handicapped student is in high school, time is a critical factor. There is a limited amount of time left for schooling. Therefore, the curriculum and instruction for the handicapped adolescent must be appropriate and efficiently and effectively delivered.

To compensate for poor reading skills, some educators have suggested using audiotaped materials (e.g., Deshler & Graham, 1980; Mosby, 1979; Wiseman, Hartwell, & Hannafin, 1980). One cannot assume, however, that learning handicapped adolescents will be able to acquire content better through verbatim audiotape recordings. The students may not have the listening skills to accomplish such a task. Therefore, the audiotaped materials consist of the tape itself as well as the text material. Deshler and Graham (1980) have developed an approach for the use of tapes to deliver content materials to handicapped youth. They suggest the following six steps: (a) decide what is to be taped; (b) use the taped materials to teach text usage and study skills; (c) use a marking system to aid students in the coordination of tape recordings with text materials; (d) apply principles of learning when using this instructional technique (e.g., reinforce behavior that you want to increase; incorporate the use of summaries, analogies, etc., to facilitate comprehension); (e) conduct a mechanically correct recording; and (f) evaluate the effectiveness of the taped materials. Keep in mind that the students may not have time to listen to verbatim recordings, so the teacher must carefully select what is to be recorded verbatim, what is to be paraphrased, and what is to be omitted. In addition, the text materials must indicate what is omitted, paraphrased, and so on, so as not to confuse the student.

Organizational Techniques. In addition to compensatory techniques, which may help the handicapped adolescent learn from grade-level reading material, it may also be useful for the consultant to use techniques that will help the handicapped youth to compensate for poor organizational skills. The use of a note-taking format, previously discussed, could help a student compensate for poor spatial organization. Many students also experience problems with time management. The consultant, therefore, may find it necessary to help the adolescent structure time.

When developing a time schedule for the handicapped adolescent, it is important to accommodate the handicapped student's need for simplicity and consistency. Without simplicity and consistency, the handicapped youth may not be able to understand or follow through with the plan. Alley and Deshler (1979) discuss a time reminder technique that attempts to impose some organization on the student's time without trying to assign a task for every minute of the day. Alley and Deshler (1979) suggest daily use of a 3 × 5 card on which critical daily activities are listed. In addition, a brief notation of long-term planning activities could also be placed on the card for future reference.

The consultant may also want to help the handicapped youth plan for longer periods of time. For example, as many academic assignments are given on a weekly basis, the consultant may find it necessary to help the handicapped youth develop a weekly schedule. In doing so, the consultant will have to work with the student in determining what tasks need to be accomplished in a week and estimate, with the student, the amount of time it will take to accomplish each task. Estimating the length of time for a task, that is new, is very difficult. But it is a necessary skill for the adolescent to develop. The consultant can help the student estimate the amount of time needed by reviewing with the student previous similar tasks and how long they took to accomplish as well as teacher estimates of the amount of time needed to complete the task. If the secondary student has realistic goals established for task completion and can experience the efficient completion of tasks, the student will experience the positive benefits of completing a task in a timely fashion (e.g., more time for other activities) and experience increased motivation for task completion.

Figure 7.4 provides a sample time-management procedure, which was developed by modifying a simple calendar called the "Uncalendar" (People Systems, 1977). Fred goes to school and works four hours a day. His school assignments reflect daily homework as well as a weekly assignment (i.e., book report). The management plan accommodates Fred's busy schedule by allotting a little time each day to work on daily homework assignments as well as the weekly assignment. In addition, the plan tries to accommodate Fred's interests (e.g., Friday night free and minimum homework over the weekend). The Comments section is provided to encourage Fred to note any problems and/or additional resources that he may need to complete an assignment. Then Fred is to incorporate an action plan into his schedule (e.g., obtaining Patty's help).

Effective Group Instruction

In addition to the use of learning strategies and/or compensatory techniques, regular education teachers can organize group lessons to meet the needs of all the students in their classes, including the student who is experiencing learning problems. The findings of the effective schools research in regular education (e.g., Anderson, Evertson, & Brophy, 1979; California State

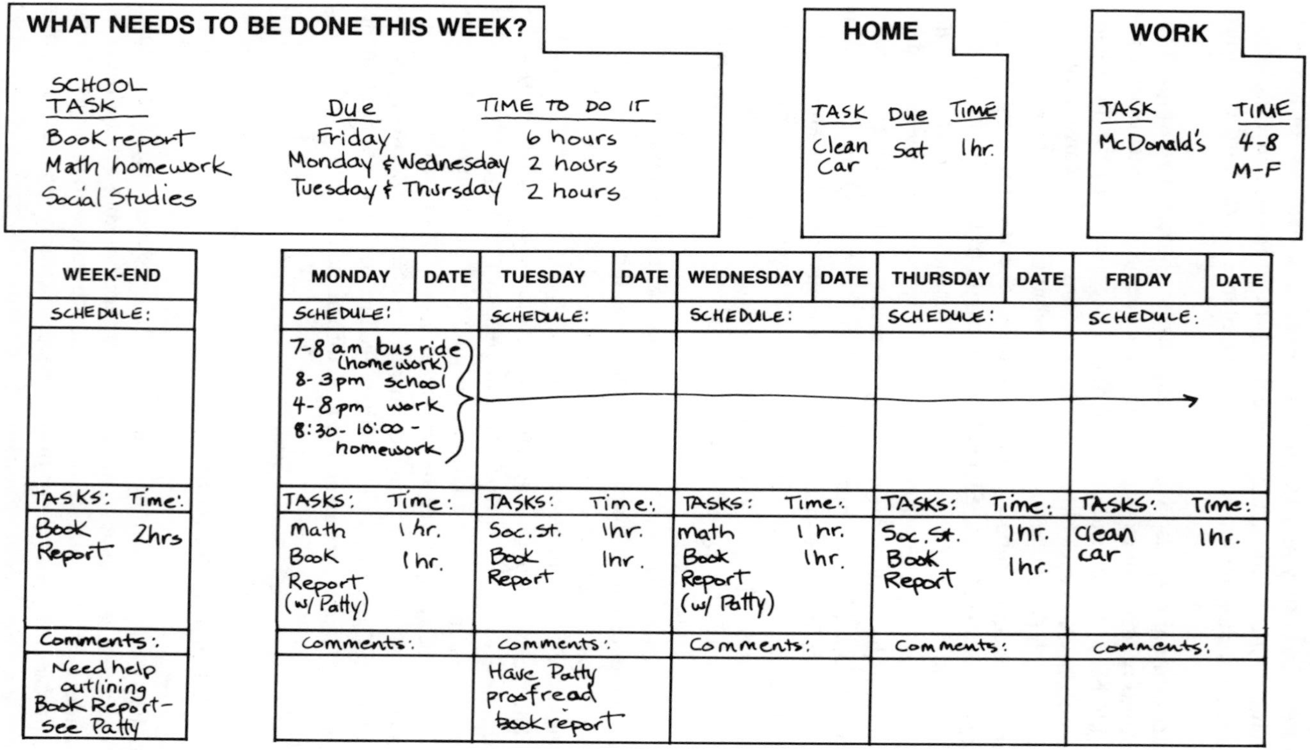

FIGURE 7.4. Sample time-management calendar. From "The Uncalendar" by People Systems, 1977. Adapted by permission.

Department of Education, 1977; Soar, 1973; Stallings & Kaskowitz, 1974) have identified several instructional factors that appear to contribute to successful school achievement. Among the important factors are a focus on academic learning, teacher-directed learning activities, high teacher expectations for academic progress, and student accountability and cooperation (Weil & Murphy, 1982).

In a review of the literature, Rosenshine (1983) indicates that teachers are most effective with students who are having problems learning when they apply the following strategies:

> structure the learning;
> proceed in small steps but at a brisk pace;
> give detailed and redundant instructions and explanations;
> provide many examples;
> ask a larger number of questions and provide overt, active practice;
> provide feedback and corrections, particularly in the initial stages of learning new material;
> have a student success rate of 80% or higher in initial learning;
> divide seatwork assignments into smaller assignments;
> provide for continued student practice so that students have a success rate of 90–100% and become rapid, confident, and firm. (p. 337)

Rosenshine (1983) noted that this approach is best used when the student has problems learning, the teacher is starting to teach new content, and/or the content being taught is hierarchical or difficult (e.g., mathematics, science facts, etc.).

Table 7.7 provides a lesson organization for secondary educators that may facilitate their ability to effectively teach mainstreamed handicapped youth. There are three essential components to this lesson organization: explain the context of the new lesson, teach the content and skills, and provide practice for students. When explaining the context, teachers should be sure to relate new information to previously learned content and provide a purpose for learning. Especially at the secondary level, without motivation to engage in an activity, handicapped students experience great difficulty starting as well as maintaining involvement in academic tasks. When teaching, the skills to be learned should be modeled. This is particularly helpful for the handicapped student who may not clearly comprehend a verbal description of a skill. If the skill is modeled and the student has the opportunity to perform the same skill with teacher feedback, the student is more likely to learn the new skill. Finally, students, especially students who have problems learning, need to practice the newly acquired skill so as to master it. This practice should be guided by the teacher so as to provide feedback necessary to assure that the student is mastering the skill correctly. In addition, to facilitate mastery, students should be provided with independent practice that will help them to overlearn the skill as well as practice generalizing the skill across different situations.

TABLE 7.7
Organization of Group Lessons

EXPLAIN	1. STRUCTURING PHASE Review Lesson Objective Activities Relation to: • old concepts/skills • culture Purpose
TEACH	2. DEMONSTRATION PHASE Teacher Models Student Rehearses Teacher Demonstrates: • similarity and difference • use • examples and nonexamples Student: • discriminates/explains • responds with more than 80% accuracy
PRACTICE	3. CONSOLIDATION PHASE Guided Practice • brisk pace • frequent questions • appropriate reinforcement • measured student performance • regular review Independent Practice • mastery • variety • active monitoring

CONCLUSION

Academic and nonacademic curriculum modifications and instructional strategies for secondary students have been presented. These curriculum modifications and instructional strategies were chosen because they represent the most commonly found educational approaches for handicapped youth. Readers are encouraged to apply these approaches to meet the individual needs of students. Practitioners should not assume that any one curriculum modification or instructional strategy will meet the needs of all students. In fact, educational consultants may want to seriously consider drawing from any one or more of these approaches in developing appropriate and effective programs for secondary students. Consultants are encouraged to use a decision-making strategy that will help them recognize when approaches can be combined and the extent to which programs are successful.

SUMMARY OF KEY POINTS

Educational Consultation at the Secondary Level

1. In developing a framework for educational consultation at the secondary level, one should consider the context of the environment.

2. The individuals involved in the life of the secondary student include the student, the secondary educators, the parents, and community members.

3. The environmental context for the secondary student includes the regular education high school program; the community program, which includes activities such as work and leisure; the home environment; and the individualized educational program for the handicapped student, which attempts to address all aspects of the youth's environment so as to facilitate generalization of skills.

Curriculum

4. Among the academic curriculum modifications that secondary educators can consider are the remedial and tutorial models.

5. The remedial approach focuses on the remediation of basic skills (i.e., reading, writing, and arithmetic).

6. The tutorial approach provides assistance to the student in meeting the needs of the regular education curriculum by specifying and developing study skills.

7. Since the secondary student will be in school for only a few more years, the need to also consider nonacademic curriculum modifications is immediate. The nonacademic curriculum modifications discussed are career education, functional curriculum, and communication/social skills development.

8. Career education for the secondary student involves career identification and preparation.

9. Consultants can assist in meeting the objectives of a career education curriculum by providing input into the vocational assessment of students, the development of the vocational program for students, and the coordination among regular, special, and vocational educators in determining appropriate placement for students.

10. The functional curriculum focuses on developing basic skills needed to function within contexts that the student will experience (e.g., the basic skills needed to be an employee, a member of a community, a contributing resident at home, or an enjoyable leisure activity partner).

11. The development of communication skills and social skills is essential for the secondary student, since it is at this time in the student's life that group membership is most important.

12. Consultants should help educators develop the communication and social skills of secondary students by identifying communication and social skills objectives that can be met within the context of the existing curriculum.

Instructional Strategies

13. Individual and group instructional strategies were presented. Two individual instructional strategies were considered: the learning strategies approach and compensatory techniques.

14. The learning strategies approach is designed to teach students how to learn. After the strategies have been learned, they can be applied to any content area.

15. Compensatory techniques are strategies that help an individual compensate for a specific skill deficit. Examples of techniques to compensate for poor basic academic skills include the use of a calculator and the use of audiotaped materials. Techniques to compensate for poor organizational skills include note-taking formats and time-management calendars.

16. Consultants are encouraged to help secondary educators construct group lessons that best meet the needs of students who have problems learning. Each group lesson should include activities designed to explain the context of the lesson, teach skills, and provide experiences for students to practice skills.

QUESTIONS

1. Describe the remedial, tutorial, and functional curricula. Within your description include: the major characteristics of each curriculum, the potential strengths and weaknesses of each curriculum, the similarities and differences between the three curricula, and an applied example of the appropriate use of each curriculum.

2. Describe compensatory and learning strategies instructional techniques. Within your description, include major characteristics and potential strengths and weaknesses.

3. Describe a program for a secondary handicapped student. Within your description, identify the curriculum and instructional strategies to implement the curriculum. Specify exactly how you would incorporate a generality component into this program. Consider a systems perspective in program development (i.e., consider the school, home, and job/community in describing your program).

DISCUSSION POINTS AND EXERCISES

1. You are faced with helping a secondary educator develop skills for students in one of the following areas. The secondary educator neither wants nor has the time to teach this skill area as a separate curriculum. Match one of the skill areas with one of the curricula. Demonstrate the integration of the selected skill area within the selected curriculum. Be sure to clearly define the curriculum and skill area goals.

Skill Areas	*Curricula*
Communication	Remedial
Social	Tutorial
	Functional

2. Visit a junior or senior high school to determine the curricula and instructional strategies that are used to accommodate handicapped students. Discuss with the principal, special educators, and regular teachers their perceptions of the efficacy of the approaches in use.

3. Attend an IEP meeting for a handicapped junior or senior high school student. Based on the student's current levels of achievement and future potential, discuss with team members the most appropriate curriculum and instructional strategies to use with the student.

4. Conduct an interview with an upper-division, mainstreamed handicapped student. Determine from the student the type of program he or she is receiving and obtain the student's evaluation of the educational approach the school has used.

8

Assessment Strategies for Educational Consultants

Consultants are frequently called upon to assess a variety of individuals and situations. Assessments are usually conducted for one of two purposes: to assist with the identification of a student problem or to evaluate an ongoing program or intervention.

This chapter discusses several assessment strategies an educational consultant could use to help teachers develop and implement effective instructional programs. Descriptive as well as measurement techniques are presented. Throughout the chapter appropriate uses for each of the various techniques will be provided.

OBJECTIVES

After reading this chapter, the reader should be able to:

1. describe the general purposes for assessment.

2. distinguish between formative and summative evaluation.

3. identify at least three considerations when planning and implementing program evaluation activities.

4. describe the psychometric and ethnographic traditions of assessment and observation.

5. identify and describe three techniques that can be used to obtain descriptive and explanatory information regarding student and teacher behavior.

6. identify and describe five techniques that can be used to measure specific behavior.

KEY TERMS

Identification	Sociogram
Survey level	Checklist
Specific level	Rating scale
Evaluation	Interaction analysis
Formative evaluation	Flanders Interaction Analysis
Qualitative data	Applied behavior analysis
Quantitative data	Permanent product measures
Summative evaluation	Frequency
Ethnographic approach	Percentage
Multimodal data	Rate
Psychometric approach	Interval recording
Field observation	Time sampling
Narrative recording	Duration recording
Interview	Event recording
Ethnographic interview	Reliability check
Stimulated recall	Brophy-Good Dyadic Interaction System
Ecological assessment	
Sociometric assessment	

PURPOSES OF ASSESSMENT

Traditionally, special educators, resource specialists, and/or educational consultants have been responsible for the diagnosis and assessment of students referred for special education services. This chapter, however, will not focus on using assessment tools for diagnosis and direct instruction. Other authors provide an in-depth treatment of this topic (e.g., Galagan, 1985; Gickling & Thompson, 1985; McLoughlin & Lewis, 1981, 1987; Salvia & Ysseldyke, 1985). Instead, this chapter focuses on the assessment strategies an educational consultant could use to help teachers develop and implement effective instructional programs.

Within an educational setting, the consultant will have occasion to assess a variety of individuals and situations. For example, if a student is experiencing difficulty in a particular educational placement, the consultant might assess the student's behavior to help determine the nature of the problem and, thereby, play a role in solving it.

On the other hand, the consultant may be required to assess groups rather than individuals. For example, the school administration may be interested in the effect of placement of mainstreamed handicapped students. The consultant may be asked to assess the effect upon students as well as teachers. In addition to assessing individuals and groups, the consultant may be asked to focus on programs. The consultant may have to evaluate an inservice teacher program, a specific educational intervention, and/or the effectiveness of the educational consultation program implemented in the school. We shall consider two levels of assessment: identification and evaluation.

Identification

Two levels of *identification* can be defined: survey and specific. At the *survey level*, the consultant attempts to identify the problem. The focus can be an individual, a classroom, or the whole school. Sometimes the referral a consultant receives about a problem situation is vaguely worded, for example, "Sally misbehaves." Here it is necessary to observe the situation before the consultant can specify the exact nature of the misbehavior. Only after the problem has been accurately identified can it be assessed and procedures begun to remedy the situation. To cite another example, a teacher may complain that students in the classroom are always fighting. The teacher feels frustrated when teaching them. The consultant, in this case, would need to identify the factors that contribute to the fighting. Through observation, the consultant may discover that a few students instigate most of the fights and that the problem is not as widespread as the teacher believes. It is also possible that some ingredient that should be present in a successful classroom situation is missing. The consultant, after observing the classroom of our frustrated teacher and talking with the teacher about events observed, may find that the teacher attends to the few students who misbehave far more frequently than the teacher attends to the appropriate behavior of the rest of the class.

It is at the *specific level* that the consultant tries to assess the factors contributing to the problem. A necessary consequence of this assessment is the development of a program designed to remedy the situation. Today the strengths and weaknesses of handicapped students are routinely assessed to develop appropriate individual educational programs for them. If a handicapped student shows maladjusted behavior in class, the consultant may observe the student to determine the nature and degree of inappropriate behavior. For example, a handicapped secondary student may be described by the algebra teacher as having a "poor attitude." During observation the consultant may note that the teacher provides few initiations to the student, waits only a short period of time for oral responses, and does not use prompting procedures effectively.

The consultant might then observe the frequency of both teacher and student behaviors in the algebra class. After obtaining the results, a program could be developed and implemented to improve the student's attitude. Subsequent observation of both student and teacher would reveal whether the attitude had indeed been changed and whether there was any change in the teacher's reaction to the student. Thus, the systematic use of an observation technique could help a consultant assess the success of an intervention program.

Evaluation

In addition to specifying and assessing problems, the consultant may also be asked to evaluate students and programs in the school. Educators are demanding the evaluation of educational intervention programs as well as materials (Bell, 1985; Deshler, Schumaker, Lenz, & Ellis, 1984).

Evaluation provides the means to determine effectiveness of a given course of action. Program evaluation can provide valuable information for decision making (Angrist, 1975). Traditionally, program evaluation has relied on the use of standardized measures of student achievement, such as test scores. Usually, a pretest of either the children or the teachers is made, the innovative program is implemented, and a posttest is administered at the conclusion. However, there has been a growing dissatisfaction among educators with this approach. Perhaps one of the most vocal protests was made by parents, teachers, and evaluation researchers during the First Annual Conference on Educational Evaluation and Public Policy (North Dakota Study Group on Evaluation, 1977). An opinion frequently expressed at this conference was that the trend in evaluative practices tends to discount educational outcomes that are not easily quantified through standardized testing. A plea was made for the use of evaluation measures that are sensitive to the goals of each program. Therefore, a need for a wide variety of evaluation methods to match the wide variety of program goals is apparent.

Many programs attempt to affect the process of teaching (interaction between teachers and students) and not just the products (test scores). Therefore, the assessment of process variables becomes as important as the assessment of product variables. Assessment techniques can be employed to measure a host of process variables, that, in turn, may lead to a more refined picture of the teaching act. Evaluation, therefore, can be conceptualized as part of an ongoing feedback loop in which program outcomes are judged against both process and product program goals (Angrist, 1975).

Formative Evaluation. *Formative evaluation* is conducted during the actual implementation of the program (the intervention mutually agreed upon by the teacher and the consultant). In formative evaluation the consultant determines whether the plan is being implemented as intended and the effectiveness of the plan for changing behavior. Formative evaluation allows for "midcourse correction." If the plan is implemented as intended, yet no functional effect on the targeted behavior is noted, another strategy can be initiated immediately.

Three general arguments have been advanced to support the formative evaluation: (a) formative evaluations are necessary to better understand and avoid the pitfalls of previous outcome evaluations; (b) traditional outcome evaluations (i.e., experimental and quasi-experimental designs involving groups of students) require large scale interventions to show statistically significant effects; and (c) formative evaluation approaches yield more useful information for decision making (Gersten & Hauser, 1984).

Summative Evaluation. *Summative evaluation* is conducted at the end of the intervention. The question the consultant seeks to answer then is, "Did the plan have a functional effect?" If the teacher's (or students') behavior changed a significant amount in the desired direction and adequate controls were used to eliminate competing explanations for the change, then the consultant can be reasonably confident that the plan accounted for the change.

Combined Approach. Gersten and Hauser (1984) contend that evaluations of special education programs should produce information useful for program improvement. Measurements should be used that are sensitive to the process as well as program outcomes. These authors discuss the use of behavioral observations and teacher ratings as viable outcome measures. They argue that two critical areas need to be assessed to improve evaluation results: program implementation and measurement of outcome. Assessing program implementation is important for two reasons: (a) It provides information on the extent to which the program was implemented as intended; and (b) the data can be used to establish the relationship between the program and its intended outcome, that is, how much or what quality of the intervention is associated with what level of outcome.

This combination of formative and summative evaluation can be used for groups and individuals. For example, the IEP process demands a yearly or summative evaluation. However, short-term objectives for each annual goal and methods for evaluating those objectives are also written into an IEP. If during implementation it is found that these short-term objectives are not being met, steps can be taken to modify the educational program. The appropriateness of the instructional methodology or the assessment instrument itself may be examined. Rather than waiting a year to determine whether the IEP has been successful for the student, a formative evaluation of short-

term objectives can indicate program success (or failure) and suggest altera-
tions in the IEP that could increase the probability of overall success.

Considerations for Planning Program Evaluation Activities.   There are many
issues to consider when conducting program evaluations, including: influence
of professional and personal viewpoints in deciding what is of value in a program (Caro, 1971); the match of evaluator with program clients and
implementers (North Dakota Study Group on Evaluation, 1977); and the
effect of evaluation at both the individual and program levels (Angrist, 1975).
However, the concern here is with methodological issues. Several program
evaluation models have been developed over the years (e.g., DEM —
Discrepancy Evaluation Model, Yavorsky, 1978; GAS — *Goal Attainment
Scaling*, Maher, 1983). However, even when using an evaluation model, one
must determine program evaluation activities. The following suggestions for
planning and conducting program evaluation activities are offered to the educational consultant:

1. Clearly identify program goals (Knowlton, 1983; Maher, 1983).

2. Clearly identify desired outcomes of the program (Knowlton, 1983) as
   well as the process of program implementation.

3. Specify measurable objectives that will reflect desired program outcomes
   as well as the process of program implementation.

4. Evaluate the usefulness of program evaluation activities, that is, the extent
   to which the efforts serve the program development and improvement
   needs of users (Maher & Bennett, 1984).

5. Assure the propriety of valuation activities, that is, the legal and ethical
   considerations (Maher & Bennett, 1984).

6. Assure the accuracy of program evaluation data collection activities, that
   is, assure that activities are technically defensible (Maher & Bennett,
   1984).

7. Identify the resources available within or outside the institution to conduct program evaluation (Knowlton, 1983).

8. Include, as a source of evaluative information, consumers of the program.

The rest of this chapter is devoted to a description of techniques that
can be used alone or in combination to generate information useful for identification and evaluation activities.

ASSESSMENT TECHNIQUES

As previously indicated, the techniques discussed in this chapter are those that the consultant may find useful in helping teachers and administrators implement effective programs for students. We have selected, for discussion, techniques that will help the consultant describe and understand situations as well as techniques designed to measure specific types of behaviors.

There is much controversy in the field of education regarding the use of qualitative and quantitative information (e.g., Howe, 1985). Simply, one could distinguish between the two by defining *qualitative data* as narrative recordings designed to describe and understand a given situation. In contrast, *quantitative data* are numerical and are designed to measure the occurrence of specific behaviors. Educators disagree as to whether these two approaches to obtaining information should be distinct or should be combined (Reichardt & Cook, 1979; Smith, 1983a; Smith, 1983b). We take the position that both approaches provide useful information to the consultant, depending upon the purpose of assessing a situation. In our opinion, the techniques discussed represent not only the traditional methods for assessing situations but the emerging methods as well. Further, these approaches can be used to observe process variables (e.g., teacher-student interactions) as well as product variables (e.g., achievement scores). In discussing assessment techniques useful for program implementation, we distinguish between two major traditions, ethnography and psychometry (Table 8.1).

The *ethnographic approach*, which is based in a social-anthropological tradition, is designed to provide the data collector with a means to understand and describe a given situation rather than merely quantifying it. The data collector attempts to analyze the context in which behavior occurs. Two aspects characterize ethnographic approaches. First, data are collected on-site and always include observational data (e.g., field notes). This distinguishes an ethnographic approach from surveys and interviews (Smith, 1979). Second, to lend objectivity to the information collected, a multimodal format of data collection is generally used (Wilson, 1977). *Multimodal data* means that more than one source of data (e.g., observing the teacher as well as students, parents, etc.) and more than one type of data (e.g., observations plus interviews) are used. As Florio (1981) pointed out, the ethnographer must be able to report more than just a travelogue. The ethnographer provides a description of the focus of observation and obtains a sufficient amount of data to understand the meaning of the observed behavior. Therefore, obtaining data from several sources through the multimodal nature of educational ethnography provides meaning as well as lends objectivity to the data collection effort. Examples of ethnographic approaches can be found in the discussion of field observation, interview, and stimulated recall.

TABLE 8.1

A Comparison of the Characteristics, Purposes, and Techniques of Ethnography and Psychometry

ETHNOGRAPHY	PSYCHOMETRY
Characteristics Focus open-ended, not pre-specified behaviors, though will focus upon individual group, program, institution. Data multimodal	*Characteristics* Focus on specified, exhibited behaviors, objectivity achieved through separation of observer and observed Assessment tabulation and/or computation Focus on individual and/or group behavior
Purpose Identification/understanding as well as behavioral description	*Purpose* Reduce behavior to smaller scale units of measurement
Sample Techniques Field Observation Interview Stimulated Recall	*Sample Techniques* Ecological Assessment Sociometric Assessment Checklists and Rating Scales Interaction Analysis Applied Behavior Analysis

The *psychometric approach*, obtaining numerical or quantitative data suitable for statistical or graphical analysis, has been the dominant system used in this country (Hamilton & Delamont, 1974). According to Hamilton and Delamont, this tradition has the advantages of simplicity and reliability and is flexible enough that it can be used in large scale studies. It has, however, several distinct disadvantages. First, the context in which the data are collected is sometimes ignored. Second, data are usually gathered over short periods of time (e.g., minutes or hours vs. days). Third, predetermined behaviors may preclude the examination of secondary effects that originally may have been unforeseen. Finally, focusing on preestablished behaviors often needlessly binds the observer to a specific theoretical position.

The psychometric approach is represented in the chapter by the following techniques: ecological assessment, sociometric assessment, checklists and rating scales, Brophy-Good Dyadic Interaction System, Flanders Interaction Analysis, and Applied behavior analysis.

The ethnographic approach attempts to minimize some of the disadvantages of psychometric measurement. With an ethnographic approach, the context of the behaviors of interest is documented and used to help understand behaviors (Wilson, 1977). Second, data are gathered over a sufficiently long period of time to allow behavior patterns to emerge (Gutmann, 1969; Harrington, 1973; Yinger, 1977). Third, the ability to extend data collection activities beyond prespecified behaviors promotes the identification and examination of secondary effects.

ETHNOGRAPHIC APPROACHES

The three approaches discussed in this section (i.e., field observation, interview, and stimulated recall) are used to describe and understand the behavior of individuals within given a situation. These techniques rely upon the use of qualitative information, and can be used best when a thorough description of a situation is necessary before measurement takes place.

Field Observation

Field observation has also been referred to by educators as educational ethnography, participant observation, qualitative observation, field study, and case study (Smith, 1979; Smith & Geoffrey, 1968; Stake, 1978). It is useful when the consultant wants to understand the context in which specific behaviors are being measured, wants to define problems or behaviors to be measured, or needs additional information before proceeding with specific assessment activities. Field observation may involve a considerable investment of time and energy by the consultant. Therefore, it is used most efficiently when important judgments or decisions need to be made or nebulous problems defined.

The field study is based on the assumption that human behavior is significantly influenced by the settings in which it occurs (Wilson, 1977). Its purpose is to provide an on-site, holistic study of a group, program, or individual that furnishes a rich description of the situation. This description can be used to generate further observation and measurement of relevant specific behaviors.

Essential Elements. There are three essential elements of the field observation. First, the focus of observation must be identified (Stake, 1978). The focus could be a person, an institution, or a program. The purpose is not to measure prespecified behaviors but rather to identify behaviors that may need to be measured. What is happening and deemed important with respect to the person, institution, or program determines what is measured.

Second, it is essential that the consultant conduct observations on-site (i.e., at the school). As the purpose of the field observation is to identify behaviors in need of further definition or assessment, the consultant draws upon observations to determine any additional information that needs to be collected to understand the situation under study.

Finally, the data are based upon a narrative description, but the approach is constructed to allow and actually foster multimodal data collection. That is, the consultant may begin with a narrative description of what is happening in a given situation for a period of time, similar to an anecdotal record. Observations are usually conducted over a long enough period of time (hours and weeks as opposed to minutes and days) to ascertain patterns of behavior. The descriptive narrative then provides the basis for other means of data collection. *Narrative recording* is used to generate questions and to help the consultant learn what additional data will be necessary to answer questions. Since multimodal data come from many sources, they provide the consultant with a wider data base and lend objectivity to this method.

Procedure.   Wilson (1977) describes the procedure generally used in field observation. First, the consultant, acting as observer, must establish a role within a particular situation. For example, if the consultant intends to study an elementary, self-contained, special education classroom for learning disabled students, the consultant would first establish a role in the classroom as an unobtrusive observer. An educational consultant can become an accepted part of the classroom environment in many ways. For example, the consultant could model the behavior of other adults in the classroom (e.g., aides or parent volunteers), who are there to assist the teacher and students. The consultant needs to effectively use verbal and nonverbal communication skills to enter and gain acceptance into the classroom. Otherwise, the observations the consultant makes of the classroom environment could reflect the participants' reactions to the consultant and not the existing educational environment. The reader is encouraged to review the work of experts regarding entry into field study situations (e.g., Dobbert, 1982; Erickson, 1973; Spradley, 1980; and Spindler, 1970). Consultants are urged to carefully consider appropriate entry and acceptance into an educational environment when conducting any of the many varied activities they are called upon to perform.

Second, the data must be collected. Since the data are multimodal, the consultant may attempt to describe the physical setting; describe how that setting changes with modification in activity or personnel; and describe both the form and content of verbal as well as nonverbal interactions between participants. The various modes of data collection evolve from the basic narrative in the field notes. The consultant develops questions based on these notes and, in the process, develops additional sources of data to answer these questions. For example, the consultant might record activities that the classroom aide performs. After reflecting on the descriptions of the activities, the consultant may question whether the teacher uses the aide primarily for instructional or clerical assistance. The consultant may then decide to engage the teacher in a simulated activity whereby the teacher is asked to plan for the same class at the same point in time during the year, but without the aide's assistance. Or the consultant may decide to interview the teacher about the aide's duties in the classroom. Either activity would provide an additional data source to the field notes about the role of the aide in the room.

Third, a representative sampling of information is made to achieve objectivity. It is established by using long-term and multimodal data collection and interpreting the data in terms of the context in which they were gathered. The observer must be sure to conduct field observations in all relevant situations and over a sufficient period of time to detect behavioral patterns. For example, in a field observation of a class of elementary learning disabled students, the physical setting of the classroom, playground, lunchroom, and gym as well as various aspects of the teacher-student and student-student interaction, the amount of time spent on academic tasks, and the nature of the educational program should be observed.

Boehm and Weinberg (1977) suggest conducting observations about the physical features, objects, people, and activities for any given situation as a means of obtaining information about the key components of a setting. Such an initial observation could be used by the consultant for many different purposes (e.g., to determine specific activities to be observed at later dates, to generate questions for the teacher regarding material and equipment use in the room, and/or to provide preliminary information about the educational environments for a specific student who had been referred due to a behavior problem).

Fourth, the data are analyzed. Data analysis involves a logical comparison of information but can reflect a variety of approaches (Miles & Huberman, 1984). Smith (1979) describes himself when analyzing the field observation data as being engaged in two processes: (a) comparing and contrasting information and (b) looking for antecedents and consequences. He actively searches for overall patterns. For Smith (1979), the final analysis of the field observation involves understanding the particular situation in comparison to his general knowledge of all situations of this type.

Example of Field Observation.   The field note excerpt found in Table 8.2 was taken from observations conducted of a junior high school resource teacher (Harris, 1981). As this was a unique program in the school (i.e., two special educators working together in one resource program with one aide), the consultant was interested in knowing how services were provided to handicapped students in this program.

TABLE 8.2
Example of a Field Observation

Situation: Third period, 10:00 a.m.

Six students around table with teacher. Tony and Nate (students) each at separate tables. (COMMENT: How are schedules arranged for students?)

TEACHER: (*Passes out paper*): "Are we ready to begin?"

SUE (*student*): "Won't be ready until the end of the period."

TEACHER: (*Writes math problem on board*): "I'm going to count this as a quiz, OK? For a grade, OK?

AIDE: Boy reading out loud to aide at back table Station 3. This is one of Sharon's (another teacher) students. Prior to this there was some discussion between two teachers and aide about what aide should do. Sharon made a comment about having plenty for the aide to do, starting with the bulletin board, the one that had been decorated by one of the students, Tom. (COMMENT: Does not seem that aide is given much instructional responsibility.) Students finish papers independently. As students state that they're finished, teacher takes their papers and grades them.

TEACHER: "Careless mistake here, Marvin—multiply."

MARVIN (*student*): "Don't mark it wrong."

TEACHER: "2 times 8 is not 10."

JIMMY (*student*): "Don't mark it wrong, please!" (*whining*) (COMMENT: Explore basis and importance of grades.)

TEACHER: "Fair is fair. I'll give you another chance tomorrow."

TEACHER: "Good job, people. Very good. Tony, one or two careless errors. Don't mess up tomorrow." (COMMENT: What happens tomorrow? Planning for this lesson—does it represent a modification of plan? Look at yesterday's assignment.)

This excerpt demonstrates the process of field observation (i.e., describing what is observed and noting questions and additional information that must be explored to understand the situation under study). In the field note excerpt in Table 8.2, the consultant was observing one of the resource teachers during math period. The consultant described what was said and recorded questions to ask the teacher at a later date (e.g., Comment: How are schedules arranged for students?; Comment: Explore basis and importance of grades; Comment: What happens tomorrow: Planning for this lesson — does it represent a modification of plan?) as well as impressions to be confirmed or negated by additional observation (e.g., Comment: Does not seem that aide is given much instructional responsibility).

Consultants should be aware that ethnographic techniques such as field observation can be used successfully to study problems in special education, particularly those in which an understanding of a situation is needed. If, for example, school district personnel believe that the mainstreaming program in a given school district is not working based on measures of number of students mainstreamed and the grades of those students mainstreamed, there is still a need to identify why the program is not working. One cannot develop an intervention or even measure the problem behavior if that behavior is not clearly defined. It may be possible to define the variables affecting the mainstreaming program by use of an ethnographic approach. Once variables have been identified and defined, then measurement of their effect can occur.

Interview

An *interview* allows an individual, usually the participant in a given situation, to express his or her perceptions. An interview is often used in field study to obtain a deeper understanding of the situation. McCallon and McCray (1975) included the following among the most common uses of interviews: to serve as a check on the reliability of information obtained through other techniques; to obtain information from individuals who represent a group under study; to obtain information from individuals considered authorities in their field; and to understand a problem and its underlying causes.

To understand a given situation, it is believed that an unstructured interview is most appropriate. An unstructured interview sets the occasion for a conversational approach. It permits a discussion of those aspects believed to be most important by the interviewee. In contrast, a structured approach requires "formal" questions, which might provide a measure of a given situation but not necessarily an in-depth description of that situation. A structured interview should be used to provide relevant information once there is a thorough knowledge of the problem or situation under study (McCallon & McCray, 1975). A structured approach for the measurement of participants' perceptions is described in the section on rating scales later in this chapter.

A form of unstructured interview is the *ethnographic interview*. The educational consultant may want to engage in an ethnographic interview as an aid in understanding the social system of a given school. For the educational consultant, ethnographic interview would be most useful when trying to work within a school environment that is new. By using ethnographic interview techniques and effective communication skills, the educational consultant can obtain a greater understanding of the perceptions of the people who function within the school and, therefore, a greater understanding of the school as a social system. Such an understanding is essential if the educational consultant wishes to help produce change within the school.

Spradley (1979) describes the ethnographic interview as a series of friendly conversations. The interviewer slowly introduces new elements to obtain further information from interviewees. It is suggested that this process be slow and friendly so as to establish and maintain rapport. According to Spradley (1979), there are three important elements: explicit purpose, explanations, and questions.

Explicit Purpose.   When the interviewer and the interviewee meet to conduct an ethnographic interview, the situation is informal and conversational. However, if the interviewer wants to know the interviewee's perceptions about a given topic, it is the responsibility of the interviewer to introduce the topic. For example, without sounding authoritarian, the consultant may ask about the grading system at the school. The consultant would engage the teacher in conversation about the grading system and also be responsible for keeping the conversation focused upon the grading system of the school.

Explanations.   In an ethnographic interview, the interviewee is essentially informing the interviewer about the culture or social system in question. The interviewer, then, must help the interviewee with this process. Explanations as to why one is engaged in this conversation help. For example, the consultant may want to make general statements concerning the reason for engaging the teacher in conversation (e.g., "I'm new in this school, and I really want to know how things operate"). Or the consultant may want to understand the terminology the teachers use related to grading or other activities. In addition, to clarify understanding of the topic being discussed, the consultant may ask the teacher to show examples of grade cards and how they are completed.

Questions.   The type of questions the consultant asks helps to establish an environment for communication. Spradley (1979) discusses three main types of ethnographic questions: descriptive, structural, and contrast. Descriptive questions help the interviewer to obtain the interviewee's perspective on the situation as well as identify terminology the interviewee uses in discussing the topic. An example of a descriptive question might be, "Could you tell me what you do when grading?" Structural questions show how the interviewee organizes the topic under discussion. For example, the consultant may ask, "What are the steps involved in completing a grade for a student?" Sometimes, structural questions are repeated to facilitate understanding the situation (e.g., "Can you think of any other things to do to get the grade card completed?"). Contrast questions help the interviewer to understand the terminology used in the discussion. For example, the consultant may ask, "What is the difference between an S and an $S+$?"

There are other situations when the consultant may want to conduct an interview for more specific purposes. For example, the consultant may want to engage a student in discussion about a given learning situation as part of a clinical teaching method (Opper, 1977). Or the consultant may want to engage a teacher in discussion about a given teaching technique as part of a study of that teacher's classroom. In both of these situations, the purpose of the interview is narrower than that described in the ethnographic interview, and, understandably, the interview process can usually be completed within a shorter period of time (i.e., one or two brief sessions).

Example of an Unstructured Interview. Table 8.3 provides an example of an actual interview conducted with a resource teacher (Harris, 1981). This excerpt was selected to illustrate the consultant's reliance upon the teacher's comments when formulating questions during an interview. The purpose of the interview was to understand the teacher's use of standardized assessments. The reader should be aware that other issues raised during the conversation (e.g., the importance of spelling in an academic curriculum) were later addressed by the consultant.

After explaining the purpose of the interview, the consultant asked a few predetermined questions (e.g., "How did you determine what *Kottmeyer* to give?" "Okay, could you talk with me about your use of the *Woodcock* in first period today?"). However, many more questions were asked by the consultant (e.g., "Why is that test used? What happens if you have kids who you think are at a higher level?") These questions were suggested by the teacher's responses to predetermined questions and provided information the consultant needed to understand the teacher's use of standardized assessments. This type of unstructured interview is a communicative activity in which the consultant actively participates in the conversation.

Regardless of the purpose of an unstructured interview, it is suggested that the consultant carefully communicate the purpose of the interview, engage the interviewee in conversation that will allow the identification and pursuit of topics deemed important by the interviewee, and ask questions that will help to clarify the interviewee's intent. The effective use of communication skills will greatly facilitate this process.

Stimulated Recall

Stimulated recall is a technique that allows an individual to express his or her perceptions. A person is given a record of his or her behavior and is asked to recall and discuss the situation. Stimulated recall techniques have been used by educators for many years. Bloom (1954) noted that stimulated recall had been used in several investigations and had proved promising. This method

TABLE 8.3
Example of an Unstructured Interview

Situation: Interview

Purpose: Use of standardized assessments; Basis for teacher's decision making

CONSULTANT*: "How did you determine what *Kottmeyer* to give?"

TEACHER: "There's the two levels. (*pause*) I figured all our kids fit into the above." (*pause*)

CONSULTANT**: "Why is that test used?"

TEACHER: "Gee, I don't know. (*pause*). It's the one Sharon had in there (*pause*) ascertain a grade level." (*pause*)

CONSULTANT**: "I think that only goes up to the sixth grade. What happens if you have kids who you think are at a higher level?"

TEACHER: "We do have a couple, Donna and Tommy, above a sixth grade level."

CONSULTANT**: "What happens with them?"

TEACHER: "Well, at that point, levels aren't that important; spelling is not that important, I guess, in how it relates to the kid's expression. For example, Tommy can express himself clearly in writing."

CONSULTANT*: "Okay, could you talk with me about your use of the Woodcock in first period today?"

TEACHER: "Yeh. I looked in the Woodcock just to see if I could pick up any patterns of theirs." (*pause*)

CONSULTANT**: "Did you look at the tests that the kids from the first period took?"

TEACHER: "Yeh. I picked up Piccolo's, Votor's, and Zap's. I didn't pick up Tommy's." (*pause*)

CONSULTANT**: "Any reason for that order?"

TEACHER: "No, just the first one I came to. The first thing I put on the board, *slip* and *slap*, was something that Votor had missed last week in the World of Vocabulary . . .

CONSULTANT**: "The *bite-site* stuff from the Woodcock?"

TEACHER: "Yeh, and Rick said '*invited*' for *inventor*."

CONSULTANT**: "This was on the Woodcock?"

TEACHER: "Yeh, so I wanted to set that pattern. I just felt like teaching them something after all that testing."

---

* Predetermined questions
** Generated questions

was shown to be useful for recalling and reliving a given event because the individual is provided with cues that occurred during the original situation.

Stimulated recall is a technique used in conjunction with other types of information-gathering techniques, for example, field notes (Smith & Geoffrey, 1968) and videotape (MacKay & Marland, 1978; McNair, 1978–79; Peterson, Marx, & Clark, 1978). The intent is to provide the person with a recounting of an incident so as to help the person produce an explanation and/or elaboration of the incident. Since this technique is used in conjunction with a more objective recording of the incident, the stimulated recall technique allows two perceptions (i.e., that of the observer as well as that of the person observed) to be incorporated into the understanding of the behavior.

Example of a Stimulated Recall Activity. Table 8.4 provides an example of a stimulated recall activity. In general, the consultant followed suggestions of Smith and Geoffrey (1968) in conducting the stimulated recall activity. First, the consultant read through field notes and stopped at each point where comments and/or questions were noted. Second, the consultant took the field note and the date of occurrence. Third, the consultant shared the field note, minus comments and/or inferences, with the teacher. Fourth, the consultant asked the teacher to provide reasons or perceptions about the behavior reported. Fifth, the consultant and the teacher talked about the teacher's perceptions and the consultant's comments and/or questions.

This stimulated recall activity was conducted because the consultant noticed that sometimes when the aide provided instruction, the consultant did not understand the aide's role in that instruction. The consultant asked the teacher in the interview about the aide's activities, but a clear understanding from the teacher's viewpoint was not evident.

Table 8.4 shows that the teacher did not feel comfortable with the aide's instructional ability. Yet the aide was very conscious of the teacher's feelings and did want to support her in her activities in the resource room. The information obtained through this stimulated recall activity, as well as other information obtained through subsequent discussions between the teacher and consultant, was used to construct a training program for the aide that also included monitoring by the teacher.

PSYCHOMETRIC APPROACHES

The approaches discussed in this section (i.e., ecological assessment, sociometric assessment, checklists, rating scales, interaction analysis, and applied behavior analysis) will provide the consultant with techniques useful for measuring specific behavior of individuals within given situations. These techniques rely upon the use of quantitative information. It is our opinion that

TABLE 8.4
Example of Stimulated Recall Activity

Directions: Reflect on incident described. Note any clarification, comments, perceptions, questions, etc.

FIELD NOTES

Date: 3-7-80 **Period:** 3

TEACHER: "Miss T (*student*), please correct these. Where's Ned? There's Ned (*lounge chairs*). Listen, gang. Today each of you is going to be working individually. Some of you will be working on division. For most of you, it will be a review. Listen carefully to the directions each of you will get." (*students at various points calling out "Mr. M"—(teacher). Teacher stationed at aide's table with Ned. Aide helping students at table near board. Anna disagreeing with aide about division problem.*)

TEACHER: (*walking over to table*) "What's the problem, Anna?"

ANNA: "She said she did that one."

TEACHER: "Who did that one? Mrs. H (aide), Anna?"

TEACHER'S RESPONSE

"Third period math class (*pause*) let's see (*pause*). It's pretty much a transcript of a conversation back and forth between myself and the kids. Let's see. I noticed here that you focused a little bit on Anna and her contact with Mrs. H. My reaction to that is two-fold. One with Anna, one concerning Anna and one with Mrs. H. Anna, is a, as I told you in some of our conversations, tends to get kind of frustrated with she doesn't pick up something right away. She needs to, she likes to learn things quickly and get them right away. If that isn't the case, then, she tends to rush through, make careless mistakes and really not go back and look over and see the way, the correct way, that certain operations should be done. In this instance, Mrs. H went over to help her, and, you know, that's one of the things I need to be a little cautious of because, Mrs. H is familiar with doing all the operations but, you know, from what, she brings in several short cuts that are fine if the kids understand the basic procedure, concepts, involved but, you know, if they, if they're having a problem with the basic work, I don't particularly want her showing the kids a lot of short cuts and crossing this out and doing that and doing the other thing. You know, it tends to cause confusion when I'm telling them one thing and she's telling them another. That particular thing happened here a little bit so I had to explain to Anna, you know, to kind of, to do it the way I had originally explained. I tried tactfully so that Mrs. H wouldn't feel that I was undercutting her, or putting her down in any way, because I certainly do appreciate it when she helps."

these techniques can best be used when the consultant wishes to measure behaviors that have been identified and clearly defined.

Ecological Assessment

Ecological assessment can be defined within two broad perspectives. First, the individual's behavior is considered interactive. That is, a change in performance of one behavior may affect other behaviors. Second, behavior is viewed in relation to its environmental context. That is, a change in one setting or context may produce changes in other environments and, in turn, affect an individual's performance (Rogers-Warren & Warren, 1977).

Ecological assessment is usually conducted when a sample of a student's behavior and environment that extends beyond the classroom is desired (Glass, Christiansen, & Christiansen, 1982). As Hardin (1978) suggests, before an effective intervention can be conducted, the student and his or her relationship to the environment must be assessed.

A basic assumption in an ecological approach is that there is an intrinsic order to human events and behavior and that behaviors and events occur within and in response to the surrounding environment (Gutmann, 1969). As Brandt (1975) notes, it then becomes the task of the data collector to gather enough information to make this order and behavioral consistency apparent.

Procedure. Due to the comprehensive nature of an ecological assessment, the consultant should consider the student's behavior in several settings. Wiederholt, Hammill, and Brown (1978) have identified the school, the home, and the community as the major environments in an ecological assessment. Harris and Little (1982) suggest that the student, peers, family, employers, community members, teachers, school administrators, and school staff be considered when conducting an ecological assessment. For example, the consultant may find it necessary to assess a student's behavior in the regular classroom, the special education setting, the gym, the lunchroom, and/or the playground. Heron and Heward (1982) note the possible importance of the physical aspects of a given classroom: that is, the amount of space each student has, how the seating is arranged, the amount of classroom lighting, and the noise level. These variables have been shown to affect student performance. In addition, academic responding time (i.e., the time during which a student is actively performing academic tasks such as reading, writing, and asking or answering questions) has been found to be positively correlated with academic achievement (Borg, 1980; Cooley & Leinhardt, 1980; Gaver & Richards, 1979; Good & Grouws, 1977; McKinney, Mason, Perkerson, & Clifford, 1975).

Heron and Heward (1982) also identify other factors that seem related to student performance. These include student physiological aspects (e.g., medical history, medication, or dietary consideration); the nature of student-student interaction; the nature of teacher-student interaction; and the previous reinforcement history of the student. The last is considered worth study, since current student behavior can be affected by the behaviors that have been reinforced across the various settings of the regular classroom, the special education placement, or the home in the past.

To conduct a comprehensive ecological assessment, several sources of data may need analysis. One readily available source of information is the student's permanent record. According to Heron and Heward (1982), student records should indicate the level (and possibly the rate) of student achievement as well as provide important information on pertinent physical or psychological characteristics. Such records should not be viewed as the sole source of information, nor should they be viewed as the verification of a student's problem. Rather, student records should serve as a stimulus to continue the inquiry.

Also, a consultant can probe areas identified through student records by interviewing relevant individuals, such as teachers, students, parents, or physicians. Through interview, the consultant can confirm, clarify, and possibly add to information in the student records.

Another useful way to investigate student behavior and the environment is direct observation. For instance, the use of interaction analysis might help the consultant define the nature of teacher-student interactions. Student-student relationships can be explored through sociometric analysis. Direct, daily observation can be used to assess physical aspects of an environment, such as the amount of space in the room, as well as the behavioral aspects of an environment, such as the frequency and duration of student behavior. The consultant can select among all the assessment techniques discussed in this chapter.

When is it appropriate to conduct a full-scale ecological assessment? Heron and Heward (1982) suggest that this time-consuming activity be undertaken only when a planned intervention has the potential to produce unexpected consequences; it could presumably be jeopardized if salient ecological variables were ignored.

Example of an Ecological Assessment. A consultant may wish to conduct an ecological assessment if faced with the following type of situation. Suppose a new student moves into the school district, and he is suspected of having a handicapping condition. He has not been previously classified as handicapped in his other school placements. However, two of his teachers at the new school have reported serious behavior problems.

There are a number of avenues that the consultant may wish to explore in an effort to define this problem. Interviews with teachers mentioned in the student's school record might determine whether he experienced earlier school problems. Also, it may be helpful to talk to the parents to find out whether the student had undergone any recent changes in diet or medication. The consultant might learn, too, from the parents whether the student had difficulties in other schools. The parent might be able to describe the previous school setting so that the consultant could compare it with the current placement to determine any differences between the two that could account for the student's behavior. Observations made of teacher-student and student-student interaction, as well as the physical structure of the classroom, might yield significant information regarding the student's behavior. Finally, the consultant may wish to talk directly with the student to gain his perspectives on the situation and to see whether he perceives himself as exhibiting inappropriate behaviors.

This assessment strategy combines the use of qualitative and quantitative data. Through qualitative data collection efforts (e.g., interviews), the consultant identifies behaviors that will then need to be measured to confirm the inappropriateness of the student's behavior and to develop an effective intervention plan.

Sociometric Assessment

Among the many assessment techniques consultants can use to measure social acceptance are measures of teacher-student interaction and measures of peer relationships (McLoughlin & Lewis, 1987). *Sociometric assessment* provides data about the attitudes of group members toward one another and is often used for finding out how well special students are accepted by peers (Asher & Taylor, 1981). Students may be asked to rate their classmates, choose between pairs of students, or nominate a peer. The peer nominating technique was originally developed by Moreno (1953). In this procedure each child's social position in the class is determined by analyzing his or her responses with respect to specific questions. For example, each student might be asked to name someone with whom he or she would like to play. It is assumed that the student who is named most frequently enjoys the highest status in the class.

Sociometric measurements can provide the teacher and consultant with information useful for understanding classroom dynamics or interactions because it focuses on student-student interaction in the classroom.

Procedure.   In a sociometric assessment, each student may be asked to choose two or three children in the class with whom he or she would most (or least) like to play or most (or least) like to work with on a project. The students' responses are confidential. Students are not asked to make their nominations aloud but usually write the names of their choices on pieces of paper. An alternative is to assign a number to each child. Then each student, in response to a question, writes on paper the number of the selected child. It is also possible to provide a multiple-choice situation. That is, for each question, the students may have the names or numbers of the other students before them, and then indicate their selections by circling or underlining the appropriate name or number. Whatever the method, it should take into account each student's response capability.

Once the peer nominations have been made, they are plotted on a *sociogram*. A sociogram is a schematic representation of all student responses. Figure 8.1 shows a schematic representation of the responses by a third-grade class to the question, "Who would you most like to sit next to?" This sociogram shows us that Yolanda was not picked by any student nor did she select any student to sit near. Irene chose two students, Sean and Lynn, but was not chosen herself. Also, one may suspect that Kathleen and Christine, Blaine and Marge, and Lee and Lynn are close friends, since they chose each other.

After the sociogram is analyzed, the consultant might help the teacher plan a program to change for the better the social relationships of the students in the classroom.

Example of Sociometric Assessment. It is apparent from Figure 8.1 that Yolanda is an isolate in this class. If Yolanda also exhibited withdrawn

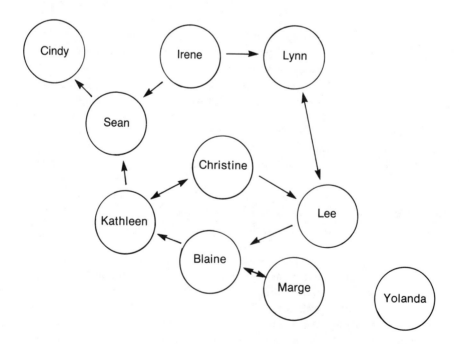

FIGURE 8.1. Example of a sociogram.

behavior (e.g., she did not participate in class discussions, raise her hand, or talk with her teacher or classmates outside the classroom), the results of this sociometric analysis might confirm why and help the consultant understand how Yolanda's peers felt about her and she about them. Steps could then be taken to engineer positive social interactions between Yolanda and one or two selected classmates. A subsequent sociometric analysis could measure any change that might result in the social status of Yolanda with respect to her peers and vice versa. In this way, some estimate as to the success of the consultant's intervention plan for Yolanda and her classmates could be made.

Checklists and Rating Scales

According to Brandt (1975) observational data can generally be reduced to three types: narratives, checklists, and rating scales. Narrative observation was discussed earlier in this chapter under Field Observation. A *checklist* reflects the the presence or absence of a particular characteristic according to some predetermined set of categories, and a *rating scale* represents an estimate of the degree to which a particular characteristic is evident along a basic continuum. Therefore, if the degree or frequency of behavior is important, a checklist would not be appropriate. Checklists are suggested for use as initial sources of assessment data, not as definitive sources (Wallace & Larsen, 1978). Checklists covering the varieties of observable behavior among children in special education are available commercially and are also being developed locally by teachers and consultants (Bush & Waugh, 1982).

Checklists. Checklists can be used by consultants for a variety of purposes, including measurements of environmental characteristics of schools (Wang & Birch, 1984). To measure the presence or absence of critical program dimensions for the *Adaptive Learning Environments Model*, Wang and Birch identified 96 performance indicators, which were then incorporated into a checklist. Critical program dimensions included the creation and maintenance of instructional materials, record keeping, diagnostic testing, and interactive teaching.

Checklists are frequently used to measure student behavior, including student academic behavior (Saracho, 1984) as well as student problem behavior (Bower & Lambert, 1976).

Bower and Lambert (1976) in their discussion of teacher-made behavior checklists suggest that they include three general areas: (a) behaviors seen in the target child; (b) behaviors seen in the target child's interaction with other students in the class; and (c) behaviors seen in the teacher's interaction with the target child. Based on recommendations from teachers, Wiederholt, Hammill, and Brown (1978) have developed these same three areas into a sample checklist. The authors suggest that the sample checklist serve as a guide for teachers (Table 8.5).

In addition to checklists designed to indicate the presence or absence of problem behaviors, consultants and teachers can develop checklists that will indicate the presence and absence of specific skills, such as those related to student readiness for school, self-help (dressing, grooming, toileting), arithmetic, and reading.

Some sample items that might be found on a school readiness scale are the following:

1. Does the child appear to be in good general health?

2. Can the child name the days of the week?

3. Can the child count aloud from 1 to 20?

4. Does the child follow classroom rules?

Laurent (1978) proposes the following guidelines for developing informal assessment checklists for handicapped students: (a) Skills should be sequenced according to difficulty under their appropriate subject heading; (b) the range of skills should be broad enough so that almost all students in the class will be included; and (c) the skills should be based on the curriculum.

Listed below are some sample items from an informal checklist.

Basic Knowledge	*Achievement Date*
1. Identifies body parts	____
2. Sorts by color, shape, size, and class	____
3. Counts ten subjects	____
4. States name, address, and phone number	____
5. Selects coins to make sums up to $1.00	____

The consultant may also tap knowledge of specific arithmetic and reading skills with a teacher-made checklist. The teacher can list, hierarchically, those skills necessary to master a particular reading or arithmetic program and check off mastery of each skill as the child achieves it. Some sample items from an arithmetic skills checklist that may be used at the elementary level follow. (Note: The items are not arranged hierarchically.)

1. Sort according to a particular quality (physical property, form, color, size, shape)

TABLE 8.5
Teacher-made Checklist for Measuring Problems in Social and Emotional Development

This list was designed to be used by teachers in any classroom to make them more aware of their students' behavior. It can help identify behavior that otherwise might be overlooked or misunderstood. From here the teacher may want to take frequency counts of identified behavior, or in some other way further analyze the situation.

	Frequently	Not Frequently

I. Self-image
   A. Makes "I can't" statements
   B. Reacts negatively to correction
   C. Gets frustrated easily
   D. Makes self-critical statements
   E. Integrity: cheats, tattles, steals, destroys property
   F. Makes excessive physical complaints
   G. Takes responsibility for actions
   H. Reacts appropriately to praise

II. Social Interaction
   A. Seeks attention by acting immaturely:
      thumbsucking, baby talking, etc.
   B. Interacts negatively
   C. Fails to interact
   D. Initiates positive interaction
   E. Initiates negative interaction
   F. Reacts with anger, verbally
   G. Reacts with anger, physically

III. Adult/Teacher Relationships
   A. Seeks attention by acting immaturely
   B. Excessively demands attention
   C. Reacts appropriately to teacher requests
   D. Inappropriately reacts to authority figures

IV. School-Related Activities
   A. Attends to task
   B. Exhibits off-task behavior
   C. Interferes with other students' learning
   D. Shows flexibility to routine changes

Date the checklist and complete one for each child. Once the checklist has been completed and reviewed, a narrative report can be written with explanations and suggestions for the future. For the list to be effective, the teacher must use the results to actually make changes in the classroom.

From *The resource teacher* (pp. 212–213) by J. L. Wiederholt, D. D. Hammill, & V. Brown (1978), Boston: Allyn & Bacon. Reprinted by permission.

2. Count from 1 to 20

3. Add two place numbers by counting objects

4. Rewrite subtraction problem as an addition problem

5. Demonstrate that multiplication is repeated addition

6. Demonstrate successful understanding of division using 2, 3, or 4 place divisors

Rating Scales.   Rating scales are a widely used measuring instrument (Ary, Jacobs & Asghar, 1985). An individual may be asked to complete a rating scale as a measurement of his or her behavior or perceptions or as a measurement of someone else's behavior. There are different types of rating scales. A numerical rating scale includes the assignment of a numerical value to points along a continuum (Figure 8.2). A category rating scale consists of a number of categories, hierarchically arranged, that provide a measure of a given characteristic. For example, a consultant may ask a student to rate the fairness of a teacher by giving the student the following question:

How fair is this teacher? (check one)
exceptionally fair	_____
very fair	_____
fair	_____
not fair	_____
not at all fair	_____

Rating scales can be used by consultants for a number of different purposes. Often, consultants use rating scales with teachers to determine the teacher's judgment of student behaviors.

A rating scale developed by Iscoe and Payne (1972) for evaluating exceptional children with respect to environmental influences focuses on three general areas. They are the physical domain, the adjustment domain, and the educational domain, areas of particular relevance to the successful functioning of the handicapped student. Each domain is divided into the categories of visibility, locomotion, and communication (Figure 8.3).

In each of the nine resulting subareas, Iscoe and Payne (1972) have established a seven-point rating scale, one indicating the absence of a problem and seven indicating extreme problems. Each exceptional child is judged with respect to a normal peer. Inspection of Figure 8.3 shows a hypothetical rating profile for Ted. Based upon the summary information in this table, we can conclude that Ted has no apparent difficulties in academic achievement, but he is experiencing some problems relating to his classmates, and his adjustment problem may be related to a highly visible handicap that interferes with his mobility.

Sample Questions
Special Education Questionnaire: Teachers
Place an X in the rectangle that describes how you feel
about each question.

---

1. How do you feel about having a special education staff person come into your classroom?

1 2 3 4 5 6 7
(I do not like it)   (I like it very much)

2. When a special education teacher is in one of your classes and gives your students help, do you feel comfortable?

1 2 3 4 5 6 7
(very comfortable)   (very uncomfortable)

Sample Questions
Special Education Questionnaire: Students

Place an X in the space that describes how you feel
about each question.

1. How do you feel about having special education teachers come into your regular education classes?

1 2 3 4 5 6 7
(I do not like it)   (I like it very much)

2. How do you feel when a special education teacher comes into your regular education classroom and helps you with your classwork?

1 2 3 4 5 6 7
(very comfortable)   (very uncomfortable)

FIGURE 8.2. Questions measuring teacher and student satisfaction with consultation model.

	Visibility	Locomotion	Communication
Physical Domain	**7**	**5**	**2**
	Peer	Family	Self
Adjustment Domain	**4**	**2**	**2**
	Motivation	Achievement	Potential
Education Domain	**1**	**2**	**1**

FIGURE 8.3.   Hypothetical rating profile according to the Iscoe-Payne classification system.

Consultants can also use rating scales to measure the effectiveness of consultation services. For example, as part of an inservice activity, consultants should assess the needs of participants as well as evaluate the effectiveness of the inservice activity. Rating scales can be appropriately used for both of these functions. For example, in constructing a needs assessment for an inservice activity, consultants may want to list topic areas and ask teachers to prioritize their interest in the listed topic areas by circling one of the following responses for each topic area:

1. very interested

2. interested

3. slightly interested

When designing an evaluation form for an inservice activity, Idol-Maestas (1983) suggests the following: Ask concrete and specific questions that will yield useful information for follow-up activities, keep the evaluation brief, and include more than one type of response in the evaluation form (e.g., use rating scales as well as open-ended questions).

As a measure of student and teacher satisfaction with a consultation model implemented in a high school, local special education teachers developed a questionnaire that used a rating scale as the measurement technique (Harris et al., 1986). These questionnaires were administered to students and regular education teachers. Examples of the questions can be found in Figure 8.2. In constructing these questionnaires, an attempt was made to ask at least two questions related to the same concept so as to obtain more than one judgment of a given concept. Also, similar questions were asked on both questionnaires so that teacher and student responses could be compared.

Summary. Checklists and rating scales can provide very useful information to the consultant, especially when used in conjunction with other data collection activities. However, when deciding on the use of checklists and rating scales, consultants should consider the reliability of these measurements. To foster the reliability of checklist measurements, it is recommended that consultants use operational definitions of behaviors to be measured and request that individuals complete checklists at the time the behavior occurs. The longer the time between behavior occurrence and checklist completion, the greater the risk of inaccuracy, because the person completing the checklist must then have to rely on his or her memory of events.

When rating scales are used to measure the behavior of another individual, they are susceptible to error (Ary, Jacobs, & Asghar, 1985). Errors commonly happen when a general impression of a subject influences ratings on specific behaviors; when a rater, if unsure, gives the subject the benefit of the doubt; and when a rater tends to avoid either extreme and rates all individuals in the middle of the scale. There are ways to reduce the chance of error. One way is to provide raters with training and discuss with them the possibility of making these types of errors. In addition, when actually performing the rating, give raters a clearly developed rating sheet, be available to answer questions raters may have, and provide enough time for the raters to complete the rating scale.

Interaction Analysis

Interaction analysis refers to the observation of teacher behaviors with individual students or with the entire class. Measurement of teacher-student interaction has received considerable attention in the educational literature as a consequence of the recent interest in effective teaching (Brophy, 1979). There are many interaction analysis techniques that can be used in the classroom. In this chapter, we present an overview of the Brophy-Good Dyadic Interaction System and Flanders Interaction Analysis. These two systems were chosen because they are used frequently and because each measures a different type of teacher-student interaction.

Brophy-Good Dyadic Interaction System.   The *Brophy-Good Dyadic Inter-action System* was introduced in 1969 (Brophy & Good, 1969). One of the reasons for its popularity is that it affords the observer the opportunity to code several types of dyadic interactions, exchanges between a teacher and an individual student. Also, the system treats each individual as a separate unit of analysis.

The dyadic interaction system has a number of distinct advantages over applied behavior analysis observation systems and observation approaches that use the whole classroom as the unit of analysis. First, the system measures the verbal interactions that take place between the teacher and student. Second, as we shall discuss later, the system is designed to record many behaviors. Of course, the more behaviors that are measured, the more information that is obtained. Third, it is relatively easy to learn how to code behaviors within this system. Given practice, anyone with experience as a classroom observer should be able to use the system competently. Fourth, adequate reliability scoring between observers is facilitated by the clear description of each behavioral category in the training manual. The 80% reliability level can be readily achieved.

Unlike applied behavior analysis, which permits the teacher to collect the observation data, the Brophy-Good system requires additional personnel. This may be a disadvantage, especially in districts where consultants are not readily available. A second disadvantage is that only verbal interaction can be measured. Experienced supervisors and teachers realize the powerful effects nonverbal behaviors have on student behavior, but the Brophy-Good system simply does not measure them.

Procedure.   The Brophy-Good system measures five types of dyadic interactions in the classroom: (a) response opportunity, (b) recitation, (c) procedural contacts, (d) work-related contacts, and (e) behavioral contacts. These categories are broadly defined below. The reader is referred to the Brophy-Good manual for a more detailed description of each category.

For an interaction to be coded as a response opportunity, three criteria must be met: (a) The interaction between the teacher and student is public and heard by the entire class; (b) the teacher initiates the interaction by asking questions; and (c) only one child responds to the teacher. Choral responses, students responding in unison, or student "call-outs" to teacher questions are not considered response opportunities.

If a child reads aloud, makes an oral presentation to the class, or recounts an incident to the class in response to a teacher direction, a recitation response is scored.

Procedural contacts are scored when there is an interaction between teacher and child that facilitates the management of personal needs or the distribution of supplies. In a sense, the teacher or child is obtaining the other's compliance in performing a task. Procedural contacts initiated by the teacher may include asking the child to be a messenger, pass out papers, or take roll. Procedural contacts initiated by the child might be asking the teacher's permission to sharpen a pencil, to go to the bathroom, or calling the teacher's attention to a specific object or event.

Any interaction between the teacher and child that relates specifically to some aspect of classwork, homework, or other assigned tasks in the classroom is coded as a work-related contact.

Any verbal statement made by the teacher to a student that makes reference to his or her classroom behavior would be coded as behavioral contact. The three categories under behavioral contact include praise, behavioral warnings, or behavioral criticism.

Example of use of the Brophy-Good Dyadic Interaction System. It would be appropriate to use the Brophy-Good Dyadic Interaction System in situations where the consultant wanted to record the amount of praise given by teachers not only to entire classes but also to individual students, especially mainstreamed handicapped students. Suppose that after conducting observations in two classrooms, it was found that both teachers praised their students during 80% of the observed intervals. At first it might appear that the two teachers were comparable in terms of the amount of praise they issued to the students in their rooms. If data were obtained using the dyadic interaction code, it is possible that a different interpretation of the data could be obtained. That is, the first teacher might distribute praise across all students in the classroom, while the second teacher might praise only a small minority of students. In short, 10% of the students might receive 80% of the praise. By looking at individual interactions, using the dyadic system, the consultant could determine that the interaction patterns in the two classrooms were different.

Flanders Interaction Analysis System. The *Flanders Interaction Analysis System* is one of the early structured observation systems to measure teacher-student interaction (Flanders, 1975). As with the Brophy-Good System, the teacher and student behaviors measured are strictly verbal. One category of measurement within the system is reserved for silence or confusion. Again, like Brophy-Good, a basic assumption is that the verbal behavior of the teacher or student is an adequate sample of his or her total behavior.

Although teacher-student verbal behaviors are observed, the primary focus of this approach is on the teacher. The purpose is to determine the teacher's influence upon pupil participation in class by recording and analyzing his or her spontaneous verbal behavior.

Procedure. The use of this system requires an observer who is not engaged in classroom interaction. According to Flanders (1975), the observer sits in the classroom in the best position to see and hear the classroom participants. At the end of a three-second period, the observer decides which of ten categories best represents the interaction just completed. Seven itemized categories relate to teacher verbalizations, and two categories (eight and nine) are reserved for student talk. The tenth category is for silence or confusion. The observer records the appropriate category number in a column as teacher and student behavior is observed. Whenever there is a major transition in the classroom, like a change in activity, the observer indicates the time on the recording form, because changes in interaction patterns may coincide with changes in activity. When the observation is completed, the observer leaves the classroom and writes a general description of each observation period. The description provides the observer with an overall view of the classroom and supplements the data obtained in the observation.

One can receive training to use the Flanders Interaction Analysis System. The training involves three basic steps. First, the trainees memorize the teacher and student categories. Second, the trainees attempt to code taped recordings of classroom verbal interactions. Here group discussion can lead to the development of more reliable judgments. The third step in the training process involves direct classroom observation. The presence of an experienced trainer during the observation facilitates the recording of reliable data. The trainer is able to answer questions regarding the recording of teacher or pupil talk. Hence, higher levels of agreement can be achieved.

Example of use of Flanders Interaction Analysis System. The use of the Flanders Interaction Analysis System would yield helpful information in many different situations. Suppose success in the mainstream classroom can be fostered by teachers who provide structure and direction for all students, especially the handicapped. The Flanders Interaction Analysis System could be used by the consultant to quantify the amount of direct teacher influence on a handicapped child.

The consultant may also be faced with a situation where it may be necessary for the success of a mainstreamed placement to identify a teacher who exhibits an indirect influence upon students. Sometimes handicapped students react negatively when faced with a teacher who is directive. In such a case, it may be helpful to place this student with a teacher who uses students' ideas and accepts the feelings of students rather than a teacher who manages the class by primarily lecturing and issuing directions. The Flanders Interaction Analysis System can help identify a teacher with this particular teaching style.

Summary. Interaction analysis systems are used commonly to provide feedback to teachers on their behavior. Since each system analyzes classroom events from a different perspective and uses different recording procedures, each can be of value to the teacher who is interested in developing specific interaction skills. Morine (1975) suggests that teachers be provided with feedback from a variety of systems, thereby exposing them to different perspectives.

Consultants should also recognize that the teacher behaviors selected for observation will probably reflect the evaluator's viewpoint. For the most accurate evaluative use, the interaction analysis system should also reflect the views of the teacher being evaluated.

The consultant should also be aware that interaction analysis systems may seem to the teacher to lack relevance. The teacher may simply not be interested in the data generated by the system because the teacher does not view interaction patterns as particularly good indicators of successful teaching. For whatever purpose an interaction analysis system is chosen, it is advisable to survey several techniques before making the most appropriate choice for each teacher. Observation systems differ in the extent to which they can be applied to situations other than those for which they were designed (Kerlinger, 1964). Therefore, in selecting an appropriate observation system for measuring teacher-student interaction, the consultant is urged to select an observation system that is flexible enough so that the behavior of interest is measured but specific enough so that reliable observations can be conducted. When using the observation system, consultants are urged to (a) observe a representative sample of the behaviors to be measured and (b) make a complete accurate record of the observed behavior (Medley & Mitzel, 1963).

Applied Behavior Analysis

Applied behavior analysis techniques provide measurements of discrete behaviors and represent an assessment approach that provides accurate information regarding the performance of specific, predetermined behaviors. The distinguishing features of applied behavior analysis (ABA) are the emphasis on the repeated and precise observation of the behavior, systematic intervention to determine treatment effects, and determination of the reliability of observation.

An obvious advantage of ABA techniques is that the observer can record any behavior of interest whenever it occurs as well as the conditions before and after its occurrence. ABA techniques are flexible, highly reliable, and can be used by most teachers after training and practice. However, unless the behavior under evaluation is sampled systematically, an erroneous estimate of its "true" level might be obtained. Instructional decisions made on sketchy or incomplete data could affect program decisions for handicapped students.

Permanent Product Measures. Permanent product measures can be obtained on any student behavior that is written, tape-recorded, or videotaped. In effect, a *permanent product measure* is a performance result that can be reviewed repeatedly. Also, a helpful feature is that the observer does not have to witness the behavior as it occurs. Measures can be taken after the fact. Common examples of permanent product measures include student math papers; number of sentences that were recorded on an audiotape; or the number of correct spelling words written on a weekly spelling test. Typically, permanent product measures are collected in one of three ways: frequency, percentage, and rate.

Frequency. *Frequency* is simply a tally of the number of responses emitted by the student in a unit of time. Frequency data could be obtained on the number of math problems or workbook pages a handicapped student completed. While frequency data may yield important information on the number of items the student completes, other types of data can, and should, be used to give the teacher an accurate index of the student's achievement. Frequency counts can be plotted on both noncumulative and cumulative graphs (Figures 8.4 and 8.5).

Percentage. *Percentage* correct is the ratio of the number of correct responses emitted divided by the number of items attempted. For example, if a learning disabled student were issued 20 math problems and completed 10

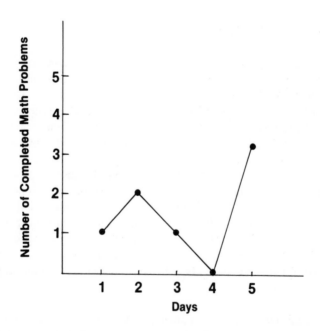

FIGURE 8.4. Number of math problems completed each day during baseline.

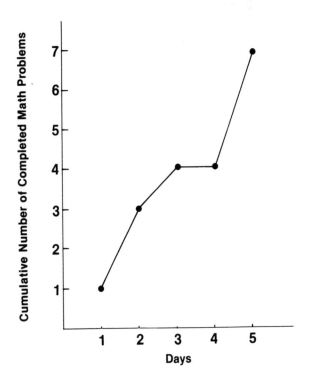

FIGURE 8.5. Cumulative number of math problems completed each day during baseline. Data are the same as Figure 8.4.

of them correctly, his percentage correct would be 50%. Percentage is usually considered in index of accuracy, that is, how well a student responds to given stimulus items. If a student were given 50 math problems and he attempted 20, and answered 15 out of the 20 correctly, his percentage correct would be 75%, not 30%. If the percentage is calculated on number issued rather than number attempted, a child's ability might be underestimated. Figure 8.6 provides an example of percentage correct for a student during a daily reading period.

Rate.   Whereas percentage is an index of accuracy, *rate* is an index of proficiency. The information that rate data provide is how well a student performs per unit of time. Many handicapped students are able to success-

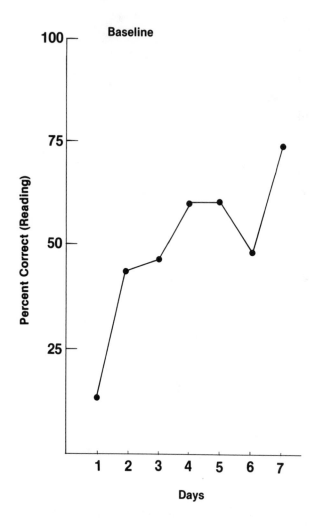

FIGURE 8.6. Percentage correct on daily reading comprehension questions.

fully complete an assigned task in the regular classroom. Their problem, however, is that it takes an inordinate amount of time to do it.

Lovitt, Kunzelmann, Nolan, and Hutten (1968) state the rate correct and rate incorrect data are essential for deciding on the functional value of an intervention program. As rate correct increases, rate incorrect should remain stable or decrease, depending on the number of problems given. Figure 8.7 shows rate correct and incorrect per minute for math.

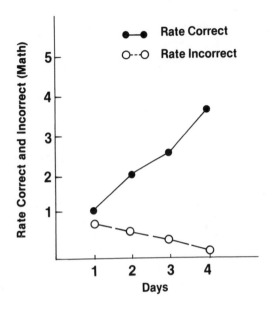

FIGURE 8.7. Rate correct and rate incorrect performance per minute in math during baseline.

Observation Measures. Not all behaviors that occur in the classroom result in permanent products. In fact, many behaviors that have a direct bearing on the success or failure of a mainstreaming program are transitory. Given the rapid pace of both teacher and student behaviors, another form of data collection, the observation system, has been developed. The principal techniques in the observation system are interval recording, time sampling, duration recording, and event recording.

Interval recording. *Interval recording* refers to an observational system where the occurrence of the target behavior at any time during a prescribed interval of time (e.g., 5 or 10 seconds) is scored. For example, if one were measuring the on-task performance of a student for one minute using 10-second intervals, only one occurrence of the behavior within any interval would be required to score that interval as an occurrence. If the target behavior did not occur at any time during the prescribed interval, then the interval would be scored as an interval of nonoccurrence of the target behavior. Hence, if the student was on-task at any time during each 10-second interval, a maximum of six intervals would be scored as occurrences.

Interval sampling is sensitive to both the frequency and duration of behavior (Cooper, 1981). Specifically, if out of six 10-second intervals, three were scored as occurrences and three as nonoccurrences, the consultant could determine that the behavior occurred at least three times, and the total duration of nonoccurrence was 30 seconds.

Time sampling.   When behaviors are recorded at the conclusion of every nth interval, the procedure is called *time sampling.* For example, if a behavior is recorded using a 30-second, time-sampling technique, it is recorded twice each minute, at the 30th second and the 60th second. The observer need not pay attention to what goes on between intervals, because it is irrelevant in this observation system.

The determination of interval length is a primary factor in the success of this approach in the classroom. If the intervals are too short, the teacher will not be able to instruct the students and observe simultaneously; if the intervals are too long, the data may not accurately reflect the "true" level of the behavior (Cooper, 1981).

Axelrod (1977) offers one variation of the time-sampling approach. He suggests that "X" number of observations take place during a given time period. A timer is set at a random interval, and when it goes off, the target behavior is recorded. The teacher then resets the timer for the next interval and so on until all the observations are made. Two advantages of this variation are (a) that the students are not likely to predict the end of interval since it is random and (b) that the teacher will have a cue, the sound of the timer, to remind her or him to record the behavior.

Duration recording.   Typically, *duration recordings*, made by an observer using a stopwatch, yield data on the total amount of a given behavior. When the desired behavior is emitted, the stopwatch is activated. When the behavior ceases, the watch is stopped. The elapsed time shown on the stopwatch is the duration of the behavior.

So, if a teacher were interested in the actual time that an educable mentally retarded student worked each day from 9:00 a.m. to 9:30 a.m., he or she would press the stopwatch button when the student worked and stop it when the student paused or finished. Since the stopwatch would show cumulative working time, the teacher would be able to determine the total number of minutes the student was on-task during the half-hour time frame.

Event recording.   *Event recording* is a tally of the number of times a given behavior occurs. For example, the number of times a student talks back or interacts appropriately with peers might be tallied this way. Some behaviors, however, may not lend themselves to accurate event recording. If, for example, a student left his seat momentarily several times during the day, event recording could be used to count this behavior. But if the student left his seat once to take a two-hour stroll around the school grounds, event recording would grossly underestimate the actual time away.

Event recording can be performed easily by classroom teachers. It has an advantage over interval and duration recording in that the teacher does not have to observe a student's behavior continuously to determine its level. Also, since teachers are familiar with the procedures of tallying the number of times a behavior occurs, they are more likely to use event recording rather than other observation measures.

Reliability. A *reliability check* is a measure taken by an independent observer, using the same observation procedure as the teacher, for the purpose of reducing or eliminating inaccuracies or bias (Axelrod, 1977). For instance, if a teacher noted 9 occurrences of a target behavior and the consultant recorded 10 occurrences of the same behavior within the same time frame, the reliability would be 90%, and the teacher could be confident that there was high agreement with the consultant on the level of the behavior. Conversely, if the teacher recorded 4 instances of the behavior and the consultant recorded 10, it would indicate that they were not observing the target behavior at the same time, or that they had differing definitions of the target behavior, or both.

To calculate reliability for interval sampling and time sampling, each observed interval must be compared to determine agreement (Figure 8.8). Once the number of agreements has been determined, the following formula can be used to calculate the reliability index:

$$\text{Reliability} = \frac{\text{Number of Agreements}}{\text{Total intervals observed}} = 100$$

Reliability over 80% is usually considered acceptable for most applied settings (Cooper, 1981). Reliability checks are not only performed on observational data, they are needed for permanent product data as well. To obtain a reliability index for product data, it is necessary for one observer to record on a separate sheet, for example, the number of math problems with correct answers, and then the reliability observer conducts a check on the same data without seeing how the other observer scored each response. In this way the reliability check is performed independently, and the reliability observer is not influenced by the primary observer's recording.

If student responses cannot be obtained with paper and pencil procedures, a tape or video recorder can be substituted. This situation occurs when the teacher wants the student to respond orally to questions or exam items. To conduct the reliability check, each observer would watch and/or listen to the tape independently to record the student's responses and then determine the number of agreements. To illustrate, suppose a teacher gave a student a 10-item oral spelling test in which the student spelled the words directly on the tape. After the test the teacher would rewind the tape and listen to each word to determine whether it was spelled correctly. The reliability

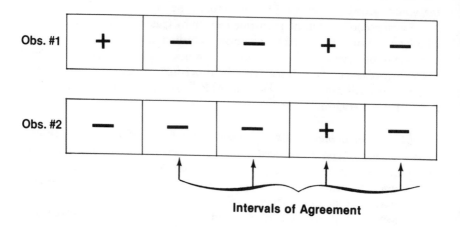

FIGURE 8.8. The number of agreements between two observers during daily 5-minute observations.

observer would follow the same procedure as the teacher, except that his or her recordings of the student's responses would be made on a separate sheet. Once both observers had scored the test, a percentage of agreement (the reliability) could be calculated. This is an effective strategy to employ when the second observer (e.g., a consultant) cannot be there to listen to the student as he or she responds.

Examples of Applied Behavior Analysis. Data obtained through permanent product measurement can be useful to the consultant who is helping teachers individualize instruction. For example, suppose that the consultant checked a student's math paper each day for a one-week period and noted that an average of eight errors was made daily. By counting the number and type of mistakes, the consultant could determine a pattern of errors and recommend to the teacher a method of instruction that would benefit the student. Also, the consultant would be able to help the teacher program more efficiently for generalization.

In permanent product measures, the consultant simply notes the number of errors in the raw data (e.g., the completed math paper). However, if data are collected by direct observation, it is usually necessary to sample the behavior over a number of days and under a number of different stimulus conditions. The consultant might note that Peter's on-task performance is high during reading and math but decreases appreciably during social studies. If this pattern continues, the consultant might suggest to the classroom teacher that the student be allowed to do his reading or math only after he completes his social studies assignments. The consultant could help the teacher plan an appropriate intervention based on the observation of the target behavior.

A general rule of thumb is that at least three to five days worth of data should be gathered before initiating or changing an instructional or behavior approach. Most educators (e.g., Cooper, 1981; Lovitt, 1977) feel that three to five days represents a "fair trial" for the observation.

For example, Figure 8.9 shows that the percentage of Ann's talking-out behavior increased over the first three sessions of baseline. Baseline refers to the magnitude of the behavior before an intervention is introduced and serves as a standard for comparing the effects of the intervention (Cooper, Heron, & Heward, 1987). These data are sufficient because a trend has been

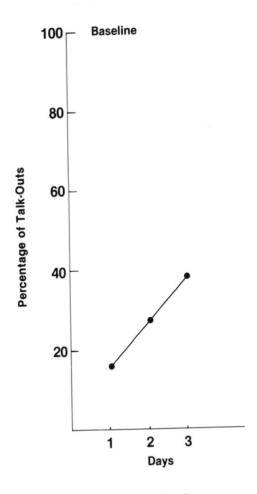

FIGURE 8.9. Percentage of talk-outs during baseline.

established; talk-outs are increasing. Since the intent of the intervention is to reverse the talking-out, the teacher could initiate an intervention after the third day.

Figure 8.10, on the other hand, shows hypothetical data on the number of times Stephen is out of his seat during a 50-minute math period. During baseline the data show a decrease, that is, a decelerating trend is evident. It would not be advisable to begin an intervention phase at this point, because the trend of the data is already in the desired direction.

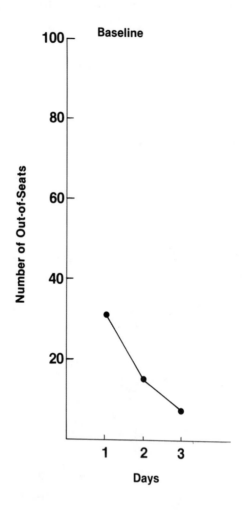

FIGURE 8.10. Number of out-of-seats during baseline.

Figure 8.11 shows hypothetical data for rate correct per minute performance in math. These data were collected to determine math proficiency. Since the data reveal a relatively stable pattern, it is acceptable to begin intervention after the fifth day.

Summary. A decision should be made to introduce an instructional or behavioral intervention only when the data show stability or movement in a direction opposite to that of the intervention. For more information on baseline trends and their meanings, the reader is referred to Cooper (1981) and Cooper et al. (1987).

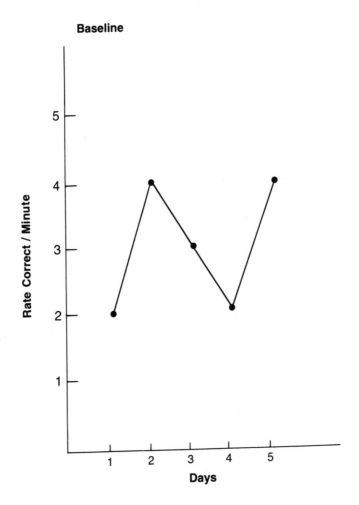

FIGURE 8.11. Rate correct per minute in math during baseline.

CONCLUSION

All assessment systems have advantages and disadvantages. Consultants interested in assisting teachers will need to decide upon the use of an assessment approach that will be sufficient to answer the proposed questions. If a consultant is able to reconcile concerns of need and efficiency, then the consultant is well on the way to deciding the type of assessment technique best suited to a particular situation.

Regardless of the assessment approach selected, the consultant should adhere to the following guidelines: (a) announce the intention to assess prior to implementing the assessment; (b) be as unobtrusive as possible; and (c) provide appropriate feedback to all interested parties following the assessment.

SUMMARY OF KEY POINTS

Purposes of Assessment

1. Two broad purposes of assessment were presented: identification and evaluation.

2. For purposes of identification, the consultant may be asked to identify the problem (survey level) or the consultant may be asked to measure the factors contributing to the problem (specific level.)

3. Evaluation provides the means to determine the effectiveness of a given course of action.

4. Formative evaluation is conducted during the implementation of the program and allows for "midcourse correction" (i.e., changes in the program before the program has been completed).

5. Summative evaluation is conducted at the end of the program, and it is designed to measure the effect of the program.

6. Consultants are encouraged to combine formative and summative evaluations into the activities of a program evaluation.

7. When planning and implementing program evaluations, consultants should clearly identify program goals; clearly identify desired outcomes as well as the process of program implementation; evaluate the utility and propriety of program evaluation activities; assure the accuracy of program evaluation data; and include as a source of evaluation consumers of the program.

Assessment Techniques

8. Qualitative data are best used to describe and understand a given situation.

9. Quantitative data are best used to measure the occurrence of specific behaviors.

10. The ethnographic approach relies on the use of narrative or qualitative data to provide a means of understanding a given situation.

11. The psychometric approach to assessment obtains numerical or quantitative data suitable for statistical or graphical analysis.

12. In selecting assessment techniques, consultants should consider whether the technique will yield information in an efficient manner that is accurate and complete.

Ethnographic Approaches

13. Ethnographic techniques are useful for describing and understanding the behavior of individuals within a given situation.

14. The three techniques discussed were field observation, interview, and stimulated recall.

15. Field observation is based upon narrative recordings, conducted on-site. However, additional data suggested by the field observation is also collected, characterizing this approach as multimodal.

16. To successfully conduct a field observation, the observer must take care to enter and become accepted into the environment under study.

17. A situation suitable for a field study would be one in which the consultant is interested in knowing all about a new school program.

18. Interview allows an individual to express his or her perceptions.

19. Interviews are used to serve as a check on the reliability of information obtained through other techniques and to obtain information from individuals who represent a group under study as well as to understand a problem and its underlying causes. Interviews are often used in conjunction with field observation.

20. When conducting an interview, the consultant should be sure to make explicit the purpose of the interview, help the interviewee to inform the consultant by explaining the reasons for conducting the interview, and ask questions to obtain the interviewee's perspective as well as clarify the information discussed.

21. In a stimulated recall activity, an individual is provided with a record of his or her behavior and is asked to recall and discuss the situation.

22. Stimulated recall allows for the perceptions of the observer as well as the person observed to be considered in interpreting the meaning of a given situation.

Psychometric Approaches

23. Psychometric techniques rely upon the use of quantitative data and are useful for measuring the specific behaviors of individuals within given situations.

24. The five measurement techniques discussed were ecological assessment, sociometric assessment, checklists, rating scales, interaction analysis, and applied behavior analysis.

25. In an ecological assessment, all environments related to the behavior in question are assessed using a variety of assessment techniques.

26. Sociometric measures provide data about the attitudes of group members toward one another.

27. In a sociometric assessment, individuals belonging to a group are asked a question about the group (e.g., "Who would you most like to sit next to?"). Results are plotted on a sociogram and visually inspected.

28. A checklist reflects the presence or absence of a particular characteristic according to some predetermined set of categories.

29. A rating scale represents an estimate of the degree to which a particular characteristic is evident along a basic continuum.

30. To maximize reliability of checklists and rating scales, consultants should use operational definitions for behaviors to be measured, request that individuals complete checklists at the time behavior occurs, and provide training and enough time for the completion of rating scales.

31. Interaction analysis refers to the observation of teacher behaviors with individual students or with the entire class.

32. Two commonly used measures of teacher-student interaction are the Brophy-Good Dyadic Interaction System and Flanders Interaction Analysis.

33. As observation systems differ in the extent to which they can be applied to situations other than those for which they were designed, consultants are urged to select an observation system that is flexible enough so that the behavior of interest is measured but specific enough so that reliable observations can be conducted.

34. Applied behavior analysis techniques provide measurements of discrete behaviors and represent an assessment approach that provides accurate information regarding the performance of specific behaviors.

35. Applied behavior analysis techniques include permanent product measures and observation measures.

36. Interval recording refers to an observation system where the occurrence of the target behavior at any time during a prescribed interval of time is scored.

37. Time sampling refers to an observation system where behaviors are recorded at the conclusion of every nth interval.

38. Duration recording refers to an observation system where data on the total amount of a given behavior is recorded.

39. Event recording is a tally of the number of times a given behavior occurs.

40. A reliability check is a measure taken by an independent observer, using the same observation procedure as the observer, for the purpose of reducing or eliminating inaccuracies.

QUESTIONS

1. What are the two broad purposes of assessment?

2. What is the difference between formative and summative evaluation?

3. What are some of the advantages of assessment techniques based in psychometry?

4. What are some of the disadvantages of psychometrically based assessment techniques for which ethnographic observation techniques attempt to account?

5. What is the difference between qualitative and quantitative data?

6. In what situations would it be appropriate to use field observation, interview, and stimulated recall as assessment techniques of choice?

7. What is the purpose of an ecological assessment?

8. What are some of the factors that should be considered in an ecological assessment?

9. What are three sources of information a consultant may draw upon in conducting an ecological assessment?

10. What is the name of an approach that can provide useful information concerning the process of student-student interaction in the classroom?

11. What is the basic difference between a checklist and a rating scale?

12. What is one purpose for which the use of an interaction analysis system would be appropriate?

13. What are three permanent product measures?

14. When would collection of frequency data yield helpful information?

15. Rate data are an index of what dimension of behavior?

16. What is the name of the observation technique whereby the occurrence of the target behavior at any time during a prescribed interval is scored?

17. What is the name of an observation technique appropriate for the determination of the total amount of a given behavior per unit of time?

18. Why is it important to conduct reliability checks?

DISCUSSION POINTS AND EXERCISES

1. Interview and observe the consultants and supervisors in your school district to determine for what purposes student observations are conducted. Identify the types of observation approaches used and what the observers feel are their strengths and weaknesses.

2. Based on a teacher referral of a student who exhibits behavior problems, devise an assessment approach that will identify and measure the problem behavior. If possible, construct and implement an intervention. Measure the effectiveness of that intervention.

3. Identify a curriculum or instructional program that teachers have been asked to implement in your school. Describe an assessment approach that will be sensitive to the way in which each teacher is implementing this program. Explain why the program is being implemented in this fashion.

4. The principal has informed you, the educational consultant, that the special education program in the school has a bad reputation. The principal wants you to do something about it. Develop a plan that will help you to assess the situation.

5. You have been asked by your principal to conduct an evaluation of your program. Design an evaluation plan. Include evaluation activities and appropriate assessment techniques.

9

Selecting and Implementing Appropriate Behavior Management Strategies

Each day teachers make innumerable decisions. They decide what lessons should be reviewed, what teaching material to use, what skills should be taught, and what behavior management strategies to employ. Similarly, parents make multiple decisions. They decide what household responsibilities the child will have, what social experiences will be permitted, and what behaviors to discipline or ignore. For both teachers and parents, these decisions are not always easy, but the decision-making process can be facilitated if a consistent management strategy is followed.

The emphasis of this chapter is on the management needs of students. Specifically, the purpose is to describe a number of procedures a consultant can recommend to teachers or parents to increase appropriate and decrease inappropriate behaviors. Training strategies are discussed along with a comprehensive decision model for changing behavior using the "least restrictive alternative" method. Examples from the authors' classroom teaching experience with handicapped and nonhandicapped populations as well as examples from research studies are presented.

OBJECTIVES

After reading this chapter, the reader should be able to:

1. define the terms *positive reinforcement* and *positive reinforcer* and give an applied example of each.

2. outline five levels of reinforcers and give an applied example of each.

3. define the terms *negative reinforcement* and *negative reinforcer* and give an applied example of each.

4. describe the appropriate steps to use to establish, maintain, and thin a token reinforcement program.

5. write a functional contingency contract with task and components.

6. describe the *Premack Principle*.

7. name two variables that enhance modeling and give an applied exampleof each.

8. list several guidelines for increasing behaviors.

9. define the term *extinction*.

10. differentiate among several positive reduction procedures and give an applied example of each.

11. define the *Doctrine of the Least Restrictive Alternative*.

12. discuss several ethical issues associated with using punishment in applied settings.

13. describe the components of a decision-making model for using punishment in applied settings.

14. distinguish among the terms *punishment, overcorrection, time out from positive reinforcement,* and *response cost*.

15. list several guidelines for decreasing behavior.

16. define the term *group-oriented contingency* and state the conditions under which it should be used.

17. list several guidelines for using a group-oriented contingency.

KEY TERMS

Positive reinforcement

Positive reinforcer

Negative reinforcement

Negative reinforcer

Unconditioned reinforcer

Conditioned reinforcer

Modeling

Extinction

Differential reinforcement of other behavior (DRO)

Differential reinforcement of low rates of behavior (DRL)

Differential reinforcement of incompatible behavior (DRI)

Punishment

Edible reinforcer

Tangible reinforcer

Exchangeable reinforcer

Activity reinforcer

Social reinforcer

Token reinforcer

Contingency contract

Overcorrection

Time out from positive reinforcement

Response cost

Gaylord-Ross Decision Model

Group-oriented contingency

Good Behavior Game

Premack Principle

PROCEDURES TO INCREASE ACADEMIC AND SOCIAL BEHAVIOR

Teachers, parents, and consultants have a number of procedures at their disposal for improving academic and social behavior. These procedures have been thoroughly researched and field tested and have been used by the authors in many classroom circumstances.

It is important for the consultant, especially consultants who work with teachers or parents of handicapped children, to be well-grounded in learning theory and applied behavior analysis because teaching handicapped children and youth is challenging, and the teachers or parents must be prepared to meet this challenge. A consultant who is skilled in applied behavior analysis will be able to assist teachers and parents competently as they jointly devise management programs.

Positive Reinforcement

According to Cooper, Heron, and Heward (1987), *positive reinforcement* is said to occur when a behavior is followed immediately by the presentation of a stimulus or event, and, as a result, that behavior is more likely to occur again in the future. Catania (1984) specifies three conditions necessary for reinforcement: (a) A response must have some consequence; (b) the response must increase in probability (i.e., the response must be more probable than when it does not have this consequence); and (c) the increase in probability must occur *because* the response has this consequence, and not for some other reason.

The stimulus or event that follows the behavior (the consequence) is known as the *positive reinforcer*. For example, if Raymond raises his hand to answer a question in class (the behavior), and the teacher praises him for his response (the reinforcer), the likelihood of the student raising his hand in the future is increased. It should be noted that a reinforcer can be so labeled only if it alone increases the likelihood of the behavior's recurrence. Table 9.1 contains a list of potential positive reinforcers. Whether any one stimulus or event is an actual reinforcer for an individual student depends solely on its effect on the student's behavior. Reinforcers are determined in a functional manner. What might be a reinforcer for one student may not work for another. What may be reinforcing for one student at one given time may not produce the same increase in behavior at another time.

Negative Reinforcement

Probably no term is misused or misunderstood more often than negative reinforcement. Simply stated, *negative reinforcement* occurs when a stimulus is removed contingent upon the performance of a particular behavior. Consequently, the likelihood of that particular behavior occurring in the future

TABLE 9.1
Potential Positive Reinforcers for School-Aged Students

Elementary Level Students	Intermediate Level Students	Secondary Level Students
Popcorn	Graphs of Behavior	Soft drinks
Soft drinks	Points/tokens	Radio listening time
Crayons	Calculators	Popular magazines
Comic books	Science activities	Free time in gym
Play money	Fast food gift certificates	Romantic novels
Stars/stickers	Pictures of TV stars	Graphs of behavior
Graphs	Radio listening time	Praise
Toy	Structured free time	Rock star posters
Notes home	Sports and car magazines	T-shirts
Balls	Soft drinks	Plants
Raisins	Diary	Calculators
Chalkboard work	Games	Tickets to sports events

quently, the likelihood of that particular behavior occurring in the future is increased. Negative reinforcement has the effect of increasing the desired behavior, not decreasing it. Negative reinforcement is not synonymous with punishment. In fact, it has the opposite meaning and effect. Cooper et al. (1987) clarify the misconception regarding the terminology associated with positive and negative reinforcement.

> The term reinforcement always means an increase in response rate and that the modifiers positive and negative describe the type of stimulus change operation that best characterizes the consequence (i.e., adding or withdrawing a stimulus). (p. 25)

Negative reinforcement can be used by skilled classroom teachers to improve student performance. For example, suppose a teacher says, "If each person in the class receives 85% or better on the first two math pages today, the third page of the assignment will be canceled." In effect, the teacher is removing the stimulus (the third page of math) contingent upon the successful completion of the first two pages. The *negative reinforcer*, the stimulus that is removed, is the third page of math.

Consultants should not hesitate to recommend a negative reinforcement contingency to a regular classroom teacher. In many instances, the use of a negative reinforcement procedure can serve the teacher's purpose as well as a positive reinforcement procedure. For example, suppose that a learning disabled student consistently returned homework that was sloppy and inaccurate. The consultant might suggest that the teacher set up a contingency whereby neater and more accurate papers were negatively reinforced by the removal of the student's homework requirements one day per week.

Types of Reinforcers

Some reinforcers affect an individual's behavior without the individual having prior experience with them. The first type of reinforcer is termed an unconditioned reinforcer. An *unconditioned reinforcer* is biologically determined and tends to satisfy basic human needs. The great majority of reinforcers are of the second type: conditioned reinforcers. A *conditioned reinforcer* acquires its reinforcing capability when paired repeatedly with unconditioned reinforcers or previously acquired conditioned reinforcers. According to Cooper et al. (1987), the major types of unconditioned and conditioned reinforcers have associated subcategories (Figure 9.1).

It is important for the consultant to be aware of these types and subcategories so that he or she can contribute recommendations to the teacher or parent that will work within school or home settings. Further, the consultant must be able to recognize conditions in the classroom or home that would suggest a shift to more natural or generalized reinforcers such as social praise.

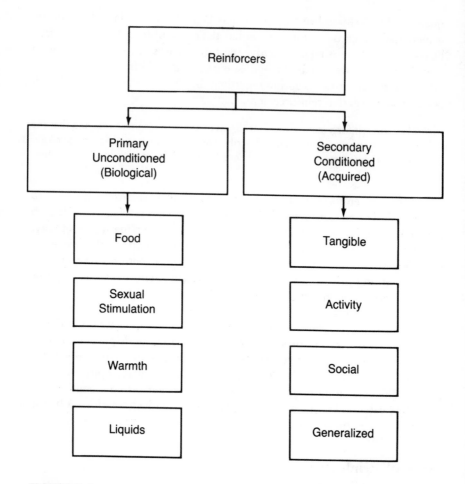

FIGURE 9.1   Types of potential reinforcers. From *Applied Behavior analysis* (p. 261) by J.O. Cooper, T.E. Heron, & W.L. Heward (1987), Columbus, OH: Merrill. Reprinted by permission.

The more commonly used subcategories of reinforcement are presented in this section. An analysis also illustrates the role of the consultant in dealing with a particular management problem in a classroom or home setting.

Edible Reinforcers.   An *edible reinforcer* can be defined as any food item that is delivered contingent on the occurrence of a behavior and that increases the likelihood that the behavior will occur again in the future. Willis, Hobbs, Kirkpatrick, and Manley (1975) used an edible reinforcer (snacks) to reduce the number of out-of-seat and talk-out behaviors of 27 highly disruptive seventh-grade students. Essentially, their reversal design study consisted of four conditions. During Baseline$_1$ the number of out-of-seat and talk-out behaviors were measured. During Treatment$_1$ students were informed that a 5-minute snack break would be available at the end of the class period if they did not leave their seat or call out during the first 15 minutes of class. Baseline$_1$ conditions were reinstated. During Treatment$_2$, Treatment$_1$ conditions were reinstituted. Finally, during Treatment$_3$ students were told that snacks would still be provided contingent on the absence of out-of-seat or talking-out behavior, but the snack would not be provided every day. Students did not know from day to day whether a snack was going to be provided. The results of the study indicated that when the snack condition was in effect, the number of out-of-seat and talk-out behaviors was reduced to near zero. Likewise, the study showed that during the third snack condition, which provided reinforcement on a variable interval schedule, the reduced levels of out-of-seat and talking-out behavior were maintained.

Before implementing a program using edible reinforcers, the consultant should confer with the teacher, staff person, or parent. First, from an ethical viewpoint it is critical that these persons make sure that there is no medical condition that might preclude the use of edible reinforcers. For example, if a handicapped student were allergic to chocolate or sugar and the teacher issued chocolate bits for appropriate behavior, a serious situation could develop. Second, edible reinforcers can lose their effectiveness quickly as a student becomes satiated. That is, the student has received an overabundance of a reinforcer. A soda break is not as likely to be as effective as a reinforcer immediately after lunch as it might be during mid-afternoon. Finally, even though edibles can be used successfully to establish desired behavior, to maintain performance over long periods of time it is usually advisable to switch to other reinforcers in the hierarchy, such as praise, that occur more naturally in the environment. The teacher should use edible reinforcers only in those situations where other reinforcers in the hierarchy are not likely to be effective.

Tangible Reinforcers. A *tangible reinforcer* can be considered any type of physical object presented subsequent to the occurrence of a behavior which has the effect of increasing the future probability of that behavior. For example, if a learning disabled student cleaned his or her desk each week, the teacher might reinforce the student with a puzzle or small trinket. Recall Table 9.1 and its list of reinforcers. Many of these reinforcers can be considered tangible, because the student receives a physical object contingent upon performance. Anecdote 9.1 describes how a regular classroom teacher structured tangible reinforcers for two physically handicapped students based on a prior discussion with the consultant.

ANECDOTE 9.1

TEACHER: Nancy and Barbara, I've noticed that you have a difficult time getting your work completed each day.

NANCY: That's for sure. There is so much to do, I barely have time to breathe.

BARBARA: That's right. It seems like I am always working.

TEACHER: Well, to help you get more done I want to present a plan to you. I've discussed the plan with Mr. Bobb, the consultant, and we both feel that it's worth a try. When you complete your assigned tasks for the week, you'll earn a cassette tape on which I've recorded your favorite records. The tape will be yours to keep.

BARBARA: That sounds great.

NANCY: And we get to keep the tape?

TEACHER: That's right, and to get things off to a good start, here is a cassette tape bin to store your tapes. I think you'll be earning a number of them.

GIRLS: You bet!

The consultant and teacher had jointly agreed to use the cassette tapes, because they knew the students enjoyed listening to music. They also chose tapes because they are powerful reinforcers, can be prepared easily, and can be used in other environments, such as the home. Also, a teacher may want to issue a noncontingent reinforcer, one the students do not have to earn, to prime them to respond. In this case, the tape bin served as the noncontingent reinforcer. The teacher could just as easily have made the first few assignments simple enough so that the students could have earned the tape bin. Either strategy is acceptable.

Exchangeable Reinforcers.   A token, check mark, or star that is earned by a student for appropriate behavior and later traded for another reinforcing object or event is considered an *exchangeable reinforcer*. Exchangeable reinforcers serve a dual function. First, they reinforce the target behavior immediately, and second, they can be exchanged by the student for a stronger reinforcer in the future. More descriptions of token reinforcers and an illustration of how tokens serve as exchangeable reinforcers are found later in this chapter.

Activity Reinforcers. An *activity reinforcer* can be defined as any game, free time, or social event that is used contingently to increase the future occurrence of the behavior that preceded it. Phillips, Phillips, Fixsen, and Wolf (1971) demonstrated that providing access to activities contingent upon performance can increase appropriate academic and social behavior. In their study, students earned points for promptness, cleanliness, and academic work that were exchangeable for hobbies and games, television viewing time, and sports events. Phillips et al. (1971) report that the activity reinforcers improved performance across each of the target behaviors.

It is important to remember that when using activity reinforcers (free time, field trips, etc.) students should not have access to the activity at other times. It would hardly be effective to say to a student who had an articulation problem that contingent upon three correct verbal initiations to another student she would earn 15 minutes of free time, if access to free time were available at recess or lunch. Students will more likely perform under the stated contingencies if other sources of activity reinforcers are controlled.

Anecdote 9.2 shows how a consultant and regular class teacher structured an activity reinforcer for a hard-of-hearing student mainstreamed into a regular junior high school class. The student has concomitant speech difficulties.

ANECDOTE 9.2

TEACHER: Mrs. Frank, I'm having a problem with one of my students in the class. I thought you might be able to help me.

CONSULTANT: I'll be glad to help if I can. What seems to be the difficulty?

TEACHER: Megan, a hearing-impaired student in the class, has extreme difficulty talking to the other students. I think she is afraid they will either ignore her or make fun of her.

CONSULTANT: I see.

TEACHER: There are a few students who talk to her occasionally, but most of the students ignore her.

CONSULTANT: I see. How about if we get together in a couple of days to discuss the situation?

TEACHER: Okay.

CONSULTANT (*meeting with the teacher a few days later*): I recall you said that there were a few students who talked a little bit to Megan.

TEACHER: Yes, that's right.

CONSULTANT: How would you feel if we designed a program whereby these students could earn extra points if they interacted with Megan?

TEACHER: That would be fine, since all of my students earn points for one thing or another in class. I'm sure we could extend the present program in this direction.

CONSULTANT: Good.

CONSULTANT AND TEACHER (*approach the two students who occasionally talk to Megan*): Chris and Bill, we have an idea that might interest the two of you.

BILL: Really? what is it?

CONSULTANT: As you know, Megan has difficulty talking to other students.

CHRIS: We know. She's hard to understand sometimes.

TEACHER: We realize that some of what Megan says is difficult to understand, but we'd like the two of you to make an effort to talk to her, maybe between classes or during project work in class. Whenever either of you says something to Megan, you'll earn one extra point toward your weekly total.

BILL: That's all we have to do?

CONSULTANT: That's right. Any time either of you begins a conversation with Megan, each of you will earn one extra point.

MEGAN (*approaches the teacher some time later*): Mrs. Jones, things have really gotten better. Two students in my classes are talking to me more, and even listening to me when I talk. School isn't such a drag anymore.

The consultant and the teacher could have arranged the contingency the other way around. That is, they could have made point acquisition for Megan contingent upon her initiating conversations with other students. The rationale for structuring the activity for the nonhandicapped students is that the teacher knew that the points would be a powerful reinforcer for Chris and Bill, and there might be more occasions for Chris and Bill to initiate a conversation with Megan than the reverse. Clearly, though, as time goes by the teacher and the consultant would continue to refine the program so that Megan would have more responsibility for initiating and maintaining interactions.

Social Reinforcers.   Social reinforcement is the least intrusive level of reinforcement that a classroom teacher can use to establish and maintain behavior. Praise is the foremost example of a *social reinforcer*. Other types of social reinforcement include smiles, pats on the back, facial gestures, and teacher attention. The use of contingent praise has been demonstrated frequently in the literature (Broden, Bruce, Mitchell, Carter, & Hall, 1970; Hall, Lund, & Jackson, 1968; Kazdin & Klock, 1973). Surprisingly, however, social praise is not given in the classroom with the frequency that one might expect, despite its demonstrated effectiveness. While "hard data" still remain to be gathered, some researchers (e.g., Madsen & Madsen, 1974; Stuart, 1971) indicate that a functional ratio of about four praise statements to one disciplinary statement should be the goal of teachers in most learning settings. These data are in contrast to Madsen, Madsen, Saudargas, Hammond, and Egar's (1970) study, which found that approximately 77% of teacher interactions with children were negative whereas 23% were positive.

Hall, Lund, and Jackson (1968) conducted a classic study showing the effects of praise on student behavior. When elementary-aged students engaged in study behavior, the teacher either verbally praised them, patted them on the back, or came close to their desks. If a student was not studying, the teacher did not attend to him or her. Figure 9.2 clearly shows the effects of positive praise and attention on the study behavior of one of the students. When the contingency was in effect, study behavior increased. When it was not in effect, study behavior decreased.

The consultant recommending social praise as an alternative to building behaviors can remind the teacher that it is the most natural reinforcer that a teacher can use, and it has a number of distinct advantages over other levels of reinforcement. First, given the variety of praising statements that teachers can use, satiation is unlikely to occur. Second, praise and attention are cost-effective. The teacher does not have to spend money to deliver the reinforcement. With other levels of reinforcers (edibles, tangibles, and exchangeables), the cost of purchasing items is a factor. Third, social reinforcers are convenient and efficient. Teachers do not have the potential messiness associated with edible reinforcers, nor do they have to be concerned with the potential delays in student response while the candy is eaten or the exchangeable reinforcers are handled. Finally, student performance is much more likely to be maintained in different learning settings under social reinforcement than under other levels of reinforcement.

Token Reinforcers

According to Cooper et al. (1987) token reinforcers can be considered generalized reinforcers, because they are associated with a large number of reinforcers. A *token reinforcer* can be a physical object, such as a chip or a star, or it can be a written symbol, such as a check mark. Tokens can be reinforcing themselves, and they acquire stronger reinforcing capability when they are exchanged for back-up reinforcers, such as free time or activity reinforcers.

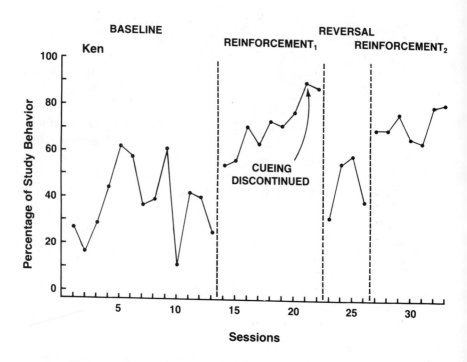

FIGURE 9.2. A record of study behavior for Ken. From "Effects of teacher attention on study behavior" by R. V. Hall, D. Lund, & D. Jackson (1968) in *Journal of Applied Behavior Analysis, 1*(1), 6. Copyright 1968 by Society for the Experimental Analysis of Behavior. Reprinted by permission.

Initiating and Maintaining a Token Economy in the Classroom.   Token economies have been used in a wide variety of settings including classrooms with hyperactive (Robinson, Newby, & Ganzell, 1981); culturally diverse (Wolf, Giles, & Hall, 1968); and normal students (McLaughlin, 1981).

When initiating a token economy, the first step is to determine the target behavior to be modified. Once the target behavior has been identified in observable and measurable terms, the teacher describes the rules of the token economy. The teacher tells the students the conditions under which tokens can be earned, the back-up reinforcers that are available, and the exchange procedure. Frequent token exchanges are recommended when initiating a token economy program.

Finally, Cooper et al. (1987) suggest that consideration be given to selecting an appropriate token for the individual or group. The token should be safe (i.e., not likely to swallowed by young children) and not likely to be counterfeited. Also, it should be durable, reusable, and inexpensive.

Once the token system is established, maintaining it is a relatively simple task. The teacher needs only to follow the rules that were initially formed. Reinforcing students with the token immediately after the occurrence of the desired behavior, providing a variety of back-up reinforcers, and maintaining a functional exchange procedure are essential components of maintenance. Also, it is to the teacher's advantage to begin to increase the response requirements while simultaneously decreasing the amount of tokens earned. It is important to incorporate this strategy, because the primary goal of the token program should be to move to a higher level of reinforcement (e.g., praise) as soon as possible. By repeatedly pairing praise with the delivery of the token, the praise will acquire the reinforcing capability of the token. For a complete description of the guidelines for establishing and maintaining token economy systems in the classroom, the reader is referred to Kazdin (1977), Kazdin & Bootzin (1972), and Cooper et al. (1987).

Financing a Token Economy. Consultants who recommend the use of token economies or other exchangeable systems must be able to suggest ways for teachers to finance these systems. A few alternatives are presented.

Grant-in-aid. Many state and local departments of education offer grants for teachers to develop, implement, and evaluate instructional approaches. If the use of the tokens or exchangeable reinforcers are essential components of the overall instructional methodology, the cost of these items could be incorporated into the budget. The obvious disadvantage of this approach is that competition for funding is often keen, and because many proposals have to be reviewed, there may be a considerable delay between the application and the reward of the grant. Waiting to implement the token program until a decision is rendered by the granting source may be counterproductive.

District support. Some school districts allocate money each year for expendable items, such as reinforcers. Often the principal has a petty cash account that might be used to reduce the cost of the token economy.

Parent-teacher groups. In many districts parent-teacher associations (PTAs) sponsor fund-raising events each year to reduce or eliminate costs for worthwhile school projects. Petitioning the PTA to sponsor a fund raiser to support a token economy might help.

Personal expenditure. Many teachers purchase exchangeable reinforcers with their own money. While this is an undesirable option from a cost standpoint, many teachers feel that the benefit the students derive from having the program outweighs the cost it incurs. To avoid incurring expenditures for exchangeable reinforcers, teachers or parents should ensure that the available reinforcement menu includes a variety of no cost options (i.e., free time, classroom privileges, fast food coupons). If free time, classroom privileges, or coupons are reinforcers for the students, costs are eliminated.

Contingency Contracting

Contingency contracting refers to a behavioral approach in which tasks and reinforcers are specified before the assignment is begun. The use of contracts is frequent in our daily lives. Examples of contracts are paying a mortgage, purchasing items with credit cards, and signing an employment agreement. Although each of these activities is different, a common feature exists. In any contract there are specifications about the terms of the agreement and responsibilities of each party. According to Cooper et al. (1987), specifying the terms of the contract is an important consideration when establishing a contingency contract. Teachers and parents who might use contracts must realize that the personal exchange between the parties is an important dimension of the process. Cooper et al. (1987) put it succinctly.

> The warning against the oversimplification of contracting is important. Contracting is not as simple as it is so often presented whether used with delinquent teenagers or well behaved third graders. The negotiation/compromise process is not an adjunct to, but rather an integral component of contingency contracting as a behavior change intervention. (p. 16)

Educators (notably Cooper et al., 1987; Homme, Csanyi, Gonzales, & Rechs, 1969; Kelley & Stokes, 1982) have outlined guidelines for using contracts in school environments. Homme et al. (1969), for example, outlined 10 specifications for contracts and suggested that contracts can be used with any population of students for any subject matter (Table 9.2).

Taken as a whole, Homme et al.'s (1969) specifications provide the consultant with clear guidelines for assisting teachers in developing working contracts. Embedded in the rules are the behavioral procedures of immediate reinforcement, systematic application, and fairness.

Teachers who use contingency contracting according to Homme et al.'s (1969) guidelines become more directive teachers, even for subject areas in which contracts are not employed. Teachers begin to recognize the value of positive directions, immediate feedback, frequent reinforcers, and consistency. In classrooms where handicapped students are enrolled, teachers frequently report that the shared responsibility of developing the contract, in conjunction with the monitoring process, increases student academic and social performance.

More recently, Dardig and Heward (1976), Heward, Dardig, and Rossett (1979), and Cooper et al. (1987) have indicated that contracts can be used

TABLE 9.2
Homme et al.'s Ten Rules for Contingency Contracting

Rule 1. The contract payoff (reward) should be immediate.

Rule 2. Initial contracts should call for and reward small approximations.

Rule 3. Reward frequently with small amounts.

Rule 4. The contract should call for and reward accomplishment rather than obedience.

Rule 5. Reward the performance after it occurs.

Rule 6. The contract must be fair.

Rule 7. The terms of the contract must be clear.

Rule 8. The contract must be honest.

Rule 9. The contract must be positive.

Rule 10. Contracting as a method must be used systematically.

From *How to use contingency contracting in the classroom* by L. Homme, A.P. Csanyi, M.A. Gonzales, & J.R. Rechs (1969), Champaign, IL: Research Press. Reprinted by permission.

with children in home or school settings to increase and maintain a wide variety of behaviors. These authors suggest that contracts be written so that the task and reinforcement components are clearly specified.

As Figure 9.3 shows, four items are completed under the task component portion: Who, What, When, How Well. Under the reward component, the items Who, What, When, and How Much reinforcement are listed. In this contract Ron must attend to his tasks each day with a minimum of two prompts from the teacher. When this behavior occurs, he will earn 10 minutes of free time from his teacher, Mrs. Pauley.

Ideally, contracts should be written jointly with students. Students specify tasks or reinforcers. For example, when beginning to contract with students, the teacher or the parent may specify the task components, while the student completes the reinforcement categories. As the student develops more and more competence in task completion, the teacher or parent may have him or her suggest tasks as well. As a student becomes more self-directed, more responsibility is provided for stating the terms of the contract.

As Dardig and Heward (1981a) suggest, contracts can also be employed across settings. For example, a handicapped student who completes his or her work on time and at criterion in the regular classroom might have reinforcers issued at home. In a variation of home contracting, Trovato and Bucher (1980) found that reading deficient elementary-aged students made twice the

---

Contract

Task	Reward

Task

WHO: Ron Johnson

WHAT: Attending to task,

WHEN: Each school day

HOW WELL: Not more than two reminders may be given each day

Reward

WHO: Mrs. Pauley

WHAT: Extra free time

WHEN: Each day

HOW MUCH: 10 minutes

Sign Here: _Ronald Johnson_   Date ___1|5|87___

Sign Here: _Mrs. J. Pauley_   Date ___1/5/87___

Task Record

FIGURE 9.3. A sample contract. From *Sign here: A contracting book for children and their parents* (unnumbered page in text) by J. C. Dardig & W. L. Heward (1981a) Bridgewater, NJ: F. Fournies & Associates. Reprinted by permission.

achievement gains of peers participating in in-class tutoring when the in-class peer tutoring was supplemented with a home-based contingency contract. In their study, improved reading performance produced a variety of reinforcers specified by the contract, including preferred goods, being able to invite a friend to the house, or going out to eat dinner with the family.

Contracts have been used at the elementary and secondary level for students for whom previous types of reinforcement strategies failed. Kelley and Stokes (1982) provide an excellent illustration of how contingency contracting was used with junior- and senior-level high school dropouts attending a vocational training center. During baseline conditions, the students earned money for attending daily class sessions. During Contracting$_1$, students were paid for completing a negotiated amount of workbook items on a daily and/or weekly basis. For instance, their contract might require the completion of

5 daily assignments and/or 25 weekly assignments. Students earned their pay for attendance and work completion. Baseline$_2$ conditions were introduced approximately halfway through the study during which the contingency contracts were removed. Finally, Contingency Contracting$_2$ was reinstated.

Figure 9.4 shows that the contingency contracting was an effective procedure for improving the academic productivity of the students. During the contingency contracting condition of the study, the number of correct items completed by the students increased, whereas during baseline conditions the improvement was lost. Anecdotally, the students indicated they preferred the contracts because they knew exactly how much work was expected of them to earn the reinforcer.

Consultants who recommend contingency contracting should emphasize that it may take a couple of trials with students before the contracting process is completely successful. They must also stress to teachers that contracting is a mechanism to increase student performance when other procedures have failed, as it provides students with a voice in determining either the tasks they have to perform or the reinforcement they will earn. For many handicapped students, having a say about the curriculum can enhance their performance within it.

Premack Principle

The *Premack Principle* is often dubbed "Grandma's Law" and is best explained in Grandma's own words: "When you finish your meat and beans, you will be able to have your ice cream." In the present context, the Premack Principle means that access to a high-frequency behavior (eating ice cream) is contingent upon the performance of low-frequency behavior (eating meat and beans). Teachers can use the Premack Principle in their classrooms if they can determine high- and low-frequency behaviors.

One of the easiest ways to determine high- or low-frequency behaviors is to observe student activity during free time. For example, during recess or lunchtime, what activities does the student engage in? Does he or she like to play games, listen to records, talk to a friend, or read a book?

Another way a teacher can determine high- or low-frequency behavior is to ask the student, "What do you (or don't you) like to do when you have free time?" According to Cooper et al. (1987), however, asking students what reinforcer they prefer does not guarantee that an accurate answer will be made. What a student claims to be a reinforcer at one time or under one set of conditions may not be a reinforcer at another time or under a different set of conditions.

Finally, a third way to determine high- and low-frequency behavior is to systematically arrange tasks for students to choose. For example, a teacher could repeatedly give a student the option of doing one of three possible tasks,

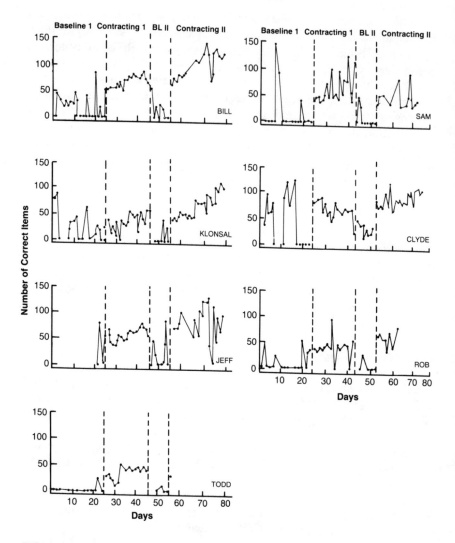

FIGURE 9.4. Number of items completed by students during baseline and contracting conditions. Missing data points represent student absences. From "Contingency contracting with disadvantaged youths: Improving classroom performance " by M.L. Kelley & T.F. Stokes (1982) in *Journal of Applied Behavior Analysis, 15*(3), 452. Copyright 1968 by *Society for the Experimental Analysis of Behavior*. Reprinted by permission.

such as writing a report, preparing a collage, or listening to a slide-tape presentation. It can be inferred that the task the student chooses most often will be the one that he or she finds the most reinforcing. Conversely, the task the student chooses least often over time would be the one he or she finds less reinforcing.

Once the high- and low-frequency behaviors have been determined, the teacher need only arrange them contingently. For purposes of discussion, academic school work will be considered low-frequency behavior, conceding that the example does not hold in all cases.

It should be noted that the Premack Principle can be used with either individuals or groups and can be applied with equal success across grade levels and academic subject areas.

Modeling

In a *modeling* procedure an antecedent stimulus is presented to the learner for the purpose of having him or her imitate it. The model could be a person or a behavior. Telling a student to watch the blackboard as the teacher solves a problem would be an example of using a modeling procedure.

Despite the extensive literature that indicates the powerful effects modeling has on increasing student performance (cf. Cooper et al.,1987; Striefel, 1981), consultants may overlook this procedure when recommending strategies to teachers or parents for solving problems. Modeling may be overlooked, because consultants do not fully understand how modeling can be used.

Broden et al. (1971), for example, demonstrated the effect that contingent teacher attention has on the disruptive behavior of second-grade students. Specifically, when the teacher attended to one student, the behavior of another student also improved — albeit to a lesser degree — even though the teacher's attention was not directed to the second student. Broden et al. (1971) suggested modeling may have played a part in the improved performance of the nontarget child. In essence, the nontarget student saw the target student receive the teacher's attention only when the target student was not disrupting the class. Therefore, to gain the teacher's attention the nontarget student may have begun to imitate the behavior of the target student.

Other researchers (e.g., Bell, 1977; Blankenship, 1978) have shown how modeling can be used to teach mathematics skills to students. Bell (1977), for instance, demonstrated that when a teacher modeled the performance of a given mathematics problem (i.e., showed students how to do the problem) and gave them verbal feedback about the accuracy of their responses, student performance improved.

In summary, when students already possess many of the component skills required in a task, whether they are academic or social skills, teachers or parents can use a modeling procedure to refine the performance of the student. Striefel (1981) and Cooper et al. (1987) provide excellent guidelines for using modeling in applied settings.

PROCEDURES TO DECREASE INAPPROPRIATE BEHAVIOR

Many behaviors that occur in school and home settings cannot be changed using reinforcement procedures alone. Often, a procedure is needed to weaken an inappropriate behavior. The next section describes how extinction, positive reductive procedures, and punishment approaches can be used to reduce inappropriate behavior.

Extinction

Extinction refers to the discontinuation of reinforcement for a previously reinforced behavior (Cooper et al., 1987). When a teacher ignores a student behavior that she previously reinforced, extinction is in effect. Zimmerman and Zimmerman (1962) indicate that extinction (ignoring) will produce desirable reductions in inappropriate behavior. If the other sources of reinforcement, such as peer attention to a student's misbehavior, cannot be eliminated, however, the extinction procedure will be compromised.

The teacher's systematic use of an extinction procedure can have a dramatic effect on student performance in the classroom. Suppose that a teacher feels he or she may be reinforcing poor behavior. For example, calling on students who shout their responses may reinforce shouting. To use extinction to reduce shouting behavior, the teacher would stop attending to students who shouted. The only students who would receive attention would be those who raised their hands.

While extinction can be a powerful technique for reducing inappropriate behavior, it has shortcomings. For example, it may take several sessions to be effective. For problems that require quick solutions, such as fighting, verbal abuse, or self-destructive behavior, the consultant would be advised to recommend other alternatives to the teachers. Further, when extinction is introduced, the teacher may notice a temporary increase in the rate of the inappropriate behavior. Consultants need to advise teachers to prepare for this temporary increase, lest they abandon the procedure prematurely.

Positive Reductive Procedures

Students emit a number of behaviors in the classroom that, while not totally disruptive, could be considered annoying or obnoxious. For example, a student who sings or hums to himself or herself may distract other students who are trying to complete their work. Under different circumstances, the humming and singing could be perfectly acceptable, and the teacher might encourage such behavior. With such a student, teachers are not interested in eliminating the singing; rather, they want to reduce the level of behavior or teach the child when to sing and hum and when not to. Positive reductive procedures can be employed successfully when the teacher wants to reduce the level of behavior. Additionally, these procedures avoid the potential side effects associated with other, more restrictive techniques (e.g., punishment).

Differential Reinforcement of Other Behavior (DRO).　*Differential reinforcement of other behavior (DRO)*, or omission training, is a relatively simple procedure to reduce unwanted behavior. To use a DRO procedure, (a) choose a target behavior; (b) establish a time interval for nonoccurrence of the behavior; and (c) deliver reinforcement if the time interval passes without the target behavior occurring.

For example, a fifth-grade teacher had a learning disabled student in her classroom who did a competent job on her assignments but often daydreamed. Ms. Abbott decided to reduce the amount of daydreaming. To accomplish her objective, Ms. Abbott discussed the situation with a consultant. After that meeting, they agreed that Ms. Abbott should collect baseline data on the student's daydreaming during the last 20 minutes of each period. The consultant, along with Ms. Abbott, established a series of four 5-minute intervals for each period. At the end of each 5-minute interval, a kitchen timer sounded. If daydreaming was not occurring, the student was reinforced. However, if daydreaming behavior occurred at the end of the interval, reinforcement was postponed. Any behavior that occurred at the end of the 5-minute period except daydreaming produced reinforcement.

One of the major shortcomings of the DRO procedure is that a wide range of behaviors could occur at the close of the interval, and the teacher would still have to provide reinforcement. This student, for example, could be hitting another student at the end of the 5-minute interval, but as long as she was not daydreaming, reinforcement would follow. Inappropriate behavior, therefore, could be reinforced.

Given the possibility of adventitious reinforcement of inappropriate behavior, and the fact that differential reinforcement of other behavior requires consistent observation, consultants should recommend a DRO procedure for those behaviors that can be clearly observed (e.g., talking-out, swearing, fighting).

Differential Reinforcement of Low Rates (DRL).　Students who occasionally call out jokes, tell humorous anecdotes, or change the topic of discussion in class can help to maintain an informal atmosphere that makes learning more enjoyable. Students who engage in these behaviors constantly, however, can be annoying. To use a *differential reinforcement of low rates (DRL)* procedure, the teacher structures the management plan so that the emission of lesser amounts of the behavior leads to reinforcement.

Deitz and Repp (1973) used a DRL procedure to reduce the number of times high school girls changed the topic of conversation during a class discussion period. During baseline conditions, the number of subject changes were recorded. Then during phases 2, 3, 4, and 5, progressively fewer subject changes produced the reinforcer (free time on Friday). For instance, during phase 2, 6 or fewer changes earned free time; during phase 3, 5 or fewer changes produced reinforcement. Figure 9.5 shows how the DRL procedure produced a stepwise decrease in subject changes for the high school students.

According to Cooper et al. (1987), the DRL procedure has several advantages and disadvantages. First, it is positive. Students can earn reinforcers. Second, it is tolerant. It does not require the total elimination of a behavior. Rather, DRL is designed to progressively reduce the inappropriate behavior.

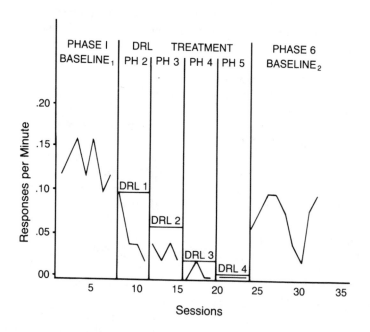

FIGURE 9.5. The rate of subject changes for a class of high school senior girls during baseline 1, treatment, and baseline 2 phases. "Free" Fridays could be earned by the group if they made fewer than the specified number of responses for each of the first four days of the week. The limit for the first treatment week was 5 or fewer responses during the 50-minute sessions (DRL 1). DRL 2 required three or fewer responses. DRL 3 required 1 or zero responses, and DRL 4 required zero responses. From "Decreasing classroom misbehavior through the use of DRL schedules of reinforcement" by S. M. Deitz and A. C. Repp (1973) in *Journal of Applied Behavior Analysis, 6,* 461. Copyright 1973 by *Society for the Experimental Analysis of Behavior.* Reprinted by permission.

Third, DRL is convenient and effective. Teachers can incorporate DRL in the classroom without rearranging their entire management program.

On the other hand, DRL is slow. It takes time to reduce the inappropriate behavior to tolerable levels. Consultants would not recommend a DRL procedure to a teacher to reduce aggressive or violent behavior. Also, this procedure focuses on the inappropriate behavior. Teachers who are not careful might fall into the trap of attending to undesirable behavior more than to desirable behavior and, in effect, inadvertently reinforce it.

Differential Reinforcement of Incompatible Behavior (DRI).   When a teacher reinforces a behavior that is incompatible with another behavior, *differential reinforcement of incompatible behavior (DRI)* is said to be in effect. Skilled consultants recommend DRI, because they have learned that it accomplishes a two-fold purpose: An inappropriate behavior is reduced or eliminated, and an appropriate behavior is strengthened. Reinforcing incompatible behaviors blends the best features of reductive and reinforcement procedures (Cooper et al., 1987).

How does one choose an incompatible behavior? Usually, all that is required is to select a behavior that physically cannot occur at the same time as the target behavior. For instance, if a student with developmental disabilities roams around the room, in-seat behavior would serve as an incompatible response to reinforce. Likewise, if a student repeatedly blurts out answers, the teacher might choose quiet hand-raising as the incompatible behavior. Ayllon and Roberts (1974) found that disruptive behavior decreased when students were consistently reinforced for appropriate academic performance.

Punishment Procedures

Four common punishment strategies are used in applied settings: punishment by the contingent presentation of a stimulus, overcorrection, time out from positive reinforcement, and response cost. The first two procedures are referred to as Type I punishment, because a stimulus or event is presented immediately after the occurrence of a behavior. The last two are referred to as Type II punishment, because they refer to the withdrawal of positive reinforcement. All punishment procedures have one feature in common: The future probability of a behavior is reduced.

Punishment by Contingent Presentation of a Stimulus.   *Punishment by contingent presentation of a stimulus* means that a stimulus or event is presented subsequent to the occurrence of a behavior, and the future probability of the behavior decreases (Azrin & Holz, 1966; Cooper et al., 1987). Hall et al. (1971) report a study in which punishment was used to stop a 7-year-old girl with mental retardation from biting and pinching herself. The teacher simply pointed to the student and shouted "No!" following each self-inflicted bite or pinch. Figure 9.6 shows that the student's biting and pinching were virtually eliminated when the punishment condition was in effect and that high levels of biting and pinching were evident when the punishment condition was absent.

One of the more popular uses of punishment by the contingent presentation of a stimulus occurs under conditions of corporal punishment. In corporal punishment, the misbehaving student receives swats for rule infractions in the presence of a witness. According to Rose (1983), despite the long history of the use of corporal punishment in schools, there is little empirical evidence of its effectiveness. Likewise, he reports that when corporal punishment is administered, it is usually done by a noninstructional staff member, not the teacher. From the consultant's standpoint, it would advisable to be well versed on district policy relating to how and under what conditions corporal punishment is administered, particularly since it is apparently conducted for ill-defined behaviors (Rose, 1983).

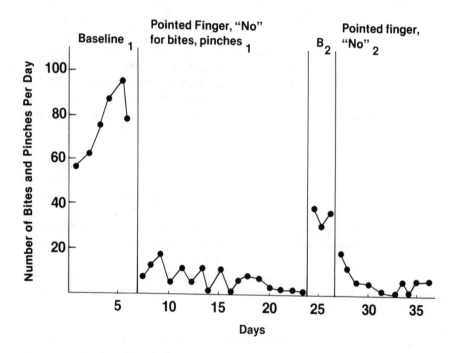

FIGURE 9.6. The number of times Andrea bit or pinched herself or others each day. From "The effective use of punishment to modify behavior in the classroom" by R. V. Hall, S. Axelrod, M. Foundopoulus, J. Shellman, R. A. Campbell, & S. S. Cranston (1971) in *Educational Technology, 11*(4), 25. Reprinted by permission.

Overcorrection. According to Cooper et al. (1987), *overcorrection* consists of one or both of two components: restitutional overcorrection and positive practice overcorrection. In restitutional overcorrection the individual restores the damaged environment to a state better than existed prior to the disruption or infraction. For instance, if Lyle wrote his name on his desk with his pencil, he would be required to clean his own desk and all of the other desks in the room. Positive practice overcorrection means that the individual engages in the appropriate behavior repeatedly. To continue with our example, under a positive practice overcorrection procedure the student would be required to repeatedly write his name on a piece of paper or on the blackboard.

Despite research that shows the efficacy of overcorrection for reducing inappropriate behavior (Cooper et al., 1987; Foxx, 1982; Foxx & Bechtel, 1983), consultants should not be too eager to recommend this form of punishment to teachers or parents. The presence of adequately trained staff, the strong possibility of student resistance, the likelihood of inadvertent reinforcement of the current inappropriate behavior, and the chance that collateral behaviors will be affected outweigh the wholesale endorsement of this reductive approach for all but the most serious of behaviors. Readers interested in learning more about this reductive approach are referred to Cooper et al., 1987; Foxx and Bechtel, 1983; and Azrin and Besalel (1980).

Time Out from Positive Reinforcement. According to Cooper et al. (1987), *time out from positive reinforcement*, or simply *time out*, is defined as "the withdrawal of the opportunity to earn positive reinforcement or the loss of access to positive reinforcers for a specified period of time, contingent upon the occurrence of a behavior; the effect is to reduce the future probability of that behavior" (p. 440). Procedurally, there are two types of time out variations that can be considered: exclusion time out and nonexclusion time out.

Exclusion time out. When time out consists of the physical removal of the student from the environment, it can be done successfully only under certain conditions. For example, the time-in environment (e.g., the classroom) must be positive and reinforcing. If the time out environment is more appealing, it is unlikely that the procedure will be effective. If a teacher sends a student to the principal's office only to have the student talk with school staff, visitors, or other students, time out will be ineffective. Also, the time away from the classroom should be relatively short. Cooper et al. (1987) recommend time out durations that do not exceed 15 minutes. Longer time out intervals become self-defeating because students have the opportunity to engage in other behaviors that may not be desirable. Exclusion time out, however, need not mean that the student is always physically removed from the classroom. Foxx (1982) recommends using a partition to separate an offending student for a brief period of time from his or her classmates but which allows the student to stay in the classroom.

Nonexclusion time out. Planned ignoring, withdrawing a specific reinforcer, contingent observation, and time out ribbon are four ways nonexclusion time out can be delivered (Cooper et al., 1987). In each of these variations, the individual remains in the setting but loses the opportunity to earn reinforcers, or loses a specific amount of reinforcement. Nonexclusion time out has the obvious advantage of reducing the risk of physical confrontations with students and can be conducted within the regular classroom.

Before a time out procedure is implemented, the consultant should make sure that district policy does not preclude its use. Some school systems, reacting to public pressure and court mandates, have ruled that time out cannot be employed. Several court cases (e.g., *Morales v. Turman*, 1973) have set mandatory guidelines and time limitations for physically secluding students from their normal environment. The reader is referred to Budd and Baer (1976) for a review of the legal implications of time out and to Brantner and Doherty (1983) and Cooper et al. (1987) for a complete discussion of procedures for using time out.

Response Cost. *Response cost* is defined as the loss of a specific amount of positive reinforcement contingent upon a behavior. The response or behavior is going to "cost" the child something he or she finds reinforcing. Like other forms of punishment, a response-cost contingency has the effect of temporarily reducing or suppressing the inappropriate behavior. Response cost does not involve the application of any physical stimulus.

There are a number of examples that demonstrate the efficacy of the response-cost procedure. For instance, Gallagher, Sulzbacher, and Shores (1976) and Leonardi, Duggan, Hoffheins, and Axelrod (1972) demonstrated how a response-cost technique can be used to reduce inappropriate behaviors in the classroom. In both studies the teachers wrote a series of numbers on the blackboard that indicated the amount of available free time. When a student disrupted the class, the teacher placed a slash through the highest remaining number on the blackboard, indicating that one minute of free time had been lost. Anecdote 9.3 shows how a building principal worked collaboratively with a teacher who had two behaviorally disordered students mainstreamed into her junior high school classroom.

ANECDOTE 9.3

TEACHER: Mrs. Jackson, the two boys who are mainstreamed into my classroom have completely disrupted my regular program.

PRINCIPAL: Does the problem lie with only these two students or are there other students involved?

TEACHER: Initially, it was just the two students, but the problem has spread to many others as well. I've tried talking to the boys, talking to their parents, and reinforcing them for their good behavior, but nothing seems to be working. I'm afraid someone is going to get hurt.

PRINCIPAL: You feel there is a danger that someone might get injured?

TEACHER: I do. Several arguments have already broken out. I'm afraid that a fight might break out at any time.

PRINCIPAL: Given the circumstances, would you consider trying a response cost procedure?

TEACHER: At this point I'd be willing to try almost anything. Frankly, I have run out of ideas.

PRINCIPAL: I know what you mean. I have days like these myself! Let me describe a procedure to try, and see what you think of it.

TEACHER: Okay

PRINCIPAL: First, place the numbers 20 to 1 on the chalkboard so that everyone can see them. Then tell the students that any time anyone in the classroom is out-of-seat or calls-out that the top number will be crossed off. Emphasize that the number left after the period is over indicates the amount of free time they'll have in class the next day, or that day, if possible. Teach the class as you normally do (i.e., continue to reinforce appropriate behavior), and make certain that every time one of the disruptive behaviors occurs you cross of the highest remaining number. Any questions so far?

TEACHER: What happens if the disruptive behavior continues?

PRINCIPAL: Let's wait to see what happens before we plan other alternatives. I'm prepared to recommend some options, but I'll hold off until after you've had a chance to try this procedure.

TEACHER: I'm willing to try it for a day or so.

PRINCIPAL: Let's meet again tomorrow.

In this case the principal recommended the response cost procedure because the threat of student injury in the classroom was high. He made his decision knowing that the response cost procedure has several possible advantages, including rapid suppression of the behavior, possible long lasting effects, and ease of application for the teacher (Cooper et al., 1987).

While an informed principal would be aware of the disadvantages of response cost — it may generate escape or aggressive behavior — he or she might choose not to outline these at the time to the teacher. Perhaps here the principal felt that the teacher could implement the procedure more effectively if the possible disadvantages were outlined at a later time. Planning a meeting for the next day would give the teacher time to field test the principal's recommendation and report the findings.

Ethical Considerations

Given court decisions (e.g., *Ingraham* v. *Wright*, 1977; *Wyatt* v. *Stickney*, 1972), school boards are more careful how they sanction or condone the use of any punishment contingency, especially those that might involve the use of an aversive stimulus. Sometimes, however, student behavior can be physically harmful, and an efficient and reliable means must be employed to suppress it quickly.

Consultants must temper their recommendations to use any type of punishment procedure because of the potential for unpredictable effects. Heron (1978b) proposed several guidelines that would aid the consultant in deciding when and how to recommend punishment procedures to teachers with handicapped children in their classrooms (Table 9.3). These guidelines summarize the major limitations and procedures for using punishment.

From an ethical and legal perspective, consultants must be aware that punishment procedures to reduce behavior should be used only as a last resort and only after obtaining informed consent (Carr & Lovaas, 1983; Longo, Rotatori, Kapperman, & Heinze, 1981). Programmatically, before a punishment procedure is implemented, all other "least restrictive alternatives" — for example, extinction, differential reinforcement of incompatible behavior (DRI) — should have been tried and have been shown to be ineffective.

A Decision Making Model for Using Punishment.   The *Gaylord-Ross decision model* (1980) provides an excellent illustration of procedures to consider when deciding the point at which punishment is introduced. His model suggests that five areas be addressed before punishment is implemented (Figure 9.7).

Assessment.   The assessment component of the model is designed to determine the severity of the inappropriate behavior. For example, is the behavior harmful to the individual or to others? If medical reasons are associated with the behavior, this stage allows for their identification and treatment without further steps.

Reinforcement.   The purpose of the reinforcement component is to determine if the inappropriate behavior is being maintained by reinforcement. If so, these reinforcers are identified, presented contingently, and/or withheld

TABLE 9.3
Limitations of and Recommended Procedures for Punishment

Limitations

1. Disruptive or inappropriate behavior can be reduced using punishment procedures. However, if students are motivated to perform the punished behavior, and have the opportunity to perform the punished behavior, it is likely that the inappropriate behavior will occur again in the future.

2. If a teacher uses a punishment technique to remove an aversive stimulus (e.g., yelling at students to be quiet), the teacher may be negatively reinforced. He or she may tend to use punishment again in the future to reduce inappropriate student behavior.

3. Punishment may produce undesirable side effects. Student aggression, escape, or avoidance behavior may result. If punishment occurs in the same environment repeatedly (e.g., in the classroom), the environment may become a conditioned aversive setting that students avoide.

4. Punishment may produce "spillover effects." That is, the behavior of nontarget students may be adversely affected by punishment directed toward target students.

Procedures

1. Vary the types of punishments that are used. If the same type of aversive stimuli are used repeatedly, the students may become satiated.

2. Use a high enough intensity of punishment to suppress the behavior, but refrain for gradually increasing the intensity lest the student develop a tolerance for punishment.

3. Punishment delivered at the beginning of a sequence of disruptive or inappropriate behaviors will often reduce the level of that behavior faster than punishment delivered at the end of the sequence.

to determine if the behavior changes in the desired direction. Assuming that reinforcers cannot be identified or that the behavior cannot be altered measurably using a reinforcement approach (e.g., differential reinforcement of incompatible behavior), the next component of the model is introduced.

Ecology.   Given that many educators have reported that ecological variables (e.g., noise level, seating arrangement) affect student performance (Heron & Heward, 1982; Rogers-Warren & Warren, 1977), the practitioner at this stage searches for variables that might be setting the occasion for, or reinforcing, the inappropriate behavior. For instance, moving a student's seat

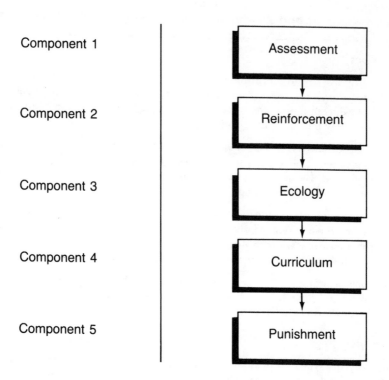

FIGURE 9.7. Gaylord-Ross decision-making model for punishment. From "A decision model for the treatment of aberrant behavior in applied settings" by R. Gaylord-Ross (1980) in *Methods of instruction for severely handicapped students* (p. 138), edited by W. Sailor, B. Wilcox, & L. Brown, Baltimore: Paul H. Brookes. Reprinted by permission.

from the back to the front of the room might reduce off-task and/or disruptive behavior by itself. Each suspected ecological variable should be altered before proceeding to the next step in the model.

Curriculum. The scope and sequence of the curriculum might set the occasion for inappropriate behavior. Changing the design of instructional materials (Vargas, 1984), the sequence of instruction (Engelmann & Carnine, 1982), or the pace of instruction (Carnine, 1976) might substantially reduce the occurrence of inappropriate behavior. Carnine (1976), for example, showed that when questions were asked at a fast pace (12 questions per minute), students correctly answered 80% of the time and were off-task only 10% of the time. Conversely, when a slow pace was used (5 questions per minute), the students correctly answered only 30% of the time and were off-task 70% of the time.

Punishment. The last phase in the Gaylord-Ross (1980) model prescribes punishment. To reiterate, this phase should be used only after the variables within the model discussed above have been investigated exhaustively. Even so, Gaylord-Ross (1980) recommends that the least restrictive form of punishment be used (e.g., Type II) before more restrictive forms are initiated (e.g., Type I). Furthermore, he recommends that punishment be combined with reinforcement for appropriate behavior or that punishment be reduced or eliminated as soon as the inappropriate behavior is under control.

GROUP CONTINGENCIES IN THE CLASSROOM

Thus far a number of procedures for increasing appropriate and decreasing inappropriate behavior in the classroom have been discussed. It should be noted that many of these procedures can be employed with individuals within a group context. Teachers, however, who have serious problems with many students in the room usually do not have the time to apply a series of individual contingencies. Teachers need an effective and convenient approach to deal with multiple misbehaviors. A *group-oriented contingency* serves this purpose, because the contingency is applied to the whole class regardless of individual behavior and it allows the teacher to take advantage of peer group influences. Some authors have legitimately outlined the dangers of using peers as change agents (Shapon-Shevon, 1979); still, peers have been shown to be effective agents for constructive change (Gresham & Gresham, 1982).

Advantages of Group-Oriented Contingencies

A group-oriented contingency has a number of advantages that teachers might find appealing. First, most students enjoy playing games, and group games usually generate enthusiasm. As Axelrod (1977) indicates, teachers can capitalize on student willingness to participate in these games. Second, many student behaviors, appropriate and inappropriate, are the result of conformity to peer pressure. For older students, especially junior and senior high school students, performance of appropriate and inappropriate social behavior may be reinforced by the peer group (Minuchin, Chamberlain & Graubard, 1967). Academic behavior, as well, may be controlled by peer pressure (Hamblin, Hathaway, & Wodarski, 1971). In the latter study, when group reinforcement was based on the improved performance of the bottom three students on a test, the more able students helped to tutor the low-scoring students. This contrasts with data acquired during the study's individual contingency phase, where the more able students did not tutor the other students. Third, group contingencies are often easy to carry out in the classroom. Axelrod (1973), for example, compared individual and group contingencies in two classrooms to determine which would be more efficient in reducing disruptive behavior. He found that both techniques were equally effective, but that the group consequence was far easier to implement in the room, since the consequence for any inappropriate behavior had to be administered only to the group rather than to each individual. Finally, simpler record keeping can be facilitated using group consequences (Long & Williams, 1973). Individual data would not have to be gathered on 30 to 40 students; instead, the occurrence of each target behavior would be recorded for the class as a whole.

Disadvantages of Group-Oriented Contingencies

The most obvious disadvantage for the use of a group-oriented contingency in the classroom is that all students, regardless of behavior, share the same outcome. For example, when a teacher uses a response cost group contingency in a class to reduce call-outs, all students lose a minute of recess for each call-out. Students who do not call out share the same punishment as those who do. However, if only a few students in the class are responsible for the call-outs, the teacher could set up a specific response-cost contingency just for them. In this case, the rest of the class would not be penalized for the inappropriate behavior of a few students.

Second, group procedures may not be sensitive to individual student performance. If a teacher uses only group data, individual student performance will be masked.

Finally, peer group pressure may be generated. Students who lose reinforcement because of a peer's behavior may threaten or intimidate that peer to force him or her to conform to group standards. Consultants who recommend a group-oriented contingency to teachers need to emphasize that peer pressure can work both for and against them. All parties engaged in the design and implementation of a group-oriented contingency must be aware of the potential effects of this approach for all students.

Litow and Pumroy (1975) suggest that group-oriented contingencies can be arranged according to (a) dependent group-oriented systems, where the whole class is reinforced if one student performs the stated behavior; (b) independent group-oriented systems, where individuals are reinforced if they *each* perform the desired behavior; and (c) interdependent group-oriented systems, where the whole class is reinforced when all students perform the acceptable behavior.

Dependent Group-Oriented Systems

Gresham (1983) conducted a dependent group-oriented contingency study that would be of interest to consultants who must arrange management programs across home and school environments. Billy, the 8-year-old target of the study, earned good notes for nondestructive behavior at home (not setting fires, not destroying furniture). The notes, which served as a daily report card, were exchangeable at school for juice, recess, and tokens. After Billy earned 5 tokens, he was allowed to serve as the host for a class party. So, Billy's good performance at home earned a reinforcer at school for him and his classmates. The results of the study indicate that Billy's destructive behavior at home was greatly reduced.

Independent Group-Oriented Systems

Independent group-oriented procedures are most typically represented by token reinforcement or contingency contracting programs in which the performance of each student does not depend on the rest of the members of the group.

Robinson, Newby, and Ganzell (1981) provide a useful illustration of an independent group-oriented contingency to improve the academic performance of 18 hyperactive third grade boys. Students earned colored disks (red, green, yellow, and white) for teaching themselves or a partner sight words or the use of the words in sentences. Each student could earn 15 minutes of free time after earning the red token, designating that he or she had taught another student to use words in a sentence. Using a reversal design, the data indicated that when the token system was in effect, student reading and math improved. When the independent group-oriented contingency was not in effect, performance decreased markedly (Figure 9.8).

Interdependent Group-Oriented Systems

An interdependent group-oriented contingency can be accomplished in one of four ways: (a) The group as a whole meets the criterion (Gola, Holmes, & Holmes, 1982); (b) reinforcement is delivered when a group mean score is achieved (Baer & Richards, 1980); (c) a single student earns reinforcement for the group (Speltz, Shimamura, & McReynolds, 1982); and the Good Behavior Game is used (Barrish, Saunders, & Wolf, 1969). Of these four procedural variations, the Good Behavior Game provides the consultant with the most flexibility for school or home application.

According to Barrish et al. (1969), the *Good Behavior Game* begins by dividing the group into two (or more) groups or teams. Each team is told that whichever team has the fewest marks against it when the game ends is the winner. The teams are also told that they can both win if they both meet the criterion specified by the teacher. Figure 9.9 shows the results of the Barrish et al. (1969) study. When the Good Behavior Game was in effect, the

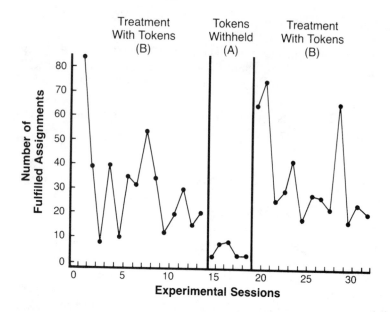

FIGURE 9.8. Total number of completed assignments for an 18-member class of hyperactive students. From "A token system for a class of underachieving hyperactive children" by P. W. Robinson, T. J. Newby, & S. L. Ganzell (1981) in *Journal of Applied Behavior Analysis, 14*, 311. Copyright 1981 by *Society for the Experimental Analysis of Behavior*. Reprinted by permission.

percentage of intervals of talking-out and out-of-seat during reading and math decreased.

The Good Behavior Game is an example of a "package" group contingency, because it combines punishment (behavior decreases), differential reinforcement of lower rates of behavior (the criterion for performance is changed by the teacher), stimulus control (the marks on the board indicating an infraction), and reinforcement (a reinforcer is delivered for the team that meets the criterion). Its applicability in a wide variety of classroom situations makes it a desirable alternative for the consultant working with group problems.

CONCLUSION

This chapter summarized a number of procedures to manage behavior, including the behavior of groups of individuals. Given that consultants are often called upon to assist with increasing or decreasing a wide range of responses, consultants must be skilled in the application of these principles and procedures.

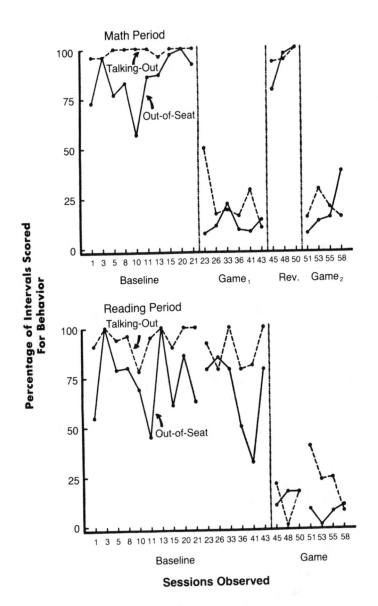

FIGURE 9.9. Percent of one-minute intervals scored by an observer as containing talking-out and out-of-seat behaviors occurring in a classroom of 24 fourth-grade students during math and reading. From "Good Behavior Game: Effects of individual contingencies for group consequences on disruptive behavior" by H. H. Barrish, M. Saunders, & M. M. Wolf (1969) in *Journal of Applied Behavior Analysis*, 2(2), 122. Copyright 1969 by *Society for the Experimental Analysis of Behavior*. Reprinted by permission.

Even more so, consultants must recognize conditions under which certain procedures are warranted. The Gaylord-Ross (1980) model serves as one illustration of a decision-making process that is based on the concept of the least restrictive alternative. Finally, group-oriented contingencies offer the consultant another set of management procedures that can be applied in a variety of settings.

SUMMARY OF KEY POINTS

Positive Reinforcement

1. Positive reinforcement is defined as the presentation of a stimulus or event subsequent to the performance of a behavior which results in the increase in the probability of the behavior occurring again.

2. The stimulus or event that follows the behavior and that is responsible for the increase in behavior is the positive reinforcer.

Negative Reinforcement

3. Negative reinforcement is defined as the removal of a stimulus contingent upon a response and has the effect of increasing the probability of the behavior in the future.

4. The stimulus or event that is removed is the negative reinforcer.

Types of Reinforcers

5. Reinforcers can be of several types: edible, tangible, exchangeable, activity, or social. Reinforcers are determined solely by their effect on behavior.

Token Reinforcers

6. A token reinforcer is a physical object or symbol that is exchangeable for a back-up reinforcer.

7. Tokens can be employed in classroom situations where conventional reinforcers have been ineffective.

8. Token programs permit the teacher to use a wide variety of back-up reinforcers to establish and maintain behavior. Tokens should be paired with social praise so that when the tokens are reduced or removed, student performance will be maintained by the social praise.

Initiating and Maintaining a Token Economy in the Classroom

9. To initiate a token economy, identify the target behavior; describe the rules for earning tokens; and ensure that the tokens are durable, reusable, and exchanged frequently.

10. Token programs can be maintained by following the rules designated for the program, providing a variety of back-up reinforcers, and using an intermittent exchange program.

Financing a Token Economy

11. A token economy might be financed through a grant-in-aid, district support, parent-teacher groups, or personal resources.

Contingency Contracting

12. Contingency contracting refers to a behavioral approach in which the task and reinforcement components for the teacher and student are specified in advance.

13. Contracts should be written, and, if possible, students should help to write them. Contracts can be employed with individuals or groups of students and should be drawn using appropriate guidelines.

Premack Principle

14. The Premack Principle states that access to a high-frequency behavior is contingent upon the performance of low-frequency behavior.

15. High-frequency behavior can be determined by observing, asking, or arranging choices.

Modeling

16. When a teacher wants to increase the performance of students who already possess many components of target behaviors, a modeling procedure may be employed.

17. Modeling can be effective for a wide range of academic or social behavior.

Extinction

18. Extinction refers to the discontinuation of reinforcement for a previously reinforced behavior.

19. Extinction must be used cautiously in the classroom, because other sources of reinforcement for inappropriate student behavior might interfere.

20. Extinction usually has a delayed effect on behavior rather than an immediate one.

Positive Reductive Procedures

21. There are three positive reductive procedures: differential reinforcement of other behavior, differential reinforcement of low rates of behavior, and differential reinforcement of incompatible behavior.

Punishment Procedures

22. Punishment procedures can be divided into four categories: punishment by the contingent presentation of a stimulus, overcorrection, time out from positive reinforcement, and response cost.

23. Punishment by the contingent presentation of a stimulus and overcorrection are referred to as Type I punishment. Time out and response cost are referred to as Type II punishment.

Ethical Considerations

24. Punishment of any type should not be administered without informed consent or before all other nonintrusive approaches have been attempted.

A Decision-Making Model for Using Punishment

25. A five-step decision-making model for using punishment specifies that before punishment is used, assessment, reinforcement, ecology, and curriculum variables must be used. Only after these variables have been tried and have been shown to fail should punishment be implemented.

Group Contingencies in the Classroom

26. A group-oriented contingency is designed to reduce the inappropriate and increase the desirable behavior of a class as a whole.

27. A group-oriented contingency can be applied to a variety of academic or social problems.

28. Group-oriented contingencies can be classified into three categories: dependent, independent, and interdependent.

QUESTIONS

1. Define and give one example of positive reinforcement, negative reinforcement, punishment (including overcorrection, time out and response cost), and extinction.

2. Identify the components of a contingency contract. Why are contracts effective when other management procedures are sometimes not?

3. List three ways to decrease inappropriate social behavior. Focus your response on positive reductive procedures.

4. Why is it important for the consultant to be well versed with the ethical issues surrounding some types of behavioral interventions?

5. How can Gaylord-Ross's (1980) decision-making model be used at the elementary, middle, and senior high school levels? Would any modifications in the model need to be made?

6. Describe three ways in which a group-oriented contingency could be placed into effect. What are the advantages and disadvantages of each approach?

DISCUSSION POINTS AND EXERCISES

1. Discuss the value of objective data in teaching in terms of (a) deciding whether or not a problem exists; (b) determining appropriate intervention strategies; and (c) the effect of an applied intervention.

2. Identify your school system's procedures for dealing with truant students, students who abuse drugs and alcohol, and destructive students. Do the data indicate that existing procedures are effective?

3. How would you apply the procedures outlined in the chapter to a student who is consistently late for class, a student who will not attempt assigned work, or a student who has difficulty establishing and maintaining appropriate social relationships?

4. List five potential reinforcers for students at each of the following grade levels: primary, intermediate, junior high, and high school.

5. Present regular teachers who have a handicapped student in their classrooms with a blank contract (see Figure 9.3). Ask the teachers to complete the full contract for one handicapped student and for one nonhandicapped student in the classroom. Check each contract for consistency with Homme et al.'s (1969) recommendations and Dardig and Heward's (1981a) guidelines. Praise teachers for correct performance.

6. During an inservice presentation demonstrate how to pair social praise with the delivery of tokens. Stress how to remove tokens once performance begins to improve. Have teachers practice token delivery during inservice sessions and monitor their performances in the classroom.

7. Show a videotape of a skilled teacher using response cost and time out procedures with handicapped and nonhandicapped students. Have

teachers in attendance identify the specific teaching behaviors that make these approaches work. Solicit their opinions as to how these techniques could be used in their classrooms.

10

Multicultural Considerations in Educational Consultation

Educational consultants are frequently called upon to assist with the development, implementation, and evaluation of programs for linguistically and culturally diverse exceptional students. Not only is the consultant faced with the usual challenges of accommodating the special learning needs of the student, but now these needs must be met in a manner consistent with the language and culture of these students.

After presenting several multicultural considerations, we will discuss issues related to curriculum, instruction, parent training, and the coordination of services for multicultural handicapped students. Examples from the literature and the authors' experience related to these topics are provided.

OBJECTIVES

After reading this chapter, the reader should be able to:

1. describe four types of bilingual education programs.

2. define an English as a second language (ESL) program.

3. distinguish two types of language proficiency.

4. identify the major components of a culture.

5. distinguish three levels of ethnic identity.

6. describe three curriculum and instructional modifications that are sensitive to language and culture.

7. identify three reasons for limited participation by multicultural parents in educational programs.

8. identify at least five different staff members who may be able to provide educational services for multicultural handicapped students.

KEY TERMS

Limited English Proficient (LEP)	Second language acquisition
Bilingual Education Act	Language proficiency
Bilingual education	Basic interpersonal communication skills (BICS)
Transition program	Cognitive/Academic Linguistic Proficiency (CALP)
English as a second language	Traditional community
Maintenance program	Dualistic community
Restoration program	Atraditional community
Anglo-American culture	Ethnic identity
Enrichment program	Multisensory approaches

MULTICULTURAL CONSIDERATIONS

More and more, schools are faced with providing education for diverse student populations. As reported in *Education Week* (Today's Numbers, 1986), Americans now are "more racially and ethnically diverse than any previous generation in American history" (p.14). For instance, of the students enrolled in school in September of 1986, 25% were from families who lived in poverty; 15% were physically or mentally handicapped; 15% were immigrants speaking a language other than English; and 10% had poorly educated, even illiterate, parents.

Though these demographic statistics may be misleading in the sense that children from these families may not need special services in school, clearly it is inferred that many of the students represented by these characteristics are "at-risk" children who might require special services to succeed in school.

Linguistically different individuals are scattered throughout the entire country (Baca & Cervantes, 1984). Approximately 10% of the entire school population (estimated to be approximately 40 million students in 1982) is linguistically different. Of these, approximately 600,000 students are linguistically different and handicapped. It is anticipated that this group will double by the year 2000.

The single largest group of linguistically different students is Hispanic, representing approximately 75% of the *Limited English Proficient* (LEP) population of students (i.e., those students who have limited skills in English reading, writing, speaking, and understanding). Another sizable group is that of refugees (Baca & Cervantes, 1984). Characteristically, these people are poor and, therefore, must contend with the problems of culture, language, and poverty.

To accommodate the cultural and linguistic diversity in this nation, the *Bilingual Education Act* was passed in 1968. This act, amended three times (1974, 1978, 1984), assures appropriate education for LEP students. Though the law recognizes the value of using native language and culture in instruction, the emphasis of the Bilingual Education Act is the development of English proficiency. Limited English Proficient students who are also exceptional are entitled to receive services under the Bilingual Education Act, the Education of All Handicapped Children Act of 1975, and the Rehabilitation Act (Baca & Cervantes, 1984). In effect, linguistically different exceptional children are entitled to bilingual education and special education services. It is important that consultants facilitate the appropriate education of these students by considering the role bilingual education can take in the educational program of exceptional multicultural students. Consultants are encouraged to work closely with school district personnel who work in these fields and to examine the writings of authorities in these fields (Baca & Cervantes, 1984; Chinn, 1979; Cummins, 1981a, 1981b, 1984a, 1984b; Garcia, 1982; Jones, 1976; Krashen, 1981, 1982; Omark & Erickson, 1983; Terrell, 1981; Thonis, 1981) to best understand how to coordinate services for these students.

CURRICULUM

To help design an appropriate curriculum for a multicultural handicapped student, the educational consultant must consider several factors: the language proficiency of the student; the culture of the student; the regular education curriculum; and the bilingual education curriculum. Whether the student is in a special education setting or a mainstreamed setting, it is necessary to determine the appropriate language for instruction to develop a curriculum that is culturally meaningful to the student. Also, if the student is in a special education setting, it will be necessary to incorporate relevant components of the regular education and bilingual education curricula to ensure that the student receives an appropriate program. This program should be commensurate with that being received by the student's peers and should facilitate the generalization of skills to less restrictive settings. If the student is mainstreamed, it is appropriate to assume that a bilingual education program may be necessary. Therefore, it is essential that the consultant know the philosophy, curriculum, goals, and instructional methodology of the bilingual education program in the school.

We have considered aspects of the regular education curriculum, at the elementary and secondary levels, in chapters 6 and 7. In this chapter, we shall briefly present some issues related to bilingual education, language, and culture that are necessary to provide effective consultation services for culturally and linguistically different exceptional students.

Bilingual Education

Bilingual education is defined as an education program in which the teacher uses two languages to provide instruction (Baca & Cervantes, 1984). The process of providing effective bilingual education is controversial, and not all educators agree on the most effective process. However, it seems that bilingual education programs using both English and non-English languages for instruction are more beneficial in promoting English and academic achievement in LEP students than those that emphasize the use of only one language (Carpenter, 1983; Chan & So, 1982).

The goals of a bilingual education program involve cognitive and affective development, linguistic growth, and culture (Baca & Cervantes, 1984). These goals are reflected in a number of different bilingual education programs.

Transition Programs.   *Transition programs* use the native language and culture of a student to teach the student how to function in a regular school curriculum, and ultimately to become proficient in English. Most federally funded bilingual education programs are transition programs. Students are taught basic skills in their native language with *English as a Second Language (ESL)* instruction. When students demonstrate English proficiency, they are transitioned into regular education programs where instruction is provided in English.

Maintenance Programs.   *Maintenance programs* promote English proficiency as well as literacy in the student's native language. An example of a maintenance program is one that continues to provide native language instruction after the student demonstrates English proficiency and is receiving instruction in English. Maintenance programs help to ensure that individuals have the skills necessary to function bilingually in professional endeavors. This type of program is successful in developing truly proficient bilingual individuals.

Restoration Programs.   *Restoration programs* attempt to develop the language and culture of the student's ancestors. With this philosophical orientation toward bilingual education, the student who is a second- or third-generation resident of this country, and who may have been assimilated into the *Anglo-American culture*, receives instruction in the language and culture of his or her heritage. The custom among Jewish communities of sending their children to Hebrew school is an example of a restoration program.

Enrichment Programs. *Enrichment programs* teach a new language and culture to a group of monolingual children. This is a common practice in many European countries. Schools in the United States provide foreign language instruction, usually at the secondary level. However, some elementary schools, in keeping with the national emphasis of supporting a culturally pluralistic society, are introducing foreign language instruction and culture as an enrichment program to grade-school students as part of the regular education curriculum.

English as a Second Language (ESL)

English as a second language is not a bilingual approach per se, because it relies exclusively on English as the language of teaching and learning. In schools, ESL instruction can be offered as an independent program, or it can be incorporated as a method of promoting English fluency in bilingual programs. Baca & Cervantes (1984) consider bilingual education and ESL compatible, and they recommend the use of both programs in developing appropriate educational programs for linguistically different students.

When developing an individualized program for an exceptional linguistically different student, the consultant is urged to consider language and culture as the means to provide an appropriate program and not as ends in themselves (Baca & Cervantes, 1984). Consultants should be familiar with the bilingual program available in the school and the goals of the program and attempt to match the goals of the bilingual program with the individual learning goals of the linguistically different exceptional student. Before making a placement recommendation, the consultant should also take into account the parents' choice and the student's attitude toward instruction in English and instruction in the native language (Ortiz, 1986).

Language

Whether the multicultural handicapped student is in a special education setting or a mainstreamed setting, there are several factors to consider in deciding the language of instruction. The educational consultant should be aware of the nature of *second language acquisition*[1] and the *language proficiency* of the exceptional student. Two key features of second language acquisition warrant emphasis. First, Cummins (1981a, 1984) suggests that language proficiency is composed of two distinguishable components: everyday conversational skills (*Basic Interpersonal Communication Skills, BICS*) and abstract skills characteristic of academic instruction (*Cognitive/Academic Linguistic Proficiency, CALP*). It is important for the teacher to know the level and type of proficiency (e.g., BICS or CALP) of the student to decide what language to use when providing different types of instruction. If the student has mastered BICS in English but not CALP, the student may be able to converse in English. However, that is no guarantee that the student will be able to learn academic content in English. CALP seems to be acquired only after a five- to seven-year period of exposure to the new language — in this case, English.

The next point is that the second language is acquired when the student receives comprehensible input in a low-anxiety situation. Therefore, language instruction should be comprehensible, interesting, and relevant (Krashen, 1982).

Cautions   These key points have implications for bilingual education, ESL instruction, and instruction in content areas such as science and social studies. Specifically, in bilingual education transition programs, educators are cautioned to ensure that students have mastered CALP before making a transition into an all-English program. In ESL instruction, English should be taught so that the vocabulary is comprehensible and motivating to the student. For example, one may start with food words and accompany the lesson with the actual food objects to reinforce mastery of the vocabulary. At the secondary level, educators are urged to ensure that content is truly comprehensible to the LEP student, because second language acquisition is facilitated only if the student can understand the lesson. This is usually not the case in secondary classes where the academic content is aimed at native language speakers.

Educators are also urged to determine the student's mastery of CALP before relying upon English as the language of instruction for complex academic subjects like those usually found in secondary classes. Harris (in press) found that some secondary special educators assume that the multicultural handicapped student, if the student speaks English, has acquired the English proficiency needed to handle secondary subject matter instruction in English. However, if Cummins' (1981a, 1984) estimate of five- to seven-year exposure to the new language is correct, secondary special educators should seriously question the extent of each secondary LEP student's English language mastery when developing appropriate individualized programs for these students.

---

[1] J. Cummins and S.D. Krashen are two well-known experts in the field of *second language acquisition*. The reader is referred to their works for an understanding of this complex topic.

Assessment. Determining language proficiency is a difficult task and one that educators have been addressing for several years (cf. Carpenter, 1983; Langdon, 1983). It is beyond the scope of this text to discuss standardized assessment procedures. However, we would like to mention possible uses of other types of assessment data that may provide valuable supplementary information regarding the language use of students.

Ecological inventories can be extended to address specific factors related to language use. Langdon (1983) suggests that, in addition to the standard information obtained regarding educational, family, and health history, educators obtain information related to the length of time in this country. Payan (1984) also suggests obtaining information related to the level of language involvement with the disability, language skills upon entering school, the method and language used in measuring academic achievement, amount and type of language input received in the home environment, and success in any previous bilingual programs.

Several authors (e.g., Baca & Cervantes, 1984; Langdon, 1983) suggest that educators use observational and interview data to obtain additional information regarding language use. As suggested by Baca and Cervantes (1984), the key question to address concerns whether "the difficulties [noted are] related to bilinguality" (p. 178). Langdon (1983) suggests interviewing parents or guardians to obtain more information about home language use, the parents' perception of the problem, and the parents' perception of the child's motivation to know and learn another language.

In summary, the consultant is urged to collect as much information as possible concerning students' language use in home, school, and community situations and to apply knowledge of second language acquisition in determining the language of instruction for a LEP exceptional student. Ortiz and Yates (1984) sum up the situation: "The language of instruction should be the language through which the child learns best. The language in which the child learns best may be situation specfic" (p. 207).

Culture

When developing an individualized program for an LEP exceptional student, or when consulting with a teacher and an LEP student, it is necesary to remember that the student's language is inextricably bound to his or her culture. Culture provides meaning for verbal communication.

Aragon (1973) defines five major components that define a culture: the communication patterns reflected in a common language; a diet and way of preparing food; common dress; socialization patterns (e.g., the expected roles and interactions of family members, school personnel, etc.); and common values. Many of these components are explicit, that is, clearly observable in the behavior of individuals representing a given culture. However, other components are not readily apparent and require some probing and sensitivity to detect. For example, the values and socialization patterns may not be readily apparent to someone who is unfamiliar with the culture. That is why it is recommended that educators take some time to get to know students and their families. Once the educator understands the characteristics of the child's home and community environment, he or she is more likely to be able to develop a meaningful instructional program for the child and maximize communication with the child and the child's family. Field observation techniques, described in Chapter 8, may assist educators in accomplishing this objective.

Ortiz and Yates (1984) advise the educator to refrain from applying stereotypical characteristics to all individuals representing a given cultural group. Students are individuals. Though they are influenced by the cultures of their families, all students may not be influenced in the same way. Also, different generations reflect different aspects of a given culture. Ortiz and Yates (1984) discuss three types of culturally organized communities. A *traditional community* is one in which immigrants congregate and maintain the language and culture. The primary language used by the family, children, and community is the native language, not English. A *dualistic community* is one in which there is evidence of the influence of Anglo-American values. English may be spoken by the children but not by the parents. The children are bilingual. The children may be not only using two languages, but also living within two cultures — the family culture and the Anglo-American culture. An *atraditional community* is one in which natives are bicultural. The family is living within a primarily Anglo-American community. For the family to transmit their native culture, it may be necessary to provide special experiences for the children. For example, the parents may provide special native language instruction or specific activities to teach ethnic culture (e.g., special celebrations where the food and dress of the native culture are taught and celebrated).

Consultants should help teachers to ascertain the *ethnic identity* of the students in the class and engage the class in activities that reflect experiences ranging from traditional to atraditional life-styles. In this way, the curriculum can accommodate diversity among members of the same ethnic group, reduce stereotyping, and be a more meaningful way to provide instruction for multicultural handicapped students.

Benavides (1980) provides guidelines for developing cultural awareness in teachers. The consultant should help the teacher to (a) understand how the teacher's own cultural perspective affects the ongoing teaching/learning relationship; (b) promote an atmosphere in which cultural differences can be explored and approached intellectually as well as attitudinally; (c) draw upon the cultural experiences of students and parents; and (d) help students expand their knowledge of their own culture as well as the cultures of other students.

In summary, to provide effective and appropriate instruction for multicultural handicapped students, the educator must consider the cultural background these students bring to the educational setting. The teacher should develop a curriculum in consideration of the following characteristics of the child: (a) What is the student's familiarity and identity with the Anglo-American culture, (b) what is the student's familiarity and identity with his or her own native culture, (c) what is the student's expectation of the educational environment, and (d) has the student been successful in becoming part of the educational community?

Defining the exceptional multicultural child is a difficult task (Chinn, 1979). Few empirical data are available that describe this population. Generally, educators have merged the characteristics of handicapping conditions with the general characteristics of ethnic and racial groups (Carpenter, 1983).

Several authors have discussed differences in the behaviors of children who are representative of the Anglo-American culture and children from other ethnic/racial groups. The following are some examples.

> Most Afro-Americans...speak "standard" English...in settings where it is appropriate to conform to the dominant society's norm. However, when socializing with less assimilated relatives and friends, they often use many words and phrases that linguists call "Black English." (Banks, 1984, p. 57)

> Very few Asians engage in free participation in group discussion. (Kitano, 1973, p. 14)

> Indian students learn more through observation or visual means rather than verbal. (Pepper, 1976, p. 140)

> Hispanic students prefer cooperative activities, are concerned with immediate tasks, and are characterized by close family ties (Aragon & Marquez, 1973; Condon, Peters, & Sueiro-Ross, 1979; Rodriguez, Cole, Stile, & Gallegos, 1979; Sierra, 1973).

Consultants are urged to be mindful of the behaviors students exhibit that may be indicative of a cultural identity. This awareness is necessary so that, when designing programs for handicapped multicultural students, instruction will be provided "within a relevant cultural context so that expectations can be understood by the student" (Payan, 1984, p. 97).

INSTRUCTION

When providing an appropriate individualized program to multicultural handicapped students, consultants should carefully consider the presentation of instruction, grouping of students, and modification of materials that address the characteristics of multicultural handicapped students.

Presentation of Instruction

In deciding how to instruct an LEP exceptional student, the language of instruction is an important consideration. If it is decided that the student should be taught using two languages (i.e., English and the student's native language), language can be used in various ways (Baca & Cervantes, 1984). For instance, the teacher can alternate the times when a given language is used in the classroom. In the alternate-day plan, the native language is used one day, and English is used the other day. The half-day plan involves the use of the native language for one part of the school day and the use of English for the other part of the school day. In a mixed schedule some subjects are taught in the native language, and other subjects are taught in English. The authors have found that teachers of LEP exceptional students prefer the mixed schedule. The teachers found that if they were able to select the language of instruction for specific subjects, it was more likely that they would be able to make a match between the student's language proficiency and the language of instruction. Also, for some students, clearly separating language use is preferable when they are still developing proficiency in native language and English.

According to Collier and Kalk (1984), *multisensory approaches* to instructional presentation are helpful in establishing a meaningful lesson for LEP handicapped students. If a teacher does not have mastery of the student's native language, then it is essential that the teacher use as many modalities as possible to present content. In this way, the learning experience for the student is maximized. If the student does not clearly understand the language of instruction and the teacher demonstrates the skill to be mastered using auditory, visual, and concrete materials, the student has a greater chance of grasping the concept. Further, if a teacher uses many modes in presenting content, he or she has a better chance of matching the learning style of the student with the mode of presentation of the lesson. However, teachers are urged to consider individual learning styles as well as cultural learning styles, especially for those students who have a strong cultural identity.

There is some literature to suggest that cultural identity may be related to learning style. For instance, Ramirez and Castaneda (cited in Ortiz & Yates, 1984) report that children from traditional communities are likely to be field sensitive, while children from dualistic communities may use both field sensitive and field independent strategies. Collier and Kalk (1984) suggest that teachers become knowledgeable about the cultural characteristics of students with strong cultural identities and then determine the best mode of instruction by asking questions such as the following: "Does it seem more culturally appropriate to use physical demonstrations and experience activities rather than diagrams and verbal/visual directions?" (p. 244).

Teachers should also consider the strength of the student's cultural identity in determining the best response mode for a student. For example, if the teacher is presenting a lesson that requires student initiation for participation, the lesson may not be consistent with an Asian student's response mode. Teachers should not automatically attribute lack of participation by an LEP handicapped student as a sign of disinterest. Rather, teachers should carefully consider the response modes of students in light of their cultural identity. However, teachers are also urged to use good judgment and recognize the dangers of stereotyping and overgeneralizing cultural characteristics to all children from a particular group.

Grouping Strategies

The literature suggests that students from different cultural groups have different reactions to grouping patterns and activities (e.g., Delgado-Gaitan & Trueba, 1985; Pepper, 1976). For example, students with a strong American Indian cultural identity may perform best in cooperative group activities. The American Indian cultural norm is that excellence is related to how one performs as a group member and that group cooperation is more desirable than individual competition (Pepper, 1976). Likewise, Delgado-Gaitan and Trueba (1985), in their study of Mexican children in northern California, found that the children naturally formed cooperative groups for doing home chores as well as for conducting play activities.

Kagan (1986), in a review of the research of the academic achievement of multicultural groups, found "strong achievement gains among minority pupils in cooperative classrooms" and that "minority students show far greater gains in the cooperative compared to traditional methods" (p. 245). A number of studies have also examined the performance of high-, medium- and low-achieving students. Results indicate that medium and low achievers benefit from the cooperative methods, while high achievers seem to perform equally well in cooperative classrooms and traditional classrooms. It should also be noted that "both majority and minority students gained more using student teams" (Kagan, 1986, p. 246).

These findings suggest that grouping strategies may be appropriate and effective teaching techniques for multicultural handicapped students. The consultant should help teachers develop their skills in the use of a variety of grouping strategies. In Chapter 6, the use of peer tutoring and cooperative learning strategies was discussed. Cooperative grouping techniques can be appropriately used in special and mainstreamed settings, with all age groups. It is for the consultant and teacher to decide how to form the cooperative learning situations so as to best meet the cultural and skill needs of multicultural handicapped students. Kagan (1986) reports that improved ethnic relations among students have been a consistent finding in the cooperative learning research.

Modification of Materials

It is often necessary to modify materials to meet the needs of exceptional learners. When modifying materials for exceptional multicultural learners, it is also necessary to consider language and culture. The following criteria may be applied when deciding the appropriatenesss of curriculum material: (a) Does it reinforce learning; (b) is the material logically sequenced; (c) is the material comprehensible; and (d) is the material culturally sensitive (Collier & Kalk, 1984; Ortiz & Jones, 1982)?

Points a and b have been addressed in previous chapters. Points c and d are specific to multicultural handicapped students. When determining if the material is comprehensible, it is necessary for the educator to determine if the language level of the material matches the language proficiency of the student. It is also necessary to determine if the language concepts expressed in the material are consistent with the language concept development of the student. For example, in some languages there is no distinction between sexes. Sex is determined by the sensitivity of the culture to different sex roles, not by a word to denote sex. Therefore, the teacher will need to incorporate culturally appropriate activities and teach the concepts of *he* and *she*; otherwise, the student may become confused (Collier & Kalk, 1984).

In addition to determining if the language is comprehensible, the educator should also determine if the curriculum material is culturally sensitive. For example, many materials depicting different cultural groups may present general stereotypes. The teacher should be careful to discuss materials used and note which are indicative of modern-day cultural groups and which are not. The teacher should encourage the students to help identify and explain the cultural values depicted in curriculum materials.

In addition, the educator should use curriculum materials in a culturally sensitive fashion. As discussed by Collier & Kalk (1984), the educator should not assume that what is true in one culture is true in another. For example, the teacher may, in teaching the colors white, black, and brown, use different groups of people as examples. However, in many non-Western cultures, the words for white, black, and brown are never applied to human beings.

The following are examples of modified curriculum and instruction for multicultural handicapped students at the elementary and secondary levels. These approaches have been discussed in the literature and used with culturally and linguistically different students.

Modified Curriculum and Instruction (Elementary). Collier and Kalk (1984) discuss the use of the "integrated curriculum" at the elementary level. The principles of the approach could be applied at the secondary level as well. When using the integrated curriculum, the teacher selects a topic drawn from the life of the students. The teacher then develops specific skills through lessons developed around these topics. Collier and Kalk (1984) provide an example of an integrated curriculum around the general topic of "The Family at Home."

1. Math and science skills ("How does your father measure the logs for the corral? How is adobe made? How does your grandfather [or uncle] determine the proper time and season to tell stories. . . to shear the sheep?. . . to plant the crops or harvest? What about the treatment of illness?" "Let's make some fry bread, sopapillas, or rice.").

2. Language arts skills ("Tell us about when you helped your grandmother." "Tell or write about where your home is located." "How does your mother teach you about what to do in the morning?" "Let's all read Kee's story about taking the lambs to water. . .").

3. Motor/visual development (drawing pictures of family, home, maps of the area; building models or hooghans or wickiups; dioramas of the environments. Traditional games and activities that build coordination, such as dancing or drama). (pp. 252, 253)

Modified Curriculum and Instruction (Secondary). In *Monograph for Bilingual Vocational Instructor Competencies* (1981), the nature of bilingual vocational training for secondary age LEP students is discussed. The content is taught bilingually, and job-specific ESL instruction is taught concurrently. The purpose of the training is to prepare LEP students to perform successfully in work environments that require English language skills. The programs attend to the language needs of students by providing ESL instruction in vocabulary that is job specific as well as providing content instruction in the native language. The instructional materials are written in the trainee's native language or in simple, concrete English. Educators in these programs report that students acquire job skills quickly. The content being learned is comprehensible. The content is also meaningful, as it is directly related to employment for these students.

In summary. The modification of curriculum materials requires the educator to be sensitive to the learning, language, and cultural characteristics of students. It requires the educator to know about content area, learning problems, and compensatory strategies as well as language and cultural characteristics. The consultant can assist the teacher by providing resources for the teacher to increase knowledge in areas of weakness as well as by assisting the teacher in determining the individual needs of multicultural handicapped students. As stated by Collier and Kalk (1984), "The use of multisensory approaches coupled with multicultural materials and cross-cultural techniques is a good beginning in bridging the bilingual/bicultural and special learning needs of culturally and linguistically different exceptional children" (p. 245).

WORKING WITH PARENTS OF MULTICULTURAL EXCEPTIONAL STUDENTS

There are many reasons why parents from diverse cultural populations may not be involved in the educational programs of their children. Some of these reasons may be related to language and culture. For example, a parent who is not a fluent English speaker and/or is unfamiliar with the educational system in this country may be reluctant to participate in school-sponsored activities. There may also be a specific cultural value in conflict with Anglo-American expectations for parental participation. Ortiz and Yates (1984) state that "among some traditional Hispanics, there is a transfer of authority to the teacher. . . . Parents perceive teachers and other school personnel as experts in academic matters and, once they have transferred their responsibility to the educational expert, it is not their prerogative as a parent to interfere or to question decisions or actions of school authorities" (p. 191).

Another reason for lack of parental participation may be environmental constraints. Many parents of refugee children are poor. Parents in lower socioeconomic classes may have duties and responsibilties that take immediate priority over their child's education. Parents' poverty may also result in transportation or babysitting problems as well as a lack of time to participate (Lynch, 1981).

A third reason why parents may not participate may be lack of knowledge. Interviews with parents revealed that a large majority of parents did not know their rights concerning their children (Delgado, 1982). A survey conducted by Lynch (1981) with lower socioeconomic parents of special education students revealed that parents of mildly handicapped students participated in their child's educational program far less than parents of severely handicapped children. If lack of knowledge is a factor prohibiting parental participation in school-sponsored activities, consultants are encouraged to develop specific "outreach" programs to inform parents about the nature of handicapping conditions, educational programs available for multicultural handicapped students, and the expectations of the school personnel regarding the parents' involvement in their child's educational program.

An example of a training program for multicultural parents is the Mississippi Choctaw Bilingual Education Program (cited in Baca & Cervantes, 1984). In this program, parents assumed different roles, including members of the advisory board, community aides, and participants in a literacy program and a writer's workshop. The program design was based on the ATSEM model. ATSEM stands for the phases of the program: the *acquaint* phase, the *teach* phase, the *support* phase, the *expand* phase, and the *maintain* phase. In the acquaint phase, the family was introduced to the program by requesting that family members participate as advisory board members and as community aides. One of the activities of the community aides was to determine concepts that were related to their culture.

In the teach phase the bilingual family members learned new skills, which they then used to teach the younger children. In the Mississippi Choctaw Bilingual Education Program, the parents were taught to read and write and then helped the student learn to read and write.

The support phase was activated whenever family members needed emotional, social, or economic support. In the Mississippi Choctaw Bilingual Program, the family members belonged to advisory groups and support groups and helped each other with child rearing as well as financial problems. The support phase could also be used to identify resources to help parents with their handicapped child.

Family members enter the expand phase when they are completely comfortable with the program and are ready to become more involved. For example, a parent who comes to school and tells a story to the whole class from Choctaw folklore, without embarassment, would have achieved the expand phase.

The maintain phase of the model serves to keep family members involved and help bring new family members into the program. For example, family members who have been involved in the program may now help to acquaint new families with the program.

The model provides a framework for introducing and then actively involving the participants in the program. An interesting feature of this program is its flexibility and consideration of all members of the bilingual family. The flexibility of the program allows family members to participate at various levels of involvement, depending upon their needs and comfort with the program. Involving all members of the family is consistent with the culture and supports the involvement of the older siblings with the development of the younger children.

In summary, there are many reasons why parents from different cultural groups may not be actively involved in the educational programs of their children. Consultants are encouraged to work with parents and educators to involve them in the educational process to the maximum extent possible. However, parent-training programs should be implemented with Kroth's (1980) framework in mind and be consistent with parents' language, culture, knowledge, and environmental constraints.

COORDINATING SERVICES

As previously discussed, LEP handicapped students are entitled to special education, bilingual education, and regular education services. Therefore, determining the most appropriate program for an LEP handicapped student requires coordination of services. According to Martinez (1982), it is necessary to establish communication between departments of Bilingual Education/ESL and Special Education. These departments must agree that there is a need to develop specialized programs. They must commit resources and energy to work cooperatively to identify, design, and implement programs. The role of the consultant involves establishing and maintaining open lines of communication with resource personnel.

According to Baca and Cervantes (1984), "A model placement for the bilingual exceptional student should be one where the student could receive maximum instruction in the primary language within a relevant cultural context and where the student would be maximally integrated into the public school setting" (p. 272). To accomplish this goal, the educational consultant should consider the learning characteristics of the student, the expectations of the educational environment as well as factors specific to culture and language. These factors include the student's language proficiency in English and in the student's native language, the degree of social maturity in both native and Anglo-American culture, the wishes of the student and parent, and the available services (Baca & Cervantes, 1984). If the consultant obtains information relative to each of these areas, it will be possible to identify appropriate educational resources and develop a suitable individualized program for a multicultural handicapped student.

Evaluating Resources

Using the assessment strategies presented in Chapter 8, the consultant may want to apply the guidelines provided by Benavides (1985) for analyzing the educational resources available for handicapped multicultural students.

Benavides (1985) suggests a five-stage process. First, specify the objectives of the service delivery. In the case of services for LEP handicapped students, a goal of the service delivery system may be that all LEP handicapped students be provided appropriate education by certified teachers who are bilingual and biliterate in the student's native language.

Second, the consultant will determine the resources available to accomplish the objectives. In this case, the consultant would want to take a frequency count of the number of LEP handicapped students in special day classes, mainstreamed regular education settings, and mainstreamed bilingual education settings. The consultant would also want to determine the number of certified teachers in each of these settings and their level of proficiency in different languages.

Third, if the resources are not sufficient to provide the necessary services, the consultant must determine alternatives. For example, the consultant may decide that pairing bilingual and biliterate paraprofessionals with certified monolingual English teachers may provide a satisfactory alternative.

Fourth, the consultant evaluates the resources available to implement the alternative goal, using procedures similar to those used to evaluate resources in step two. The consultant would also want to determine what additional staff training may be required to implement the alternatives and estimate the cost and effectiveness of implementing the alternative plan.

Fifth, the alternative plan is implemented. The consultant would evaluate the effectiveness of the alternative plan, considering formative and summative evaluation procedures.

The consultant may also want to consider developing long-term and short-term plans. For example, a suitable alternative may not be possible with existing resources. The consultant may develop interim alternatives (e.g., sharing of aides between the bilingual and special education departments) until the educational staff is adequately trained to implement a more effective service delivery program for multicultural handicapped students.

Staffing Alternatives

It is important for the consultant to consider the adequacy of resources to serve this population and initiate programs that may be necessary to improve the quality of service for multicultural handicapped students. Because many districts are faced with an inadequate staff to implement the ideal program for multicultural handicapped students, they have developed alternative staffing patterns. Two examples of alternative staffing patterns are discussed below. One program, in Los Angeles Unified School District (LAUSD), provides guidelines for staffing and program construction of a special education self-contained program for LEP handicapped students. The other program, in San Jose Unified School District (SJUSD), considers ways of combining educational staff to provide a number of program options for LEP handicapped students.

In LAUSD three personnel options for the provision of services for LEP handicapped students in self-contained special education classes were identified: (a) A bilingual special education teacher is teamed with a monolingual special education assistant/trainee; (b) a monolingual special education teacher is teamed with a bilingual special education assistant/trainee; or (c) a monolingual special education teacher is teamed with a monolingual special education assistant/trainee and a bilingual aide who is assigned to the program.

The preferred personnel option from the list above is a. However, due to the limited number of bilingual special education teachers, alternative staffing arrangements may be implemented. Presumably, when an alternative is implemented, the district provides training activities for staff to increase their ability to provide effective services for multicultural handicapped students.

When implementing personnel staffing options b or c in LAUSD, LEP handicapped students who are being served in self-contained special education programs might benefit from the following staffing patterns. The monolingual special education teacher provides ESL instruction, and sheltered English for subjects such as math computation, science, and social studies. Cross-cultural activities and classes in art, music, and physical education are provided. The bilingual assistant/trainee provides primary language, reading, primary oral and written language, and math (problem solving). This alternative will require considerable training for the special education teacher and the assistant. That is, the special education teacher will have had to master directive teaching skills and skills needed to teach ESL. Also, the bilingual aide will need training in teaching primary language skills, since she or he will be responsible for teaching in this area.

The consultant may consider teaming with the bilingual educator when training the special education teacher and the aide. The training program could incorporate the bilingual educator's knowledge of primary language instruction and the consultant's knowledge of curriculum and instructional modifications.

The program in San Jose Unified School District (SJUSD) has staffing arrangements for providing services to LEP handicapped students in mainstreamed and special education settings. These arrangements include (a) exchanging a bilingual aide and a special education aide up to two hours daily to meet language needs; (b) having a team composed of a special educator and a bilingual educator who consult and share areas of expertise; (c) having a nonspecial education student model appropriate behavior to the special education student under the direction of a resource specialist; (d) providing alternative classes at the elementary level that are multigraded; (e) grouping LEP special education students in the resource room with bilingual materials for one or two periods per day; and (f) assigning a bilingual aide to the resource specialist program when the teacher and the aide speak English only.

The Role of the Interpreter

In addition to the special, regular, and bilingual education staff, the multicultural handicapped student may need to receive services from interpreters. In previous chapters we discussed the role of the special educator and the regular educator in providing instruction for handicapped students. In this chapter, we discussed different types of instruction provided by bilingual education/ESL educators. We shall now consider the role of the interpreter as it relates to educational services for multicultural handicapped students.

According to Medina (1982). "The main function of an interpreter . . . is to make it possible for all participants to communicate with one another despite language and cultural differences. The interpreter . . . facilities communication" (p. 34). Interpreters generally facilitate communication for school personnel by interpreting during parent conferences, parent interviews, and testing situations. However, bilingual paraprofessionals, secretaries, and other staff members may also be asked to serve as interpreters for monolingual English teachers and students who do not speak English. Since individuals who are not trained as interpreters may be asked to serve as interpreters, it is important for the consultant to be familiar with the skills needed by interpreters and the skills needed by educators to work successfully with interpreters.

Medina (1982) lists several minimal qualifications that interpreters should have. She states that the interpreter should be bilingual and biliterate with proficiency in both English and the target language. The interpreter should also be able to adjust to different levels of language use (i.e., the interpreter should be able to function if the situation involves colloquial language or literary language). This also necessitates that the interpreter be familiar with the appropriate educational terminology, the culture of the school, and the culture of the student. Finally, and most important, the interpreter should be familiar with the ethics of interpretation. This includes maintenance of the confidentiality of information and interpreting responses and questions without elaboration.

The following represents a modification of Langdon's (1983) discussion of skills one should have when working with interpreters. First, the educator should be familiar with the dynamics of interpretation. This includes familiarity with procedures for establishing rapport with multicultural participants; knowledge of the kinds of information that can easily be interpreted and not lost in the interpretation process; understanding of the authority position of the educator; use of appropriate and culturally sensitive nonverbal communication methods; and understanding of the need to obtain translations that do not include the personal input of the interpreter. Second, the educator should be able to plan and conduct pre- and post-sessions with the interpreter. During these sessions, the educator orients the interpreter to the purpose and procedures of a given educational situation. Third, the educator should be able to help the interpreter follow ethical procedures of interpretation.

If the person responsible for interpreting and the educator involved in the interpretation process do not have the necessary skills to successfully work together, the consultant should seek resources and training for the educational staff. This is most important if the services provided the educational staff will directly affect the adequacy of the educational program for a multicultural handicapped student.

CONCLUSION

Providing appropriate services for multicultural handicapped students requires sensitivity to the language and culture of the student as well as sensitivity to the student's learning strengths and weaknesses. Consultants have an obligation to help teachers prepare adequately to teach multicultural handicapped students. This requires that the teachers of these students be linguistically and culturally proficient as well as flexible in the use of curriculum and instructional strategies. To provide the best possible educational service for multicultural handicapped students, consultants should work closely with the families of the multicultural handicapped students and with all educational staff members who may be able to provide needed services. This coordination will require the consultant to use his or her best collaborative problem-solving techniques.

SUMMARY OF KEY POINTS

Curriculum

1. To help design an appropriate curriculum for a multicultural handicapped student, the educational consultant must consider several factors: the language proficiency of the student; the culture of the student; the regular education curriculum; and the bilingual education curriculum.

Bilingual Education

2. Bilingual education involves the use of two languages to provide instruction.

3. There are four types of bilingual education programs.

4. Transition programs teach students basic skills in their native language while developing English language proficiency. Students are transitioned into English instruction after they demonstrate English language proficiency.

5. Maintenance programs provide native language instruction even after a student demonstrates English language proficiency.

6. Restoration programs develop the language and culture of a student's ancestors.

7. Enrichment programs teach a new language and culture to a group of monolingual children.

8. English as a second language (ESL) is not bilingual instruction, as it relies exclusively on English for teaching and learning.

Language

9. Basic Interpersonal Communication Skills (BICS) is proficiency in everyday conversational skills.

10. Cognitive/Academic Linguistic Proficiency (CALP) is proficiency in the abstract skills needed for academic instruction.

Culture

11. The major components of a culture include language, food, dress, social norms, and values.

12. Three different levels of ethnic identity can be found among members of traditional communities, dualistic communities, and atraditional communities.

Instruction

13. A multicultural curriculum is one that is culturally sensitive and introduces students to a variety of cultures.

14. Cross-cultural techniques use instructional strategies that are consistent with learning styles across cultural groups.

Grouping Strategies

15. Grouping strategies are effective teaching alternatives for multicultural handicapped students. Cooperative learning strategies can be used in regular and mainstreamed settings.

Modification of Materials

16. Before modifying materials for multicultural exceptional learners, consideration must be given to language and cultural factors.

Parental Participation

17. Three reasons why parents of multicultural handicapped students may be minimally involved in their child's educational program are language and culture, environmental constraints, and lack of knowledge.

Coordinating Services

18. Multicultural handicapped students may require the services of the following staff members: special educators, bilingual/ESL educators, aides, interpreters, and regular educators.

19. When evaluating the adequacy of educational services for multicultural handicapped students, consultants should be able to identify the objectives of the program, determine the resources available, determine the adequacy of resources, develop an alternative plan, evaluate the resources available to implement the alternative plan, implement the plan, and evaluate the effectiveness of the implemented plan.

20. Consultants should consider developing long-term and short-term plans for providing appropriate services for multicultural handicapped students.

21. A possible short-term plan for providing services to multicultural handicapped students might involve coordinating services from bilingual and special educators.

The Role of the Interpreter

22. Interpreters should be bilingual and biliterate, knowledgeable in educational terminology and culture, flexible, and ethical.

23. The primary role of the interpreter is to facilitate communication. Interpreters should be familiar with procedures for establishing rapport, the use of nonverbal communication, and colloquial expressions.

24. When working with interpreters, educators should be able to establish rapport with all participants, use appropriate nonverbal communication, and conduct pre- and post-sessions with the interpreter.

QUESTIONS

1. Describe an educational situation that would necessitate use of a bilingual aide. How would you help the teacher work with the bilingual aide to provide appropriate instruction for a multicultural handicapped student?

2. Describe the characteristics of a group of students who represent more than one culture and language. As an educational consultant, what assessment techniques could you use to help the teacher determine the appropriate curriculum and instructional strategies to use with these students? Why would you use these techniques?

3. Describe a situation that would involve the family of a multicultural handicapped student. How would you work with this family to increase their involvement in the educational program of the multicultural handicapped student?

4. Describe an educational situation that would require the modification of instructional materials for multicultural handicapped students. What kinds of modifications would you make and why?

DISCUSSION POINTS AND EXERCISES

1. Develop a special education referral process for students in your school who are members of a cultural and/or linguistic minority.

2. Design a training program for the families of the multicultural handicapped pupils in your school.

3. Design a cultural awareness training program for the monolingual English special education teachers in your school.

4. Coordinate a training program designed to develop curriculum and instructional modification skills among special educators, bilingual educators, and aides.

5. Identify a school. Evaluate the adequacy of this school to meet the needs of the multicultural handicapped students who attend the school. Develop a long-term and short-term plan for improving the quality of service in the school.

11

Litigation and Legislation: Why and How it Affects Consultation

Educational services that handicapped children and youth presently receive are, in part, a direct result of litigative and legislative action. Decisions rendered by courts and federal laws enacted by Congress have greatly influenced the structure and operation of our nation's schools. For example, in the past, laws concerning the treatment of the handicapped were permissive. That is, educational service for a school-aged child may or may not have been offered. The state department of education or the local school district had complete discretionary power. With the enactment of recent legislation, however, educational services for the school-aged child are mandated.

Seeking recourse through the courts or through the Congress represents an important change in the way educational services are typically secured. No longer can local school districts or state departments of education exclude handicapped children from an education. To the contrary, the specific procedures that local districts must employ to identify and serve the handicapped in the least restrictive setting are delineated in the rules and regulations that accompany federal statutes.

The purpose of this chapter is to define the terms litigation *and* legislation *and to establish their importance in the educational process. The implications that these court rulings and federal and state laws have for consultants are addressed. In addition, a discussion of funding is presented. After reading the chapter, consultants working with regular and special education teachers should be aware of key issues regarding the right to education and how these rights affect their relationships with teachers, administrators, and parents.*

OBJECTIVES

After reading this chapter, the reader should be able to:

1. define the term *litigation*.

2. define the term *legislation*.

3. cite two important lawsuits concerning the right to education.

4. discuss the meaning and trend of educational opportunity in the United States.

5. discuss the relevance of Section 504 of the Rehabilitation Act of 1973 to the right of education of the handicapped.

6. define the provisions of Public Law 94-142.

7. distinguish between the terms *substantive due process* and *procedural due process*.

8. discuss three components of a handicapped child's free and appropriate educational program.

9. cite at least one lawsuit pertinent to the assurance of a free and appropriate education for handicapped students.

10. identify the components of a due process hearing.

11. identify several methods of funding educational programs for handicapped students.

KEY TERMS

Litigation

Class action suit

Consent decree

Pennsylvania Association for Retarded Children v. the Commonwealth of Pennsylvania (1972)

Mills v. Board of Education (1972)

Legislation

Rules and regulations

Right to education

Brown v. Board of Education (1954)

Section 504 of the Rehabilitation Act of 1973

Public Law 93-380

Public Law 94-142

Substantive due process

Procedural due process

Diana v. State Board of Education (1970)

Larry P. v. Riles (1972)

LeBanks v. Spears (1973)

Nondiscriminatory evaluation

Impartial hearing process

DEFINITION OF LITIGATION

Litigation refers to the act or process of bringing a court suit against another party for the purpose of redressing an alleged injustice. Suits bring a plaintiff and a defendant before a judge or panel of judges. The judge, or panel, is empowered to decide upon an appropriate course of action based on present facts and past precedents. According to Ysseldyke and Algozzine (1982), special education litigation has had two focuses: (a) correcting the denial of opportunity for education and (b) correcting the failure to provide an appropriate educational experience.

Litigative suits can be filed by individual citizens on their own behalf, or by individuals on the behalf of others in similar circumstances. The latter is referred to as a *class action suit*.

Class Action Litigation

There have been many class action suits involving handicapped individuals. For example, *Pennsylvania Association for Retarded Children v. Commonwealth of Pennsylvania* (1972); *Mills v. Board of Education* (1972); and *Maryland Association for Retarded Children v. State of Maryland* (1974) were class action suits brought before the court by one individual on behalf of other individuals with a similar situation. There are no specified number of plaintiffs required to initiate a class action suit (*Stoner v. Miller*, 1974). Rule 23(a) of the Federal Rules of Civil Procedure (28 USC.A.) lists the following requirements for filing class action suits: (a) There are too many members to have codefendants or co-plaintiffs in an individual suit; (b) there are questions of law or fact common to the class; (c) the claims of the defense of the representative parties are typical of the claims of the defenses of the class; and (d) the representative parties will fairly and adequately protect the interest of the class.

Advantages of Class Action Suits. Compared to individual lawsuits, class action suits are economical. That is, if an individual or small group succeeds in persuading the court, a much larger number of people benefit from the action. Likewise, the court's calendar is not consumed with cases having essentially the same grievance. For example, suppose a class action suit is filed for a mentally retarded individual on behalf of all mentally retarded persons alleging that a free and appropriate public education has been denied. If the court agrees with the plaintiff (i.e., the mentally retarded individual), a decision would be rendered that would affect not only the plaintiff but also the population of retarded individuals specified in the suit.

Disadvantages of Class Action Suits. A distinct disadvantage of the class action suit occurs when the individual or group fails to achieve a favorable court decision. In effect, the ability of other individuals or groups similarly situated to file suits, individually or collectively, might be compromised. As Abeson (1976) indicates, litigated cases are lost despite the presence of competent attorneys and "what seems the most noble of causes" (p. 241). Even if a class action suit is lost, however, future cases might not need to be filed if public policymakers and legislators take steps to correct the injustice through legislation. Such action extends the process, and the plaintiff is usually not provided with relief during the interim.

Main Effects of Litigation

As Turnbull and Turnbull (1978) indicate, litigation has been the primary method used to establish and maintain the educational rights of exceptional children and youth. The litigative decisions or *consent decrees* — agreements between or among parties based on negotiations — have set the precedent for appropriate legislation. Consent decrees do not represent judicial decisions resulting from a fully litigated case. Rather, a consent decree represents a compromise achieved outside of the court. It has the same effect as a fully litigated case and can serve as a legal precedent for future cases. The PARC decision (*Pennsylvania Association for Retarded Children v. Commonwealth of Pennsylvania*, 1972), a class action suit representing the school-age mentally retarded children of the state of Pennsylvania, was resolved with a consent decree.

Whether the case is fully litigated through the court, or resolved by means of a consent decree, the net effect for the plaintiffs is identical. If a favorable decision is rendered, the case is won. If an unfavorable decision is obtained, the plaintiffs' grievances will probably continue.

Other Effects of Litigation

Although a court may render a decision in favor of handicapped students, increased services are not automatically provided. The defendants have the right to appeal, and even if their appeal is lost, they are not immediately compelled to comply with the court order. The implementation of several decisions has been delayed because defendants failed to comply with the court mandates (Turnbull & Turnbull, 1978). An important case in the field of special education that illustrates this is *Mills v. Board of Education* (1972).

Mills v. Board of Education (1972). This class action suit was filed by the parents of seven handicapped students against the District of Columbia Board of Education, Department of Human Resources, and the Mayor for failure to provide all children with a public education. The court ruled in favor of the parents and issued a court order on December 20, 1971, stating that by January 3, 1972, all plaintiffs must be provided with a publicly supported education. The defendants (i.e., the Board of Education and the Mayor) failed to comply, and further action by the plaintiffs was required. The defendants claimed, in response to this latter action, that they were unable to comply with the court order due to insufficient funds. The court did not find that to be an adequate defense. The following court response resulted:

> The District of Columbia's interest in educating the excluded children clearly must outweigh its interest in preserving its financial resources. If sufficient funds are not available to finance all of the services and programs that are needed and desirable in the system, then the available funds must be expended equitably in such a manner that no child is entirely excluded from a publicly supported education consistent with his needs and ability to benefit therefrom. The inadequacies of the District of Columbia public school system, whether occasioned by insufficient funding or administrative inefficiency, certainly cannot be permitted to bear more heavily on the "exceptional" or handicapped child than on the normal child. (*Mills v. Board of Education*, 1972, p. 876)

Although the court ruled in favor of the parents in the first action, provision of services did not result until further litigative action had been sought by the plaintiffs. The reader is referred to Turnbull and Turnbull (1978) for a full discussion of options available to plaintiffs in cases where court mandates have been ignored or noncompliance with the court order has occurred.

DEFINITION OF LEGISLATION

Legislation refers to the act or process whereby elected representatives embody within a single document the law that becomes applicable to the general public. The intent of a federal or state statute is to serve the common good, the greatest majority of the citizens. Whereas litigative action is an attempt to solve a specific problem through a court remedy, legislative action is designed to solve broader societal problems. Bersoff (1979) sums up the distinction between these two avenues of social change:

> Courts develop rules of conduct in piecemeal fashion and only after litigants have presented legally cognizable issues. Rulemaking bodies such as legislatures and government agencies, on the other hand, need not wait for complaining litigants. When, among other reasons, problems need a broader solution than courts can provide, or they affect many people, lawmakers enact statutes and administrators promulgate regulations that have comprehensive effect. (Bersoff, 1979, p. 77)

To accomplish this objective, a legislative process has been devised that encourages public participation. One process that a bill — a draft of proposed legislation — might follow before it is enacted into law is shown in Figure 11.1.

Figure 11.1 illustrates that before a bill is enacted into law, the specific provisions within the bill are examined by subcommittees, committees, and finally the full house. At any of these stages, the bill is subject to amendments prompted by citizens' groups, lobbyists, congressional representatives, or the bill's sponsors. Conference committees are established to resolve discrepancies between House and Senate versions of a bill. At the federal level, the President has the option to veto a bill, and the Congress has an option to override the veto.

After any federal law is passed, proposed *rules and regulations* are published. These are proposed statements indicating how that law will be implemented and interpreted. Definitions for key terms in the law are provided as well as regulations for implementing the law. The general public is informed of proposed rule changes through the *Federal Register*, a daily publication of the United States Government, and public responses to the proposed changes are solicited for a period of months. After reviewing and commenting upon oral and written testimony, the governmental office responsible for the legislation publishes the final rules and regulations relative to the statute.

Often, when federal legislation is enacted, state law is changed so that it conforms to the new federal law. However, the enactment of legislation does not always guarantee that compliance will occur. Implementation is greatly dependent on the publication of clear regulations that specify the consequences for noncompliance.

From an educational perspective it is clear that litigative decisions and federal and state statutes have the potential to affect the population and nature of consultation services. For example, mentally retarded children, who prior to the PARC decision were excluded from school, are currently receiving a free public education. Teachers instructing these children are benefiting and presumably will continue to benefit from direct or indirect consultation services. Further, if educational institutions or systems do not comply with court decisions or federal and state statutes, educational services that may have been offered could be postponed, and consultants would find little demand for the educational service they were trained to supply.

Legislation pertinent to the right to education and, more broadly, to the equal protection of the handicapped can be found in a number of federal statutes (Table 11.1). Of the 195 federal laws specific to the handicapped enacted in 1975, 61 of these laws were passed in the period from March, 1970, through November, 1975. In 1974 alone, 36 federal bills that directly or indirectly affected the handicapped were signed into law (LaVor, 1976). It is interesting to note that previous legislation regarding education was primarily permissive, that is, states could provide educational services if they so desired. Legislation in the 1970s, especially P.L. 94-142, has mandated

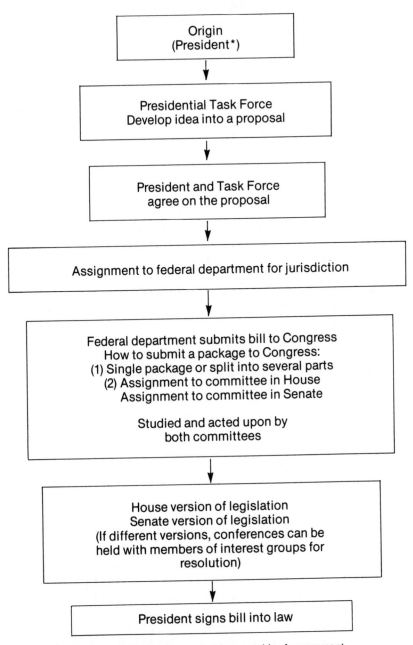

*Idea for a bill can originate anywhere —inside or outside of government

FIGURE 11.1. Decision points in the development and passage of a bill.

the education of school-aged handicapped children. The enactment of mandatory legislation could be viewed as a reflection of the changing societal approach to providing services for handicapped individuals.

THE RIGHT TO EDUCATION

Many view the movement in the courts by advocates for the handicapped as part of the trend to increase the civil rights of all minority groups. A number of major court decisions have been rendered over the last 20 years which have greatly influenced the type, variety, and duration of services to handicapped individuals.

The following section will briefly cite litigative and legislative actions pertinent to the *right to education*, the principle that states that all children are entitled to receive free and appropriate instruction. Some of the benefits that have followed will be discussed. This discussion of specific laws or court decisions is not intended to be exhaustive. Only landmark court cases and legislation relevant to the right to education for handicapped individuals will be presented. It is felt that these litigative and legislative actions have had a significant impact upon the quantity and quality of educational services provided to exceptional individuals. Consultants who are well grounded in these cases and laws might have a better understanding of their role and function within the school, and how that role and function were determined.

Brown v. Board of Education (1954)

The classic case of separate but equal educational opportunity was tested in *Brown v. Board of Education* (1954). This litigation was a class action suit, representing all black children of school age in Topeka, Kansas. Thus, not just one black girl, but all school-age black children in the city of Topeka were represented.

Essentially, the case focused on the legality of separate but equal educational opportunity. The plaintiffs contested that their rights under the equal protection clause of the Fourteenth Amendment, Section 1 (i.e., "nor deny to any person within its jurisdiction the equal protection of the laws") were violated. Equal protection, according to Weintraub and Abeson (1974), means that whatever action is taken with some individuals must be taken with all individuals on equal terms. Judge Warren, ruling on the Brown case, stated that separate educational facilities are inherently unequal. In addition, Judge Warren stated, "it is doubtful that any child may reasonably be expected to succeed in life if he is denied the opportunity of an education" (*Brown v. Board of Education*, 1954, p. 493).

TABLE 11.1
Federal Legislation
Pertinent to the Education of the Handicapped

Title	Comments
Title I, Elementary and Secondary Education Act of 1965, P.L. 89–10	In light of the special educational needs of children of low income families, this act provides federal assistance to local education agencies for the improvement of educational programs in low income areas.
National Technical Institute for the Deaf Act of 1965, P.L. 89–36	This act provides for the construction and operation of a residential institution for post-secondary technical training and education for deaf individuals. The goals of education are to prepare deaf individuals for successful employment.
Vocational Education Amendments of 1968 (Title I—Vocational Education), P.L. 90–576	This act provides that 10% of vocational education funds are to be spent for handicapped individuals.
Developmental Disabilities Services and Facilities Construction Amendments of 1970, P.L. 91–517	This act amends the Mental Retardation Facilities and Community Health Centers Construction Act of 1963 (P.L. 88–164). It provides for assistance to states to furnish comprehensive services to persons affected by mental retardation and other developmental disabilities originating in childhood.
Higher Education Amendments of 1972, P.L. 92–328	This act provides for grants and contracts with institutions of higher education to assist youths with academic potential who are from low-income families but who may lack adequate secondary school preparation or who may be physically handicapped.
The Economic Opportunity Act Amendments of 1972, P.L. 92–424	This act affects preschool services (i.e., it makes enrollment in Headstart available to handicapped children).
The Rehabilitation Act of 1973, P.L. 93–112	This act replaces all Vocational Rehabilitation Act Amendments since P.L. 66–236. It establishes the basis for the Rehabilitation Services Administration. It provides for an individualized written rehabilitation program for each handicapped individual (similar to the IEP required in P.L. 94–142).

TABLE 11.1. continued

Title	Comments
The Education of the Handicapped Act of 1970, P.L. 91–230	This act extends the powers of the Bureau for the Education of the Handicapped. It provides authorization to disburse funds for training and research.
Title III, Elementary and Secondary Education Act of 1965 (P.L. 89–10) as amended by P.L. 93–380 (1974), Educational amendments of 1974	This act provides funding for supplementary educational programs, including programs for handicapped children.
Education of the Gifted and Talented, P.L. 93–380, Title IV, Section 404	P.L. 93–380 provides for the establishment of an administrative unit within the Office of Education to coordinate programs and activities related to the gifted and talented as well as a national clearinghouse to collect and disseminate relevant information.
The Developmentally Disabled Assistance and Bill of Rights Act of 1974, P.L. 94–103	This act amended P.L. 91–517. Changes made include the following: The definition of the term developmental disability was broadened to include autism and dyslexia; however, the latter individuals must also suffer from mental retardation, cerebral palsy, or autism; all developmental disabilities grantees must take affirmative action to employ and advance qualified handicapped individuals; a comprehensive performance-based system for the evaluation of services must be provided.
The Education for All Handicapped Children Act (1975), P.L. 94–142	This act contains the major financial support mechanism and represents the essential educational rights guarantees for handicapped individuals.

The reader is referred to Ballard (1976), La Vor (1976) and Ysseldyke and Algozzine (1982) for a discussion of these federal education laws.

Judge Warren's statement had a great impact upon the education of handicapped populations, because in the past there had been legal precedent for excluding the handicapped from educational instruction. For example, The Wisconsin Supreme Court in the case of *State ex. rel. Beattie v. Board of*

Education of City of Antigo (Wis.) (1919) upheld the decision that a child's cerebral palsied condition "was harmful to the best interests of the school" (p. 154). The major argument presented by the Board of Education was that such a condition produced "a depressing and nauseating effect on the teachers and school children and that he [the student] required an undue portion of the teacher's time" (p. 154).

The *Brown v. Board of Education* (1954) case served as the catalyst for providing equal educational opportunity for handicapped students. Also, *Brown v. Board of education* laid the foundation for the eventual reduction of self-contained classrooms for placement of handicapped students.

Pennsylvania Association for Retarded Children v. Commonwealth of Pennsylvania (PARC) (1972)

The exclusion of handicapped individuals from educational opportunity was challenged directly in the PARC (1972) case, a class action suit representing school-age mentally retarded children in the Commonwealth of Pennsylvania.

The right of this population to a free public education was argued on several grounds, including the equal protection clause of the Fourteenth Amendment. Essentially, Pennsylvania law stated that a proper education should be provided for all handicapped children. However, the law also stated that children who were uneducable and untrainable, and who had not yet attained a mental age of 5 years, may be excluded from the public schools (Gilhool, 1973). The plaintiffs used two primary arguments in their case. One argument was based upon the legal decision rendered in *Brown v. Board of Education* (1954). The second was based upon the expert testimony of witnesses who stated that handicapped individuals could benefit from an education.

It is important to mention that in the PARC case, expert witnesses challenged the historical arguments for exclusion or segregation of the handicapped from public education. Kubetz (1972) summarizes these historical arguments as follows: (a) Retarded individuals could not profit from instruction; (b) retarded students would cause harm to the welfare of other students; and (c) instruction of such individuals, if attempted, would be impractical.

Expert witnesses countered these arguments by testifying that systematic education programs for retarded children would produce learning, and also that education could not be defined solely in terms of academic gains. Rather, "education must be seen as a continuous process by which individuals learn to cope and function within their environment. Thus, for children to learn to clothe and feed themselves is a legitimate outcome achievable through an educational program" (Weintraub & Abeson, 1974, p. 527). This statement of educational goals, developed by experts in the PARC case, should be considered in light of the meaning of equal educational opportunity.

Educational Opportunity.   Weintraub and Abeson (1974) trace the evolution of the meaning of equal educational opportunity in this country. Initially, as a populist concept, equal education opportunity meant equal access to resources with equal opportunity to meet common objectives. In other words, the resources were the same, the goals were the same, and everyone had equal access to goals. Each student went through the same educational program to achieve his or her educational goal — for example, the ability to master the skills to achieve a high school diploma. In the 1960s the concept was changed to mean equal access to differing resources to meet common objectives. For everyone to master the skills necessary to achieve a high school diploma, students would not necessarily go through the same educational program. Rather, those who needed it would receive additional remedial assistance. Finally, in the 1970s and 1980s the meaning changed once again. Now, educational opportunity means equal access to differing resources for the attainment of different objectives. In other words, not only will there be different educational services provided depending on needs, but also the goals of education may not be the same for all students. One need not receive educational services only to achieve a high school diploma; it is also legitimate to receive educational services to learn to clothe and feed oneself.

Thus, the major impact of the PARC case on the education of handicapped children is illustrated by noting the revised definitions of educational opportunity. In short, not only could different educational services be provided, depending on the student's need, but the basic goal of education for each student might not be the same. As Reynolds and Rosen (1976) point out, in the PARC case the court clearly indicated that the enhancement of individual development, rather than potential returns to society, is the critical object of education.

The Rehabilitation Act of 1973, Section 504

Section 504 of the Rehabilitation Act of 1973 (P.L. 93-112) is the first federal civil rights law that specifically protects the rights of the handicapped against discrimination on the basis of physical or mental handicap. The specific wording of Section 504 attests to its comprehensive civil rights mandate.

> No otherwise qualified handicapped individual in the United States . . . shall, solely by reason of his handicap be excluded from participation in, be denied the benefits of, or be subjected to discrimination under any program or activity receiving Federal financial assistance.

The nondiscriminatory provisions of the law are almost identical to the nondiscriminatory provisions related to race, that are included in Title VI of the Civil Rights Act of 1964, and to Title IX of the Education Amendments of 1972, Public Law 92-318. Originally, Section 504 was restricted primarily to employment. In 1974, Public Law 93-156 was passed, amending Section 504 to include educational services.

In April, 1977, the final regulations for Section 504 were issued for all recipients of funds from the Department of Health, Education and Welfare (HEW), including elementary and secondary schools, colleges, hospitals, social service agencies, and, in some instances, doctors. In a Section 504 Fact Sheet published in July, 1977, the term *handicapped* was defined, and the rights of the handicapped were outlined.

The term *handicapped* includes such diseases or conditions as speech, hearing, visual, and orthopedic impairments, cerebral palsy, epilepsy, muscular dystrophy, multiple sclerosis, cancer, diabetes, heart disease, mental retardation, emotional illness, and specific learning disabilities such as perceptual handicaps, dyslexia, minimal brain dysfunction, and developmental aphasia as well as alcohol and drug addiction. It was noted that physical or mental impairments do not constitute a handicap unless they are severe enough to limit one or more of the major life functions.

Several rights for the handicapped are included under Section 504 of the Rehabilitation Act. These rights will be examined briefly.

Program Accessibility.   Programs as a whole must be accessible to handicapped persons. Structural changes are required to make the program accessible only if an alternative, such as reassignment of classes or home visits, is not possible. The deadline for making structural changes in existing facilities to achieve program accessibility was June 23, 1980.

Free and Appropriate Education.   Every handicapped child at the preschool, elementary, secondary, and adult educational levels is entitled to a free and appropriate public education, regardless of the nature or severity of handicap. School systems have the responsibility of providing transportation for handicapped students to and from educational programs. The compliance date for providing a free and appropriate education for children ages 3 tc 21 was September 1, 1978, for public elementary and secondary schools.

Colleges and Other Postsecondary Institutions.   Recruitment, admissions, and the treatment of students must be free of discrimination. Quotas for admission of handicapped persons are not permissible.

Health, Welfare, and Social Services.   The provisions for accessibility and reasonable accommodation also apply to health, welfare, and social services. Benefits and services may not be denied on the basis of handicap.

General Employment Provisions.   Employers may not refuse to hire or promote handicapped persons solely because of their disability. Also, accessibility to the employment location is required, and, therefore, reasonable accommodation may have to be made to the person's handicap. The compliance date for those employers who receive federal funds and who employ 15 or more persons was September 2, 1977.

Failure to Comply with Section 504.   Another major component of the Section 504 rules and regulations is the provision for failure to comply. The primary consequence for violating Section 504 is that federal funds can be withheld from the state agency, institution, or district until such time as full compliance with Section 504 is achieved.

The Education of All Handicapped Children Act of 1975 (P.L. 94-142)

The right to education is embodied within The Education of All Handicapped Children's Act of 1975 (P.L. 94-142). This federal statute is a comprehensive law that states as one of its central provisions that all handicapped children are entitled to a free and appropriate public education designed to meet their unique needs. According to the statute,

> It is the purpose of this Act to assure that all handicapped children have available to them . . . a free appropriate public education that emphasizes special education and related services designed to meet their unique needs, to assure that the rights of handicapped children and their parents or guardians are protected, to assist States and localities to provide for the education of all handicapped children, and to assess and assure the effectiveness of efforts to educate handicapped children.

Impact of Litigation and Legislation for Consultants

The impact of right to education litigation and legislation for consultants is evident in several areas. First, these court rulings and federal and state laws have provided the opportunity to serve, directly and indirectly, populations of handicapped children who were not receiving services previously (e.g., trainable mentally retarded children). Second, the structure and administrative procedures of many schools changed as a function of these rulings and laws. Physical barriers for the handicapped have been greatly reduced or eliminated, and administrative procedures for identification, placement, and delivery of service are now required. Finally, consultants should be aware of compliance requirements for Section 504, federal regulations, and state standards. By noting inconsistencies or inadequacies in their districts' programs, and making recommendations to change these deficiencies, consultants might be able to avoid a federal or state citation for noncompliance and, therefore, prevent existing programs for the handicapped from being jeopardized.

ASSURING THE RIGHT TO EDUCATION FOR ALL HANDICAPPED STUDENTS

Two federal statutes have been instrumental in assuring the right to an appropriate education for all handicapped individuals. P.L. 93-380 established a national policy of equal educational opportunity by declaring that every citizen is entitled to an education at public expense that is designed to achieve the individual's full potential. P.L. 94-142 is an amendment to P.L. 93-380 and extends equal educational opportunity specifically to handicapped populations. It has been described as the "Bill of Rights for the Handicapped," because it is designed to correct inequities on behalf of handicapped students.

Brimer and Barudin (1977) outline four basic principles common to both P.L. 93-380 and P.L. 94-142 that are designed to assure that the rights of all handicapped students are observed: (a) due process; (b) a free and appropriate public education for all handicapped children; (c) financial assistance to states, and (d) federal training and technical assistance. A close examination of the first three principles follows. The fourth principle, training and technical assistance, is not examined, because this area has been the responsibility of the former Bureau of Education for the Handicapped, now under the auspices of the Office of Special Education and Rehabilitation Programs (OSERP). Since passage of P.L. 94-142, OSERP has been responsible for the explanation and implementation of this provision. Suffice it to say that training and technical assistance have been provided to state directors, parents, and teachers.

Due Process

Due process can be defined as a vehicle for judicial protection of liberty and property against unreasonable governmental action. This protection is embodied within the Fifth Amendment of the Constitution: ". . . nor shall any State deprive any person of life, liberty, or property, without due process of law." Essentially, due process consists of two components, substantive and procedural. Each is addressed below.

Substantive Due Process.   *Substantive due process* refers to the threatened or actual denial of life, liberty, or property. It weighs fundamental fairness against arbitrariness or unreasonableness. That is, a court decision cannot be based on whim, but must follow a logical process. Also, a decision that is made must be enforced equally and fairly. Substantive due process can be viewed as the degree of protection under a given set of circumstances before a decision is rendered. The court determines the cut-off point for deciding to hear a case based on alleged violations of substantive due process by weighing the seriousness of the offense and the harm to the individual (Goldstein, 1975). So, as Brimer and Barudin (1977) point out, due process is not a dichotomous situation that is appropriate in some cases and inappropriate in others, but rather a continuum of procedures that offers the appropriate protection of the rights of the individual. As Fischer (1970) emphasizes, due process helps to protect a person from an arbitrary or capricious judgment.

Procedural Due Process.   *Procedural due process* refers to the standards specifying how due process is to be applied. The procedural safeguards delineated in P.L. 94-142 provide an example of procedural due process. This act provides handicapped children and their parents or guardians with procedural safeguards with respect to the provision of free appropriate public education. A summarization of these procedural safeguards is found in Table 11.2.

As Brimer and Barudin (1977) point out, many of the plaintiffs' arguments in the PARC case were based upon procedural due process infringements. The parents in the PARC case were not notified as to why their children were excluded from school; neither were they afforded a hearing to counter the school's action. In support of these two arguments, the plaintiffs in the PARC case quoted judicial decisions from prior litigation (i.e., Supreme Court Justice Frankfurter, who stated, "The right to be heard before being condemned to suffer grievous loss of any kind. . . . is a principle basic to our society" (*Joint Anti-Facist Committee v. McGrath*, 1951, p. 168).

Another procedural due process argument used in the PARC case was concerned with the issue of labeling. The point was that the label mentally retarded stigmatized the child and should not have been attached without prior notice to the parents and without allowing the parents an opportunity to challenge the labeling. Justice Douglas of the United States Supreme Court in a previous case related to labeling (*Wisconsin v. Constantineau*, 1971) rendered the folloiwng decision: "Where a person's good name, reputation, honor or integrity are at stake because of what the government is doing to him, notice and opportunity to be heard are essential" (p. 437). Thus, the Supreme Court made it clear that a label is a stigma and as such cannot be imposed without due process of law.

A fourth argument presented in PARC was that the educational process is a fundamental interest and should not be deprived without notice of the

TABLE 11.2
Summarization of the Procedural Safeguards Specified in P.L. 94–142

---

1. The parents or guardian of a handicapped child are to be provided with the opportunity to examine all records relevant to the educational programming of their child,* as well as the opportunity to obtain an independent educational evaluation of the child, if they so desire.**

2. If there is no parent or guardian of the handicapped child, an individual who is not involved in the education of the child will be appointed to act as the surrogate for the parents or guardian.

3. Written notice is to be provided to the parent or guardian of a handicapped child when an educational agency proposes or refuses to initiate or change the child's educational program.

4. The parents or guardian of a handicapped child must have the opportunity to present complaints with respect to any matter related to the educational programing of their child.

5. If the parents or guardian of a handicapped child make a complaint regarding the educational programing of their child, they shall have the opportunity for an impartial due process hearing.

---

*The Buckley Amendment of 1975 (Title V, Sec. 513, 514, P.L. 93–380) gave to parents of public school students under 18 the right to see, correct, and control access to school records.

**A list of independent evaluators can be obtained from the superintendent of the school district or county program.

impending deprivation and a chance to be heard. This argument relates to both substantive due process (i.e., the notion of fair play) as well as procedural due process (i.e., the right to be heard before a fundamental interest, such as education, can be denied).

A Free and Appropriate Public Education for All Handicapped Children

According to P.L. 93-380, the education for all children is to be commensurate with each child's needs and in a least restrictive setting. Additionally, parents and guardians are to be involved to the maximum extent possible. P.L. 94-142 expanded procedures of P.L. 93-380 in that an Individualized Educational Program would be used to determine an education commensurate with a handicapped child's needs. This educational program must also meet state educational agency standards. The educational program is to be provided at public expense.

But, what constitutes an appropriate education for a handicapped student? Two lawsuits, *Rowley v. Hendrick Hudson District Board of Education* (1980) and *Armstrong v. Kline* (1979) (*Battle v. Commonwealth*), address this key question.

Rowley v. Board of Education.   The main issue in the *Rowley* case was whether Amy Rowley, a hearing-impaired student, was entitled to the services of a sign language interpreter as part of her Individualized Education Program. Briefly, Amy was an entering first-grade student who, because of the nature of her hearing loss (she had approximately 50% residual hearing), needed special education services in the regular classroom. The district provided her with a hearing aid, speech therapy, and a tutor. The district also provided her a sign language interpreter but discontinued this service after the interpreter reported that Amy resisted her services. That is, Amy looked at the teacher to read her lips and asked the teacher to repeat instructions, rather than looking at the interpreter. The parents' claim was that because Amy was not provided with a sign language interpreter, she missed 50% of her instruction, and therefore was denied an appropriate public education, even though she was making satisfactory progress in school and passing from grade to grade.

The case reached the Supreme Court of the United States, where in a 6-3 decision it was ruled that the school district did not have to provide a sign language interpreter to Amy. Judge Rehnquist, writing for the majority and basing his decision on his interpretation of congressional intent when writing the legislation, stated that P.L. 94-142 was written to provide an education opportunity for handicapped students, consisting of instructions and related services to provide "educational benefit" to the child. He stated:

> By passing the Act, Congress sought primarily to make public education available to handicapped children. But in seeking to provide such access to public education, Congress did not impose upon the States any greater substantive standard than would be necessary to make such access meaningful.

The court's ruling essentially overturned the U.S. District Court of Appeals' ruling, which had decided that P.L. 94-142 was designed so that each child would achieve his or her maximum potential. In short, the U.S. Supreme Court ruled that "the aim of P.L. 94-142 is to develop a handicap child's self-sufficiency rather than to allow a handicap child his full potential commensurate with the opportunity provided to other children" (*Rowley v. Board of Education*, 1980).

Armstrong v. Kline. *Armstrong v. Kline* (1979) was a class action suit brought to the court on behalf of three severely handicapped children and their parents. The purpose of the suit was to challenge the Pennsylvania Department of Education's policy, which stated that programs for handicapped students would not be funded for a longer period of time than those for nonhandicapped students (i.e., 180 school days).

The plaintiff's position was that the "180-day rule" violated provisions of P.L. 94-142 regarding a free and appropriate public education, because the policy prohibited hearing officers from formulating funded IEPs that extended beyond 180 days.

In June 1979, the U.S. District Court for Eastern Pennsylvania ruled that the 180-day rule was illegal because the rule made it extremely difficult for students to achieve self-sufficiency and independence. In essence, the court ruled that the 180-day rule denied these children a free and appropriate public education (Stotland & Mancuso, 1981).

On July 15, 1980, the U.S Third Circuit of Appeals in *Battle v. Commonwealth* upheld the lower court's ruling. In part, the court of appeals ruled that "inflexible application of a 180 day maximum prevents the proper formulation of appropriate educational goals for individual members of the plaintiff class" (p. 28).

According to Stotland and Mancuso (1981), in order for a program to be termed "appropriate" it must "be based on an individualized assessment and an individual planning process that must result in an individualized program designed to meet each child's unique needs." (p. 270). With respect to providing an individualized program, we shall consider three aspects: (a) nondiscriminatory evaluation and the placement decision, (b) the Individualized Education Program, and (c) educational placement in the least restrictive environment.

Nondiscriminatory Evaluation and the Placement Decision. There has been a long-standing concern with the nature of programs for children who are provided with special education services. According to Hoffman (1975), special classes during the early part of the 20th century were often considered a hodgepodge. Non-English speaking students, for example, as well as mentally and behaviorally disordered children, were all grouped together. Classes were disproportionately filled with minority children because of faulty diagnosis and poor administration.

In the 1980s there is still the concern that special education programs are used indiscriminately. It is felt that many minority group children may be inappropriately placed. Advocates for these children are attempting to deal with the problem through the judicial process. Parents are demanding the right to question the appropriateness of a school's classification of their children, and they are demanding the right of due process. A brief discussion of three key lawsuits conducted in the 1970s pertinent to this aspect of educational programming will be presented.

In *Diana v. State Board of Education of California* (1970), it was argued that nine Mexican-American public school students had been improperly placed in classes for the mentally retarded on the basis of inaccurate and discriminatory tests. That is, individualized intelligence tests were administered to these Spanish-speaking children by an English-speaking examiner. It was argued that the tests relied primarily on verbal aptitude in English, thereby ignoring learning abilities in Spanish. In addition, it was alleged that the intelligence tests were standardized on Americans and were therefore inappropriate for Spanish-speaking, Mexican-American students. The court sustained these arguments.

Further, subsequent legislation passed in California prohibited IQ scores from being used to place students in special education classrooms. The decision rendered in *Diana* set the occasion for subsequent federal legislation, P.L. 94-142, that included provisions that intelligence test scores can be used as only one measure of a multifactored evaluation, and tests must be given in the student's native language.

In *Larry P. v. Riles* (1972), the plaintiffs sought an injunction restraining the San Francisco school district from administrating intelligence tests for purposes of determining the placement of black students in classes for the educable mentally retarded. It was alleged that misplacement in classes for the mentally retarded carried a stigma and a life sentence of illiteracy. The injunction was upheld if the use of the intelligence tests resulted in racial imbalance in the composition of such classes.

In the litigated cases of *Diana* and *Larry P.*, the use of standardized tests, especially intelligence tests, for making placement decisions was a main issue. According to Singletary, Collings, and Dennis (1978), two factors that expand on this issue are (a) no child can be placed in a special education program on the basis of an intelligence test if that placement results in racial imbalance, and (b) those students already enrolled in special programs must be reevaluated periodically.

The *LeBanks v. Spears* (1973) case was a class action suit representing students ages 5 through 21 in the public school district of Orleans Parish, Louisiana, who were described as, identified as, or suspected of being retarded. The plaintiffs asserted that they were denied publicly supported educational programs. A preliminary consent agreement was ordered on May 3, 1973, that expanded the dimension of nondiscriminatory evaluation. The consent decree delineated the steps necessary to ensure that appropriate services were afforded to mentally retarded children.

Subsequent legislation, Section 504 of P.L. 93-112, was based on the rulings issued in *LeBanks v. Spears*. In Section 503, procedures for nondiscriminatory materials and evaluation were provided. A summarization of these procedures is found in Table 11.3.

TABLE 11.3
Nondiscriminatory Materials and Evaluation Procedures as Specified in Section 504 of P.L. 93–112

1. Tests and evaluation materials are to be validated and administered by qualified evaluators.

2. Texts and other evaluation materials are to assess specific areas of educational need.

3. The tests are to be selected and administered so as not to reflect impairment but accurately reflect aptitude and/or achievement.

4. For educational placement, one must draw upon a variety of sources, carefully document and consider all information, and make group placement decisions.

5. Educational programming must undergo periodic reevaluation.

Nondiscriminatory evaluation, specified in Section 503 and P.L. 94-142, means that the standardized tests used to evaluate children and youth should be normed or standardized for that child's particular age, ethnic, or cultural group. Also, testing must be conducted using the child's primary language, and written permission must be obtained from the parents prior to testing.

There are several important implications for educational consultants with respect to nondiscriminatory evaluation. First, the consultant might be responsible for administering standardized tests to students. Based on the outcome of previous litigation and recent legislation, it is imperative that measures be taken to ensure that the test is age- and culture-appropriate. In addition, the evaluation of the child must assure the careful assessment of all areas of weakness, not just overall general aptitude. If the child's primary language is not English, or if the child does not use expressive language, then provisions must be made to test the child through his or her primary language or mode of communication. Second, the consultant might be responsible for observing that the due process procedures established by the district are carried out. It is important that procedures be followed exactly, especially those procedures that specify the parents' rights. Third, educational placement must be based on a careful consideration of all data obtained through a multifactored evaluation. The placement decision should reflect the consensus of the placement team, and if there are dissenting opinions regarding the placement, these opinions must be documented. Finally, the consultant might be responsible for scheduling a periodic review. The purpose of the review is to reexamine the student's need based on progress observed since the last review. The review is an integral part of the child's Individualized Education Program.

The Individualized Education Program. As stated previously, an Individualized Education Program must be developed for all children who receive special education and related services. The IEP is a written document that specifies the child's educational program, based on assessed need, for a specified period of time, usually an academic year. As defined in Federal regulations, an IEP must contain the following:

1. a statement of the child's present level of educational performance
2. annual goals and short-term objectives
3. the special education and related services needed by the child
4. the extent to which the child will participate in a regular education program
5. dates for initiation and duration of services
6. evaluation criteria, schedules, and procedures (*Federal Register*, Vol. 42, No. 163, August 23, 1977, 121a346)

There is a considerable amount of literature describing suggested steps to generate an IEP as well as the guidelines that may be used to assure due process procedures (Meyen, 1978; Turnbull, Strickland, & Brantley, 1982). Basically, all parties involved in the process must come to agreement on the content of the written document, that is, its development and implementation. If there is a disagreement, a hearing may be conducted according to due process safeguards. A hearing may be requested by any party in disagreement.

In the *impartial hearing process*, three hierarchical steps are available to the dissenting party. First, a hearing may be called at the local level to review all pertinent information (e.g., assessment results, placement, related service needs). If the dissenting party is not satisfied, a state level review may be called. Again, if the dissenting party is still aggrieved, civil action through a state or federal district court may be taken. As noted by Abeson, Bolick, and Hass (1975), an impartial hearing includes the right of the dissenting party to receive timely and specific notice of the hearing, all pertinent records, an independent evaluation, if desired, and representation by counsel. Also, the plaintiff is entitled to cross-examine witnesses, and bring witnesses of his or her own.

Hearing officers are involved in the first two levels. The role of a hearing officer is not to place blame or determine right or wrong, but to achieve resolution of the conflict with a final determination of an appropriate program for the child. As Abeson et al. (1975) note, the specification of criteria to be used in selecting effective hearing officers in all settings is difficult because of changing circumstances. Nevertheless, the authors provide general guidelines, which are presented in Table 11.4.

Dissatisfaction with a decision at the local or state level can result in litigation. It is probable that the courts will become involved in litigation, contesting aspects of the IEP process.

TABLE 11.4
Guidelines for Selecting Hearing Officers

1. The hearing officer should not have been involved in decisions already made about a child regarding identification, evaluation, placement, or review.

2. The hearing officer should possess special knowledge, acquired through training and/or experience, about the nature and needs of exceptional children. An awareness and understanding of the types and quality of programs that are available for exceptional children are essential.

3. The hearing officer should be sufficiently open-minded so that he or she will not be predisposed toward any decisions that he or she must make or review. However, the hearing officer must also be capable of making decisions.

4. The hearing officer should possess the ability to objectively, sensitively, and directly solicit and evaluate both oral and written information that needs to be considered in relation to decision making.

5. The hearing officer should have sufficient experience to effectively structure and operate hearings in conformity with standard requirements and limits, and to encourage the participation of the principal parties and their representatives.

6. The hearing officer should be free enough of other obligations to give sufficient priority to hearing officer responsibilities. He or she must be able to meet the required deadlines for conducting hearings and reporting written decisions.

7. The hearing officer should be aware that this role is unique and relatively new. It will require constant evaluation of the hearing processes and the behavior of all the principals involved, including the hearing officer's.

From "A primer on due process: Education decisions for handicapped children" by A. Abeson, N. Bolick, & J.A. Hass (1975) in *Exceptional Children, 42,* 72–73. Reprinted by permission.

The IEP and impartial hearing processes have several implications for consultants. For example, if a consultant served as the representative from the local education agency during the IEP conference, he or she would share responsibility for seeing that the services prescribed were actually delivered. Also, the consultant might bear some responsibility for monitoring the instructional program of the child. The monitoring process might consist of brief contacts or more extensive discussions with the teacher (Bergan, 1977). Further, the consultant might be responsible for scheduling the periodic or annual review. If he or she is, arrangements for testing may have to be made so that current information would be available for the team.

Finally, in the event that a due process proceeding (i.e., impartial hearing) is initiated, the consultant might be required to document all the steps taken with the student and his or her parents. It would be important for the consultant to be able to communicate these data effectively to the hearing officer so that an impartial decision could be rendered (Turnbull et al., 1982).

Educational Placement in the Least Restrictive Environment.   Ennis (1976) stated that the notion of the least restrictive environment is the legal corollary of the social science principle of normalization, that is, existence as close as possible to normal. Wolfensberger (1972) reformulated the normalization principle for application to human management, specifically, the management of mentally retarded individuals. He defines normalization as the use of means that are as culturally normative as possible, in order to establish or maintain personal behaviors and characteristics that conform to the cultural norm.

There has been considerable litigation concerning the issue of the least restrictive environment, some of that predates P.L. 94-142 (cf. *Warren v. Nussbaum*, 1974; *Panitch v. State of Wisconsin*, 1974). In *Lake v. Cameron* (1966), it was made clear that the government may not elect a convenient alternative of service if another would be a more appropriate choice. In this case, the plaintiff was confined to a hospital for the insane. She was described as senile, with a poor memory, and unable to care for herself, but not insane. The plaintiff was in a hospital because her family was unable to provide care. The ruling in this case was that it is the obligation of the state to explore other possible alternatives to meet the individual's needs. This case demonstrated that the government cannot overextend protection of the individual to the point of deprivation of personal liberty. In other terms, the state was obliged to find the least restrictive placement for the plaintiff, that is, a setting less restrictive than a hospital, but that would meet the plaintiff's needs.

Since 1975, one case, *Mattie T. v. Holladay* (1981), has focused primarily on the provision of the least restrictive environment. In this case, it was asserted that placement in a self-contained classroom effectively removed handicapped students from the opportunity to interact with their nonhandicapped peers thus not meeting the educational needs of students. The case was settled by consent decree in favor of the plaintiffs.

Financial Assistance to States

According to Kimball, Heron, and Weiss (1984a), the federal government plays a necessary role in funding special education programs. In their view, "Without adequate [federal] funding, it is impossible to implement the law as designed" (p. 29). Kimball et al. (1984b) emphasize that funds should be earmarked for model research and demonstration grants and other technical assistance projects.

With respect to fiscal allocation of funds, the distribution of handicapped children and youth affects the cost of programs and related services. States or local school districts with small populations of handicapped students receive less money proportionally from the federal government than states or districts with larger handicapped populations.

Also, the degree of a child's handicap affects the cost of special education services. Generally speaking, the more severe the handicap, the more likely the child is to need related services (e.g., speech, occupational, or physical therapy and transportation), and the more costly the program becomes.

Rossmiller, Hale, and Frohreich (1970) produced a cost index for various handicapping conditions. The cost index is the ratio of the average pupil expenditure for a category of exceptionality (e.g., blind, deaf, or learning disabled) to the average pupil cost for children in the regular elementary program. Rossmiller et al.'s data indicate that programs for the gifted involved the least cost, while programs for the physically handicapped were the most expensive. Given the broad range of program options for handicapped students, it is unclear whether the relative expenditures for special services for each exceptionality will remain the same. Nevertheless, there are basic costs, common across exceptionalities, that can be identified. Marinelli (1976) cites the expenditures that follow:

Building Block Resources.   These resources involve time, space, equipment, and supplies. Time may be converted into fixed dollar cost, especially if personnel salaries are used.

Organizational Units.   Instruction, pupil personnel services, transportation, and food services are included in this category. Rossmiller et al. (1970) found that salaries of teachers and teacher aides were the largest single expenditure. Instructional support is an expensive component since guidance, counseling, and rehabilitation personnel, psychologists, therapists, doctors, and nurses are widely used. Also, transportation costs for the physically handicapped are high, because orthopedically impaired children require specially equipped buses.

Cost of Delivery Systems.   The educational placement of a handicapped child is often a function of the type and severity of the handicap. Usually, the more severe the handicap, the higher the cost. Marinelli (1976) indicates that determining the actual costs is difficult due in part to the trend away from the conventional classroom and toward individualized student programs with many student grouping patterns and differentiated staffs.

Federal Government Funding Procedures

As Abeson and Ballard (1976) point out, in 1977 it was estimated that an additional 4 to 5 billion dollars was needed to achieve full service for all exceptional children, so the federal appropriation of about $400 million annually was inadequate. However, P.L. 94-142 authorizes a gradual increase in the federal contribution. A funding formula established by P.L. 94-142 is based on an escalating percentage of the national average expenditure per public school student multiplied by the number of handicapped children being served in the school districts of each state.

Basically, the formula taxes the National Average Per Pupil Expenditure (NAPPE) for students in public schools and multiplies that figure by the number of handicapped children served in school districts. The formula became effective in fiscal year 1978 and was scheduled to reach 40% of NAPPE in 1982.

The actual allocation to a state is based on the appropriation made by Congress and the total number of handicapped children identified each year. The state's share of pass-through funds after 1979 is 25% and is earmarked for technical assistance and support service programs. The remaining 75% is paid directly to eligible local education agencies (Section 611, P.L. 94-142).

State Funding for Special Education

Marinelli (1976) noted that despite the increase of federal funds for special education, the monies would probably not be enough to meet the mandates for educating all handicapped children. State or local funds have been used to cover the deficit.

Historically, programs for special education were financed by categorical state aid that paid for the extra costs. The sources of funding were the regular state funds — a flat amount to pay for a portion of the salary of the special education teacher — and funds generated from local taxes. States also subsidized partial costs of instructional materials, transportation, and personnel. The level of funding and the distribution process were not subjected to special education cost analysis to determine the adequacy or equity of funding (McClure, 1975).

There are several methods of funding special education services. Crowner (1985) proposed a taxonomy of special education finance that delineated four categories: bases, formulae, types, and sources (Table 11.5). According to Crowner, "base" refers to the elements upon that funds are calculated, "formulae" refers to the way revenue dollars are determined, "type" refers to the restrictions placed on the use of funds, and "source" refers to the authorization agent of the funds.

TABLE 11.5
A Taxonomy of Special Education Finance

Bases	Types
Pupil	Continuing
Resource	Noncontinuing
Service	Targeted
Cost	Discretionary
Unit	Inside formula
	Outside formula
	Matching
	Mixed

Formula	Sources
Weighted	Federal
Straight sum	State
Excess cost	Local
Percent of cost	Private
Mixed	

From "A taxonomy of special education finance" by T.T. Crowner (1985) in *Exceptional Children*, 51(6), 503-508. Reprinted by permission.

Bases

Pupil base.   Funds are allocated on a pupil basis by determining the number of students served.

Resource base.   Here funds are generated for teachers, support personnel, supplies, equipment, and facilities. Usually, this base produces a set amount of dollars per year.

Service base.   With this base, dollars are produced based on the kind of service provided (e.g., resource room or self-contained classroom).

Cost base.   Here the actual cost of the district's special education program is used as the measure. Unfortunately, actual costs are often difficult to determine. According to McCarthy and Sage (1982), system costs are predicated on several varying factors — including salaries, transportation, food service, and maintenance — making actual cost determinations difficult.

Unit base.   A unit is defined as a predetermined number of children assigned to a special education class. By this method of funding, two or more of the other bases are combined. The unit system has prompted the growth of special classes.

Formulae

Extra cost pattern. Excess cost is the amount by which the per pupil expenditure for an exceptional child exceeds the per pupil expenditure for all other children. Calculating excess cost for handicapped children who receive a number of services may be difficult. As stated previously, data on the true cost of the resources used by the special education student are often unavailable.

Percentage reimbursement. In this approach, the state reimburses a district for a set percentage of all costs incurred in providing special education programs. According to Crowner (1985), Wisconsin's percentage reimbursement is limited to 70% of allowable costs.

Straight sum reimbursement. This procedure is simply a set amount of money, which may vary according to exceptionality, allocated by the state for each child in a district. A disadvantage of this approach is that school districts are reinforced monetarily for identifying handicapped children.

Weighted formula. According to this method, special education programs are funded according to a system of weights. The per pupil cost of the least expensive school program (i.e., regular elementary program) serves as a base of 1. Each category of exceptionality is weighted. This weight is multiplied by the regular per pupil cost to determine the amount of funding for that special education program. For example, a physically handicapped student receiving therapy may have a weight of 1.8, which means that his program would cost .8 more than the student in the regular program.

Mixed formula. With this formula one or more of the formulae identified in the table are combined and cost reimbursement is based on that figure. For example, students within a hearing impaired program might receive a weight of 1.9, but the state might reimburse only 80% of the cost for that student.

Types

Continuing funds. Year-to-year funds are called continuing funds. These funds represent a relatively stable source of revenue for the district. Financial reimbursement based on pupil attendance is an example of this type of funding.

Noncontinuing funds. Noncontinuing funds are one-time monies that are usually designated for specific purposes (e.g., special equipment).

Targeted funds.   Targeted funds, sometimes referred to as nondiscretionary funds, must be spent for a particular item. If the funds are not used for the intended purpose, they are returned to the funding agent.

Discretionary funds.   Discretionary funds provide the district with the widest possible latitude for spending. Discretionary funds allow a district to use monies for any purpose it earmarks.

Inside formula funds.   These are funds from other sources that must be deducted before reimbursement from a second source can be accomplished. Inside formula funds are designed to reduce the base amount on which final calculations for reimbursement are made.

Outside formula funds.   Outside formula funds are the opposite of inside formula funds. That is, these are dollars that are not deducted from a base before calculating the final reimbursement figure.

Matching funds.   Matching funds apply when one agency or group "matches" or equals the funds contributed by another agency or group. If an equal, or ratio, of the match is not met, funds are withheld.

Mixed funds.   Mixed funds represent a combination of any of the seven formulas.

Sources

Federal.   Federal monies for special education services can be obtained through several sources (e.g., P.L. 94-142 monies, P.L. 89-313 monies for transitional students, and special grants). Dollars from the federal government can be received directly, or indirectly through the state education agency.

State.   The State Education Agency (SEA) allocates monies to local districts across special education programs.

Local.   Local funds usually are obtained by using an existing tax mechanism (e.g., property tax) to generate funds.

Private.   Private funds are obtained through charitable or volunteer associations. These funds are usually donated with minimal or no cost accounting requirements attached.

Despite various methods of funding, most states seem to use some form of the categorical label for each handicapping condition to allocate funds. Even in noncategorical funding arrangements, when funds for exceptional children are included in the general fund for use by special education, the local educational agency (LEA) is in a position to direct some of those funds to other educational programs, unless a strict accounting of the use of those funds for special education is required.

CONCLUSION

The terms litigation and legislation have been defined to assist the reader in understanding litigative and legislative influences upon education for exceptional children and youth. Major litigative and legislative milestones relevant to handicapped populations have been discussed in light of the right to education and the assurance of an appropriate education for all exceptional students.

Landmark litigative and legislative actions pertinent to the right to education were examined with respect to the developing notion of equal educational opportunity in this country. The assurance of that educational opportunity for handicapped individuals was examined in the context of P.L. 94-142, the key law affecting the education of handicapped children and youth. Aspects of due process, nondiscriminatory testing, free and appropriate education, and funding were discussed in an effort to provide the consultant with an understanding of how that right to education for handicapped individuals can be sustained.

SUMMARY OF KEY POINTS

Definition of Litigation

1. Litigation refers to the act or process of bringing a court suit against another party for the purpose of redressing an alleged injustice.

2. A class action suit refers to a suit brought by one or more individuals on behalf of others in similar circumstances.

3. One of the main effects of litigation is that rights for handicapped individuals have been obtained.

Definition of Legislation

4. Legislation refers to the act or process whereby elected representatives embody within a single document the law that becomes applicable to the general public.

5. Once a federal law is enacted, state law is usually changed to be in compliance with the federal statute.

6. Rules and regulations that describe how the procedures for the law will operate are written after a law is enacted.

The Right to Education

7. The Right to Education is based on the principle that all children are entitled to a free and appropriate public education.

8. The Right to Education is based on litigative rulings and federal statues.

9. Section 504 of the Rehabilitation Act is termed the civil rights law for the handicapped because of its comprehensive and far-reaching implications. Section 504 specifically prohibits discrimination in education and employment based on handicapping condition.

Assuring the Right to Education for All Handicapped Students

10. The right to an educational experience is assured by the following provisions of law: due process, free and appropriate public education, nondiscriminatory evaluation, the IEP, and the least restrictive environment.

Financial Assistance

11. Financial assistance to state or local education agencies is usually based on the severity of the handicapping condition. The more severe the handicapping condition, the more assistance is needed. Other factors, such as the number of students to be served and associated costs for serving students, also enter into cost calculations.

Funding Procedures

12. Several methods for funding special education programs are available. These include the bases of the cost, the formula to calculate the cost, the type of funding available, and the source of the funds.

QUESTIONS

1. What are some advantages and disadvantages of class action suits?

2. Define the term *litigation*.

3. Distinguish between a fully litigated case and a case that has been resolved by a consent decree.

4. Define the term *legislation*.

5. Explain the meaning of the term *educational opportunity* over the past 30 years. Provide reasons for any change in meaning.

6. What litigative action had an impact upon the current meaning of educational opportunity in this country?

7. What are two major components of the Section 504 Rules and regulations?

8. What law is crucial to the assurance of an appropriate education for all handicapped children?

9. What are the basic principles, as outlined by Brimer and Barudin (1977), of P.L. 93-380 and P.L. 94-142?

10. What is a basic distinction between substantive and procedural due process?

11. What are two aspects of nondiscriminatory evaluation resulting from litigated cases?

12. What three hierarchical steps are available to the dissenting party in the impartial due process hearing procedures?

13. According to Ennis (1976), the notion of the least restrictive environment is the legal corollary of what social science principle?

14. List three factors that affect the cost of educating an exceptional child.

15. Describe a taxonomy for funding that could be used to provide services for handicapped students in local educational systems.

DISCUSSION POINTS AND EXERCISES

1. Compare the special education programming that existed in your school district in the 1970s with the program that exists today.
   a. What are some of the similarities?
   b. What are some of the differences?
   c. Identify federal and state legislation and/or district policy that has affected educational programming in your district.
   d. What have been the consequences of this legislation and/or policy?
   e. Have any problems ensued that could result in litigative action?
   f. What would be the nature of that litigation?
   g. Could you foresee the need to amend recent legislation?
   h. What would be the nature of such amendments?

2. As a consultant in your school district, you are involved in the implementation of special education programming. You are requested to make a presentation at the next parent-teacher meeting outlining the service delivery system to your school district. State how all children, handi-

Litigation and Legislation 359

capped and nonhandicapped, will receive a quality education. Points to consider:

a. Factors essential for quality education.
b. Factors unique to handicapped students.
c. The service delivery procedure best suited to meet the needs of all children in the school district.

3. There has been a complaint regarding the educational program of a main-streamed special education student in your school system. You are requested to attend a local hearing. What would be the nature of the information you, as a consultant, supervisor, or local education agency representative, should be prepared to supply?

References

Abeson, A. (1976). Litigation. In F. J. Weintraub, A. Abeson, J. Ballard, & M. L. LaVor (Eds.), *Public policy and the education of exceptional children* (pp. 240–257). Reston, VA: Council for Exceptional Children.

Abeson, A., & Ballard, J. (1976). State and federal policy for exceptional children. In F. J. Weintraub, A. Abeson, J. Ballard, & M. L. LaVor (Eds.), *Public policy and the education of exceptional children* (pp. 83–95). Reston, VA: Council for Exceptional Children.

Abeson, A., Bolick, N., & Hass, J. A. (1975). A primer on due process: Education decisions for handicapped children. *Exceptional Children, 42,* 68–74.

Adamson, D. R. (1983). Linking two worlds: Serving resource students at the secondary level. *Teaching Exceptional Children, 15*(2), 70–76.

Adelman, H. (1971). The not so specific learning disability population. *Exceptional Children, 37*(7), 528–533.

Adelman, H. S. (1978). The concept of intrinsic motivation: Implications for practice and research related to learning disabilities. *Learning Disability Quarterly, 1,* 43–54.

Affleck, J. Q., Lowenbraun, S., & Archer, A. (1980). *Teaching the mildly handicapped in the regular classroom* (2nd ed.). Columbus, OH: Merrill.

Alessi, C. (1985). *Effects of a home-school communication system on the writing performance of learning disabled students.* Unpublished master's thesis, The Ohio State University, Columbus, OH.

Allen, A. R., & Boraks, N. (1978). Peer tutoring: Putting it to the test. *The Reading Teacher, 31,* 274–278.

Alley, G., & Deshler, D. (1979). *Teaching the learning disabled adolescent: Strategies and methods.* Denver: Love.

Alpert, J. L. (1977). Some guidelines for school consultants. *Journal of School Psychology, 15*(4), 308–319.

Alves, A. J., & Gottlieb, J. (1986). Teacher interactions with mainstreamed handicapped students and their nonhandicapped peers. *Learning Disability Quarterly, 9*(1), 77–83.

Anderson, L. M., Evertson, C. M., & Brophy, J. E. (1979). An experimental study of effective teaching in first-grade reading groups. *Elementary School Journal, 79,* 193–222.

Angrist, S. S. (1975). Evaluation research: Possibilities and limitations. *The Journal of Applied Behavioral Science, 11*(1), 75–91.

Aragon, J. (1973). Cultural conflict and cultural diversity in education. In L. A. Bransford, L. Baca, & K. Lane (Eds.), *Cultural diversity and the exceptional child* (pp. 24–31). Reston, VA: Council for Exceptional Children.

Aragon, J., & Marquez, L. (1973). Highlights of institute on language and culture: Spanish-speaking component. In L. A. Bransford, L. Baca, & K. Lane (Eds.), *Cultural diversity and the exceptional child* (pp. 20–21). Reston, VA: Council for Exceptional Children.

Armstrong v. Kline, 476 F. Supplement 583 (E.D. PA 1979).

Aronson, E., Blaney, N., Stephan, C., Sikes, J., & Snapp, M. (1978). *The jigsaw classroom*. Beverly Hills, CA: Sage.

Ary, D., Jacobs, L. C., & Asghar, R. (1985). *Introduction to research in education* (3rd ed.). New York: Holt, Rinehart and Winston.

Asher, S. R., & Taylor, A. R. (1981). Social outcomes of mainstreaming: Sociometric assessment and beyond. *Exceptional Education Quarterly, 1*(4), 13–30.

Axelrod, S. (1973). Comparison of individual and group contingencies in two special classes. *Behavior Therapy, 4*, 83–90.

Axelrod, S. (1977). *Behavior modification for the classroom teacher*. New York: McGraw-Hill.

Ayllon, T., & Roberts, M. D. (1974). Eliminating discipline problems by strengthening academic performance. *Journal of Applied Behavior Analysis, 7*, 71–76.

Azrin, N. H., & Besalel, V. A. (1980). *How to use overcorrection*. Austin, TX: PRO-ED.

Azrin, N. H., & Holz, W. E. (1966). Punishment. In W. K. Honig (Ed.), *Operant behavior: Areas of research and application* (pp. 380–447). New York: Appleton-Century-Crofts.

Azrin, N. H., & Lindsley, O. R. (1956). The reinforcement of cooperation between children. *Journal of Abnormal and Social Psychology, 52*, 100–102.

Babcock, N. L., & Pryzwansky, W. B. (1983). Models of consultation: Preferences of educational professionals at five stages of service. *Journal of School Psychology, 21*, 359–366.

Baca, L. M., & Cervantes, H. T. (1984). *The bilingual special education interface*. Columbus, OH: Merrill.

Baer, D., Wolf, M., & Risley, T. (1968). Some current dimensions of applied behavior analysis. *Journal of Applied Behavior Analysis, 1*, 91–97.

Baer, G. G., & Richards, H. C. (1980). An interdependent group-oriented contingency system for improving academic performance. *School Pyschology Review, 9*, 190–193.

Bailey, M. N., & Raimondi, S. L. (1984). Technology and special education: A resource guide. *Teaching Exceptional Children, 16*(4), 273–277.

Ballard, J. (1976). Active federal education laws for exceptional persons. In F. J. Weintraub, A. Abeson, J. Ballard, & M. L. LaVor (Eds.), *Public policy and the education of exceptional children* (pp. 133–146). Reston, VA: Council for Exceptional Children.

Bandura, A. (1969). *Principles of behavior modification*. New York: Holt, Rinehart and Winston.

Bandura, A. (1971). *Social learning theory*. New York: General Learning Press.

Banks, J. A. (1984). *Teaching strategies for ethnic studies* (3rd ed.). Boston: Allyn and Bacon.

Barbe, W. & Swassing, R. H. (1979). *Teaching through modality strengths: Concepts and practices.* Columbus, OH: Zaner-Bloser.

Barrish, H. H., Saunders, M., & Wolf, M. M. (1969). Good behavior games: Effects of individual contingencies for group consequences on disruptive behavior in a classroom. *Journal of Applied Behavior Analysis, 2,* 199–224.

Barsch, R. H. (1969). *The parent teacher partnership.* Arlington, VA: Council for Exceptional Children.

Baskin, O., & Aronoff, C. (1980). *Interpersonal communication in organizations.* Santa Monica, CA: Goodyear.

Battle v. Pennsylvania, 629 (3rd Cir. 1980).

Becker, H. J. (1984). Computers in schools today: Some basic considerations. *American Journal of Education, 93*(1), 22–39.

Bell, L. (1977). *Effects of modeling and verbal feedback on math performance of educable mentally retarded children.* Unpublished master's thesis, The Ohio State University, Columbus, OH.

Bell, M. E. (1985). The role of instructional theories in the evaluation of microcomputer courseware. *Educational Technology,* March, 36–40.

Benavides, A. (1980). Cultural awareness training for the exceptional teacher. *Teaching Exceptional Children, 13*(1), 8–11.

Benavides, A. (1985). Planning effective special education for exceptional language minorities. *Teaching Exceptional Children, 17*(2), 127–132.

Bender, M., & Valletutti, P. J. (1982). *Teaching functional academics: A curriculum guide for adolescents and adults with learning problems.* Austin, TX: PRO-ED.

Bergan, J. R. (1977). *Behavioral consultation.* Columbus, OH: Merrill.

Bergan, J. R., & Tombari, M. L. (1976) Consultant skill and efficiency and the implementation and outcomes of consultation. *Journal of School Psychology, 14*(1), 3–14.

Bersoff, D. N. (1979). Regarding psychologists testily: Legal regulation of psychological assessment in the public schools. *Maryland Law Review, 39,* 27–120.

Bijou, W. W., Birnbrauer, J. S., Kidder, J. D., & Tague, C. (1967). Programmed instruction as an approach to teaching reading, writing, and arithmetic to retarded children. In S. W. Bijou & D. M. Baer (Eds.), *Child development: Readings in experimental analysis.* New York: Appleton-Century-Crofts.

Bilingual Education Act, P.L. 90-247, 81 Stat. 783 816 (Jan. 2, 1968).

Bilingual Education Act, as amended by the Elementary and Secondary Education Amendments of 1978, P.L. 95-561, 92 Stat. 2268 (Nov. 1, 1978).

Bilingual Education Act as amended by Title II of P.L. 98-511 (October 19, 1984).

Bittle, R. G. (1975). Improving parent-teacher communication through recorded telephone messages. *Journal of Educational Research, 69,* 87–95.

Blankenship, C. S. (1978). Remediating systematic inversion errors in subtraction through the use of demonstration and feedback. *Learning Disability Quarterly, 1,* 12–22.

Bloom, B. S. (1954). The thought process of students in discussion. In S. J. French (Ed.), *Accent on teaching: Experiments in general education* (pp. 23–46). New York: Harper and Brothers.

Boehm, A. E., & Weinberg, R. A. (1977). *The classroom observer: A guide for developing observation skills*. New York: Teachers College Press.

Bonning, R. A. (1968). *Specific skill series*. New York: Barnell-Loft.

Borg, W. (1980). Time and school learning. In C. Denham & A. Lieberman (Eds.), *Time to learn* (pp. 33–72). Washington, DC: National Institute of Education.

Bowe, F. (1980). *Rehabilitating America*. New York: Harper and Row.

Bowe, F. G. (1984). *Personal computers and special needs*. Berkeley, CA: Sybex.

Bower, E. M., & Lambert, N. M. (1976). In-school screening of children with emotional handicaps. In N. J. Long, W. C. Morse, & R. G. Newman (Eds.), *Conflict in the classroom* (pp. 95–100). Belmont, CA: Wadsworth.

Boyer, E. L. (1983). *High school*. New York: Harper and Row.

Brandt, R. M. (1975). An historical overview of systematic approaches to observation in school settings. In R. A. Weinberg & F. H. Wood (Eds.), *Observation of pupils and teachers in mainstream and special education settings: Alternative strategies* (pp. 9–37). Reston, VA: Council for Exceptional Children.

Brantner, J. P., & Doherty, M. A. (1983). A review of timeout: A conceptual and methodological analysis. In S. Axelrod & J. Apsche (Eds.), *The effects of punishment on human behavior* (pp. 87–132). New York: Academic Press.

Brimer, R. W., & Barudin, S. I. (1977). *Due process, right to education and the exceptional child: The road to equality in education*. Unpublished manuscript, University of Missouri-Columbia, Columbia, MO.

Broden, M., Bruce, C., Mitchell, M. A., Carter, V. C., & Hall, R. V. (1970). Effects of teacher attention on attending behavior of two boys in adjacent desks. *Journal of Applied Behavior Analysis, 3*, 199–203.

Broden, M., Copeland, G., Beasley, A., & Hall, R. V. (1977). Altering student responses through changes in teacher verbal behavior. *Journal of Applied Behavior Analysis, 10*, 479–487.

Brolin, D. E., & Carver, J. T. (1982). Lifelong career development for adults with handicaps: A new model. *Journal of Career Education, 8*, 281–292.

Brolin, D. E., & D'Alonzo, B. J. (1979). Critical issues in career education for handicapped students. *Exceptional Children, 45*, 246–253.

Brolin, D. E., & Kokaska, C. (1974). Critical issues in job placement of the educable mentally retarded. *Rehabilitation Literature, 35*, 174–177.

Brolin, D. E., & Kokaska, C. J. (1979). *Career education for handicapped children and youth*. Columbus, OH: Merrill.

Brophy, J. (1979). Teacher behavior and its effects. *Journal of Educational Psychology, 71*, 733–750.

Brophy, J. E., & Good, T. L. (1969). *Teacher-child dyadic interaction: A manual for coding classroom behavior*. Austin, TX: The Research and Development Center for Teacher Education, The University of Texas at Austin.

Brophy, J. E., & Good, T. L. (1974). *Teacher-student relationships: Causes and consequences*. New York: Holt, Rinehart and Winston.

Brown v. Board of Education of Topeka. (1954). 347 U.S. 483.

Brown, D., Reschly, D., & Wasserman, H. (1974). Effects of surreptitious modeling upon classroom behaviors. *Psychology in the Schools, 11*(3) 366–369.

Brown, D., Wyne, M. D., Blackburn, J. E., & Powell, W. C. (1979). *Consultation: Strategy for improving education*. Boston: Allyn and Bacon.

Brown, J. M., & Yuh-Sheng Chang, G. (1982). Supplementary reading materials for vocational students with limited reading ability. *Journal of Reading, 26*(2), 144–149.

Brown, V. L. (1977). "Yes, but. . ." A reply to Phyllis Newcomer. *The Journal of Special Education, 11*(2), 171–177.

Bryan, J., & Bryan, T. (1977). The social-emotional side of learning disabilities. *Behavior Disorders, 2,* 141–145.

Bryan, T. (1974a). An observational analysis of classroom behaviors of children with learning disabilities. *Journal of Learning Disabilities, 7,* 26–34.

Bryan, T. H. (1974b). Peer popularity of learning disabled children. *Journal of Learning Disabilities, 7,* 620–625.

Bryan, T. H. (1976). Peer popularity of learning disabled children: A replication. *Journal of Learning Disabilities, 9,* 307–311.

Bryan, T. H. (1977). Learning disabled children's comprehension of nonverbal communication. *Journal of Learning Disabilities, 10,* 501–506.

Bryan, T. H. (1982). Social skills of learning disabled children and youth: An overview. *Learning Disability Quarterly, 5*(4), 332–333.

Bryan, T. H., & Bryan, J. H. (1978). Social interactions of learning disabled children. *Learning Disability Quarterly, 1,* 33–38.

Bryan, T., Cosden, M., & Pearl, R. (1982). The effects of cooperative goal structures and cooperative models on LD and NLD students. *Learning Disability Quarterly, 5*(4), 415–421.

Bryan, T., Wheeler, R., Felcan, J., & Henek, T. (1976). "Come on Dummy": An observational study of children's communication. *Journal of Learning Disabilities, 9*(10), 661–669.

Bruininks, V. L. (1978a). Actual and perceived peer status of learning disabled students in mainstreamed programs. *Journal of Special Education, 12*(1), 51–58.

Bruininks, V. L. (1978b). Peer status and personality characteristics of learning disabled and nondisabled students. *Journal of Learning Disabilities, 11,* 484–489.

Bucknam, R. B., & Brand, S. G. (1984). EBCE really works. *Educational Leadership, 40*(6), 66–71.

Budd, K., & Baer, D. M. (Summer, 1976). Behavior modification and the law: Implications of recent judicial decisions. *The Journal of Psychiatry and Law,* 171–244.

Budoff, M., Thormann, J., & Gras, A. (1984). *Microcomputers in special education.* Cambridge, MA: Brookline.

Bush, W. J., & Waugh, K. W. (1982). *Diagnosing learning problems* (3rd ed.), Columbus, OH: Merrill.

California State Department of Education. (1977). *California school effectiveness study: The first year, 1974–1975.* Sacramento, CA: Author.

Campbell, A., & Sulzer, B. (February, 1971). *Naturally available reinforcers as motivators toward reading and spelling achievement by educable mentally handicapped students.* Paper presented at the meeting of the American Research Association meeting, New York.

Carlson, S. A., & Alley, G. R. (1981). *Performance and competence of learning disabled and high achieving high school students on essential cognitive skills* (Research Report No. 53). Lawrence, KS: The University of Kansas Institute for Research in Learning Disabilities.

Carnine, D. W. (1976). Effects of two teachers' presentation rates on off-task behavior, answering correctly, and participation. *Journal of Applied Behavior Analysis, 9,* 199–206.

Caro, F. G. (1971). Issues in the evaluation of social programs. *Review of Educational Research, 41,* 87–114.

Carpenter, L. (1983). *Bilingual special education: An overview of issues.* Los Alamitos, CA: National Center for Bilingual Research.

Carr, E. G., & Lovaas, I. O. (1983). Contingent electric shock as a treatment for severe behavior problems. In S. Axelrod & J. Apsche (Eds.), *The effects of punishment on human behavior* (pp. 221–245). New York: Academic Press.

Cartledge, G., Frew, T., & Zaharias, J. (1985). Social skill needs of mainstreamed students: Peer and teacher perceptions. *Learning Disability Quarterly, 8*(2), 132–140.

Catania, A. C. (1984). *Learning* (2nd ed.) Englewood Cliffs, NJ: Prentice-Hall.

Cavallaro, C. C. (1983). Language interventions in natural settings. *Teaching Exceptional Children, 16*(1), 65–70.

Cegelka, P. T. (1979). Career education. In D. Cullinan & M. H. Epstein (Eds.), *Special education for adolescents: Issues and perspectives* (pp. 155–184). Columbus, OH: Merrill.

Chan, K. S., & So, A. Y. (1982). *The impact of language of instruction on the educational achievement of Hispanic children* (Technical Note No. 6). Los Alamitos, CA: National Center for Bilingual Research.

Chandler, L. A. (1980). Consultative services in the schools: A model. *Journal of School Psychology, 18*(4), 399–401.

Chapman, J. (1978). *Improving parent-teacher communication through the use of recorded messages.* Unpublished master's thesis, The Ohio State University, Columbus, OH.

Chapman, R. B., Larsen, S. C., & Parker, R. M. (1979). Interaction of first- grade teachers with learning disordered children. *Journal of Learning Disabilities, 12*(4), 20–25.

Chinn, P. C. (1979). The exceptional minority child. Issues and some answers. *Exceptional Children, 19,* 61–71.

Chinn, P. C. (1984). *The education of culturally and linguistically different children.* Reston, VA: Council for Exceptional Children.

Clayton, I. (1983). Career preparation and the visually handicapped student. *Education of the Visually Handicapped, 14*(14), 115–120.

Cloward, R. D. (1967). Studies in tutoring. *Journal of Experimental Education, 36,* 14–25.

Coleman, R. A. (1970). A conditioning technique applicable to elementary school classrooms. *Journal of Applied Behavior Analysis, 3,* 293–297.

Collier, C., & Kalk, M. (1984). Bilingual special education curriculum development. In L. M. Baca & H. T. Cervantes, *The bilingual special education interface* (pp. 233–268). Columbus, OH: Merrill.

Committee on Youth Development of the President's Committee on Employment of the Handicapped (Ed.). (1984, January). *A codified report of the Pathways to Employment meeting series: Needs and strategies for preparing disabled youth for their first job.* Washington, DC: PCEH.

Condon, E. C., Peters, J. Y., & Sueiro-Ross, C. (1979). *Special education and the Hispanic child: Cultural perspectives.* Philadelphia, PA: Teacher Corps Mid-Atlantic Network, Temple University.

Conlon, M. F., Hall, C., & Hanley, E. (1972). The effects of a peer correction procedure on the arithmetic accuracy for two elementary school children. In G. Semb (Ed.), *Behavior analysis and education.* Lawrence, KS: The University of Kansas Support and Development Center for Follow Through.

Conoley, J. C., & Conoley, C. W. (1982). *School consultation: A guide to practice and training.* New York: Pergamon.

Cooke, N. L., Heron, T. E., & Heward, W. L. (1983). *Peer tutoring: Implementing classwide programs in the primary grades.* Columbus, OH: Special Press.

Cooley, W., & Leinhardt, G. (1980). The instructional dimensions study. *Educational Evaluation and Policy Analysis, 2,* 7–24.

Cooper, J. O. (1981). *Measuring behavior* (2nd ed.), Columbus, OH: Merrill.

Cooper, J. O., & Edge, D. (1981). *Parenting: Strategies and educational methods.* Louisville, KY: Eston Corp.

Cooper, J. O., Heron, T. E., & Heward, W. L. (1987). *Applied behavior analysis.* Columbus, OH: Merrill.

Cooper, L., Johnson, D. W., Johnson, R., & Wilderson, F. (1980). Effects of cooperative, competitive, and individualistic experiences on interpersonal attraction among heterogeneous peers. *Journal of Social Psychology, 111,* 243–252.

Corman, L., & Gottlieb, J. (1978). Mainstreaming mentally retarded children: A review of research. *American Journal of Mental Deficiency, 3,* 251–275.

Cossairt, A., Hall, R. V., & Hopkins, B. L. (1973). The effects of experimenter's instructions, feedback, and praise on teacher praise and student attending behavior. *Journal of Applied Behavior Analysis, 6,* 89–100.

Cox, J. (1980). Operation divert: A model program for learning disabled juvenile offenders. In R. H. Riegel & J. P. Mathey (Eds.), *Mainstreaming at the secondary level: Seven models that work.* Plymouth, MI: Wayne County Intermediate School District.

Crowner, T. T. (1985). A taxonomy of special education finance. *Exceptional Children, 51*(6), 503–508.

Cummins, J. (1981a). Age on arrival and immigrant second language learning in Canada: A reassessment. *Applied Linguistics, 2*(2), 131–149.

Cummins, J. (1981b). The role of primary language development in promoting educational success for language minority students. In *Schooling and language minority students: A theoretical framework* (pp. 3–49). Los Angeles: Evaluation, Dissemination and Assessment Center, California State University, Los Angeles.

Cummins, J. (1984). *Bilingualism and special education: Issues in assessment and pedagogy.* Clevedon, Avon, England: Multilingual Matters.

Custer, J. D., & Osguthorpe, R. T. (1983). Improving social acceptance by training handicapped students to tutor their nonhandicapped peers. *Exceptional Children, 50*(2), 173–174.

D'Alonzo, B. J., Marino, J. F., & Kauss, M. W. (1984). Mesa public school comprehensive career and vocational education program for disabled students. *Career Development for Exceptional Individuals, 7,* 22–29.

Dardig, J. C., & Heward, W. L. (1976). *Sign here: A contracting book for children and their parents.* Kalamazoo, MI: Behaviordelia.

Dardig, J. C., & Heward, W. L. (1981a). *Sign here: A contracting book for children and their parents* (2nd ed). Bridgewater, NJ: F. Fournies and Associates.

Dardig, J. C., & Heward, W.L. (1981b). A systematic procedure for prioritizing IEP goals. *The Directive Teacher, 3*(2), 6,8.

Davis, M. (1972). Effects of having one remedial student tutor another remedial student. In G. Semb (Ed.), *Behavior Analysis and Education-1972.* Lawrence: University of Kansas, Department of Human Development.

Davis, W. E. (1983). *The special educator: Strategies for succeeding in today's schools.* Austin, TX: PRO-ED.

deGrandpré, B. B., & Messier, J. M. (1979). Helping mainstreamed students stay in the mainstream. *The Directive Teacher, 2*(2), 12,15.

Deitz, S. M., & Repp, A.C. (1973). Decreasing classroom misbehavior through the use of DRL schedules of reinforcement. *Journal of Applied Behavior Analysis, 6,* 457–463.

Delgado, T. (1982). A parent's point of view in working with special education children. *Proceedings of the conference on special education and the bilingual child* (pp. 104–105). San Diego, CA: National Origin Desegregation Law Center, San Diego State University.

Delgado-Gaitan, C., & Trueba, H. T. (1985). Ethnographic study of participant structures in task completion: Reinterpretation of "handicaps" in Mexican children. *Learning Disability Quarterly, 8*(1), 67–75.

Delquadri, J. C., Greenwood, C. R., & Hall, R. V. (1979). *Opportunity to respond: An update.* Paper presented at the Fifth Annual Meeting of the Association for Behavior Analysis, Dearborn, MI.

Delquadri, J. C., Greenwood, C. R., Whorton., D., Carta, J. J., & Hall, R. V. (1986). Classwide peer tutoring. *Exceptional Children, 52*(6), 535–542.

Deshler, D. D., Alley, G. R., & Carlson, S. A. (1980). Learning strategies: An approach to mainstreaming secondary students with learning disabilities. *Education Unlimited, 2*(4), 6–11.

Deshler, D. D., & Graham, S. (1980). Tape recording educational materials for secondary handicapped students. *Teaching Exceptional Children, 12,* 52–54.

Deshler, D. D., Lowrey, N., & Alley, G. R. (1979). Programming alternatives for learning disabled adolescents: A nationwide survey. *Academic Therapy, 14,* 389–397.

Deshler, D. D., Schumaker, J. B., Alley, G. R., Warner, M. M., & Clark, F. L. (1982). Learning disabilities in adolescent and young adult populations: Research implications. *Focus on Exceptional Children, 15*(1), 1–12.

Deshler, D. D., Schumaker, J. B., Lenz, B. K., & Ellis, E. (1984). Academic and cognitive interventions for LD adolescents: Part II. *Journal of Learning Disabilities, 17*(3), 170–179.

Deterline, W. C. (1970). *Training and management of student-tutors: Final report.* Palo Alto, CA: General Programmed Teaching (ERIC Document Reproduction No. 048-133).

Devine, T. (1981). *Teaching study skills.* Boston: Allyn and Bacon.

Diana v. State Board of Education of California. (N.D. Cal., January 7, 1970, and June 18, 1973). Civil No. C-70, 37 RFP.

Dineen, J. P., Clark, H. P., & Risley, T. R. (1977). Peer tutoring among elementary students: Education benefits to the tutor. *Journal of Applied Behavior Analysis, 10*, 231–238.

Dishon, D., & O'Leary, P. W. (1985). *A guidebook for cooperative learning: A technique of creating more effective schools.* Holmes Beach, FL: Learning Publications.

Dobbert, M. L. (1982). *Ethnographic research: Theory and application for modern schools and societies.* New York: Praeger.

Donahue, M., & Bryan, T. (1984). Communicative skills and peer relations of learning disabled adolescents. *Topics in Language Disorders,* March, 10–21.

Duncan, M., & Biddle, B. (1974). *The study of teaching.* New York: Holt, Rinehart and Winston.

Edwards, J., Norton, S., Taylor, S., Weiss, M., & Van Dusseldorp, R. (1975). How effective is CAI? A review of the research. *Educational Leadership, 33*, 147–153.

Egner, A., & Lates, B. J. (1975). The Vermont consulting teacher program: Case presentation. In C. A. Parker (Ed.), *Psychological consultation: Helping teachers meet special needs* (pp. 31–64). Minneapolis, Minnesota: Leadership Training Institute/Special Education.

Ellis, D. E. (1980). *Peer tutoring: The effect of praise on the academic achievement and social structure of a first-grade classroom.* Unpublished master's thesis, The Ohio State University, Columbus, OH.

Englemann, S., & Carnine, D. (1982). *Theory of Instruction: Principles and applications.* New York: Irvington.

Englert, C. S. (1984). Effective direct instruction practices in special education settings. *Remedial and Special Education, 5*(2), 38–47.

Ennis, B. J. (1976). Reaction comment to Strauss. Due process in civil commitment and elsewhere. In M. Kindred, J. Cohen, D. Penrod, & T. Shaffer (Eds.), *The mentally retarded citizen and the law.* New York: The Free Press.

Epstein, M. H. (1982). Special education programs for the handicapped adolescent. *The School Psychology Review, 11*(4), 384–390.

Erickson, F. (1973). What makes school ethnography ethnographic? *Council on Anthropology and Education Newsletter, 4*, 10–19.

Evans, I., & Meyer, L. H. (1985). *An educative approach to behavior problems: A practical decision model for interventions with severely handicapped learners.* Baltimore: Paul H. Brookes.

Evans, S. (1980). The consultant role of the resource teacher. *Exceptional Children, 46*(5), 402–404.

Federal Register, Vol. 42, No. 163, August 23, 1977, 121a.346.

Federal Register. (August 23, 1977). Vol. 42, No. 163, paragraph 121a.533.

Federal Register. (August 23, 1977). Vol. 42, No. 163, paragraph 121a.550 (1), (2).

Federal Rules Civil Procedure, Rule 23 (a), 28 United States Code Annotated.

Ferrante Alexander, D. (1986). Drilling basic math facts: From drudgery to delight. *Teaching Exceptional Children, 18*(3), 209–212.

Fischer, T. C. (1970). *Due process in the student-institution relationship.* Washington, DC: American Association of State Colleges and Universities. (ERIC Document Reproduction Service No. ED 041 189)

Flanders, N. A. (1975). The use of interaction analysis to study pupil attitudes toward learning. In R. A. Weinberg & F. H. Wood (Eds.), *Observation of pupils and* teacher in mainstreamed and special education settings: Alternative strategies (pp. 41–74). Reston, VA: Council for Exceptional Children.

Florio, S. (1981). Very special natives: The evolving role of teachers as informants in educational ethnography. East Lansing, MI: Institute for Research on Teaching, Michigan State University. (ERIC Document Reproduction Service No. ED 204-342)

Foxx, R. M. (1982). Decreasing behaviors of severely retarded and austistic persons. Champaign: IL: Research Press.

Foxx, R. M., & Bechtel, D. R. (1983). Overcorrection: A review and analysis. In S. Axelrod & J. Apsche (Eds.), The effects of punishment on human behavior (pp. 133–220). New York: Academic Press.

Frager, S., & Stern, C. (1970). Learning by teaching. The Reading Teacher, 23, 403–417.

Friend, M. (1985). Training special educators to be consultants. Teacher Education and Special Education, 8(3), 115–120.

Functions of the placement committee in special education: A resource manual. (1976). Washington, DC: National Association of State Directors of Special Education.

Galagan, J. E. (1985). Psychoeducational testing: Turn out the lights, the party's over. Exceptional Children, 52(3), 288–299.

Gallagher, P. A. (1985). Inservice! A mandated special education course and its effects on regular classroom teachers. Teacher Education and and Special Education, 8(2), 59–65.

Gallagher, P. A., Sulzbacher, S. I., & Shores, R. E. (March, 1976). A group contingency for classroom management of emotionally disturbed children. Paper presented at the meeting of the Kansas Council for Exceptional Children, Wichita.

Gallessich, J. (1982). The profession and practice of consultation. San Francisco: Jossey-Bass.

Garcia, R. (1982). Teaching in a pluralistic society: Concepts, models, strategies. New York: Harper & Row.

Gardner, D. P. (1983). A nation at risk: The imperative for education reform. Washington, DC: The National Commission on Excellence in Education.

Gast, D., & Wolery, M. (1987). Severe maladaptive behaviors. In M. E. Snell (Ed.), Systematic instruction of people with severe handicaps (3rd ed., pp. 300–332). Columbus, OH: Merrill.

Gaver, D., & Richards, H. (1979). Dimensions of naturalistic observation for the prediction of academic success. Journal of Educational Research, 72, 123–127.

Gaylord-Ross, R. (1980). A decision model for the treatment of aberrant behavior in applied settings. In W. Sailor, B. Wilcox, & L. Brown (Eds.), Methods of instruction for severely handicapped students (pp. 135–158). Baltimore: Paul H. Brookes.

Gersten, R., & Hauser, C. (1984). The case for impact evaluations in special education. Remedial and Special Education, 5(2), 16–24.

Gickling, E. E., & Thompson, V. P. (1985). A personal view of curriculum-based assessment. Exceptional Children, 52(3), 205–218.

Gilhool, T. K. (1973). Education: An inalienable right. *Exceptional Children, 39,* 597-609.

Gillet, P. (1980). Career education in the special elementary education program. *Teaching Exceptional Children, 13*(1), 17-21.

Gillet, P. (1983). It's elementary! Career education activities for mildly handicapped students. *Teaching Exceptional Children, 15*(4),199-205.

Glass, R. M., Christiansen, J., & Christiansen, J. L. (1982). *Teaching exceptional students in the regular classroom.* Boston: Little, Brown.

Gleason, G. (1981). Microcomputers in education: The state of the art. *Educational Technology, 21*(3), 7-18.

Gola, T. J., Holmes, P. A., & Holmes, N. K. (1982). Effectiveness of a group contingency procedure for increasing prevocational behavior of profoundly mentally retarded residents. *Mental Retardation, 20*(1), 26-29.

Goldstein, A. P., & Sorcher, M. (1974). *Changing supervisor behavior.* New York: Pergamon.

Goldstein, A. P., Sprafkin, R. P., Gershaw, N. J., & Klein, P. (1980). *Skillstreaming the adolescent: A structured learning approach to teaching prosocial skills.* Champaign, IL: Research Press.

Goldstein, S., Strickland, B., Turnbull, A. P., & Curry, L. (1980). An observational analysis of the IEP conference. *Exceptional Children, 46*(4), 278-286.

Goldstein, S. R. (1975). Due process in school disciplinary proceeding: The meaning and implication of *Goss v. Lopez. Educational Horizons, 54,* 4-9.

Good, T., & Grouws, D. (1977). Teaching effects: A process-product study in 4th grade mathematics classrooms. *Journal of Teacher Education, 28,* 49-54.

Good, T. L., Biddle, B. J., & Brophy, J. E. (1975). *Teachers make a difference.* New York: Holt, Rinehart and Winston.

Goodlad, J. I. (1983). *A place called school: Prospects for the future.* New York: McGraw-Hill.

Goodman, H., Gottlieb, J., & Harrison, R. (1972). The social acceptance of EMR's into a nongraded elementary school. *American Journal of Mental Deficiency, 76,* 412-417.

Goodman, L. (1985). The effective schools movement and special education. *Teaching Exceptional Children, 17*(2), 102-105.

Goodman, L., & Mann, L. (1976). *Learning disabilities in the secondary schools: Issues and practices.* New York: Grune & Stratton.

Gottlieb, J., & Leyser, Y. (1981). Friendship between mentally retarded and non-retarded children. In S. Asher & J. Gottman (Eds.), *The Development of Children's Friendships* (pp. 150-181). Cambridge, MA: Cambridge University Press.

Graubard, P. S., Rosenberg, H., & Miller, M. B. (1971). Student applications of behavior modification to teachers and environments or ecological approaches to deviancy. In E. A. Ramp & B. L. Hopkins (Eds.), *A new direction for education: Behavior analysis 1971* (pp. 80-101). Lawrence: University of Kansas.

Greenspan, S., & Shoultz, B. (1981). Why mentally retarded adults lose their jobs: Social competence as a factor in work adjustment. *Applied Research in Mental Retardation, 2,* 23-38.

Greenwood, C. R., Delquadri, J. C., & Hall, R. V. (1984). Opportunity to respond and student academic achievement. In W. L. Heward, T. E. Heron, D. S. Hill,

& J. Trap-Porter (Eds.), *Focus on behavior analysis in education* (pp. 58–88). Columbus, OH: Merrill.

Greenwood, C. R., Sloane, H. N., Jr., & Baskins, A. (1974). Training elementary aged peer behavior managers to control small group programmed mathematics. *Journal of Applied Behavior Analysis, 7,* 103–114.

Gresham, F. M. (1981). Social skills training with handicapped children: A review. *Review of Educational Research, 51,* 139–176.

Gresham, F. M. (1982). Misguided mainstreaming: The case for social skills training with handicapped children. *Exceptional Children, 48*(5), 422–433.

Gresham, F. M. (1983). Use of a home-based dependent group contingency system in controlling destructive behavior: A case study. *School Psychology Review, 12*(2), 195–199.

Gresham, F. M. (1984). Social skills and self-efficacy for exceptional children. *Exceptional Children, 51*(3), 253–261.

Gresham, F. M., & Gresham, G. N. (1982). Interdependent, dependent, and independent group contingencies for controlling disruptive behavior. *Journal of Special Education, 16*(1), 101–110.

Gresham, F. M., & Reschly, D. J. (1986). Social skills deficits and low peer acceptance of mainstreaming learning disabled children. *Learning Disability Quarterly, 9*(1), 23–32.

Gutmann, D. (1969). Psychological naturalism in cross-cultural studies. In E. P. Willems and H. L. Rausch (Eds.), *Naturalistic viewpoints in psychological research* (pp. 162–176). New York: Holt, Rinehart and Winston.

Hagen, D. (1984). *Microcomputer resource book for special education.* Reston, VA: Council for Exceptional Children.

Hall, R. V., Axelrod, S., Foundopoulos, M., Shellman, J., Campbell, R. A., & Cranston, S. (1971). The effective use of punishment to modify behavior in the classroom. *Educational Technology, 11,* 24–26.

Hall, R. V., Cristler, C., Cranston, S. S., & Tucker, B. (1970). Teachers and parents as researchers using multiple baseline designs. *Journal of Applied Behavior Analysis, 3,* 247–255.

Hall, R. V., Delquadri, J., Greenwood, C. R., & Thurston, L. (1982). The importance of opportunity to respond in children's academic success. In E. B. Edgar, N. G. Haring, J. R. Jenkins, & C. G. Pious (Eds.), *Mentally handicapped children: Education and training* (pp. 107–140). Austin, TX: PRO-ED.

Hall, R. V., Lund, D., & Jackson, D. (1968). Effects of teacher attention on study behavior. *Journal of Applied Behavior Analysis, 1,* 1–12.

Hallahan, D. P., & Reese, R. E. (1980). Selective attention and distractibility. In B. K. Keogh (Ed.), *Advances in special education* (Vol. 1, pp. 141–181). Greenwich, Conn.: JAI.

Hamblin, R. L., Hathaway, C., & Wodarski, J. S. (1971). Group contingencies, peer tutoring, and accelerating academic achievement. In E. A. Ramp and B. I. Hopkins (Eds.), *A new direction for education: Behavior Analysis 1971,* (Vol. 1, pp. 41–53), University of Kansas, Lawrence, Kansas.

Hamilton, D., & Delamont, S. (1974). Classroom research: A cautionary tale. *Research in Education, 11,* 1–16.

Hannaford, A. E. (1983). Microcomputers in special education: Some new opportunities, some old problems. *The Computing Teacher, 10*(6), 11–17.

Hardin, V. (1978). Ecological assessment and intervention for learning disabled students. *Learning Disability Quarterly, 1*(2), 15–20.

Harrington, C. (1973). Pupils, peers, and politics. In American Ethnological Society. *Proceedings of the 1972 Annual Spring Meeting of the American Ethnological Society: Learning and culture.* Washington: University of Washington Press.

Harris, K. C. (in press). Ethnography of a program: Curriculum and instruction for mildly handicapped Hispanic youth. *Proceedings of the Fourth Annual Symposium: Bilingual Special Education Research.* Boulder, Colorado: Bueno Center for Multicultural Education, University of Colorado.

Harris, K. C. (1981). *The classroom program of a special education teacher: A case study.* Unpublished doctoral dissertation, Temple University, Philadelphia, PA.

Harris, K. C., Garcia, L., Harvey, P., Innes, D., Jenkins, K., Munoz, D., & Stoica, R. (1986). *Evaluation of pilot consultation model.* Unpublished raw data.

Harris, K. C., & Little, J. (1982, September). *The emotionally disturbed mentally retarded student in the classroom.* Paper presented at the Matthew J. Guglielmo Endowed Chair in Mental Retardation Special Education Conference: Los Angeles.

Harris, V. W., Sherman, J. A., Henderson, D. G., & Harris, M. S. (1972). Effects of peer tutoring on the spelling performance of elementary classroom students. In G. Semb (Ed.), *Behavior analsyis and education.* Lawrence, KS: The University of Kansas Support and Development Center for Follow Through.

Hassett, M. E., Engler, C., Cooke, N. L., Test, D. W., Weiss, A. B., Heward, W. L., & Heron, T. E. (1984). A telephone-managed, home-based summer writing program for LD adolescents. In W. L. Heward, T. E. Heron, D. S. Hill, & J. Trap-Porter (Eds.), *Focus on behavior analysis in education* (pp. 89–103). Columbus, OH: Merrill.

Haubrich, P. A., & Shores, R. (1976). Attending behavior and academic performance of emotionally disturbed children. *Exceptional Children, 42*(6), 337–339.

Havighurst, R. J. (1952). *Developmental tasks and education* (2nd ed.). New York: McKay.

Hawisher, M. F., & Calhoun, M. L. (1978). *The resource room. An educational asset for children with special needs.* Columbus, OH: Merrill.

Hawkins, R. P., & Sluyter, D. J. (1970). *Modification of achievement by a simple technique involving parents and teachers.* Paper presented at the AERA convention, Minneapolis, MN.

Heath, R. W., & Nielson, M. A. (1974). The research basis for performance-based teacher education. *Review of Educational Research, 44,* 463–484.

Heron, T. E. (1978a). Maintaining mildly handicapped children in the regular classroom: A decision-making process. *Journal of Learning Disabilities, 11,* 210–216.

Heron, T. E. (1978b). Punishment: A review of the literature with implications for the teacher of mainstreamed children. *Journal of Special Education, 12,* 243–252.

Heron, T. E., & Axelrod, S. (1976). Effectiveness of feedback to mothers concerning their children's work recognition performance. *Reading Improvement, 13*(2), 74–81.

Heron, T. E., & Catera, R. (1980). Teacher consultation: A functional approach. *School Psychology Review, 9,* 283–289.

Heron, T. E., & Heward, W. L. (1982). Ecological assessment: Implications for teachers of LD students. *Learning Disability Quarterly, 5,* 117–125.

Heron, T. E., Heward, W. L., & Cooke, N. L. (1980). *A classwide peer tutoring system.* Paper presented at the Sixth Annual Meeting of the Association of Behavior Analysis, Dearborn, MI.

Heron, T. E., & Skinner, M. E. (1979). *Mainstreaming the learning disabled child: Effects on teacher-student interaction and student classroom behavior.* Paper presented at the Kentucky Federation Council for Exceptional Children Conference.

Heron, T. E., & Skinner, M. E. (1981). Criteria for defining the regular classroom as the least restrictive environment for LD students. *Learning Disability Quarterly, 4*(2), 115–121.

Heward, W. L., Dardig, J. C., & Rossett, A. (1979). *Working with parents of handicapped children.* Columbus, OH: Merrill.

Heward, W. L., Heron, T. E., & Cooke, N. L. (1982). Tutor huddle: Key element in a classwide peer tutoring system. *The Elementary School Journal, 83*(2), 114–123.

Heward, W. L., Heron, T. E., Ellis, D., & Cooke, N. L. (1986). Teaching first grade peer tutors to use verbal praise on an intermittent schedule. *Education and Treatment of Children, 9*(1), 5–15.

Heward, W. L., & Orlansky, M. D. (1984). *Exceptional Children* (2nd ed.). Columbus, OH: Merrill.

Hoffman, E. (1975). The American public school and the deviant child: The origins of their involvement. *Journal of Special Education, 9,* 415–423.

Homme, L. Csanyi, A. P., Gonzales, M. A., & Rechs, J. R. (1969). *How to use contingency contracting in the classroom.* Champaign, IL: Research Press.

Howe, K. R. (1985). Two dogmas of educational research. *Educational Researcher, 14*(8), 10–18.

Hughes, J. A. (1980). A case study in behavioral consultation: Organizational factors. *School Psychology Review, 9*(1), 103–107.

Hundert, J. (1982). Some considerations of planning the integration of handicapped children into the mainstream. *Journal of Learning Disabilities, 15,* 73–80.

Iano, R., Ayers, D., Heller, H., McGettigan, J., & Walker, V. (1974). Sociometric status of retarded children in an integrative program. *Exceptional Children, 40,* 267–271.

Idol, L., Paolucci-Whitcomb, P., & Nevin, A. (1986). *Collaborative consultation.* Rockville, MD: Aspen.

Idol-Maestas, L. (1983). *Special educator's consultation handbook.* Rockville, MD: Aspen.

Idol-Maestas, L., Nevin, A., & Paolucci-Whitcomb, P. (1984). *Facilitator's manual for collaborative consultation: Principles and techniques.* Reston, VA: National RETOOL Center, Teacher Education Division, Council for Exceptional Children.

Ingraham v. Wright, 430 U.S. 651 (1977).

Irmscher, W. F. (1972). *The Holt guide to English.* New York: Holt, Rinehart and Winston.

Iscoe, I., & Payne, S. (1972). Development of a revised scale for the functional classification of exceptional children. In E. P. Trapp and P. Himelstein (Eds.), *Readings on the exceptional child* (pp. 7–29). New York: Appleton-Century-Crofts.

Iwata, B. A., & Bailey, J. S. (1974). Reward versus cost token systems: An analysis of the effects on students and teacher. *Journal of Applied Behavior Analysis, 7,* 567–576.

Jackson, P. (1968). *Life in Classroom.* New York: Holt, Rinehart and Winston.

Johnson, D. W., & Johnson, R. T. (1975). *Learning together and alone: Cooperation, competition, and individualization.* Englewood Cliffs, NJ: Prentice-Hall.

Johnson, M., & Bailey, J. S. (1974). Cross-age tutoring: Fifth graders as arithmetic tutors for kindergarten children. *Journal of Applied Behavior Analysis, 7,* 223–232.

Johnson, R., Johnson, D. W., DeWeerdt, N., Lyons, N., & Zaidman, B. (1983). Integrating severely adaptively handicapped seventh grade students into constructive relationships with nonhandicapped peers in science class. *American Journal of Mental Deficiency, 87*(6), 611–618.

Johnson, R. T., & Johnson, D. W. (Eds.). (1984). *Structuring cooperative learning: Lesson plans for teachers.* Minneapolis, MN: Interaction.

Joint Anti-Fascist Committee v. McGrath. (1951). 341 US 123.

Jones, R. L. (Ed.). (1976). *Mainstreaming and the minority child.* Reston, VA: Council for Exceptional Children.

Joyce, B., & Showers, B. (1980). Improving inservice training: The message of research. *Educational Leadership, 37*(5), 379–385.

Kagan, S. (1986). Cooperative learning and sociocultural factors in schooling. In *Beyond language: Social and cultural factors in schooling language minority students* (pp. 231–298). Los Angeles: Evaluation, Dissemination and Assessment Center, California State University, Los Angeles.

Kaufman, M. J., Gottlieb, J., Agard, J. A., & Kukic, M. B. (1975). Mainstreaming: Toward an explication of the construct. *Focus on Exceptional Children, 7,* 1–12.

Kazdin, A. E. (1977). *The token economy: A review and evaluation.* New York: Plenum.

Kazdin, A. E., & Bootzin, R. R. (1972). The token economy: An evaluative review. *Journal of Applied Behavior Analysis, 5,* 343–372.

Kazdin, A. E., & Craighead, W. E. (1973). Behavior modification in special education. In L. Mann & D. Sabatino (Eds.), *The first review of special education* (pp. 51–102). Philadelphia: JSE Press.

Kazdin, A. E., & Klock, J. (1973). The effect of nonverbal teacher approval on student attentive behavior. *Journal of Applied Behavior Analysis, 6,* 643–654.

Kelley, M. L., & Stokes, T. F. (1982). Contingency contracting with disadvantaged youth: Improving classroom performance. *Journal of Applied Behavior Analysis, 15,* 447–454.

Kenowitz, L. A., Zweikel, S., & Edgar, E. (1978). Determining the least restrictive educational opportunity for the severely and profoundly handicapped. In N. G. Haring & D. D. Bricker (Eds.), *Teaching the Severely Handicapped* (Vol. 3). Columbus, OH: Special Press.

Keogh, B. K., & Levitt, M. L. (1976). Special education in the mainstream: A confrontation of limitations? *Focus on Exceptional Children, 8,* 1–11.

Kerlinger, F. N. (1964). *Foundations of behavioral research*. New York: Holt, Rinehart and Winston.

Kerr, M. M., & Nelson, C. M. (1983). *Strategies for managing behavior problems in the classroom*. Columbus, OH: Merrill.

Kimball, W. H., Heron, T. E., & Weiss, A. B. (1984a). New federalism and deregulation: Impact on special education. *Remedial and Special Education, 5*(2), 25–31.

Kimball, W. H., Heron, T. E., & Weiss, A. B. (1984b). Federal regulation: One more time. *Remedial and Special Education, 5*(2), 36–37.

Kirby, F. D., & Toler, H. C. (1970). Modification of preschool isolate behavior: A case study. *Journal of Applied Behavior Analysis, 3*(4), 309–314.

Kitano, H. (1973). Highlights of institute on language and culture: Asian component. In L. A. Bransford, L. Baca, & K. Lane (Eds.), *Cultural diversity and the exceptional child* (pp. 14–15). Reston, VA: Council for Exceptional Children.

Kitano, M. R., Steihl, J., & Cole, J. T. (1978). Role taking: Implications for special education. *Journal of Special Education, 12*(1), 59–74.

Kleck, R., Ono, J., & Hastorf, A. J. (1966). The effects of physical deviance on face-to-face interactions. *Human Relations, 19,* 425–436.

Klein, M. D., & Harris, K. C. (1986). Classroom communication functions of four learning handicapped students. *Language, Speech and Hearing Services in Schools, 17,* 318–328.

Kline, C. (1986). *Effects of guided notes on academic achievement of learning disabled high school students*. Unpublished master's thesis. The Ohio State University, Columbus, OH.

Knight, C. J., Peterson, R. L., & McGuire, B. (1982). Cooperative learning: A new approach to an old idea. *Teaching Exceptional Children, 14*(6), 233–238.

Knight, M. F., Meyers, H. W., Paolucci-Whitcomb, P., Hasazi, S. E., & Nevin, A. (1981). A four-year evaluation of consulting teacher service. *Behavior Disorders, 6,* 92–100.

Knowlton, H. E. (1983). A strategy for rational and responsive program evaluation. *Teacher Education and Special Education, 6*(2), 106–111.

Koegel, R. L., & Rincover, A. (1977). Research on the differences between generalization and maintenance in extra-therapy responding. *Journal of Applied Behavior Analysis, 10,* 1–12.

Kolstoe, O. P. (1976). Developing career awareness: The foundation of a career education program. In G. M. Blackburn (Ed.), *Colloquium series on career education for handicapped adolescents*. West Lafayette, IN: Purdue University.

Krashen, S. D. (1981). Bilingual education and second language acquisition theory. In *Schooling and language minority students: A theoretical framework* (pp. 51–79). Los Angeles, CA: Evaluation, Dissemination, and Assessment Center, California State University, Los Angeles.

Krashen, S. D. (1982). *Principles and practice in second language acquisition: Language teaching methodology series*. New York: Pergamon.

Kronich, D. (1969). *They too can succeed: A practical guide for parents of learning disabled children*. San Rafael, CA: Academic Therapy.

Kroth, R. L. (1975). *Communicating with parents of exceptional children: Improving parent-teacher relationships*. Denver, CO: Love.

Kroth, R. L. (1980). The mirror model of parental involvement. *The Pointer, 25*(1), 19–22.

Kroth, R. L., Whelan, R. J., & Stables, J. M. (1970). Teacher application of behavioral principles in home and classroom environments. *Focus on Exceptional Children, 3,* 1–10.

Kubetz, B. J. (1972). Education equality for the mentally retarded. *Syracuse Law Review, 23,* 1141–1165.

Kulik, J., Bangert, R. L., & Williams, G. W. (1983). Effects of computer-based teaching on secondary school students. *Journal of Educational Psychology, 75,* 19–26.

Kurpius, D. (1978). Consultation theory and process: An integrated model. *Personnel and Guidance Journal, 56,* 335–338.

Lake v. Cameron. (1966). 364 F. 2d. 657.

Lambie, R. A., & Hutchens, P. W. (1986). Adapting elementary school mathematics instruction. *Teaching Exceptional Children, 18*(3), 185–189.

Langdon, H. W. (1983). Assessment and intervention strategies for the bilingual language-disordered student. *Exceptional Children, 50*(1), 37–46.

Larry P. v. Riles. (1972). 343 F. Suppl. 1306.

Laurent, P. (1978). *Collecting additional information.* Unpublished paper, National Learning Resource Center of Pennsylvania.

Laurie, T. E., Buchwach, L., Silverman, R., & Zigmond, N. (1978). Teaching secondary learning disabled students in the mainstream. *Learning Disability Quarterly, 1,* 62–72.

LaVor, M. L. (1976). Federal legislation for exceptional persons: A history. In F. J. Weintraub, A. Abeson, J. Ballard, & M. L. LaVor (Eds.), *Public policy and the education of exceptional children* (pp. 96–111). Reston, VA: The Council for Exceptional Children.

Lazarus, B. (1986). *Effects of home-based parent tutoring managed by an automatic telephone answering machine on word recognition of kindergarten children.* Unpublished doctoral dissertation, The Ohio State University, Columbus, OH.

LeBanks v. Spears. (1973). 60 F.R.D. 135.

Leonardi, A., Duggan, T., Hoffheins, J., & Axelrod, S. (March, 1972). *Use of group contingencies to reduce three types of inappropriate classroom behaviors.* Paper presented at the meeting of the Council for Exceptional Children, Washington, DC.

Lerner, J. W. (1976). *Children with learning disabilities* (2nd ed.). Boston: Houghton Mifflin.

Levitan, S. A., & Taggart, R. (1976). *Jobs for the disabled.* Washington, DC: George Washington University, Center for Manpower Policy Studies.

Lichto, R. (1976). Communicating with parents: It begins with listening. *Teaching Exceptional Children, 8*(2), 67–71.

Lilly, S. (1970). *Classroom sociometry: A research related review of theory and practice.* Eugene, OR: Northwest Regional Special Education Instructional Materials Center.

Litow, L., (Pumroy, D.K. (1975). A brief review of classroom group-oriented contingencies. *Journal of Applied Behavior Analysis, 8,* 341–347.

Long, J. D., & Williams, R. L. (1973). The comparative effectiveness of group and individually contingency free time with inner-city junior high school students. *Journal of Applied Behavior Analysis, 6,* 465–474.

Longo, J., Rotatori, A. F., Kapperman, G., & Heinze, T. (1981). Procedures used to modify self-injurious behaviors in visually impaired, mentally retarded individuals. *Education of the Visually Handicapped, 13*(3), 77–83.

Lovitt, T. C. (1977). *In spite of my resistance—I've learned from children.* Columbus, OH: Merrill.

Lovitt, T., Kunzelmann, H. R., Nolan, P. A., & Hutten, W. J. (1968). The dimensions of classroom data. *Journal of Learning Disabilities, 1*(12), 20–31.

Lowenbraun, S., & Affleck, J. Q. (1976). *Teaching mildly handicapped children in regular classes.* Columbus, OH: Merrill.

Lynch, E. W. (1981). *Barriers to full participation of lower socioeconomic parents of special education students in school activities* (Executive Summary). San Diego, CA: Department of Special Education, San Diego State University.

MacKay, D. A., & Marland, P. (1978). *Thought processes of teachers.* Canada: University of Alberta. (ERIC Document Reproduction Service No. ED 151-328)

MacMillan, D. L., & Becker, L. D. (1977). Mainstreaming the mildly handicapped learner. In R. D. Kneedler & S. G. Tarver (Eds.), *Changing perspectives in special education* (pp. 208–227). Columbus, OH: Merrill.

Madsen, C. H., Becker, W. C., & Thomas, D. R. (1968). Rules, praise, and ignoring: Elements of elementary classroom control. *Journal of Applied Behavior Analysis, 1,* 139–150.

Madsen, C. H., & Madsen, C. R. (1974). *Teaching discipline: Behavior principles towards a positive approach.* Boston: Allyn and Bacon.

Madsen, C. H., Madsen, C. R., Saudargas, R. A., Hammond, W. R., & Egar, D. E. (1970). *Classroom RAID (Rules, Approval, Ignore, Disapproval): A cooperative approach for professionals and volunteers.* Unpublished manuscript, University of Florida.

Maher, C. A. (1983). Goal attainment scaling: A method for evaluating special education services. *Exceptional Children, 39,* 141–147.

Maher, C. A., & Barbrack, C. R. (1980). A framework for comprehensive evaluation of the individualized education program (IEP). *Learning Disability Quarterly, 3*(3), 49–55.

Maher, C. A. (1983). Goal attainment scaling: A method for evaluating special education services. *Exceptional Children, 4,* 529–536.

Marinelli, J. J. (1976). Financing the education of exceptional children. In F. J. Weintraub, A. Abeson, J. Ballard, & M. L. LaVor (Eds.), *Public policy and the education of exceptional children* (pp. 151–194). Reston, VA: The Council for Exceptional Children.

Marsh, G. E., & Price, B. J. (1980). *Methods for teaching the mildly handicapped adolescent.* Columbus, OH: Merrill.

Martin, E. W. (1974). Some thoughts on mainstreaming. *Exceptional Children, 41,* 150–153.

Martin, G., & Pear, J. (1978). *Behavior modification: What it is and how to do it.* Englewood Cliffs, NJ: Prentice-Hall.

Martinez, O. (1982). Developing a plan for coordinating bilingual and special education services: San Jose Unified School District Plan. *Proceedings of the Conference on Special Education and the Bilingual Child* (pp. 106–111). San Diego, CA: National Origin Desegregation Law Center, San Diego State University.

Maryland Association for Retarded Children v. State of Maryland. (Circuit Court, Baltimore, Maryland, 1974). Equity No. 100-182-77676.

Massad, V. E., & Etsel, B. C. (1972). Acquisition of phonetic sounds by pre- school children. Effects of response and reinforcement frequency. In G. Semb (Ed.), *Behavior Analysis and Education-1972* (pp. 11-13). Lawrence: The University of Kansas, Department of Human Development.

Matthews, R. M., Whang, P., & Fawcett, S. B. (1980). *Behavioral assessment of job-related skills: Implications for learning disabled young adults* (Research Report No. 6). Lawrence, KS: University of Kansas Institute for Research in Learning Disabilities.

Mattie T. v. Holladay, Civ. Act. No. DC 75-31-S (N.D. Miss., file 4/25/75).

McCallon, E., & McCray, E. (1975). *Planning and conducting interviews.* Austin, TX: Learning Concepts.

McCarthy, E. F., & Sage, D. D. (1982). State special education fiscal policy: The quest for equity. *Exceptional Children, 48*(5), 414-419.

McClure, W. P. (1975). Alternative methods of financing special education. *Journal of Education Finance, 1,* 36-51.

McDaniel L. (1982). Changing vocational teachers' attitudes toward the handicapped. *Exceptional Children, 48*(4), 377-378.

McDaniels, G. (May 23, 1980). Office of Special Education policy paper. DAS Information Bulletin, No. 64, Washington, DC.

McGinity, A. N., & Keogh, B. K. (1975). *Needs assessment for in-service: A first step for mainstreaming exceptional children in regular education.* Technical Report, University of California, Los Angeles.

McKenzie, H. S. (1972). Special education and consulting teachers. In F. Clark, D. Evans, & L. Hammerlynk (Eds.), *Implementing behavioral programs for schools and clinics* (pp. 103-125). Champaign, IL: Research Press.

McKinney, J., Mason, J., Perkerson, K., & Clifford, M. (1975). Relationship between classroom behavior and academic achievement. *Journal of Educational Psychology, 67,* 198-203.

McLaughlin, T., & Malaby, J. (1972). Reducing and measuring inappropriate verbalizations in a token classroom. *Journal of Applied Behavior Analysis, 5,* 329-333.

McLaughlin, T.F. (1981). The effects of classroom token economy on math performance in an intermediate grade school class. *Education and Treatment of Children, 4,* 139-147.

McLaughlin, T. F., & Malaby, J. E. (1972). Intrinsic reinforcers in a classroom token economy. *Journal of Applied Behavior Analysis, 5,* 263-270.

McLoughlin, J. A. (1978). Roles and practices of parents of children with learning and behavior problems. In D. Edge, B. J. Strenechy, & S. I. Mour (Eds.), *Parenting learning problem children: The professional educator's perspective* (pp. 79-87). Columbus, OH: NCEMMH, The Ohio State University.

McLoughlin, J. A. (1981). Training together to work together. *Teacher Education and Special Education, 4*(4), 45-54.

McLoughlin, J. A., & Lewis, R. B. (1981). *Assessing special students.* Columbus, OH: Merrill.

McLoughlin, J. A., & Lewis, R. B. (1987). *Assessing special students.* (second edition) Columbus, OH: Merrill.

McNair, K. (1978-79). Capturing inflight decisions: Thoughts while teaching. *Educational Research Quarterly, 3*(4), 26-42.

Medina, V. (1982). Issues regarding the use of interpreters and translators in a school setting. *Proceedings of the Conference on Special Education and the Bilingual Child* (pp. 31-37). San Diego, CA: National Origin Desegration Law Center, San Diego State University.

Medley, D. M., & Mitzel, H. E. (1963). Measuring classroom behavior by systematic observation. In N. L. Gage (Ed.), *Handbook of research in teaching* (pp. 247-328). Chicago: Rand McNally.

Medway, F. J., & Forman, S. G. (1980). Psychologists' and teachers' reactions to mental health and behavioral school consultation. *Journal of School Psychology, 18*(4), 338-348.

Mercer, C. D. (1979). *Children and adolescents with learning disabilities.* Columbus, OH: Merrill.

Meyen, E. L. (1976). *Instructional based approach system (IBAS).* Bellevue, Washington: Edmark Associates.

Meyen, E. L. (1978). *Exceptional children and youth: An introduction.* Denver: Love.

Meyen, E. L., & Lehr, D. (1980). Evolving practices in assessment and in intervention: The case for intensive instruction. *Exceptional Education Quarterly, 1*(2), 19-26.

Meyers, J. (1974). A consultation model for school psychological services. In J. P. Glavin (Ed.), *Ferment in special education* (pp. 167-177). New York: MSS Information Corporation.

Michaelis, B., & Michaelis, D. (1977). *Learning through noncompetative activities and play.* Palo Alto, CA: Learning Handbooks, Pitman Learning.

Miles, M. B., & Huberman, A. M. (1984). *Qualitative data analysis: A sourcebook of new methods.* Beverly Hills, CA: Sage.

Mills v. Board of Education of the District of Columbia. (1972). 348 F. Supp. 866.

Minskoff, E. (1975). Research on psycholinguistic training: Critique and guidelines. *Exceptional Children, 42,* 136-144.

Minuchin, S., Chamberlain, P., & Graubard, P. (1967). A project to teach learning skills to disturbed delinquent children. *American Journal of Orthopsychiatry, 37,* 558-567.

Monograph for bilingual vocational instructor competencies. (1981). Los Angeles, CA.: National Dissemination and Assessment Center, California State University, Los Angeles.

Moore, B. L., & Bailey, H. (1973). Social punishment in the modification of a preschool child's "autistic-like" behavior with a mother as a therapist. *Journal of Applied Behavior Analysis, 6,* 497-507.

Moore, J., & Fine, M. (1978). Regular and special class teachers' perceptions of normal and exceptional children and their attitudes toward mainstreaming. *Psychology in the Schools, 15,* 253-259.

Moorman, C., & Dishon, D. (1983). *Our classroom: We can learn together.* Englewood Cliffs, NJ: Prentice-Hall.

Morales v. Turman, 364, F. Supp. 166, (Ed.D., Texas, 1973).

Moran, M. R. (1980). *An investigation of the demands on oral language skills of learning disabled students in secondary classrooms* (Research Report No. 1). Lawrence, KS: University of Kansas Institute for Research in Learning Disabilities.

Moreno, J. (1953). *Who shall survive? Foundations of sociometry, group psychotherapy, and sociodrama* (2nd ed.). New York: Beacon House.

Mori, A. A. (1980). Career education for the learning disabled — Where are we now? *Learning Disability Quarterly, 3,* 91–101.

Mori, A. A. (1982). School-based career assessment programs: Where are we now and where are we going? *Exceptional Education Quarterly, 3*(3), 40–47.

Morine, G. (1975). Interaction analysis in the classroom: Alternative applications. In R. A. Weinberg & F. H. Wood (Eds.), *Observation of pupils and teachers in mainstream and special education settings: Alternative strategies* (pp. 75–95). Reston, VA: Council for Exceptional Children.

Morrison, G. M. (1981). Sociometric measurement: Methodological considerations of its use with mildly handicapped learning handicapped and nonhandicapped children. *Journal of Educational Psychology, 73,* 193–201.

Morrison, G. M., Forness, S. R., & MacMillian, D. L. (1983). Influences on the sociometric ratings of mildly handicapped children: A path analysis. *Journal of Educational Psychology, 75,* 63–74.

Morse, W. C. (1976). The helping teacher/crisis teacher concept. *Focus on Exceptional Children, 8*(4), 3–11.

Morsink, C. V. (1984). *Teaching special needs students in regular classrooms.* Boston: Little, Brown.

Mosby, R. J. (1979). A bypass program of supportive instruction for secondary students with learning disabilities. *Journal of Learning Disabilities, 12,* 187–190.

National School Public Relations Association. (1970). *Conference time for teachers and parents.* Washington, DC, National School Public Relations Association.

Neidermeyer, F. C. (1970). Effects of training on the instructional behaviors of student tutors. *Journal of Education Research, 64,* 119–123.

Nelson, C. M., & Stevens, K. B. (1979). *Mainstreaming behaviorally disordered children through teacher consultation.* Paper presented at the Third Annual Conference on Severe Behavior Disorders of Children and Youth. Tempe, AZ.

Nesselroade, J. R., & Reese, H. W. (1973). *Life span development psychology: Methodological issues.* New York: Academic Press.

Newcomer, P.L. (1977). Special education services for the "mildly handicapped": Beyond a diagnostic and remedial model. *The Journal of Special Education, 11*(2), 153–165.

North Dakota Study Group on Evaluation. (1977). *First California Conference on Educational Evaluation and Public Policy, 1976.* Grand Forks, ND: University of North Dakota, Center for Teaching and Learning.

O'Dell, S. (1974). Training parents in behavior modification: A review. *Psychological Bulletin, 81,* 418–432.

Oldridge, O.A. (1977). Future directions for special education: Beyond a diagnostic and remedial model. *The Journal of Special Education, 11*(2), 167–169.

Omark, D. R., & Erickson, J. G. (Eds.). (1983). *The bilingual exceptional child.* San Diego, CA: College-Hill Press.

Opper, S. (1977). Piaget's clinical method. *Journal of Children's Mathematical Behavior, 1*(4), 90–107.

Orlick, T. (1977). *Winning through cooperation: Competitive insanity; cooperative alternative.* Washington, DC: Hawkins.

Orlick, T. (1982). *The second cooperative sports and games book.* New York: Pantheon.

Ortiz, A. (June, 1986). Deciding the language of instruction for bilingual special education students. Paper presented at Fiesta Educativa Conference, Los Angeles.

Ortiz, A. A., & Yates, J. R. (1984). Staffing and the development of individualized educational programs for bilingual exceptional students. In L. M. Baca & H. T. Cervantes, *The bilingual special education interface* (pp. 187–212). Columbus, OH: Merrill.

Ortiz, S., & Jones, A. (1982). Using bilingual instructional materials for language minority students in special education. *Proceedings of the Conference on Special Education and the Bilingual Child* (pp. 83–87). San Diego, CA: National Origin Desegregation Law Center, San Diego State University.

Osbourne, J. G. (1969). Free-time as a reinforcer in the management of classroom behavior. *Journal of Applied Behavior Analysis, 2*, 113–118.

Ottman, R. A. (1981). Before a handicapped student enters the classroom: What the special educator can do. *Teaching Exceptional Children, 14*(1), 41–43.

Panitch v. Wisconsin, (1974) supra n.8.

Parker, C. A. (1975). *Psychological consultation: Helping teachers meet special needs.* Minneapolis: Leadership Training Institute/Special Education.

Parson, L. R., & Heward, W. L. (1979). Training peers to tutor: Evaluation of a tutor training package for primary learning disabled students. *Journal of Applied Behavior Analysis, 12*, 309–310.

Parsons, R. D., & Meyers, J. (1984). *Developing consultation skills.* San Francisco: Jossey-Bass.

Patterson, G. R. (1975). *Families: Application of social learning to family life.* Champaign, IL: Research Press.

Payan, R. (1984). Development of the bilingual special education interface. In L. M. Baca & H. T. Cervantes, *The bilingual special education interface* (pp. 75–101). Columbus, OH: Merrill.

Pennsylvania Association for Retarded Children v. Commonwealth of Pennsylvania. (1972). 343 F. Supp. 279.

People Systems, Inc. (1977). *The uncalendar.* Scottsdale, AZ: People Systems.

Pepper, F. C. (1976). Teaching the American Indian child in mainstream settings. In R. L. Jones (Ed.), *Mainstreaming and the minority child* (pp. 133–158). Reston, VA: Council for Exceptional Children.

Peterson, C. L., Dammer, F. W., & Flavell, J. J. (1972). Developmental changes in children's response to three indications of communicative failure. *Child Development, 43*, 1463–1468.

Peterson, P. L., Marx, R. W., & Clark, C. M. (1978). Teacher planning, teacher behavior, and student achievement. *American Educational Research Journal, 15*(3), 417–432.

Phillips, E. L., Phillips, E. A., Fixsen, D., & Wolf, M. (1971). Achievement place: Modification of behavior of predelinquent boys within a token economy. *Journal of Applied Behavior Analysis, 4,* 45–61.

Pierce, M. M., Van Houten, R. (1984). Preparing materials for peer tutoring. *The Directive Teacher, 6*(2), 24–25.

Polloway, E. A., Cronin, M. E., & Patton, J. R. (1986). The efficacy of group versus one-to-one instruction: A review. *Remedial and Special Education, 7*(1), 22–30.

Popham, W. J., & Baker, E. L. (1970). *Systematic instruction.* Englewood Cliffs, NJ: Prentice-Hall.

Price, M., & Goodman, L. (1980). Individualized Education Programs: A cost study. *Exceptional Children, 46*(6), 446–454.

Project CAST. (Grant No. G007804955) (1981). La Plata, MD: Charles County Board of Education, Office of Special Education. (ERIC Document Reproduction Service No. ED 242-142)

P.L. 92-318, Education Amendments of 1972, June 23, 1972.

P.L. 93-112, Rehabilitation Act of 1973, July 26, 1973.

P.L. 93-380, Education Amendments of 1974, August 21, 1974.

P.L. 93-516, Rehabilitation Act Amendments of 1974, December 7, 1974.

P.L. 94-142, The Education of All Handicapped Children Act of 1975, November, 1975.

Reichardt, C., & Cook, T. (1979). Beyond qualitative versus quantitative methods. In T. Cook & C. Reichardt (Eds.), *Qualitative and quantitative methods in evaluation research* (pp. 7–32). Beverly Hills, CA: Sage.

Reynolds, M. C., & Rosen, S. W. (1976). Special education: Past, present, and future. *The Educational Forum, 40,* 551–562.

Rios, E. T., & Hansen, W. E. (1978). *Career and vocational development of bilingual students.* Austin, TX: National Educational Laboratory.

Robinson, P. W., Newby, T. J., & Ganzell, S. L. (1981). A token system for a class of underachieving hyperactive children. *Journal of Applied Behavior Analysis, 14,* 307–315.

Robinson, V. M., Cameron, M. M., & Raethel, A. M. (1985). Negotiation of a consultative role for school psychologists: A case study. *Journal of School Psychology, 23,* 43–49.

Rodriguez, R. C., Cole, J. T., Stile, S. W., & Gallegos, R. L. (1979). Bilingualism and biculturalism for the special education classroom. *Teacher Education and Special Education, 2*(4), 69–74.

Rogers-Warren, A., & Warren, S. F. (1977). *Ecological perspectives in behavior analysis.* Austin, TX: PRO-ED.

Rose, T. (1983). A survey of corporal punishment of mildly handicapped students. *Exceptional Education Quarterly, 3,* 9–19.

Rosenshine, B. (1983). Teaching functions in instructional programs. *Elementary School Journal, 83,* 335–352.

Rossmiller, R. A., Hale, J. A., & Frohreich, L. E. (1970). *Educational programs for exceptional children: Resource configurations and costs.* (National Educational Finance Project Study No. 2). Madison, WI: Department of Educational Administration, University of Wisconsin.

Rowley v. Board of Education of the Hendrick Hudson Central School District, 632 F. 2d. 945 (2nd. 1980).

Russell, B. E. (1982). Calculators in the special education classroom. *The Directive Teacher,* 4(1), 6,11.

Rynders, J., Johnson, R., Johnson, D. W., & Schmidt, B. (1980). Effects of cooperative goal structuring in productive positive interaction between Down's Syndrome and nonhandicapped teenagers: Implications for mainstreaming. *American Journal of Mental Deficiency, 85,* 273–286.

Sabornie, E. J. & Kauffman, J. M. (1985). Regular classroom sociometric status of emotionally disturbed adolescents. *Behavioral Disorders, 10,* 191–197.

Sabornie, E. J., & Kauffman, J. M. (1986). Social acceptance of learning disabled adolescents. *Learning Disability Quarterly, 9*(1), 55–60.

Safer, N. & Hobbs, B. (1980). Developing, implementing, and evaluating individualized education program. *School Psychology Review, 9*(3), 212–220.

Salend, S. J. (1984). Factors contributing to the development of successful mainstreaming programs. *Exceptional Children, 50*(5), 409–416.

Salend, S. J., & Lutz, J. G. (1984). Mainstreaming or mainlining: A competency based approach to mainstreaming. *Journal of Learning Disabilities, 17*(1), 27–29.

Salvia, J., & Ysseldyke, J. E. (1985). *Assessment in special and remedial education* (3rd ed.). Boston: Houghton Mifflin.

Sandoval, J., Lambert, N., & Davis, J. M. (1977). Consultation from the consultee's perspective. *Journal of School Psychology, 15*(4), 334–342.

Sapon-Shevon, M. (1979). *The ethics of group contingencies.* Paper presented at the Annual Meeting of the Association for Behavior Analysis, Dearborn, MI.

Saracho, O. N. (1984). Using observation to assess young children's reading attitudes. *Reading Horizons, 25*(1), 68–71.

Saski, J., Swicegood, P., & Carter, J. (1983). Notetaking formats for learning disabled adolescents. *Learning Disability Quarterly, 6,* 265–272.

Schmuck, R. A., & Schmuck, P. A. (1975). *Group Processes in the classroom.* Dubuque, IA: William C. Brown.

Schmuck, R. A., & Schmuck, P. A. (1983). *Group Processes in the classroom* (2nd edition). Dubuque, IA: William C. Brown.

Schumaker, J. B., Deshler, D. D., Alley, G. R., & Warner, M. M. (1983). Toward the development of an intervention model for learning disabled adolescents: The University of Kansas Institute. *Exceptional Education Quarterly, 4*(1), 45–74.

Schumaker, J. B., Hazel, J. S., Sherman, J. A., & Sheldon, J. (1982). Social skill performances of learning disabled, non-learning disabled, and delinquent adolescents. *Learning Disability Quaterly, 5*(4), 388–397.

Schumaker, J. B., Sheldon-Wildgen, J., & Sherman, J. A. (1980). *An observational study of the academic and social behaviors of learning disabled adolescents in the regular classroom* (Research Report No. 22). Lawrence, KS: University of Kansas Institute for Research in Learning Disablities.

Schumaker, J. B., Warner, M. M., Deshler, D. D., & Alley, G. R. (1980). *An epidemiological study of learning disabled adolescents in secondary schools: Details of the methodology* (Research Report No. 12). Lawrence, KS: University of Kansas Institute for Research in Learning Disabilities.

Scruggs, T. E., & Richter, L. (1986). Tutoring learning disabled students: A critical review. *Learning Disability Quarterly, 9*(1), 2–14.

Section 504 of the Rehabilitation Act of 1973. Fact Sheet: Handicapped persons: Rights under federal law. (1977). (Reprint No. 1977-730. 851/1687 3.1) Washington, DC: U.S. Government Printing Office.

Sewall, G. T. (1982). Against anomie and amnesia: What basic education means in the eighties. *Phi Delta Kappan, 63*(9), 603–605.

Sharan, S., Hare, P., Webb, C. D., & Hertz-Lazarowitz, R. (Eds.). (1980). *Cooperation in education.* Provo, UT: Brigham Young University Press.

Shaw, S. F., & Shaw, W. K. (1972). The in-service experience plan, or changing the bath without losing the baby. *The Journal of Special Education, 6*(2), 121–126.

Shelby, C. C., & Coleman, W. T. (1983). *Educating Americans for the 21st Century.* National Science Board Commission on Precollege Education in Mathematics, Science, and Technology.

Shotel, J., Iano, R., & McGettigan, J. (1972). Teacher attitudes associated with the integration of handicapped children. *Exceptional Children, 38*, 677–683.

Shrewsberry, R. (1981). Case study number three. In J. O. Cooper & D Edge (Eds.), *Parenting: Strategies and educational methods.* Louisville, KY: Eston.

Sierra, V. (1973). Learning styles of the Mexican American. In L. A. Bransford, L. Baca, & K. Lane (Eds.), *Cultural diversity and the exceptional child* (pp. 42-50). Reston, VA: Council for Exceptional Children.

Singletary, E. E., Collings, G. D., & Dennis, H. F. (1978). *Law briefs on litigation and the rights of exceptional children, youth, and adults.* Washington, DC: University Press of America.

Siperstein, G., Bopp, M. J., & Bak, J. J. (1978). Social status of learning disabled children. *Journal of Learning Disabilities, 2,* 49–53.

Skinner, M.E. (1979). *Effects of an in-service program on the attitudes, knowledge, and student-teacher interaction patterns of regular classroom teachers.* Unpublished master's thesis, The Ohio State University, Columbus, OH.

Slate, J. R., & Saudargas, R. A. (1986). Differences in learning disabled and average students' classroom behaviors. *Learning Disability Quarterly, 9*(1), 61–67.

Slavin, R. E., Madden, N. A., & Leavey, M. (1984). Effects of cooperative learning and individualized instruction on mainstreamed students. *Exceptional Children, 50*(5), 434–443.

Slavin, R., Sharan, S., Kagan, S., Hertz-Lazarowitz, R., Webb, C., & Schmuck, R. (Eds.). (1985). *Learning to cooperate, cooperating to learn.* New York: Plenum.

Smith, D. D., & Lovitt, T. C. (1973). The educational diagnosis and remediation of b and d written reversal problems: A case study. *Journal of Learning Disabilities, 6,* 356–363.

Smith, D. D., Robinson, S., & Voress, J. (1982). The learning disabled: The transition from dependence to independence. *Topics in Language and Learning Disabilities, 2*(3), 27–39.

Smith, J. E., & Schindler, W. J. (1980). Certification requirements of general educators concerning exceptional pupils. *Exceptional Children, 46*(5) 394–396.

Smith, J. K. (1983a). Quantitative versus qualitative research: An attempt to clarify the issue. *Educational Researcher, 12*(3), 6–13.

Smith, J. K. (1983b). Quantitative versus interpretive: The problem of conducting social inquiry. In E. House (Ed.), *Philosophy of evaluation* (pp. 27–51). San Francisco: Jossey-Bass.

Smith, J. O., & Arkans, J. R. (1974). Now more than ever: A case for the special class. *Exceptional Children, 40,* 497–502.

Smith, L. M. (1979). An evolving logic of particpant observation, educational ethnography, and other case studies. In L. S. Shulman (Ed.), *Review of research in education: No. 6* (pp. 316–377). Itasca, IL: F. E. Peacock.

Smith, L. M., & Geoffrey, W. (1968). *Complexities of an urban classroom.* New York: Holt, Rinehart and Winston.

Soar, R. S. (1973). *Follow through classroom process measurement and pupil growth (1970–71): Final report.* Gainesville, FL: University of Florida Institute for Development of Human Resources.

Speece, D.L., & Mandell, C.J. (1980). Interpersonal communication between resource and regular teachers. *Teacher Education and Special Education, 3*(4), 55–60.

Spekman, N. J., & Roth, F. P. (1982). An intervention framework for learning disabled students with communication disorders. *Learning Disability Quarterly, 5,* 429–437.

Speltz, M. L., Shimamura, J. W., & McReynolds, W. T. (1982). Procedural variations in group contingencies: Effects on children's academic and social behaviors. *Journal of Applied Behavior Analysis, 15*(4), 533–544.

Spindler, G. (Ed.). (1970). *Being an anthropologist: Fieldwork in eleven cultures.* New York: Holt, Rinehart and Winston.

Spock, B. (1976). *Baby and child care.* New York: Pocket Books.

Spradley, J. P. (1979). *The ethnographic interview.* New York: Holt, Rinehart and Winston.

Spradley, J. P. (1980). *Participant observation.* New York: Holt, Rinehart and Winston.

Stainback, W., Stainback, S., Courtnage, L., & Jaben, T. (1985). Facilitating mainstreaming by modifying the mainstream. *Exceptional Children, 52*(2), 144–152.

Stake, R. E. (1978). The case study method in social inquiry. *Educational Research, 2,* 5–8.

Stallings, J., & Kaskowitz, D. (1974). *Follow through classroom observation evaluation, 1972–73.* Menlo Park, CA: Stanford Research Institute.

State ex. rel. Beattie v. Board of Education of City of Antigo (Wis.). (1919). 172 NW 153.

Steinzor, B. (1950). The spatial factor in face to face discussion groups. *Journal of Abnormal Social Psychology, 45,* 552–555.

Stephens, T. M. (1976). *Directive teaching of children with learning and behavioral handicaps* (2nd Ed.). Columbus, OH: Merrill.

Stephens, T. M. (1977). *Teaching skills to children with learning and behavior disorders.* Columbus, OH: Merrill.

Stephens, T. M. (1978). A rationale for training of teacher educators. *Viewpoints in Teaching and Learning, 54*(4), 10–19.

Stephens, T. M. (1981). *Social skills in the classroom.* Columbus, OH: Cedars Press.

Stevens, R., & Rosenshine, B. (1981). Advances in research on teaching. *Exceptional Education Quarterly, 2*(1), 1–10.

Stokes, T. F., & Baer, D. M. (1977). An implicit technology of generalization. *Journal of Applied Behavior Analysis, 10*(2), 349-367.

Stokes, T. F., Baer, D. M., & Jackson, R. L. (1974). Programming the generalization of a greeting response in four retarded children. *Journal of Applied Behavior Analysis, 7,* 599-610.

Stoner v. Miller. (1974). 377 F. Supp. 177.

Stotland, J. F., & Mancuso, E. (1981). US Court of Appeals decision regarding *Armstrong* v. *Kline:* The 180 day rule. *Exceptional Children, 47*(4), 266-270.

Strain, P. S., & Kerr, M. M. (1981). *Mainstreaming of children in schools: Research and programmatic issues.* New York: Academic Press.

Strain, P., & Odom, S. L. (1986). Peer social initiations: Effective intervention for social skills development of exceptional children. *Exceptional Children, 52*(6), 543-551.

Strain, P. S., Odom, S. L., & McConnell, S. (1984). Promoting social reciprocity of exceptional children: Identification, target behavior selection, and intervention, *Remedial and Special Education, 5*(1), 21-28.

Strenecky, B., McLoughlin, J. A., & Edge, D. (1979). Parent involvement: A consumer perspective-in the schools. *Education and Training of the Mentally Retarded, 14*(2), 54-56.

Striefel, S. (1981). *How to teach through modeling and imitation.* Austin, TX: PRO-ED.

Stuart, R. B. (1971). Assessment and change of communication patterns of juvenile delinquents and their parents. In R. D. Rubin, H. Fensterheim, A. A. Lazarus, & C. M. Franks (Eds.), *Advances in behavior therapy* (pp. 183-196). New York: Academic Press.

Sugai, G. (1985). Case study: Designing instruction from IEPs. *Teaching Exceptional Children, 17*(3), 232-239.

Sulzer-Azaroff, B., & Mayer, R. (1977). *Applying behavior analysis procedures with children and youth.* New York: Holt, Rinehart and Winston.

Swick, K. J., Flake-Hobson, C., & Raymond, G. (1980). The first step — Establishing parent-teacher communication in the IEP conference. *Teaching Exceptional Children, 12*(4), 144-145.

Taber, F. M. (1983). *Microcomputers in special education: Selection and decision making process.* Reston, VA: Council for Exceptional Children.

Tawney, J. W., & Gast, D. L. (1984). *Single subject research in special education.* Columbus, OH: Merrill.

Terrell, T. D. (1981). The natural approach in bilingual education. In *Schooling and language minority students: A theoretical framework* (pp. 117-146). Los Angeles: Evaluation, Dissemination and Assessment Center, California State University, Los Angeles.

Test, D. W. (1985). Evaluating educational software for the microcomputer. *Journal of Special Education Technology, 7*(1), 37-46.

Tharp, R. G. (1975). The triadic model of consultation: Current considerations. In C. A. Parker (Ed.), *Psychological consultation: Helping teachers meet special needs* (pp. 135-151). Minneapolis, MN: Leadership Training Institute/Special Education.

Tharp, R. G., & Wetzel, R. J. (1969). *Behavior modification in the natural environment*. New York: Academic Press.

Thompson, R. H., Vitale, P. A., & Jewett, J. P. (1984). Teacher-student interaction patterns in mainstreamed classrooms. *Remedial and Special Education, 5*(6), 51–61.

Thonis, E. W. (1981). Reading instruction for language minority students. In *Schooling and language minority students: A theoretical framework* (pp. 147–181). Los Angeles: Evaluation, Dissemination and Assessment Center, California State University, Los Angeles.

Today's numbers, tomorrow's nation: Demography's awesome challenge for schools (1986, May 14). *Education Week* (pp. 14–37).

Toffler, A. (1970). *Future shock*. New York: Random House.

Torgesen, J. K. (1986). Computers and cognition in reading: A focus on decoding fluency. *Exceptional Children, 53*(2), 157–162.

Trovato, J., & Bucher, B. (1980). Peer tutoring with or without home-based reinforcement for reading reading remediation. *Journal of Applied Behavior Analysis, 13*, 129–141.

Turnbull, A. P., & Schulz, J. B. (1979). *Mainstreaming handicapped students: A guide for the classroom teacher*. Boston: Allyn and Bacon.

Turnbull, A. P., Strickland, B. B., & Brantley, J. C. (1982). *Developing and implementing Individualized Education Programs* (2nd ed.). Columbus, OH: Merrill.

Turnbull, A. P., Strickland, B., & Hammer, S. E. (1978). IEP's: Presenting guidelines for development and implementation, Part 1. *Journal of Learning Disabilities, 11*(1), 40–46.

Turnbull, A. P., Strickland, B., & Hammer, S. E. (1978). The IEP—Part 2: Translating law into practice. *Journal of Learning Disabilities, 11*(2), 67–72.

Turnbull, H. R., & Turnbull, A. P. (1978). *Free appropriate public education: Law and implementation*. Denver: Love.

Van Den Pol, R. A., Iwata, B. A., Ivanic, M. T., Page, T. J., Neef, N. A., & Whitley, F. P. (1981). Teaching the handicapped to eat in public places: Acquisition, generalization and maintenance of restaurant skills. *Journal of Applied Behavior Analysis, 14*(1), 61–69.

Van Houten, R. (1980). *Learning through feedback*. New York: Human Sciences Press.

Van Houten, R. (1984). Setting up performance feedback systems in the classroom. In W. L. Heward, T. E. Heron, D. S. Hill, and J. Trap-Porter (Eds.), *Focus on behavior analysis in education* (pp. 114–125) Columbus, OH: Merrill.

Van Houten, R., & Sullivan, K. (1975). Effects of an audio cueing system on the rate of teacher praise. *Journal of Applied Behavior Analysis, 8*, 197–202.

Vargas, J. (1984). What are your exercises teaching? An analysis of stimulus control in instructional material. In W. L. Heward, T. E. Heron, D. S. Hill, & J. Trap-Porter (Eds.), *Focus on behavior analysis in education* (pp. 126–141). Columbus, OH: Merrill.

Varone, V. A., O'Brien, R., & Axelrod, S. (1972). *Reinforcing parents for their children's academic performance*. Paper presented at the meeting of the Council for Exceptional Children, Washington, DC.

Vaughn, S., Bos, C., & Lund, K.A. (1986). . . . But they can do it in my room. *Teaching Exceptional Children, 18*(3), 176–180.

Walker, H., McConnell, S., Holmes, D., Todis, B., Walker, J., & Golden, N. (1983) *The Walker Social Skills Curriculum: The ACCEPTS program.* Austin, TX: PRO-ED.

Wallace, G., & Kauffman, J. M. (1978). *Teaching children with learning problems* (2nd ed.). Columbus, OH: Merrill.

Wallace, C., & Larsen, S. C. (1978). *Educational assessment of learning problems: Testing for teaching.* Boston: Allyn and Bacon.

Wallace, G., & McLoughlin, J. A. (1979). *Learning disabilities: Concepts and characteristics* (2nd ed.). Columbus, OH: Merrill.

Wang, M. C., & Birch, J. W. (1984). Effective special education in regular classes. *Exceptional Children, 50*(5), 391–398.

Wang, M. C., & Reynolds, M. C. (1986). "Catch 22 and disabling help": A reply to Alan Gartner. *Exceptional Children, 53*(1), 77–79.

Wang, M. C., Vaughan, E. D., & Dytman, J. A. (1985). Staff development: A key ingredient of effective mainstreaming. *Teaching Exceptional Children, 17*(2), 112–121.

Warger, C. L., & Trippe, M. (1982). Preservice teacher attitudes toward mainstreamed students with emotional impairments. *Exceptional Children, 49*(3), 246–252.

Warner, M. M., Schumaker, J. B., Alley, G. R., & Deshler, D. D. (1980). Learning disabled adolescents in the public schools: Are they different from other low achievers? *Exceptional Education Quarterly, 1,* 27–36.

Warren v. Nussbaum, 64 Wisc. 2nd 314, 219 N.W. 2d 577 (1974).

Wehman, P., Kregel, J., & Barcus, J. M. (1985). From school to work: A vocational transition model for handicapped students. *Exceptional Children, 52*(1), 25–37.

Weil, M. L., & Murphy, J. (1982). Instruction processes. In H. E. Mitzel (Ed.), *Encyclopedia of educational research* (5th ed., pp. 890–917). New York: Free Press.

Weintraub, F. J., & Abeson, A. (1974). New education policies for the handicapped: The quiet revolution. *Phi Delta Kappan, 55*(8), 526–529.

Weiss, A. B. (1984). *The effects of a telephone managed home-school program using parents as tutors on the academic achievement of learning disabled students.* Unpublished doctoral dissertation, The Ohio State University, Columbus, OH.

Weiss, A. B., Cooke, N. L., Grossman, M. A., Ryno-Vrabel, M., Hassett, M. E., Heward, W. L., & Heron, T. E. (1982). *Home-school communication.* Columbus, OH: Special Press.

Wiederholt, J. L., Hammill, D. D., & Brown, V. (1978). *The resource teacher: A guide to effective practices.* Boston: Allyn and Bacon.

Wiegner, K. K. (1982). Tomorrow has arrived. *Forbes, 129*(4), 111–119.

Wiig, E. H. (1982). *Let's talk: Developing prosocial communication skills.* Columbus, OH: Merrill.

Will, M. (1984). Bridges from school to working life. *Clearing House on the Handicapped,* 2 (ISSN 0565-2804) pp. 1–4.

Willis, J. W., Hobbs, T. R., Kirkpatrick, D. G., & Manley, K. W. (1975). Training counselors as researchers in the natural environment. In E. Ramp & G. Semb (Eds.), *Behavior analysis: Areas of research and application* (pp. 175–186). Englewood Cliffs, NJ: Prentice-Hall.

Wilson, S. (1977). The use of ethnographic techniques in educational research. *Review of Educational Research, 47,* 245-265.

Wisconsin v. *Constantineau.* (1971). 400 U.S. 433.

Wiseman, D. E., Hartwell, L. K., & Hannafin, M. J. (1980). Exploring the reading and listening skills of secondary mildly handicapped students. *Learning Disability Quarterly, 3,* 56-61.

Wolf, M. M., Giles, D. K., & Hall, V. R. (1968). Experiments with token reinforcement in a remedial classroom. *Behavior Research and Therapy, 6,* 305-312.

Wolfensberger, W. (1972). *The principle of normalization in human services.* Toronto: National Institute on Mental Retardation.

Wong, B. Y. L., & Wong, R. (1980). Role-taking skills in normal achieving and learning disabled children. *Learning Disability Quarterly, 3*(2), 11-18.

Wood, F. H. (1982). Affective education and social skills training: A consumer's guide. *Teaching Exceptional Children, 14*(6), 212-216.

Wyatt v. *Stickney,* 344 F. Supp. 387 (M.D. Ala. 1972).

Yanok, J. (1986). Free appropriate public education for handicapped children: Congressional intent and judicial interpretation. *Remedial and Special Education, 7*(2), 49-53.

Yates, J. (1973). Model for preparing regular classroom teachers for mainstreaming. *Exceptional Children, 39,* 471-472.

Yavorsky, D. K. (1978). *Discrepancy evaluation: A practitioner's guide.* University of Virginia: Evaluation Research Center.

Yinger, R. J. (1977). A study of teacher planning: Description and theory development using ethnographic and information processing methods. *Dissertation Abstracts International, 39,* p. 207-A (University Microfilms No. 78-10,138)

Ysseldyke, J. E., & Algozzine, B. (1982). *Critical issues in special and remedial education.* Boston: Houghton Mifflin.

Ysseldyke, J. E., Thurlow, M. L., Mecklenburg, C., & Graden, J. (1984). Opportunity to learn for regular and special education students during reading instruction. *Remedial and Special Education, 5*(1), 29-37.

Zelditch, M., Jr., (1969). Some methodological problems of field studies. In G. J. McCall & J. L. Simmons (Eds.), *Issues in participant observation: A text and reader* (pp. 5-9). Reading, MA: Addison-Wesley.

Zetlin, A., & Turner, J. L. (1983, March). *Coping with adolescence: Perspectives of retarded individuals and their families.* Paper presented at the Gatlingburg Conference on Research in Mental Retardation, Gatlingburg, TN.

Zimmerman, E. H., & Zimmerman, J. (1962). The alteration of behavior in a special classroom situation. *Journal of Experimental Analysis of Behavior, 5,* 59-60.

Author Index

Subject Index

Timothy E. Heron received his BA, MEd, and EdD from Temple University. He is Professor in the Department of Human Services Education at The Ohio State University. Dr. Heron also serves as an Educational Consultant to Children's Hospital Learning Disability Clinic in Columbus, Ohio. Prior to his present appointments, Dr. Heron served as a developmental and day care supervisor for cerebral-palsied students, taught learning disabled students, and supervised a training program for resource room teachers in an inner-city school. He has published several books and articles, presented numerous papers at regional, national, and international conferences, and has served as a consultant to teachers, parents, administrators on issues related to mainstreaming and applied behavior analysis.

Kathleen C. Harris received her BA from Douglass College, MEd from Rutgers University, and PhD from Temple University. She is an Associate Professor in the Division of Special Education at California State University, Los Angeles. Prior to her appointment, Dr. Harris served as a learning consultant and teacher of handicapped students in public and private inner-city schools. Dr. Harris has published several papers in the educational literature, consulted with numerous school districts, and has presented regularly at national and international conferences on issues related to minority handicapped students, especially at the secondary level, and on the use of ethnographic methodology.